Old Testament Quotations

in the New Testament

Old Testament Quotations in the New Testament

by
Gleason L. Archer
and
Gregory Chirichigno

MOODY PRESS

CHICAGO

To my gifted instructor,
    Bruce M. Metzger

                        (Gleason L. Archer)

To my family, who has given me loving support,
To Dr. Thomas McComiskey, who has given me sound counsel,
To Dr. Archer, who has generously made me his co-worker,
And especially to Diane

                        (Gregory Chirichigno)

© 1983 by
THE MOODY BIBLE INSTITUTE
OF CHICAGO

Old Testament and New Testament quotations cited in the quotation tool of this work
are from the *Biblia Hebraica Stuttgartensia*, (© 1969 and 1977), *Septuaginta*, 2 vols.,
(© 1935), and *Novum Testamentum Graece* (26th ed., © 1979). These works are
published by arrangement with the German Bible Society, Stuttgart, and are used by
permission.

ISBN: 0-8024-0236-4

1 2 3 4 5 6 7 Printing/ BC /Year 88 87 86 85 84 83
Printed in the United States of America

CONTENTS

r

PREFACE

This study was conceived for the thirty-third annual meeting of the Evangelical Theological Society, which met in Toronto, Canada on Dec. 28–30, 1981. The theme for the conference centered on the "Relationships between the Testaments." The purpose of this study is to explore the relationships that exist among the various Old Testament quotations that are found in the New Testament. It became apparent that in order to effectively examine the use of the Old Testament in the New Testament a tool would have to be created to bring together all of the New Testament verses that quote the Old Testament along with the parallel Old Testament and Septuagint citations. What is presented in this book is both a commentary and a tool to help students and scholars alike examine the lexical and syntactical relationships of the Old Testament quotations used in the New Testament. The discussions that follow will explain how to use the quotation tool and also serve as an introduction to the commentary.

INTRODUCTION

It has often been observed by careful students of the Bible that a certain number of Old Testament passages used in the New Testament are not quoted with literal exactness. Often that is accounted for by the fact that a completely literal translation of Hebrew does not make clear sense in Greek, and therefore some minor adjustments must be made for the sake of good communication. But there are a few cases where the rewording amounts to a sort of loose paraphrase. That is particularly true with quotations from the LXX (the translation of the entire Old Testament into Greek by Jewish scholars in Alexandria, Egypt during the third and second centuries B.C.). For the most part, the LXX is quite faithful to the Hebrew wording in the Old Testament, but in a small number of instances there are noticeable deviations in the mode of expressing the thought, even though there may be no essential difference in the thought itself.

Some scholars have drawn the conclusion from such deviations that the New Testament authors could not have held to the theory of verbal inspiration; otherwise they would have gone back to the Hebrew text and done a meticulous, exact translation of their own as they rendered that text into Greek. It has even been argued that the occasional use of an inexact LXX rendering in a New Testament quotation demonstrates a rejection of inerrancy on the part of the apostolic authors themselves. Their inclusion of the LXX quotations that contain elements of inexactitude would seem to indicate a cavalier attitude toward the whole matter of inerrancy. On the basis of inference from the phenomena of Scripture itself, it is therefore argued that the Bible makes no claim to inerrancy.

To that line of reasoning we make the following reply. The very reason for using the LXX was rooted in the missionary outreach of the evangelists and apostles of the early church. The LXX translation of the Old Testament had already found its way into every city of the Roman Empire to which the Jews of the Dispersion had gone. It was virtually the only form of the Old Testament in the hands of Jewish believers outside Palestine, and it was certainly the only available form for Gentile converts to the Jewish or Christian faiths. The apostles were propagating a gospel that presented Jesus Christ as the fulfillment of the Messianic promises of the Old Testament. Their audiences throughout the Near East and Mediterranean world were told that they had only to consult their Old Testament to verify the truth of the apostolic claims that Jesus in His person and by His work had fulfilled the promises of God. Had the New Testament authors quoted those promises in any other form than in the wording of the LXX, they would have engendered uncertainty and doubt in the minds of their readers, for as they checked their Old Testament, the readers would have noticed the discrepancies at once—and would have objected, "But that isn't the way I read it in my Bible!" The apostles and their Jewish co-workers from Palestine may have been well-equipped to do their own translation from the Hebrew original, but they would have been ill-advised to substitute their own more literal rendering for that form of the Old Testament that was already in the hands of their public. They really had little choice but to keep to the LXX in all of their quotations of the Old Testament.

On the other hand, the special Hebrew-Christian audience to which the evangelist Matthew addressed himself—and even more notably the recipients of the epistle to the Hebrews—did not require the constant adherence to the LXX that was necessary for Gentile readers. Hence Matthew and Hebrews often quote from the Old Testament in a non-LXX form, normally in a form somewhat closer to the wording of the Hebrew original. And it should also be observed that, at least in some cases, those Greek renderings (whether LXX or not) point to a variant reading in the original form of the text that is better than the one that has come down to us in the standard Hebrew Bible. It should be carefully noted that none of this yields any evidence whatever of carelessness or disregard on the part of the apostles with respect to the exact wording of the original Hebrew; in fact, far from it. In some instances Christ Himself based His teaching on a careful exegesis of the exact reading in the Torah. For example, in Matthew 22:32 He pointed out the implications of Exodus 3:6 ("I *am* the God of Abraham, and the God of Isaac, and the God of Jacob") on the basis of the present tense implied by the verbless clause in Hebrew. He declared that God would not have spoken of Himself as the God of mere corpses moldering in the grave

("God is not the God of the dead, but of the living"). Therefore Abraham, Isaac, and Jacob must have been alive and well in the life beyond at the time God addressed Moses at the burning bush four or five centuries after their deaths. Similarly, Christ's discussion with the Pharisees concerning the identity of the one referred to as "my lord" in Psalm 110:1 really turned on the exact terms used in that clause or sentence. He therefore asked them, "If David then calls Him Lord, how is He his son?" (Mt. 22:45). In other words, the Messiah must not only be David's lineal descendant, but He must also be his divine Lord (*kyrios*)!

Returning then to the apostolic use of the LXX, we find that this line of reasoning (that inexact quotations imply a low view of the Bible) is really without foundation. All of us employ standard translations of the Bible in our own teaching and preach- ing, even those of us who are conversant with the Greek and Hebrew originals of Scripture. But our use of any translation in English, French, or any other modern language by no means implies that we have abandoned a belief in Scriptural inerrancy, even though some errors of translation appear in every one of those modern versions. We use those standard translations to teach our listeners in terms they can verify from the Bibles they have in their own homes. But most of us are also careful to point out that the only final authority as to the meaning of Scripture is the wording of the original languages themselves. There is no infallible translation, but that fact involves no surrender of the conviction that the original manuscripts of Scripture were free from all error. We must therefore conclude that the New Testament use of the LXX implies nothing against verbal inspiration or Scriptural inerrancy.

INTRODUCTION TO THE COMMENTARY

As we approached this project we realized that some useful ends might be achieved by those concerned with a more thorough examination of this relationship between the Testaments if a listing of all such passages, with each text in Hebrew and Greek fully reproduced in parallel columns, was available. That is, if we deal with each Old Testament quotation printed in bold type in Nestle's twenty-sixth edition or the American Bible Society's third edition of the New Testament, and line up beside it the same verses in the LXX Version and Masoretic Text of the Hebrew Bible, then we can handle a variety of questions in a far more systematic and expeditious manner than is possible by laying out three different Bibles and searching out all parallel passages that may have contributed to a single conflate quotation in the New Testament.

We have therefore undertaken a complete survey of such quotations in three parallel columns, beginning with the first relevant passage in the Old Testament (there may be two or three other verses from later books that have a bearing on the New Testament quotations; such verses are printed below the main entry) and the corresponding translations in the LXX. Our primary purpose in this parallel column system is to classify each type of quotation in relationship to the Old Testament original, to see if we can regard it as virtually equivalent in meaning and therefore free from problems (category *A*). Those passages where minor deviation from the Masoretic Text is to be found in the New Testament quotation (analyzing the exact nature of each variation in each case) are placed in category *B*. Then there is that class of quotations in which the New Testament wording is actually closer to the Hebrew of the Masoretic Text than is true of the LXX itself. Those are included in category *C*. Still another type approximates the LXX in general, but shows minor deviations that need to be analyzed and accounted for. Those we have designated as category *D*. A more difficult category is those passages (relatively few in number) that seem to take questionable liberties with the Old Testament original, whether in wording or in application. Those are designated as category *E*. Finally, there is that group of passages that do not really purport to be quotations at all, but which pick up a good deal of their phraseology from

definitely identifiable passages in the Hebrew. Most of these merely allusive passages are left without treatment because they have no direct bearing on questions of the trustworthiness or inerrancy of the Holy Scriptures. But those that contain interesting insights or implications for doctrine or interpretation are occasionally included, and make up category *F*. (See the "Summary and Conclusion" for a full treatment of these categories.)

After sorting through the entire corpus of New Testament quotations from the Hebrew Bible we are in a position to set up comparative statistics for the various categories described above, to ascertain what proportion of the entire corpus shows a deviation of any significance.[1] We may also discover which of the New Testament authors show a non-LXX type of quotation, and thus go beyond the usual generalities concerning the special nature of Matthew and Hebrews in that regard. Those who wish to do special research in Field's *Hexapla* to explore possible relationships with "Proto-Theodotion" will be greatly facilitated in that search by means of this tool. This is, of course, somewhat speculative, since all of the non-Septuagintal columns in Origen's *Hexapla* were actually composed during the second century A.D. But there may be some interesting possibilities opened up with clues to other Greek translations that may have been current prior to the apostolic age but which have been subsequently lost.

Another useful product of this study is the implications it affords for textual criticism. In a few notable instances we have become convinced that the LXX or New Testament furnish important evidence for emendation of the vowel points of the Masoretic Text, and in some cases even a revision of the vowel

---

[1]Because of the nature of the commentary, the statistics based on the amount of categorized entries per category can be misleading. The number of entries is about 410; however, those do not correspond exactly to the number of New Testament quotations in the tool. Depending on the complexity of the New Testament quotation and the number of Old Testament quotations that support it, the number of entries varies. Thus a particular New Testament verse may be assigned to more than one category. Despite that fact, percentages for each category were determined, based on the number of entries (410); category *A*—268 entries, or 64.4%; category *B*—50 entries, or 11.2%; category *C*—33 entries, or 7%; category *D*—22 entries, or 6%; category *E*—13 entries, or 3%; category *F*—32 entries, or 8%.

letters (as, for example, in the case of Amos 9:12; see #297 in the tool). That is particularly the case where no viable reconciliation seems available in the solution of substantial discrepancies. Such examples are very few in number, but they are of special significance for the proper interpretation of the Old Testament passage. Our underlying presupposition is the operation of the Holy Spirit as He, through the apostles, has furnished a uniquely valid and insightful commentary on the Hebrew Scriptures. That means that the New Testament authors were guided into interpretive techniques that Bible scholars today could hardly find justification for in their own treatment of Scripture. At the same time we should understand that authorized apostolic authors enjoyed a latitude in this regard that would be nothing short of presumptuous for us to arrogate to ourselves. In other words, there is a certain sense in which Christ's chosen spokesmen were like Him guided to expound the Old Testament Scriptures "with authority, and not as the scribes." In the exercise of that prerogative, they did not hesitate to bring out the implications of the Hebrew text rather than limiting themselves to its exact wording as they translated it. Very frequently they found it useful to combine within one quotation sundry portions from Old Testament sources other than the principle passage that they were citing. We will refer to those as "conflate" quotations and appraise them on that basis.

And of course we will also bear in mind that in all literature it is permissible and perfectly proper to omit a word or two here and there in the process of quoting—provided, of course, that such omission does not in any way distort the meaning intended by the original author.

With those guiding principles in mind the reader will be able to make good and profitable use of this study, and we pray that he will be thereby assisted quite measurably in his textual and hermeneutical endeavors. Whatever proves helpful is of the gracious guidance of the Lord; whatever is disappointing or deficient is the fault of the authors. *Soli Deo gratia!*

COMMENTARY NUMERICAL PARSING SYSTEM*

Conjugation	Pers.	Perf.	Impf.	Impv.	Juss.-Cohort.	Ptcp.	Infin.	Pron. Suffix	Pers.
G - Qal	3ms	10	20	--	40	50msa	60abs	s0	3ms
Gp - Qal psv	3fs	11	21	--	41	51fsa	--	s1	3fs
D - Pi^cel	2ms	12	22	32	42	52msc	--	s2	2ms
Dp - Pu^cal	2fs	13	23	33	43	53fsc	--	s3	2fs
	1cs	14	24	--	44	--	--	s4	1cs
HtD - Hithpa^cel	3mp	15	25	--	45	55mpa	65cst	s5	3mp
H - Hiph^cel	3fp	16	26	--	46	56fpa	--	s6	3fp
Hp - Hoph^cal	2mp	17	27	37	47	57mpc	--	s7	2mp
N - Niph^cal	2fp	18	28	38	48	58fpc	--	s8	2fp
	1cp	19	29	--	49	--	--	s9	1cp

*The symbol *c* before a number designates *Waw* Conversive-Consecutive.

xiii

COMMENTARY BIBLIOGRAPHY

Baumgartner, Walter, and Koehler, Ludwig Hugo. *Lexicon in Veteris Testamenti Libros.* Leiden: E. J. Brill, 1953.

Bootium Anim.Sact., cited in Schleusner, p. 368a.

Brown, Francis, Driver, S.R., and Briggs, Charles A. *A Hebrew and English Lexicon of the Old Testament.* Oxford: Clarendon Press, 1907.

Gesenius, Friedrich Heinrich Wilhelm. *Hebräisches und aramäisches Handwörterbuch über das Alte Testament,* in Verbindung mit H. H. Zimmern, W. Max Müller, O. Weber; bearb. von Frants Buhl. Unveränderter Neudruck der 1915 erschienenen 17. Aufl. Berlin: Springer-Verlag, 1962.

Jastrow, Marcus. *A Dictionary of the Targumim, the Talmud Babli and Yerushalmi, and the Midrashic Literature; with an index of Scriptural quotations.* 2 vols. New York: Pardes Publishing House, 1950.

Liddell, Henry George, and Scott, Robert. *A Greek-English Lexicon.* Oxford: Clarendon Press, 1940.

Schleusner, Joh. Fried. *Novos Thesaurus Philologico-Criticus: sive Lexicon in LXX et Religuos Interpetes Graecos ac Scriptores Apocryphas Veteris Testamenti.* 2 vols. London: Duncan Publishers, 1829.

Zorell, Franciscus, ed. *Lexicon Hebraicum et Aramaicum Veteris Testamenti.* Roma: Pontificii Instituti Biblici, 1947.

QUOTATION TOOL
CONTENTS
OLD TESTAMENT ORDER

QUOTATION TOOL
CONTENTS
NEW TESTAMENT ORDER

How to Use This Tool

A number of the features of the layout created for the quotation tool need to be briefly explained so that the reader will gain the full benefit from the work. Before beginning that explanation, we should advise the reader that the Old Testament quotation lists from the 3d edition of the UBS and 26th edition of the Nestle Greek texts were consulted in the process of cataloging the citations used in this tool.

The tool itself consists of four parallel columns that contain (moving from left to right) the Masoretic Hebrew text, the Septuagint (LXX), the Greek New Testament, and appropriate textual commentary (consult the copyright page for the texts used in each case). After much deliberation we decided to arrange the tool in Old Testament order, but a complete listing of New Testament passages in New Testament order has been arranged in the special table of contents section of the book.

In the example below, the Arabic numeral (55) accompanying the Old Testament text refers to that text in its *Old Testament* order (the total number of entries is 312). The reference marked off in parentheses (22:28) alerts the reader to the verse number of the *English* text where that number differs from the MT versification.

New Testament citations will appear in New Testament order and will be lettered accordingly (the lettering system will facilitate cross-referencing among the New Testament citations that appear more than once in the tool). The example below contains the second reference to Mt. 15:4; the material following the reference, [see also 48*d*], directs the reader to an earlier occurrence of Mt. 15:4 (at entry 48). Of course, in this example the same is true for Mk. 7:10. The same type of cross-referencing is also used for Old Testament citations; the cross-reference will appear next to the citation, similar to the manner illustrated below (see entry #15 for an example).

---

*a*Mt 15:4 *(see also [48],d)

4 ὁ γὰρ θεὸς ⌜εἶπεν⸱*τίμα τὸν πατέρα ⸆ καὶ τὴν μητέρα ⸆, καὶ· ὁ κακολογῶν πατέρα ἢ μητέρα θανάτῳ τελευτάτω.

*b*Mk 7:10 *(see also [48],e)

10 Μωϋσῆς γὰρ εἶπεν·*τίμα τὸν πατέρα σου καὶ τὴν μητέρα σου, καί· ὁ κακολογῶν πατέρα ἢ μητέρα θανάτῳ τελευτάτω.

One final word of explanation is needed. Because in any given entry there may be additional Old Testament citations, there will be cases in which the accompanying New Testament reference(s) will apply to only a portion of the Old Testament citations in the left column of the quotation tool. In such cases the pertinent Old Testament reference will be given immediately to the right of the New Testament citation (see entry #12, right column, for an example). In those cases where the Old Testament citation may involve more than one New Testament passage, the Old Testament reference will be found to the *left* of the New Testament passages and their relationship will be indicated by a series of lines (see entry #192, Psalm 118:22, for an example). A similar procedure is used for any Old Testament citations that need this type of treatment.

55: Ex 22:27 (22:28)

27 אֱלֹהִים לֹא תְקַלֵּל וְנָשִׂיא בְעַמְּךָ לֹא תָאֹר׃

In the portion of the tool reproduced below (entry 53), the heading on the second column (Ex. 21:16), refers to the versification of the LXX where that differs from the MT. Thus, any inconsistency in the versifications of the MT, LXX, and English texts of the Old Testament will be noted at the appropriate place in the tool.

The New Testament column of the same entry illustrates the features of that portion of the tool. All

---

53: Ex 21:17

17 וּמְקַלֵּל אָבִיו וְאִמּוֹ מוֹת יוּמָת׃

(Ex 21:16)

16 ὁ κακολογῶν πατέ-
ρα αὐτοῦ ἢ μητέρα αὐτοῦ τελευτήσει θανάτῳ. —

SUMMARY AND CONCLUSIONS

Note: Some entries (e.g., 1^2) may have more than one New Testament verse listed. Those are designated by superscript numerals. In addition, some entries can be listed under two different categories (e.g., entry #117 is either A or F, and is listed under both)—eds.

Category A

These quotations consist of reasonably or completely accurate renderings from the Hebrew of the Masoretic Text (MT) into the Greek of the Septuagint (LXX), and from there (apart from word order, which sometimes deviates slightly) into the New Testament passage in which the Old Testament text is cited. This category has been further divided into three classes: A, A-, and A^d.

The class A quotations are (noted by entry): 1^2, 2, 3, 4^4, 5, 7, 8, 9, 12^2, 13^5, 14, 16, 17, 21, 22^2, 23, 24, 26, 31, 32^2, 34, 35, 36^5, 45, 46, 48^6, 49^2, 50, 51^2, 52, 53^2, 54, 55, 58, 60, 62, 63, 66, 68^7, 69, 70, 74, 77, 78, 89^2, 90^2, 92^2, 93, 94, 95^2, 106^2, 109, 111, 114, 115^2, 117, 118, 120^3, 123, 124, 125, 130, 132, 133^3, 134, 135, 136, 137^2, 138, 139^2, 141, 142^4, 144, 146^4, 148, 149, 150, 151, 152, 155, 156, 160, 161, 167, 168, 171, 172, 175^2, 178^4, 180, 185^5, 186^2, 192^5, 193^6, 207, 209, 210, 215, 216, 220, 240, 241, 246, 247^2, 248, 251, 252, 254, 256^3, 258, 260, 262^2, 264, 265, 266, 267, 270^2, 277, 279, 285^2, 288, 290^2, 291, 294, 298, 300, 304, 305, 310. There are 201 quotations that belong to class A.

Next we come to class A-, those quotations that have a slight deviation of one or two words in the LXX (consisting of a synonym of some sort or a different compounding element of the same verb) without any real change in meaning. The A- citations are: 14 (LXX's γῇ οὐκ ἰδίᾳ is γῇ ἀλλοτρίᾳ in Acts 7:6), 23, 36, 46, 95, 106, 109, 113, 114, 134 (which supports a rendition of "govern" for תרעם rather than "shatter"), 137, 139 (which supports a rendering of "angels" for אֱלֹהִים), 150, 162, 186, 258. Those total 16 entries for class A-.

Finally, class A^d includes those quotations that differ in one or two places from the LXX wording, but without any appreciable effect on the sense of the passage.

Those citations include: 11, 14, 18, 29, 40, 47, 59, 64, 74, 86, 95^2, 97^2, 100, 103^2, 109, 141, 142

(which supports "corruption" as the proper rendering of שחת), 147, 152, 154, 165, 167, 168, 169, 176, 189, 190, 203, 206, 208, 210, 217, 231^3, 232, 234, 245, 249, 250, 253, 254, 256, 262, 268, 277 (indicating that בָּעַלְתִּי comes from בעל, meaning "abhor" rather than "be married to"), 291. Those come to a total of 50 citations.

The total for the three classes of category A (A, A-, and A^d) is 268 citations.

Category B

This category includes instances where the New Testament quotation quite closely adheres to the wording of the LXX, even where the LXX deviates somewhat (though not so seriously as to distort the real meaning of the Old Testament passage as given in the MT) from the received text in the Hebrew Bible. This category also needs to be subdivided.

The first class (B) comprises cases of complete or near-complete agreement between the New Testament and LXX. Those citations include: 5, 108, 144 (where both use φθόγγος αὐτῶν for קַוָּם, either understanding the קַו as a cord in a harp or reading it as קוֹלָם), 145, 178, 180, 191, 199, 200, 201, 205, 206 (where both read as *hophal* perfects the MT's *hiphil* imperatives), 213, 233, 243, 259, 260 (in which both treat the MT's לָאֲסוּרִים as those imprisoned by blindness), 294.

The second class (B^a) consists of those passages in which the LXX is somewhat closer to the MT than the New Testament is. Those citations are: 18 and 19 (Rom. 9:9 has ἐλεύσομαι instead of the LXX's ἀναστρέψω for אָשׁוּב), 41, 42 (in which Lk. 2:23 gives the basic sense of Ex. 13:12 rather than following the literalism of the LXX here), 57, 65 (where Rom. 10:5 slightly adjusts to harmonize with its own context), 68 (where Lk. 10:27 adds διανοίᾳ to καρδίᾳ), 69 (where Acts 3:23 inserts the antecedent for needful clarification), 78, 88 (where the New Testament authors add μόνῳ after αὐτῷ for emphasis), 115 (Rom. 15:10 either inserts a clause not found in the MT of Deut. 32:43 [though it is present in the 4QDt^q fragment of this passage] or inserts it from Ps. 97:7, which does contain those words in the MT), 124, 142 (where both render שֹׁבַע שְׂמָחוֹת by πληρώσεις), 178 (where the LXX's ἐδοκίμασαν is closer to the MT's בְּחָנוּנִי than is Heb. 3:9, ἐν δοκιμασίᾳ), 180 (where the original reading of Heb. 1:12 is in doubt; ἀλλάξεις conforms to the LXX and MT, but Nestle reads ἑλίξεις for the passage), 181, 210, 258 (where ὀξεῖς [Rom. 3:15] only approximates for the MT's יְרַצּוּ, which in the LXX is τρέχουσιν), 259 (in which ἐκ Σιών [Rom. 11:26] is not as close to לְצִיּוֹן as the LXX's ἕνεκεν Σιών, but both render לְשָׁבֵי as ἀποστρέψει, as if reading it as יָשִׁיב with פֶּשַׁע as transitive), 264 (where the LXX follows the word order of the MT a little better than the New Testament does), 288 (where Rom. 9:25 implies καλέσω—God speaking—from the command He gave His prophets to address to His people).

Including B^d, which contains 4 citations (140, 222, 225, 226), there are a total of 50 citations in category B.

Category C

These are the citations in which the New Testament adheres more closely to the MT than the LXX does, indicating that the apostolic author may have consulted his Hebrew Bible directly in the preparation of his own account or letter. In at least a few cases there may be an affinity for the Proto-Theodotion Greek translation, as some modern scholars have suggested. The existence of such a preapostolic translation may be inferred from the occurrence of some terms that were preserved in the second-century A.D. translation of Theodotion himself, as distinct from the LXX.

The readings in Category C are: 40 (Rom. 9:17 is much closer to הֶעֱמַדְתִּיךָ with its ἐξήγειρά σε than is the LXX with διετηρήθης), 107 (Mt. 22:24 accurately renders יְבַמָּה by ἐπιγαμβρεύσει, which LXX omits altogether), 114 (Rom. 12:19 is literally correct for Deut. 32:35–36, in contrast with the LXX's ἐν ἡμέρᾳ ἐκδικήσεως), 124, 129 (1 Cor. 3:19 rightly renders לֹכֵד חֲכָמִים בְּעָרְמָם by δρασσόμενος ἐν τῇ πανουργίᾳ αὐτῶν in contrast to the LXX's καταλαμβάνων ἐν τῇ φρονήσει), 131 (Rom. 11:35 τίς προέδωκεν αὐτῷ is definitely better for Job 41:3 מִי הִקְדִּימַנִי than is LXX τίς ἀντιστήσεταί μοι), 145 (Mt. 27:46 omits the LXX insertion of πρόσχες μου before ἵνα τί, but note that ἠλί in Mt. is better than ἐλωί in Mk. 15:34 in view of the comment of the bystanders in Mt. 27:46 and Mk. 15:34; note that אֵל is good Aramaic as well as Hebrew, and occurs several times in the *Genesis Apocryphon*), 157, 170 (Mt. 13:35 κεκρυμμένα is better than the LXX προβλήματα for the MT חִידוֹת), 182³, 188 (2 Cor. 9:9 joins the MT in omitting the extra τοῦ αἰῶνος of the

LXX), 204 (2 Pet. 2:22 uses ἐπιστρέψας for the participle שָׁב rather than the LXX's ἐπέλθῃ), 206 (John 12:40, unlike the Synoptics, renders הֵשַׁע as an indicative perfect, τετύφλωκεν, and similarly follows the MT vowel pointing to the end of the sentence), 209 (Rom. 9:33 follows the MT rather than the LXX wording), 211 (the LXX comes closer to הַהֹלְכִים with ὁ πορευόμενος than Mt. 4:15–16 does with ὁ καθήμενος, but the LXX construes ראו as an imperative רְאוּ rather than as an aorist indicative, while Matthew renders it as εἶδεν), 215, 217 (the LXX interprets לָנֶצַח, "forever," as a *piel* infinitive, לְנַצֵּחַ, while 1 Cor. 15:54 renders it "in victory" on the basis of a later usage of נֶצַח; but its ἐξαλείψει is much closer to מָחָה than is the LXX's ἀφεῖλεν), 233, 234, 244, 248, 253, 276, 302, 308 (Zec. 12:10 אֲשֶׁר־דָּקָרוּ is faithfully reproduced by John 19:37 ὃν ἐξεκέντησειν, whereas the LXX's ἀνθ' ὧν κατωρχήσαντο resulted from misreading דקרו as רקדו), 309 (the LXX is closer to הַךְ with its πατάξατε than Mt. 26:31 is with πατάξω, which is inferred from God's command to His prophets to be tantamount to the act of God Himself; but Matthew's τὸν ποιμένα is accurate, whereas the LXX's plural, ποιμένας spoils it as a prediction of Christ's arrest; moreover Matthew's διασκορπισθήσονται is better than the LXX's ἐκσπάσατε in rendering MT's תְּפוּצֶיךָ, "and they shall be scattered"), 311. Those come to a total of 33 quotations belonging to category C.

Category D

These consist of passages in which the New Testament quotation adheres quite closely to the LXX rendering, even when it deviates somewhat from the MT. Those citations include the following:

29. Gen. 47:31 reads מִטָּה, whereas the LXX and Heb. 11:21 read מַטֶּה.

32. Ex. 2:14 reads (a) אִישׁ שַׂר for which the LXX and Acts 7:27, 35 read ἄρχοντα (which is not a bad rendering for that phrase), (b) אַתָּה אֹמֵר, rendered σὺ θέλεις instead of λέγεις. Both read ἐχθές, which does not appear in the MT.

34. Ex. 3:2 is rendered in a different word order, so far as ἄγγελος is concerned, in the LXX and Acts 7:30; מִתּוֹךְ הַסְּנֶה becomes ἐν in both, and Acts 7:30 omits κυρίου (יהוה) after ἄγγελος.

35. In Ex. 3:5 שַׁל becomes λῦσαι in the LXX, and λῦσον in Acts 7:33; the MT dual נְעָלֶיךָ becomes singular in both; both omit σου after ὑπόδημα, whereas the MT reads נְעָלֶיךָ; the MT's צְעָקָה is κραυγῆς in the LXX, but στεναγμοῦ in Acts 7:33

(the two Greek words being almost synonymous); לְהַצִּיל comes out as ἐξαγαγεῖν in the LXX, but ἐξελέσθαι in Acts 7:34.

103. Deut. 24:1 has וְנָתַן בְּיָדָהּ in the MT, but δότω αὐτῇ (rather than the strictly literal) in the LXX and Mt. 5:31; 19:7; Mk. 10:4; Deut. 24:3: MT's סֵפֶר כְּרִיתֻת comes out as βιβλίον ἀποστασίου in the LXX and Mk. and even in Mt. 19:7, but as ἀποστάσιον in Mt. 5:31; the MT's וְשִׁלְּחָהּ becomes ἐξαποστελεῖ in the LXX, but ἀπολῦσαι in Mt. 19:7 and Mk. 10:4.

107. Deut. 25:5, 7: the MT's לְהָקִים is ἀναστῆσαι in the LXX, ἀναστήσει in Mt. 22:44 and ἐξαναστήσῃ in Mk. 12:19 and Lk. 20:28; the MT's שֵׁם אָחִיו becomes ὄνομα in the LXX, but the paraphrastic σπέρμα in the New Testament passages (D^a).

156. Ps. 40:7 reads אָזְנַיִם, for which the LXX uses the literal ὠτία; but Heb. 10:5 uses synecdoche in rendering σῶμα (the ears present the body as listening to God's Word in order to obey it). Note that Ps. 40B and 40C are both in category A.

157. Psalm 41:10(:9); the MT's עָקֵב ("heel") becomes πτερνισμόν ("a tripping up, a fraud, deception") in the LXX, but πτέρναν ("heel") in Jn. 13:18 (which is literally faithful to the MT as over against the LXX), therefore D^a. But the LXX's ἐμεγάλυνεν is closer to the MT's הִגְדִּיל, though Jn. 13:18 communicates better with ἐπῆρεν (the LXX's ἐσθίων and Jn.'s τρώγων are completely synonymous.)

227. Isa. 29:16b; the MT reads "He did not make me"—לֹא עָשָׂנִי; the LXX "Thou hast not made me wisely"; Rom. 9:20: "Why hast Thou made me thus?" These seem at first glance to be quite deviant, but Paul's interpretive rendering well captures the primary thrust of the God-defying statement in the MT. And that, of course, is what this passage in Romans is all about. From that standpoint we may class this adaptation as an interpretive paraphrase.

222. Isa. 28:11-12 reads יְדַבֵּר in the MT; the LXX makes it 3rd pers. plur. λαλήσουσιν and 1 Cor. 14:21 1st pers. singular λαλήσω (which correctly adheres to Yahweh as the subject of this verb, whereas the LXX makes it virtually impersonal).

245. Almost all of Isa. 52:11 is contained in 2 Cor. 6:17, though the word order is a bit different. The same is true of the LXX wording, although it is not quite as poetic as the New Testament. (The last clause of 2 Cor. 6:17 picks up one phrase from Ex. 20:34, a passage of similar sentiment.)

288. Hos. 2:3b רַחֲמָה is rendered by the LXX ἠλεημένη but as ἠγαπημένη by Rom. 9:25 (a meaning for רחם which is more common in Aramaic than in Hebrew). The final entry in Isa. 10:22 shows

the following variants: (a) יִהְיֶה is γένηται in the LXX, but ᾖ in Rom. 9:27; וְהָיָה מִסְפַּר (by inference) becomes ἐὰν ᾖ ὁ ἀριθμός in Rom., as well as in the LXX; in some instances וְ introduces protasis; (c) יָשׁוּב after שְׁאָר in Isa. 10:22 becomes σωθήσεται. Isa. 10:22 has only יִהְיֶה עַמְּךָ in the MT and the LXX, but Rom. 9:27 inserts ἀριθμός before τῶν υἱῶν Ἰσραήλ; שְׁאָר appears as κατάλειμμα in the LXX and ὑπόλειμμα in Rom. 9:27; שְׁאָר יָשׁוּב is given a soteriological interpretation as σωθήσεται in both the LXX and the New Testament.

293. Hos. 13:14 reads קָטָבְךָ ("your sting, thorn"), for which the LXX has δίκη (probably meaning "retributive punishment" rather than "justice" in this context), but 1 Cor. 15:55 has νῖκος (in the sense of the triumph of righteousness as the wicked are smitten in judgment). Both are therefore interpretive, though not literal; שְׁאוֹל is ᾅδη in the LXX, but θάνατε in 1 Cor. 15 (slightly paraphrastic).

294. Joel 2:28-32 as quoted in Acts 2:17-21 shows the following deviations: (1) Acts 2:17 reverses the order of "youths" and "old men," whereas the LXX keeps to the order of the MT; (2) Acts 2:19 inserts ἄνω after οὐρανῷ and κάτω after γῆ—for a heightening effect (LXX = MT); (3) Acts 2:19 also inserts σημεῖα before ἐν τῇ γῇ (which is a frequent byword in connection with τέρατα, even though the LXX does not use it here); (4) the MT's נוֹרָא ("fearful") is apparently read as from רָאָה ("to see") in the niphal participle נִרְאָה, hence ἐπιφανῆ in both the LXX and the New Testament.

302. Hab. 1:5 in Acts 13:41: (a) רְאוּ בַגּוֹיִם ("look upon the nations" with gloating satisfaction) appears with the ἴδετε in the LXX and Acts 13: ἴδετε καταφρονηταί ("Behold, you despisers. . ."). The reference to Gentiles hardly fits in with Habakkuk's context here; possibly Schleussner 228ᵇ is correct in suggesting that the Vorlage of the LXX may have read בֹּגְדִים; if so it is far more appropriate in the flow of thought in this Habakkuk passage. Yet the accidental omission of two successive consonants, such as gimel and daleth, seems rather unlikely. If, however, the error occurred during the late 6th century B.C., the form of waw was rather similar to gimel; if so, we would only have to reckon with daleth as inadvertently overlooked by the scribe. It is rather significant that καταφρονέω is actually used to translate בגד in Prov. 13:16 and Hos. 6:7, so far as the LXX is concerned; (b) ἀφανίσθητε ("disappear, vanish, perish") in the LXX and the New Testament is admissible for תֵּמַהּ; it is so used in Baruch 3:11 (cf. Scleuss. 412); (c) MT's כִּי־פֹעַל פֹּעֵל ("for one is going to do a deed") may well imply that Yahweh is the

agent in this case. If so, the LXX and Heb. 12:26 are justified in inserting ἐγώ with ἐργάζομαι to bring this out; (d) the LXX seems to have pointed the consonants פֹּעֵל פֹּעַל rather than the MT's reverse order, thus furnishing a suitable object to the verb after it rather than before it (as the MT has it); from this Acts 13:41 draws in a clarifying ἔργον as antecedent of ὃ οὐ μὴ πιστεύσητε.

311. Mal. 3:1 is quoted in Mt. 11:10; Mk. 1:2; and Lk. 7:27. The following deviations occur: (a) the LXX follows the MT in rendering לְפָנַי whereas the New Testament citations make it לְפָנֶיךָ (in which apparently God is being addressed by the prophet, rather than speaking through the prophet—yet in either case it is God who is the antecedent); (b) the MT reads "My messenger, and he will prepare the way before Me..." but this appears in the New Testament as "who will prepare..."—which amounts to the same thing. But it is fair to say that the New Testament's κατασκευάσει is much closer to וּפִנָּה than is the LXX's ἐπιβλέψεται, which is clearly erroneous (Dᵃ): (c) consistent with the use of σου (rather than μου) after προσώπου is the σου which the New Testament inserts after τὴν ὁδόν (דַּרְךָ).

In addition to the entries above, nos. 47, 86, 227, and 234 are to be included in this category. That brings to 22 the number of citations belonging to category D.

Category E

This category of quotations consists of those that give the impression that unwarranted liberties were taken with the Old Testament text in the light of its context. But when due consideration is given to the basic message of the Hebrew passage and the particular purpose that the New Testament author had in mind (under the guidance of God's Spirit), in each case it will be seen that, far from wresting or perverting the original verse, the inspired servant of Jesus brings out in a profound and meaningful way its implications and connotations. The New Testament contains the Holy Spirit's commentary on the message and teaching of the Old Testament. As we keep that guiding principle in mind we shall find our way to the solution of each of the 13 passages included under this category. Those passages (except for entry 29) warrant a fuller discussion. They include:

118. In this conflate passage of Acts 13:22 we find no translation problem whatever: "And he shall perform all my desires" is accurately carried over

from the MT to the LXX and the New Testament. The problem has to do with the identity of that promised performance. In the Isaianic context the reference of Isa. 44:28 is to Cyrus, the future conqueror of Babylon and the entire Middle East, but the Acts passage clearly refers to the Lord Jesus as the future deliverer of God's people from Satan, sin, and death. It should be carefully observed here that Cyrus is predicted as God's anointed (מְשִׁיחִי) to bring about the release of captive Israel at the end of the 70 years of exile. As such, Cyrus served as a type of Christ, the divine liberator of God's people from captivity to sin. Hence the inclusion of that phrase at the end of Acts 13:22, a conflate of three Old Testament passages.

120–121. Only the first of these three New Testament quotations shows any real discrepancy; Heb. 1:5 is correct for Psalm 2:7, and Rev. 21:7 is almost perfect for 1 Chron. 17:13, except that the MT's לְאָב is made more explicit by θεός, since God is clearly the "Father" referred to in the Old Testament passage. But in 2 Cor. 6:18 there is a very striking identification made between Christ and His church. That is, 1 Chron. 17:13 ("I will be a Father to Him and He shall be a Son to Me") is interpretively enlarged to include those redeemed sinners who are united with Christ by faith: "I will be a father to you [plural] and you shall be sons and daughters to Me" (the final clause, "says the Lord Almighty," is borrowed from 2 Sam. 7:8.) The language of Hos. 1:10 (MT 2:1) includes a very similar promise: "And it will come about that in the place where it is said to them, 'You are not My people,' it will be said to them, 'Children of the living God!'" (בְּנֵי אֵל־חָי). 2 Cor. 6:18 makes explicit what was already implicit in the Old Testament passages—that a promise to true believers among men applies also to true believers among women, even though there is no Old Testament text that actually specifies women apart from men.

165. There is not much change in the wording of Psalm 68:19a as it is quoted in Eph. 4:8, but the latter verse seems significant. The MT's "Thou hast received among men" (or "taken hold of men") becomes "Thou hast given unto men" in Eph 4:8 (the LXX closely follows the MT: לָקַחְתָּ מַתָּנוֹת בָּאָדָם), leaving out any prepositional equivalent for the Hebrew בְּ. How can those changes (ἔλαβες for לָקַחְתָּ and τοῖς ἀνθρώποις for בָּאָדָם) be justified? Here is a classic example of inferential interpretation. God took those gifts, not to appropriate them for Himself, but for the purpose of distributing them *among* (a common force for בְּ) men. Or we can interpret the MT clause as meaning: "Thou hast taken gifts from

among men" (a common use of *b* in Ugaritic Canaanite), with the implication that God has taken those spiritual gifts from among believers in order to distribute them for the benefit of His people as a whole. (It is interesting that the Targum itself construes the clause in very similar fashion: סְלֶקֶתְּ לִרְקִיעַ שְׁבִיתָא שְׁבִיתָא אַלְפְּתָא פִּתְגָּמֵי אוֹרַיְתָא לְהוֹן יָהַבְתָּא מַתְּנָן לִבְנֵי נָשָׁא.).

201. The MT of Prov. 11:31*a* seems to mean: "Behold (הֶן) the righteous in the land (בָּאָרֶץ) meets with retribution (יְשֻׁלָּם)." The LXX (followed by Peter in 1 Pet. 4:18) deviates as follows: (1) הֶן is taken as a conditional particle (as in ten other instances throughout the Hebrew Bible, and usually so in the Aramaic) rather than as an interjection, (2) "in the land" is replaced by μόλις ("scarcely"), or we can take it that בָּאָרֶץ has simply been left out and that μόλις is injected to sharpen the idea of judgment visited even on believers when they fail to obey God, and (3) the intensive stem of שׁלם is taken by LXX translators to mean "bring into safety" (as in Job 8:6), even though it is less likely to be the intended meaning here. Nevertheless, though Peter chose to follow the LXX without deviation as he wrote to the Jews of the Diaspora and their fellow-believers from among the Gentiles, he did not depart from the basic thrust of the Hebrew passage. Both the MT and the LXX present the *a minori* principle—if God does not allow His children to escape punishment when they deserve it, how much severer will be His judgment on the unbelieving and the ungodly in the final day? The essential teaching of Prov. 11:31 is thus dramatically set forth. As for Prov. 11:31*b*, the force of אַף־כִּי ("how much more") is simply intensified by the paraphrastic ποῦ φανεῖται ("where shall he [the ungodly man] appear?"). The concept is faithfully preserved by that rendering in the LXX and the New Testament.

220. Hab. 2:4 is well known. It appears three times in the New Testament as a proof-text for justification by faith. The MT of that verse uses a *hapax legomenon* that is of uncertain interpretation. It is usually construed to mean: "Behold, it [the soul of the proud sinner] has become puffed up; his soul is not upright within him." The phrase could also be taken as a virtual relative clause after an indefinite antecedent (in which case the relative אֲשֶׁר may be left out): "Behold one in whom his soul has been puffed up is not upright." But it is by no means certain that the intensive verb עֻפְּלָה is related to עֹפֶל ("hill, a round eminence"). It may rather be related to the Arabic غَفَلَ ("be heedless, neglectful"), which in the causative second measure means "show heedlessness, neglect." That is a completely tenable etymology,

which was apparently followed by the LXX as it rendered the clause: "If (הֶן) one is heedless/neglectful, My [reading נַפְשִׁי instead of the MT's נַפְשׁוֹ] soul is not well disposed [לֹא יָשְׁרָה בּוֹ; cf. Zorell, *Lexicon*, p. 339*a*] toward him." Here יָשְׁרָה is construed to mean εὐδοκεῖ ("take pleasure in, approve of"). The objective data for that rendering seems to be better than the common interpretation of "be puffed up," and in view of the frequent confusion between *waw* and *yod* during the second century B.C. an alteration of נַפְשׁוֹ to נַפְשִׁי seems altogether justified. In addition, the *Vorlage* of the LXX reads that way. The remainder of Hab. 2:4 is well rendered by the LXX and the New Testament. The only question is whether it was proper for the "his" of בֶּאֱמוּנָתוֹ to be construed as ἐκ πίστεως without any αὐτοῦ. But if we understand "by faith" to refer to the personal faith of the individual believer, and if we recognize that אֱמוּנָה may mean not simply "trustworthiness" but also "faithfulness towards God in believing and trusting" (Zorell, *Lexicon*, p. 63*a*), then we have no discrepancy in meaning between the MT and the New Testament in the treatment of the clause. And it should be recognized that there was no other word for *faith* in the vocabulary of the Old Testament except אֱמוּנָה (cf. Gesenius-Buhl, *Lexicon*, p. 962).

249. As rendered in Acts 8:33, the LXX version of Isa. 53:8 (which the Ethiopian eunuch was studying when Philip met him) contained clearly erroneous renderings of מֵעֹצֶר (as ἐν τῇ ταπεινώσει) and נֶגַע לָמוֹ (as ἤχθη εἰς θάνατον). Moreover, it misconstrued מִשְׁפָּט as the subject of לֻקָּח (ἤρθη), and made γενεὰν αὐτοῦ the object of יְשׂוֹחֵחַ (poorly construed as διηγήσεται). Again, it erred in interpreting חַיִּים, a *nomen recti* after אֶרֶץ, as if it were the subject of נִגְזַר (αἴρεται). There is no hope of bringing the LXX translation of the verse into conformity with the true intent of the MT original. But there is no need to do so in this particular case, for no doctrinal teaching is based on its erroneous rendition. The Acts 8 account simply relates that the eunuch was reading the LXX of the passage and that he was puzzled by it. It then says that Philip began to unfold the messianic teaching of Isa. 53 as a whole—and that emerges very clearly even in the defective form of the LXX rendering—and that Philip showed the eunuch how Jesus of Nazareth had fulfilled the predictions of Isa. 53. All that Acts 8 contains is historically factual and completely accurate.

263. First Cor. 2:9 presents a paraphrastic summary of several different texts in the Old Testament. From Isa. 64:4 (MT v. 3) it adapts לֹא הֶאֱזִינוּ and

עַיִן לֹא רָאָתָה as "That which the eye has not seen and the ear has not heard." The Hebrew passage states that God's people have never heard of, listened to, or seen with their eyes any other god than Yahweh himself—but that is surely consonant with the hope of heaven set forth in 1 Cor. 2. There is apparently no Old Testament basis for καὶ ἐπὶ καρδίαν ἀνθρώπου οὐκ ἀνέβη except for a reading peculiar to the LXX as the final clause of Isa. 65:16: καὶ οὐκ ἀναβήσεται αὐτῶν ἔτι τὴν καρδίαν, for which the MT has וְכִי נִסְתְּרוּ מֵעֵינָי ("and surely they [my earlier afflictions] have been hidden from my eyes"). The source for that LXX reading can only be conjectured, and yet we must appreciate the poetic and beautiful wording of the sentiment itself, as woven into the tapestry of 1 Cor. 2:9. The final clause of the verse, ἃ ἡτοίμασεν ὁ θεὸς τοῖς ἀγαπῶσιν αὐτόν, may be construed as an inference from passages like Ex. 20:6, which ends (in the LXX): καὶ ποιῶν ἔλεος εἰς χιλιάδας τοῖς ἀγαπῶσίν με. To sum up, 1 Cor. 2:9 is a noteworthy example of a conflate quotation from various passages written in a paraphrastic manner, and yet in a manner that accurately brings out the teaching of each of the sources involved.

292. Mt. 2:15 presents no problem at all so far as the translation of Hos. 11:1 is concerned. Both the LXX and the New Testament renderings are quite accurate for the MT original. But the context of Hos. 11 clearly refers to the Exodus experience of Israel under the leadership of Moses, whereas Matthew refers to the return of the holy family from Egypt after the death of Herod the Great. How can the verse be justified as a fulfilled prediction pertaining to the infancy of Jesus of Nazareth? The answer is to be found in the pattern of type-antitype that is often observable in biblical prophecy. As the Messiah, Jesus occupied the status of antitype to national Israel under the Old Testament economy. That is clearly brought out by the so-called Servant Songs of Isa. 41–53. Both the covenant nation of Israel and the suffering servant who furnishes a vicarious atonement for sinners are referred to by the title "Servant of Yahweh." Apart from the Messiah there would be no foundation for a covenant of redemption between God the Father and God the Son. And apart from a covenant of redemption there could be no covenant of grace with Abraham and his descendants. Therefore, in a very real sense Jesus, the incarnate Son of God, was Israel represented and personified. As such it was essential for Him to recapitulate, as it were, the career of His nation as it experienced God's deliverance from centuries of bondage under Egyptian power. From that perspective, the correlation between the Exodus of Israel and the return of Christ from Egypt is completely justified.

296. Acts 7:42–43 seem to deviate markedly from the MT of Amos 5:25–27. The discrepancies are as follows: (1) the plural θυσίας is used for the singular מִנְחָה; (2) σκηνήν appears for the *hapax* סִכּוּת (apparently reading it as סַכַּת, whereas it may have been intended as the name of a heathen god, Sakkut); (3) the deity-name Molokh is used for the MT's מַלְכְּכֶם ("your king"); (4) ἄστρον is used for כִּיּוּן, which is more probably to be regarded as the name of a planetary god, Kaiwan. Yet in Acts 7:26 that name is spelled entirely differently: Raiphan. How can all of those deviations be reconciled with biblical inerrancy?

First, it should be remembered that Stephen is closely following the wording of the LXX here, for the simple reason that he is addressing an audience composed both of Palestinian Jews (who would have access to the Proto-masoretic Hebrew text) and of Diaspora Jews, whose knowledge of Amos would be largely confined to the LXX. It would have been inappropriate for him at that point to explain to his hearers that the LXX had used the wrong spelling of the name of the idol; it was only important to emphasize that even in the days of the Exodus their forefathers had already fallen into a clandestine idolatry.

Second, we can come to terms with each of the deviations on the basis of textual criticism: (1) the LXX may have used the plural θυσίας with the intention that it be taken as a collective singular; "to offer a meal offering" may indeed be understood as a generality rather than simply as one distinctive offering of that kind; (2) because סכות was unpointed in first-century A.D. texts (and in third-century A.D. texts as well), סַכַּת ("booth") may have been a possible reading, fitting quite well into the context. We incline toward סַכַּת, the god Sakkuth, only because the other two such nouns appear to be deity designations, but the consonants would be the same in either case; (3) as for מַלְכְּכֶם, the context in Amos is the days when Israel had no king at all. Therefore, it is a fair inference that the word would have meant "your King-God" or (even "your Moloch" with the same consonants). Amos was not referring to his own day, when both Judah and Israel had kings ruling over them; (4) ἄστρον is not bad for an introduction to כִּיּוּן, since in any case the deity named would be an astral or planetary god. As for the origin of 'Ραιφάν from Καιωάη it should be understood that an original Sopherim reading (כיון) might easily have become corrupted in the LXX-Vorlage in the course of textual transmission, so that *kaph* would have been misread as *resh* (in the late fifth century B.C.), and *waw* as *pe*, simply because in that period those letters resembled each other so markedly. There being no way of checking the accuracy of a heathen name like כַּיִן (the deity assigned to the planet Saturn), no subsequent corrector would have been able to spot those blunders on the part of the scribal copyist. By LXX times the consonants *R-Y-P-N* were fortunate to be equipped with the right vowels, so as to come out with a-ā as in Ḳaiwān.

One other discrepancy seems to have been interpretive in nature. Whereas the MT and LXX both speak of the future Babylonian captivity by the suggestive phrase ἐπέκεινα Δαμασκοῦ ("beyond Damascus"), Stephen made it more explicit— ἐπέκεινα Βαβυλῶνος ("beyond Babylon"). Amos referred to Damascus only as a stopping point on the long, weary road to Nebuchadnezzar's Babylon. But for Stephen's audience the more illuminating way of referring to the punishment of national exile was to bring out the name of Babylon itself quite explicitly.

297. There are four or five discrepancies between Amos 9:11–12 and Acts 15:16–17: (1) Acts 15:16 departs from the MT and LXX in reading "After these things" rather than "In that day." But that is simply the replacing of the Hebrew phrase with a semantic equivalent more usual in Greek narrative style; (2) in rendering the MT's אֶת־פִּרְצֵיהֶן ("their breaches") as "the tent of David" that has fallen down, James draws from the idea of breaches in the wall the inference that the wall itself (as well as its superstructure) has fallen down. Perhaps that was colored by the LXX's "the fallen parts of her"; (3) the use of ἀνοικοδομήσω in Acts 15:16 ("I shall rebuild") is really not a discrepancy at all. The corresponding Hebrew verb בָּנָה can mean either "build" or "rebuild," depending on the context; (4) Amos 9:12 reads, "In order that they may *take possession* (יִירְשׁוּ) of the remnant of *Edom*, and all the Gentiles upon whom My name is called" (italics added). Here the reference to Edom is rather puzzling, and seems to have no particular fulfillment in subsequent history. Probably it is best to take the אֶת־ before שְׁאֵרִית as a subsequent insertion, resulting from a desire to make all of the "remnant" prophecy apply to a hoped-for conquest of Edom; hence the insertion of אֶת־ as the sign of a direct definite object

(presumably lacking in the Sopherim text back in LXX times). Also, if "Edom" is a mistaken pointing, then we should take the word to be pointed אָדָם ("mankind"), in conformity with LXX's "the remainder of mankind," to which "even (καὶ) the Gentiles" is epexegetic. As for the leading verb, the LXX points to יִדְרְשׁוּ ("that they might seek") rather than to יִירְשׁוּ ("that they might possess"). The confusion of similar letters (*yod* being read for *daleth*) could easily have occurred in the Qumran period, when an oversized *yod* resembled a *daleth* (except for the more pointed angle of the latter). Thus we may reconstruct the original text of Amos 9:12a as follows: לְמַעַן יִדְרְשׁוּ שְׁאֵרִית וְכָל־הַגּוֹים אֲשֶׁר נִקְרָא שְׁמִי עֲלֵיהֶם נְאֻם יהוה. On that basis we can see that James was perfectly justified in applying the passage to God's plan for the conversion of Gentiles and their inclusion in the holy people of God, even without first becoming circumcised as Jews.

299. Micah 5:1(2) and Mt. 2:6. The deviations are as follows: (1) γῆ Ἰουδα replaces τοῦ Ἐφραθα, since that designation in the MT and LXX simply distinguished it from Bethlehem of Zebulon (Josh. 19:15); (2) οὐδαμῶς ἐλαχίστη interprets the implication of צָעִיר (LXX ὀλιγοστός), for if the Messiah was to come from that town, then regardless of its size it would become a place of major importance. Hence the litotes: "by no means the least"; (3) ἐν τοῖς ἡγεμόσιν Ἰουδα interprets the MT's אַלְפֵי as אַלּוּפֵי from אַלּוּף ("chieftain"), therefore ἡγεμών. The LXX uses ἡγεμών for אַלּוּף in Gen. 36:15; Ex. 15:1; 1 Chron. 1:50; Psalm 54:14. In the eighth century B.C. the word would have been spelled אַלְפֵי without the *waw*, so there was a possibility of confusion with אַלְפֵי from אֶלֶף. On the basis of Matthew's interpretation under divine inspiration, it is plausible to argue for correcting the MT vocalization to אַלֻּפֵי. On the other hand, it may simply have been that Matthew recorded accurately the interpretation given to the passage by King Herod's advisors. It may well have been that they were uninfluenced by the interpretation of "thousands" put on the word by the Alexandrian Jews, and that they maintained an oral tradition of their own that was much older than that of the LXX. Be that as it may, the Masoretes themselves clearly favored the Alexandrian interpretation at that point. It should also be mentioned, however, that the rendering ἡγεμών might have derived from the same vocalization as that adopted by the Masoretes. If the term "thousand" had by Micah's time acquired a special connotation as denoting a community consisting of one thousand inhabitants or more (or even

one that was large enough to furnish a contingent of one thousand troops or more for the national militia), then the commander of the contingent might well have been referred to as a רֹאשׁ אֶלֶף, or simply as an אֶלֶף for short. (Undoubtedly that was the ultimate origin of אַלּוּף itself as a term for chieftain or leader—unless, of course, it was a figure derived from the symbol of a bull who dominated his own herd.)

307. Zech. 11:12–13. There are two basic problems connected with this passage: (1) Mt. 27:9 refers the quotation to Jeremiah rather than Zechariah because of the importance of the potter's field in the actual fulfillment of the prediction. Though most of the wording of the quotation is taken from the Zechariah passage, it is only in Jer. 18:2–3 and 19:2 that a potter is prominently mentioned as employed by the temple authorities and having a workshop in the Valley of Hinnom. The prophet was directed by God to observe carefully how the potter molded the clay on his wheel, then pushed it back into a formless lump when his first attempt was marred. Of course, that furnished a parallel to Yahweh's dealings with apostate Israel and illustrated His plan to begin a new commonwealth of monotheistic believers after the Babylonian captivity was over. Here then we have a combination of elements from both Zechariah and Jeremiah. Because it was customary to refer only to the more prominent prophet when he was linked with a less prominent fellow-prophet, through a conflate quotation, Matthew was simply conforming to the usual practice in his reference to Jeremiah alone. (Mk. 1:2 does the same thing in regard to a conflate citation from both Malachi and Isaiah; only Isaiah is referred to as its author.); (2) in Mt. 27:9 an ironic parenthesis is inserted ("that fine price at which I was valued") after τὴν τιμήν. Apparently the insertion was intended to bring out

dramatically the pathos of Judas Iscariot's disillusionment with Jesus' trial and the utterly callous attitude of the high priestly party in regard to the judicial murder of Jesus. The implication seems to be that Judas had learned too late what a poor bargain it was for a man to gain the prizes of this world but to lose his own soul; (3) on a purely allusive basis καθὰ συνέταξεν κύριος is picked up from Ex. 9:12, though from a somewhat different context.

As we have studied the 13 passages belonging to category E, in no instance have we found an insoluble contradiction or discrepancy, though many cases involved bringing out the inner meaning or prophetic implication of the Old Testament verse by some kind of paraphrase.

Category F

In this class of quotations we have found many cases of close resemblance or complete identity between the Old Testament source and the New Testament application. But because they are not adduced by the New Testament writers as quotations from the authoritative Hebrew Scriptures, they pose no problem whatever in regard to the inerrancy of those Scriptures in the eyes of the New Testament writers. The entries for category F are: 9, 11, 42, 63, 67, (see 63), 75 (Mt. 9:36), 103, 117, 126, 137, 149, 158, 164, 173, 182, 187, 194, 203, 219, 255, 281, 283, 291, 298, 300, 305, 312. The total entries for this category is 32. There may be a large number of other examples of allusive language or incidentally adopted terminology in the New Testament text, but those included here are particularly interesting or noteworthy.

QUOTATION TOOL

1: Gen 1:27

²⁷ וַיִּבְרָ֨א אֱלֹהִ֤ים ׀ אֶת־הָֽאָדָם֙
בְּצַלְמ֔וֹ בְּצֶ֥לֶם אֱלֹהִ֖ים בָּרָ֣א אֹת֑וֹ זָכָ֥ר וּנְקֵבָ֖ה בָּרָ֥א אֹתָֽם׃

²⁷καὶ ἐποίησεν ὁ θεὸς τὸν ἄνθρωπον,
κατ᾽ εἰκόνα θεοῦ ἐποίησεν αὐτόν, ἄρσεν καὶ θῆλυ ἐποίησεν αὐτούς.

Gen 5:2

² זָכָ֥ר וּנְקֵבָ֖ה בְּרָאָ֑ם וַיְבָ֣רֶךְ אֹתָ֗ם וַיִּקְרָ֤א אֶת־שְׁמָם֙ אָדָ֔ם
בְּי֖וֹם הִבָּֽרְאָֽם׃

²ἄρσεν καὶ θῆλυ ἐποίη-
σεν αὐτοὺς καὶ εὐλόγησεν αὐτούς. καὶ ἐπωνόμασεν τὸ ὄνομα αὐτῶν Αδαμ, ᾗ ἡμέρᾳ ἐποίησεν αὐτούς.

2: Gen 2:2

² וַיְכַ֤ל אֱלֹהִים֙ בַּיּ֣וֹם הַשְּׁבִיעִ֔י מְלַאכְתּ֖וֹ אֲשֶׁ֣ר עָשָׂ֑ה וַיִּשְׁבֹּת֙ בַּיּ֣וֹם
הַשְּׁבִיעִ֔י מִכָּל־מְלַאכְתּ֖וֹ אֲשֶׁ֥ר עָשָֽׂה׃

²καὶ συνετέλεσεν ὁ θεὸς ἐν τῇ ἡμέρᾳ τῇ ἕκτῃ τὰ ἔργα
αὐτοῦ, ἃ ἐποίησεν, καὶ κατέπαυσεν τῇ ἡμέρᾳ τῇ ἑβδόμῃ ἀπὸ πάντων τῶν ἔργων αὐτοῦ, ὧν ἐποίησεν.

3: Gen 2:7

⁷ וַיִּ֩יצֶר֩ יְהוָ֨ה אֱלֹהִ֜ים אֶת־הָֽאָדָ֗ם עָפָר֙ מִן־הָ֣אֲדָמָ֔ה וַיִּפַּ֥ח בְּאַפָּ֖יו
נִשְׁמַ֣ת חַיִּ֑ים וַֽיְהִ֥י הָֽאָדָ֖ם לְנֶ֥פֶשׁ חַיָּֽה׃

⁷καὶ ἔπλασεν ὁ θεὸς τὸν
ἄνθρωπον χοῦν ἀπὸ τῆς γῆς καὶ ἐνεφύσησεν εἰς τὸ πρόσωπον
αὐτοῦ πνοὴν ζωῆς, καὶ ἐγένετο ὁ ἄνθρωπος εἰς ψυχὴν ζῶσαν.

4: Gen 2:24

²⁴ עַל־כֵּן֙ יַֽעֲזָב־אִ֔ישׁ אֶת־אָבִ֖יו וְאֶת־אִמּ֑וֹ וְדָבַ֣ק בְּאִשְׁתּ֔וֹ וְהָי֖וּ לְבָשָׂ֥ר
אֶחָֽד׃

²⁴ἕνεκεν
τούτου καταλείψει ἄνθρωπος τὸν πατέρα αὐτοῦ καὶ τὴν μητέρα
αὐτοῦ καὶ προσκολληθήσεται πρὸς τὴν γυναῖκα αὐτοῦ, καὶ ἔσονται
οἱ δύο εἰς σάρκα μίαν.

5: Gen 5:2

see Gen 1:27 [1]

6: Gen 5:24

²⁴ וַיִּתְהַלֵּ֥ךְ חֲנ֖וֹךְ
אֶת־הָֽאֱלֹהִ֑ים וְאֵינֶ֕נּוּ כִּֽי־לָקַ֥ח אֹת֖וֹ אֱלֹהִֽים׃

²⁴καὶ εὐηρέστησεν Ενωχ τῷ θεῷ καὶ οὐχ ηὑρίσκετο,
ὅτι μετέθηκεν αὐτὸν ὁ θεός.

a **Mt 19:4**

4 ὁ δὲ ἀποκριθεὶς εἶπεν⊤·
οὐκ ἀνέγνωτε ὅτι ὁ ⌜κτίσας ἀπ' ἀρχῆς ἄρσεν καὶ θῆλυ
ἐποίησεν αὐτούς⌐;

Gen 1:27 & Gen 5:2. (*A*)

---

b **Mk 10:6**

6 ἀπὸ δὲ ἀρχῆς κτίσεως ἄρσεν καὶ θῆλυ ἐποίησεν
⌜αὐτούς·

---

a **Heb 4:4**

4 εἴρηκεν °γάρ που περὶ τῆς ἑβδόμης οὕτως· καὶ κατέπαυσεν ὁ θεὸς ἐν τῇ ἡμέρᾳ τῇ ἑβδόμῃ ἀπὸ πάντων τῶν
ἔργων αὐτοῦ,

Gen 2:2; LXX uses plural femine suffix. (*A*)

---

a **1 Cor 15:45**

45 οὕτως καὶ γέγραπται·
ἐγένετο ὁ πρῶτος °ἄνθρωπος Ἀδὰμ εἰς ψυχὴν ζῶσαν, ὁ
ἔσχατος °¹Ἀδὰμ εἰς πνεῦμα ζῳοποιοῦν.

Gen 2:7. (*A*)

---

a **Mt 19:5**

5 καὶ εἶπεν· ἕνεκα τούτου καταλείψει
ἄνθρωπος τὸν πατέρα καὶ τὴν μητέρα καὶ ⌜κολληθήσεται τῇ
γυναικὶ αὐτοῦ, καὶ ἔσονται οἱ δύο εἰς σάρκα μίαν·¹

Gen 2:24; all four NT passages are identical. (*A*)

b **Mk 10:7–8**

7 ἕνεκεν τούτου καταλείψει ἄνθρωπος τὸν πατέρα
αὐτοῦ καὶ τὴν ⌜μητέρα □[καὶ προσκολληθήσεται πρὸς τὴν
γυναῖκα αὐτοῦ]`, **8** καὶ ἔσονται οἱ δύο εἰς σάρκα μίαν· ὥστε·
οὐκέτι εἰσὶν δύο ἀλλὰ μία σάρξ.

c **1 Cor 6:16**

16 °[ἢ] οὐκ οἴδατε ὅτι
ὁ κολλώμενος τῇ πόρνῃ ἓν σῶμά ἐστιν; ἔσονται γάρ, φη-
σίν, οἱ δύο εἰς σάρκα μίαν.

d **Eph 5:31**

31 ἀντὶ τούτου καταλείψει
ἄνθρωπος °[τὸν] πατέρα καὶ °[τὴν] μητέρα ⌜καὶ προσκολληθήσεται πρὸς τὴν γυναῖκα αὐτοῦ`, καὶ ἔσονται οἱ
δύο εἰς σάρκα μίαν.

---

a **Heb 11:5**

5 Πίστει Ἑνὼχ μετετέθη τοῦ μὴ ἰδεῖν θάνατον, καὶ οὐχ
ηὑρίσκετο διότι μετέθηκεν αὐτὸν ὁ θεός. πρὸ γὰρ τῆς
μεταθέσεως ⊤ μεμαρτύρηται εὐαρεστηκέναι τῷ θεῷ·

Gen 5:24; MT אֵינֶנּוּ = LXX οὐχ ηὑρίσκετο; MT לָקַח =
LXX μετέθηκεν (*A*) or (*B*)

Masoretic Text	Septuagint

7: Gen 12:1

וַיֹּאמֶר יְהוָה אֶל־אַבְרָם לֶךְ־לְךָ מֵאַרְצְךָ וּמִמּוֹלַדְתְּךָ וּמִבֵּית אָבִיךָ אֶל־הָאָרֶץ אֲשֶׁר אַרְאֶךָּ:

¹ Καὶ εἶπεν κύριος τῷ Αβραμ Ἔξελθε ἐκ τῆς γῆς σου καὶ ἐκ τῆς συγγενείας σου καὶ ἐκ τοῦ οἴκου τοῦ πατρός σου εἰς τὴν γῆν, ἣν ἄν σοι δείξω·

8: Gen 12:3

וַאֲבָרְכָה מְבָרְכֶיךָ וּמְקַלֶּלְךָ אָאֹר וְנִבְרְכוּ בְךָ כֹּל מִשְׁפְּחֹת הָאֲדָמָה:

³ καὶ εὐλογήσω τοὺς εὐλογοῦντάς σε, καὶ τοὺς καταρωμένους σε καταράσομαι· καὶ ἐνευλογηθήσονται ἐν σοὶ πᾶσαι αἱ φυλαὶ τῆς γῆς.

Gen 18:18

וְאַבְרָהָם הָיוֹ יִהְיֶה לְגוֹי גָּדוֹל וְעָצוּם וְנִבְרְכוּ בוֹ כֹּל גּוֹיֵי הָאָרֶץ:

¹⁸ Αβρααμ δὲ γινόμενος ἔσται εἰς ἔθνος μέγα καὶ πολύ, καὶ ἐνευλογηθήσονται ἐν αὐτῷ πάντα τὰ ἔθνη τῆς γῆς.

9: Gen 12:7

וַיֵּרָא יְהוָה אֶל־אַבְרָם וַיֹּאמֶר לְזַרְעֲךָ אֶתֵּן אֶת־הָאָרֶץ הַזֹּאת וַיִּבֶן שָׁם מִזְבֵּחַ לַיהוָה הַנִּרְאֶה אֵלָיו:

⁷ καὶ ὤφθη κύριος τῷ Αβραμ καὶ εἶπεν αὐτῷ Τῷ σπέρματί σου δώσω τὴν γῆν ταύτην. καὶ ᾠκοδόμησεν ἐκεῖ Αβραμ θυσιαστήριον κυρίῳ τῷ ὀφθέντι αὐτῷ.

10: Gen 13:15

כִּי אֶת־כָּל־הָאָרֶץ אֲשֶׁר־אַתָּה רֹאֶה לְךָ אֶתְּנֶנָּה וּלְזַרְעֲךָ עַד־עוֹלָם:

¹⁵ ὅτι πᾶσαν τὴν γῆν, ἣν σὺ ὁρᾷς, σοὶ δώσω αὐτὴν καὶ τῷ σπέρματί σου ἕως τοῦ αἰῶνος.

11: Gen 14:17–20

וַיֵּצֵא מֶלֶךְ־סְדֹם לִקְרָאתוֹ אַחֲרֵי שׁוּבוֹ מֵהַכּוֹת אֶת־כְּדָר־לָעֹמֶר וְאֶת־הַמְּלָכִים אֲשֶׁר אִתּוֹ אֶל־עֵמֶק שָׁוֵה הוּא עֵמֶק הַמֶּלֶךְ: ¹⁸ וּמַלְכִּי־צֶדֶק מֶלֶךְ שָׁלֵם הוֹצִיא לֶחֶם וָיָיִן וְהוּא כֹהֵן לְאֵל עֶלְיוֹן: ¹⁹ וַיְבָרְכֵהוּ וַיֹּאמַר בָּרוּךְ אַבְרָם לְאֵל עֶלְיוֹן קֹנֵה שָׁמַיִם וָאָרֶץ: ²⁰ וּבָרוּךְ אֵל עֶלְיוֹן אֲשֶׁר־מִגֵּן צָרֶיךָ בְּיָדֶךָ וַיִּתֶּן־לוֹ מַעֲשֵׂר מִכֹּל:

¹⁷ Ἐξῆλθεν δὲ βασιλεὺς Σοδομων εἰς συνάντησιν αὐτῷ — μετὰ τὸ ἀναστρέψαι αὐτὸν ἀπὸ τῆς κοπῆς τοῦ Χοδολλογομορ καὶ τῶν βασιλέων τῶν μετ' αὐτοῦ — εἰς τὴν κοιλάδα τὴν Σαυη (τοῦτο ἦν τὸ πεδίον βασιλέως). ¹⁸ καὶ Μελχισεδεκ βασιλεὺς Σαλημ ἐξήνεγκεν ἄρτους καὶ οἶνον· ἦν δὲ ἱερεὺς τοῦ θεοῦ τοῦ ὑψίστου. ¹⁹ καὶ ηὐλόγησεν τὸν Αβραμ καὶ εἶπεν Εὐλογημένος Αβραμ τῷ θεῷ τῷ ὑψίστῳ, ὃς ἔκτισεν τὸν οὐρανὸν καὶ τὴν γῆν, ²⁰ καὶ εὐλογητὸς ὁ θεὸς ὁ ὕψιστος, ὃς παρέδωκεν τοὺς ἐχθρούς σου ὑποχειρίους σοι. καὶ ἔδωκεν αὐτῷ δεκάτην ἀπὸ πάντων.

12: Gen 15:5

וַיּוֹצֵא אֹתוֹ הַחוּצָה וַיֹּאמֶר הַבֶּט־נָא הַשָּׁמַיְמָה וּסְפֹר הַכּוֹכָבִים אִם־תּוּכַל לִסְפֹּר אֹתָם וַיֹּאמֶר לוֹ כֹּה יִהְיֶה זַרְעֶךָ:

⁵ ἐξήγαγεν δὲ αὐτὸν ἔξω καὶ εἶπεν αὐτῷ Ἀνάβλεψον δὴ εἰς τὸν οὐρανὸν καὶ ἀρίθμησον τοὺς ἀστέρας, εἰ δυνήσῃ ἐξαριθμῆσαι αὐτούς. καὶ εἶπεν Οὕτως ἔσται τὸ σπέρμα σου.

[a]Acts 7:3

5 καὶ
εἶπεν πρὸς αὐτόν· ἔξελθε ἐκ τῆς γῆς σου καὶ ᵒ[ἐκ] τῆς συγγενείας σου, καὶ δεῦρο εἰς ᵒ¹τὴν γῆν ἣν ἄν σοι δείξω.

Gen 12:1 is accurately followed by Acts 7:3, except that "and from your father's house" is omitted, and a δεῦρο is inserted before εἰς τὴν γῆν.

[a]Gal 3:8

8 προϊδοῦσα δὲ ἡ
γραφὴ ὅτι ἐκ πίστεως δικαιοῖ τὰ ἔθνη ὁ θεός, προευηγ-
γελίσατο τῷ Ἀβραὰμ ὅτι ἐνευλογηθήσονται ἐν σοὶ πάντα
τὰ ἔθνη·

Gen 12:3. (*A*), except that in Gen 12:3 LXX reads φυλαί. But Gen 18:18 reads ἔθνη, as Gal 3:8.

[a]Acts 7:5 *(see also [17],a)

5 καὶ οὐκ ἔδωκεν αὐτῷ κληρονομίαν ἐν αὐτῇ οὐδὲ βῆμα
ποδὸς καὶ ἐπηγγείλατο δοῦναι ˢαὐτῷ εἰς κατάσχεσιν αὐ-
τήνˡ καὶ τῷ σπέρματι αὐτοῦ μετ' αὐτόν, οὐκ ὄντος αὐτῷ
τέκνου.

Gen 12:7; Acts 7:5 inserts εἰς κατάσχεσιν αὐτήν (LXX = MT τὴν γῆν ταύτην). (*F*) Gal 3:16 (*A*)

[b]Gal 3:16 *(see also [16],a)

16 τῷ δὲ Ἀβραὰμ ἐρρέθησαν αἱ ἐπαγγελίαι καὶ τῷ σπέρματι αὐτοῦ. οὐ λέγει· καὶ τοῖς σπέρμασιν, ὡς ἐπὶ πολλῶν ἀλλ' ὡς ἐφ' ἑνός· καὶ τῷ σπέρματί σου, ⌐ὅς ἐστιν
Χριστός.

From Gen 13:15 there is only a single phrase וּלְזַרְעֲךָ that has been adopted by Gal 3:16 (where the messianic fulfillment is found in the person of Christ Himself, as *the* "seed" *par excellence*, of Abraham). (*A*) and (*D*)

[a]Heb 7:1–2

7 Οὗτος γὰρ ὁ *Μελχισέδεκ, βασιλεὺς Σαλήμ, ἱερεὺς
τοῦ θεοῦ τοῦ ὑψίστου,* ⌐ὁ συναντήσας Ἀβραὰμ ὑποστρέφοντι ἀπὸ τῆς κοπῆς τῶν βασιλέων ᵀ καὶ εὐλογήσας
αὐτόν, **2** ᾧ καὶ δεκάτην ἀπὸ ⌐πάντων ἐμέρισεν Ἀβραάμ,
πρῶτον μὲν ἑρμηνευόμενος βασιλεὺς δικαιοσύνης ἔπειτα
δὲ καὶ *βασιλεὺς Σαλήμ,* ὅ ἐστιν βασιλεὺς εἰρήνης,

Gen 14:17–20—Heb 7:1: ὑποστρέφοντι, LXX: μετὰ τὸ ἀναστρέψαι, MT: אַחֲרֵי שׁוּבוֹ. (*A*ᵈ of *F*)

[a]Rom 4:18

18 Ὃς παρ' ἐλπίδα ἐπ' ἐλπίδι ἐπίστευσεν εἰς τὸ
γενέσθαι αὐτὸν πατέρα πολλῶν ἐθνῶν κατὰ τὸ εἰρημένον·
οὕτως ἔσται τὸ σπέρμα σουᵀ,

Gen 15:5; Rom 4:18. (*A*)

Gen 17:5

⁵ וְלֹא־יִקָּרֵ֥א ע֛וֹד אֶת־שִׁמְךָ֖ אַבְרָ֑ם וְהָיָ֤ה שִׁמְךָ֙ אַבְרָהָ֔ם כִּ֛י אַב־הֲמ֥וֹן גּוֹיִ֖ם נְתַתִּֽיךָ׃

⁵ καὶ οὐ κληθήσεται ἔτι τὸ ὄνομά σου Αβραμ, ἀλλ᾽ ἔσται τὸ ὄνομά σου Αβρααμ, ὅτι πατέρα πολλῶν ἐθνῶν τέθεικά σε.

13: Gen 15:6

⁶ וְהֶאֱמִ֖ן בַּֽיהוָ֑ה וַיַּחְשְׁבֶ֥הָ לּ֖וֹ צְדָקָֽה׃

⁶ καὶ ἐπίστευσεν Αβραμ τῷ θεῷ, καὶ ἐλογίσθη αὐτῷ εἰς δικαιοσύνην.

14: Gen 15:13–14

¹³ וַיֹּ֣אמֶר לְאַבְרָ֗ם יָדֹ֨עַ תֵּדַ֜ע כִּי־גֵ֣ר ׀ יִהְיֶ֣ה זַרְעֲךָ֗ בְּאֶ֙רֶץ֙ לֹ֣א לָהֶ֔ם וַעֲבָד֖וּם וְעִנּ֣וּ אֹתָ֑ם אַרְבַּ֥ע מֵא֖וֹת שָׁנָֽה׃ ¹⁴ וְגַ֧ם אֶת־הַגּ֛וֹי אֲשֶׁ֥ר יַעֲבֹ֖דוּ דָּ֣ן אָנֹ֑כִי וְאַחֲרֵי־כֵ֥ן יֵצְא֖וּ בִּרְכֻ֥שׁ גָּדֽוֹל׃

¹³ καὶ ἐρρέθη πρὸς Αβραμ Γινώσκων γνώσῃ ὅτι πάροικον ἔσται τὸ σπέρμα σου ἐν γῇ οὐκ ἰδίᾳ, καὶ δουλώσουσιν αὐτοὺς καὶ κακώσουσιν αὐτοὺς καὶ ταπεινώσουσιν αὐτοὺς τετρακόσια ἔτη. ¹⁴ τὸ δὲ ἔθνος, ᾧ ἐὰν δουλεύσωσιν, κρινῶ ἐγώ· μετὰ δὲ ταῦτα ἐξελεύσονται ὧδε μετὰ ἀποσκευῆς πολλῆς.

Ex 2:22

²² וַתֵּ֣לֶד בֵּ֔ן וַיִּקְרָ֥א אֶת־שְׁמ֖וֹ גֵּרְשֹׁ֑ם כִּ֣י אָמַ֔ר גֵּ֣ר הָיִ֔יתִי בְּאֶ֖רֶץ נָכְרִיָּֽה׃

²² ἐν γαστρὶ δὲ λαβοῦσα ἡ γυνὴ ἔτεκεν υἱόν, καὶ ἐπωνόμασεν Μωυσῆς τὸ ὄνομα αὐτοῦ Γηρσαμ λέγων ὅτι Πάροικός εἰμι ἐν τῇ ἀλλοτρίᾳ.

Ex 3:12

¹² וַיֹּ֙אמֶר֙ כִּֽי־אֶֽהְיֶ֣ה עִמָּ֔ךְ וְזֶה־לְּךָ֣ הָא֔וֹת כִּ֥י אָנֹכִ֖י שְׁלַחְתִּ֑יךָ בְּהוֹצִֽיאֲךָ֤ אֶת־הָעָם֙ מִמִּצְרַ֔יִם תַּֽעַבְדוּן֙ אֶת־הָ֣אֱלֹהִ֔ים עַ֖ל הָהָ֥ר הַזֶּֽה׃

¹² εἶπεν δὲ ὁ θεὸς Μωυσεῖ λέγων ὅτι Ἔσομαι μετὰ σοῦ, καὶ τοῦτό σοι τὸ σημεῖον ὅτι ἐγώ σε ἐξαποστέλλω· ἐν τῷ ἐξαγαγεῖν σε τὸν λαόν μου ἐξ Αἰγύπτου καὶ λατρεύσετε τῷ θεῷ ἐν τῷ ὄρει τούτῳ.

15: Gen 17:5

see Gen 15:5 [12]

[b]**Rom 4:17**   **Only Gen 17:5**

17 καθὼς γέγραπται ὅτι *πατέρα πολλῶν ἐθνῶν τέθεικά σε*, κατέναντι οὗ ἐπίστευσεν θεοῦ τοῦ ζῳοποιοῦντος τοὺς νεκροὺς καὶ καλοῦντος τὰ μὴ ὄντα ὡς ὄντα·

Gen 17:5; Rom 4:17. (*A*)

---

[a]**Rom 4:3**

3 τί γὰρ ἡ γραφὴ λέγει; *ἐπίστευσεν δὲ Ἀβραὰμ τῷ θεῷ καὶ ἐλογίσθη αὐτῷ εἰς δικαιοσύνην.*

Gen 15:6; all five NT passages are identical. (*A*)

[b]**Rom 4:9**

9 Ὁ μακαρισμὸς οὖν οὗτος ἐπὶ τὴν περιτομὴν ᵀ ἢ καὶ ἐπὶ τὴν ἀκροβυστίαν; λέγομεν γάρ· ᵀ *ἐλογίσθη τῷ Ἀβραὰμ ἡ πίστις εἰς δικαιοσύνην.*

[c]**Rom 4:22**

22 διὸ ᴼ[καὶ] *ἐλογίσθη αὐτῷ* ǀ *εἰς δικαιοσύνην.*

[d]**Gal 3:6**

6 Καθὼς Ἀβραὰμ *ἐπίστευσεν τῷ θεῷ, καὶ ἐλογίσθη αὐτῷ εἰς δικαιοσύνην·*

[e]**Jas 2:23**

23 καὶ ἐπληρώθη ἡ γραφὴ ἡ λέγουσα· *ἐπίστευσεν* ᴼ δὲ *Ἀβραὰμ τῷ θεῷ, καὶ ἐλογίσθη αὐτῷ εἰς δικαιοσύνην* καὶ ⌐φίλος θεοῦ⌐ ἐκλήθη.

---

[a]**Acts 7:6–7**

6 ἐλάλησεν δὲ ⌐οὕτως ὁ θεὸς ᵀ ὅτι *ἔσται τὸ σπέρμα αὐτοῦ πάροικον ἐν γῇ ἀλλοτρίᾳ καὶ δουλώσουσιν* ᶠαὐτὸ *καὶ κακώσουσιν ἔτη τετρακόσια·* 7 *καὶ τὸ ἔθνος* ᾧ ἐὰν ⌐δουλεύσουσιν *κρινῶ ἐγώ,* ˢ ὁ θεὸς εἶπενˡ, *καὶ μετὰ ταῦτα ἐξελεύσονται καὶ λατρεύσουσίν μοι ἐν τῷ τόπῳ τούτῳ.*

Gen 15:13–14; Acts 7:6 γῇ ἀλλοτρίᾳ = LXX γῇ οὐκ ἰδίᾳ, MT בְּאֶרֶץ לֹא לָהֶם. (*A*ᵈ), otherwise (*A*) or (*A*-)

Ex 3:12 is not quoted or alluded to in the NT, though related in sense.

16: Gen 17:7

⁷ וַהֲקִמֹתִי אֶת־בְּרִיתִי בֵּינִי וּבֵינֶךָ וּבֵין זַרְעֲךָ
אַחֲרֶיךָ לְדֹרֹתָם לִבְרִית עוֹלָם לִהְיוֹת לְךָ לֵאלֹהִים וּלְזַרְעֲךָ אַחֲרֶיךָ:

Gen 24:7

⁷ יְהוָה׀ אֱלֹהֵי הַשָּׁמַיִם
אֲשֶׁר לְקָחַנִי מִבֵּית אָבִי וּמֵאֶרֶץ מוֹלַדְתִּי וַאֲשֶׁר
דִּבֶּר־לִי וַאֲשֶׁר נִשְׁבַּע־לִי לֵאמֹר לְזַרְעֲךָ אֶתֵּן אֶת־הָאָרֶץ הַזֹּאת הוּא
יִשְׁלַח מַלְאָכוֹ לְפָנֶיךָ וְלָקַחְתָּ אִשָּׁה לִבְנִי מִשָּׁם:

⁷καὶ στήσω τὴν διαθήκην μου ἀνὰ
μέσον ἐμοῦ καὶ ἀνὰ μέσον σοῦ καὶ ἀνὰ μέσον τοῦ σπέρματός σου
μετὰ σὲ εἰς γενεὰς αὐτῶν εἰς διαθήκην αἰώνιον εἶναί σου θεὸς καὶ
τοῦ σπέρματός σου μετὰ σέ.

⁷κύριος ὁ θεὸς τοῦ οὐρανοῦ καὶ ὁ θεὸς τῆς γῆς, ὃς ἔλαβέν
με ἐκ τοῦ οἴκου τοῦ πατρός μου καὶ ἐκ τῆς γῆς, ἧς ἐγενήθην, ὃς
ἐλάλησέν μοι καὶ ὤμοσέν μοι λέγων Σοὶ δώσω τὴν γῆν ταύτην
καὶ τῷ σπέρματί σου, αὐτὸς ἀποστελεῖ τὸν ἄγγελον αὐτοῦ ἔμπροσθέν σου, καὶ λήμψῃ γυναῖκα τῷ υἱῷ μου Ισαακ ἐκεῖθεν.

17: Gen 17:8

⁸ וְנָתַתִּי לְךָ וּלְזַרְעֲךָ אַחֲרֶיךָ אֵת׀ אֶרֶץ מְגֻרֶיךָ אֵת כָּל־אֶרֶץ כְּנַעַן
לַאֲחֻזַּת עוֹלָם וְהָיִיתִי לָהֶם לֵאלֹהִים:

Gen 48:4

⁴ וַיֹּאמֶר אֵלַי הִנְנִי מַפְרְךָ וְהִרְבִּיתִךָ וּנְתַתִּיךָ לִקְהַל
עַמִּים וְנָתַתִּי אֶת־הָאָרֶץ הַזֹּאת לְזַרְעֲךָ אַחֲרֶיךָ אֲחֻזַּת עוֹלָם:

⁸καὶ δώσω σοι καὶ τῷ σπέρματί σου
μετὰ σὲ τὴν γῆν, ἣν παροικεῖς, πᾶσαν τὴν γῆν Χανααν, εἰς κατάσχεσιν αἰώνιον καὶ ἔσομαι αὐτοῖς θεός. —

⁴καὶ εἶπέν μοι Ἰδοὺ ἐγὼ αὐξανῶ σε καὶ πληθυνῶ
σε καὶ ποιήσω σε εἰς συναγωγὰς ἐθνῶν καὶ δώσω σοι τὴν γῆν
ταύτην καὶ τῷ σπέρματί σου μετὰ σὲ εἰς κατάσχεσιν αἰώνιον.

18: Gen 18:10

¹⁰ וַיֹּאמֶר שׁוֹב אָשׁוּב אֵלֶיךָ כָּעֵת חַיָּה וְהִנֵּה־בֵן לְשָׂרָה
אִשְׁתֶּךָ וְשָׂרָה שֹׁמַעַת פֶּתַח הָאֹהֶל וְהוּא אַחֲרָיו:

¹⁰εἶπεν δέ Ἐπαναστρέφων ἥξω
πρὸς σὲ κατὰ τὸν καιρὸν τοῦτον εἰς ὥρας, καὶ ἕξει υἱὸν Σαρρα
ἡ γυνή σου. Σαρρα δὲ ἤκουσεν πρὸς τῇ θύρᾳ τῆς σκηνῆς, οὖσα
ὄπισθεν αὐτοῦ.

19: Gen 18:14

¹⁴ הֲיִפָּלֵא מֵיהוָה דָּבָר לַמּוֹעֵד אָשׁוּב אֵלֶיךָ כָּעֵת
חַיָּה וּלְשָׂרָה בֵן:

¹⁴μὴ ἀδυνατεῖ παρὰ τῷ θεῷ ῥῆμα; εἰς τὸν
καιρὸν τοῦτον ἀναστρέψω πρὸς σὲ εἰς ὥρας, καὶ ἔσται τῇ Σαρρα
υἱός.

20: Gen 18:18

see Gen 12:3 [8]

21: Gen 21:10

¹⁰ וַתֹּאמֶר לְאַבְרָהָם גָּרֵשׁ הָאָמָה הַזֹּאת וְאֶת־
בְּנָהּ כִּי לֹא יִירַשׁ בֶּן־הָאָמָה הַזֹּאת עִם־בְּנִי עִם־יִצְחָק:

¹⁰καὶ εἶπεν τῷ Αβρααμ
Ἔκβαλε τὴν παιδίσκην ταύτην καὶ τὸν υἱὸν αὐτῆς· οὐ γὰρ κληρονομήσει ὁ υἱὸς τῆς παιδίσκης ταύτης μετὰ τοῦ υἱοῦ μου Ισαακ.

aGal 3:16 *(see also [9],b)

16 τῷ δὲ Ἀβραὰμ ἐρρέθησαν αἱ ἐπαγγελίαι καὶ τῷ σπέρματι αὐτοῦ. οὐ λέγει· καὶ τοῖς σπέρμασιν, ὡς ἐπὶ πολλῶν ἀλλ' ὡς ἐφ' ἑνός· καὶ τῷ σπέρματί σου, ⌜ὅς ἐστιν
Χριστός.

It is sufficient to observe that the term σπέρμα in the singular is used in both Gen 17:7 and 24:7, and this is really the main point of Paul's citation showing that while the descendants of Abraham are perhaps indicated by this language, this reference to זרע as a collective is from the prophetic standpoint significantly a singular and it was the Messiah, Christ, who was pre-eminently the σπέρμα or the "seed" of Abraham; so it is simply the question of its being a singular rather than a plural that is important here. (A)

aActs 7:5 *(see also [9],a)

5 καὶ οὐκ ἔδωκεν αὐτῷ κληρονομίαν ἐν αὐτῇ οὐδὲ βῆμα
ποδός καὶ ἐπηγγείλατο δοῦναι ˻αὐτῷ εἰς κατάσχεσιν αὐ-
τὴν˼ καὶ τῷ*σπέρματι αὐτοῦ μετ' αὐτόν, οὐκ ὄντος αὐτῷ
τέκνου.

Acts 7:5 includes portions of Gen 48:4 (none of which is distinctive for Gen 17:8 alone), converting direct address (2nd pers. sing.) into 3rd pers. sing. in a matter appropriate to the context of Stephen's speech. (A)

aRom 9:9

9 ἐπαγγελίας γὰρ ὁ λόγος οὗτος·
κατὰ τὸν καιρὸν τοῦτον ἐλεύσομαι καὶ ἔσται τῇ Σάρρᾳ υἱός.

Rom 9:9a (or b, really) quotes from Gen 18:10 the temporal phrase "at about this time"; from Gen 18:14 it picks up "I shall come, and Sarah will have a son." But ἐλεύσομαι differs a bit from ἀναστρέψω in the LXX (which is a literal rendering of MT's אָשׁוּב. (A^d)

aGal 4:30

30 ἀλλὰ τί λέγει ἡ
γραφή; ἔκβαλε τὴν παιδίσκην καὶ τὸν υἱὸν αὐτῆς· οὐ γὰρ
μὴ ⌜κληρονομήσει ὁ υἱὸς τῆς παιδίσκης μετὰ τοῦ υἱοῦ
⌜τῆς ἐλευθέρας⌝.

Gen 21:10. (A), except that Gal 4:30 omits ταύτης after τῆς παιδίσκης.

22: Gen 21:12

¹² וַיֹּאמֶר אֱלֹהִים אֶל־אַבְרָהָם אַל־יֵרַע בְּעֵינֶיךָ
עַל־הַנַּעַר וְעַל־אֲמָתֶךָ כֹּל אֲשֶׁר תֹּאמַר
אֵלֶיךָ שָׂרָה שְׁמַע בְּקֹלָהּ כִּי בְיִצְחָק יִקָּרֵא לְךָ זָרַע׃

¹²εἶπεν δὲ ὁ θεὸς τῷ Αβρααμ Μὴ σκληρὸν ἔστω τὸ ῥῆμα ἐναντίον σου περὶ τοῦ παιδίου καὶ περὶ τῆς παιδίσκης· πάντα, ὅσα ἐὰν εἴπῃ σοι Σαρρα, ἄκουε τῆς φωνῆς αὐτῆς, ὅτι ἐν Ισαακ κληθήσεταί σοι σπέρμα.

23: Gen 22:16–17

¹⁶ וַיֹּאמֶר בִּי
נִשְׁבַּעְתִּי נְאֻם־יְהוָה כִּי יַעַן אֲשֶׁר עָשִׂיתָ אֶת־הַדָּבָר הַזֶּה וְלֹא חָשַׂכְתָּ
אֶת־בִּנְךָ אֶת־יְחִידֶךָ׃ ¹⁷ כִּי־בָרֵךְ אֲבָרֶכְךָ וְהַרְבָּה אַרְבֶּה אֶת־זַרְעֲךָ
כְּכוֹכְבֵי הַשָּׁמַיִם וְכַחוֹל אֲשֶׁר עַל־שְׂפַת הַיָּם וְיִרַשׁ זַרְעֲךָ אֵת שַׁעַר
אֹיְבָיו׃

¹⁶λέγων Κατ' ἐμαυτοῦ ὤμοσα,
λέγει κύριος, οὗ εἵνεκεν ἐποίησας τὸ ῥῆμα τοῦτο καὶ οὐκ ἐφείσω τοῦ υἱοῦ σου τοῦ ἀγαπητοῦ δι' ἐμέ, ¹⁷ἦ μὴν εὐλογῶν εὐλογήσω σε καὶ πληθύνων πληθυνῶ τὸ σπέρμα σου ὡς τοὺς ἀστέρας τοῦ οὐρανοῦ καὶ ὡς τὴν ἄμμον τὴν παρὰ τὸ χεῖλος τῆς θαλάσσης, καὶ κληρονομήσει τὸ σπέρμα σου τὰς πόλεις τῶν ὑπεναντίων·

24: Gen 22:18

¹⁸ וְהִתְבָּרֲכוּ בְזַרְעֲךָ כֹּל גּוֹיֵי הָאָרֶץ עֵקֶב אֲשֶׁר שָׁמַעְתָּ בְּקֹלִי׃

¹⁸καὶ
ἐνευλογηθήσονται ἐν τῷ σπέρματί σου πάντα τὰ ἔθνη τῆς γῆς,
ἀνθ' ὧν ὑπήκουσας τῆς ἐμῆς φωνῆς.

Gen 26:4

⁴וְהִרְבֵּיתִי אֶת־זַרְעֲךָ כְּכוֹכְבֵי הַשָּׁמַיִם וְנָתַתִּי לְזַרְעֲךָ אֵת כָּל־
הָאֲרָצֹת הָאֵל וְהִתְבָּרֲכוּ בְזַרְעֲךָ כֹּל גּוֹיֵי הָאָרֶץ׃

⁴καὶ πληθυνῶ τὸ σπέρμα σου ὡς τοὺς ἀστέρας τοῦ οὐρανοῦ καὶ δώσω τῷ σπέρματί σου πᾶσαν τὴν γῆν ταύτην, καὶ ἐνευλογηθήσονται ἐν τῷ σπέρματί σου πάντα τὰ ἔθνη τῆς γῆς,

---

25: Gen 24:7

see Gen 17:7 [16]

26: Gen 25:23

²³ וַיֹּאמֶר יְהוָה לָהּ
שְׁנֵי גוֹיִם בְּבִטְנֵךְ וּשְׁנֵי לְאֻמִּים מִמֵּעַיִךְ יִפָּרֵדוּ
וּלְאֹם מִלְאֹם יֶאֱמָץ וְרַב יַעֲבֹד צָעִיר׃

²³καὶ εἶπεν κύριος αὐτῇ
Δύο ἔθνη ἐν τῇ γαστρί σού εἰσιν,
καὶ δύο λαοὶ ἐκ τῆς κοιλίας σου διασταλήσονται·
καὶ λαὸς λαοῦ ὑπερέξει,
καὶ ὁ μείζων δουλεύσει τῷ ἐλάσσονι.

27: Gen 26:4

see Gen 22:18 [24]

28: Gen 38:8

see Deut 25:5 [107]

*a*Rom 9:7

7 οὐδ' ⌐ὅτι εἰ-
σὶν σπέρμα Ἀβραὰμ πάντες τέκνα, ἀλλ'· ἐν Ἰσαὰκ κληθήσεταί σοι σπέρμα.

*b*Heb 11:18

18 πρὸς ὃν ἐλαλήθη ὅτι
ἐν Ἰσαὰκ κληθήσεταί σοι σπέρμα,

Gen 21:12. (*A*)

---

*a*Heb 6:13–14

13 Τῷ γὰρ Ἀβραὰμ ἐπαγγειλάμενος ὁ θεός, ἐπεὶ κατ'
οὐδενὸς εἶχεν μείζονος ὀμόσαι, ὤμοσεν καθ' ἑαυτοῦ
14 λέγων·
⌐*εἰ μὴν*⌐ *εὐλογῶν εὐλογήσω σε καὶ πληθύνων πληθυνῶ σε·*

Gen 22:16–17. (*A*); note that כִּי־בָרֵךְ is ἦ μὴν in LXX and εἰ μὴν in NT. (*A-*)

---

*a*Acts 3:25

25 ὑμεῖς ἐστε οἱ υἱοὶ τῶν προφητῶν
καὶ τῆς διαθήκης ἧς ⌐διέθετο ὁ θεὸς⌐ πρὸς τοὺς πατέρας
⌐ὑμῶν λέγων πρὸς Ἀβραάμ· *καὶ ἐν τῷ σπέρματί σου*⌐[ἐν-]
εὐλογηθήσονται πᾶσαι αἱ πατριαὶ τῆς γῆς.

Gen 22:18. (*A*); note that the verb ἐνευλογηθήσονται comes first in LXX, though after σπέρματί in NT (Acts 3:25).

Gen 26:4 is identical in this clause.

---

*a*Rom 9:12

12 οὐκ ἐξ ἔργων ἀλλ' ἐκ
τοῦ καλοῦντος, ἐρρέθη °αὐτῇ ὅτι *ὁ μείζων δουλεύσει τῷ
ἐλάσσονι,*

Gen 25:23. (*A*)

29: Gen 47:31

³¹ וַיֹּ֙אמֶר֙ הִשָּׁ֣בְעָה לִ֔י וַיִּשָּׁבַ֖ע ל֑וֹ
וַיִּשְׁתַּ֥חוּ יִשְׂרָאֵ֖ל עַל־רֹ֥אשׁ הַמִּטָּֽה׃

³¹ εἶπεν δέ Ὄμοσόν μοι.
καὶ ὤμοσεν αὐτῷ. καὶ προσεκύνησεν Ισραηλ ἐπὶ τὸ ἄκρον τῆς
ῥάβδου αὐτοῦ.

30: Gen 48:4

see Gen 17:8 [17]

31: Ex 1:8

⁸ וַיָּ֥קָם מֶֽלֶךְ־חָדָ֖שׁ עַל־מִצְרָ֑יִם אֲשֶׁ֥ר לֹֽא־יָדַ֖ע אֶת־יוֹסֵֽף׃

⁸ Ἀνέστη δὲ βασιλεὺς ἕτερος ἐπ᾽ Αἴγυπτον, ὃς οὐκ ᾔδει τὸν Ιω-
σηφ.

32: Ex 2:14

¹⁴ וַ֠יֹּאמֶר מִ֣י שָֽׂמְךָ֞ לְאִ֣ישׁ שַׂ֤ר
וְשֹׁפֵט֙ עָלֵ֔ינוּ הַלְהָרְגֵ֙נִי֙ אַתָּ֣ה אֹמֵ֔ר כַּאֲשֶׁ֥ר הָרַ֖גְתָּ אֶת־הַמִּצְרִ֑י וַיִּירָ֤א
מֹשֶׁה֙ וַיֹּאמַ֔ר אָכֵ֖ן נוֹדַ֥ע הַדָּבָֽר׃

¹⁴ ὁ δὲ
εἶπεν Τίς σε κατέστησεν ἄρχοντα καὶ δικαστὴν ἐφ᾽ ἡμῶν; μὴ ἀνελεῖν με σὺ θέλεις, ὃν τρόπον ἀνεῖλες ἐχθὲς τὸν Αἰγύπτιον; ἐφο-
βήθη δὲ Μωυσῆς καὶ εἶπεν Εἰ οὕτως ἐμφανὲς γέγονεν τὸ ῥῆμα
τοῦτο;

*a*Heb 11:21

21 Πίστει Ἰακὼβ ἀποθνήσκων ἕκαστον τῶν υἱῶν Ἰωσὴφ εὐλόγησεν καὶ *προσεκύνησεν ἐπὶ τὸ ἄκρον τῆς ῥάβδου αὐτοῦ.*

Between MT of Gen 47:31 and the LXX rendering (which is followed also in Heb 11:21) there is a divergence in only one word. That is to say, MT's מִטָּה "bed" is rendered in Greek by "staff," ῥάβδου. At first glance this looks like an insoluble error, but upon closer examination it turns out to be nothing more than a matter of a disputed vowel point. The LXX points the word as מַטֶּה, "staff," whereas MT points it as מִטָּה, "bed." Bearing in mind that Masoretic vowel points were not used until after A.D. 700, and that the LXX was translated nearly 1,000 years earlier, we must consider the distinct possibility that the Alexandrian Jewish translators were more correct than the Masoretes in their interpretation of this word. In the light of the context it could well be argued that Jacob would be more likely to support his weight on the top of his staff as he bowed his head in worship than that he leaned on top of his *bed.* Presumably this was an Egyptian style of bed, since he had for 17 years been living in Egyptian luxury as the father of the prime minister. If so, the numerous bas-reliefs and specimens that have been preserved show us that the head of an Egyptian bed was scarcely higher than six inches. There is therefore no way Jacob or anyone else, for that matter, could have leaned on the top (רֹאשׁ) of the bed at a time of worship. Consequently we must adopt the vowel-pointing of the LXX (correctly followed by Heb 11:21) as the true and original one. (*E*) and (*D*)

---

*a*Acts 7:18

18 ἄχρι οὗ ἀνέστη βασιλεὺς ἕτερος □[ἐπ' Αἴγυπτον]‵ ὃς οὐκ ⌜ᾔδει τὸν⌝ Ἰωσήφ.

Ex 1:8. (*A*)

---

*a*Acts 7:27–28

27 ὁ δὲ ἀδικῶν τὸν πλησίον ἀπώσατο αὐτὸν εἰπών· τίς σε κατέστησεν ἄρχοντα καὶ δικαστὴν ἐφ' ἡμῶν; **28** μὴ ἀνελεῖν με σὺ θέλεις ὃν τρόπον ἀνεῖλες ἐχθὲς τὸν Αἰγύπτιον;

Ex 2:14 is accurately rendered by the LXX, which is followed exactly by Acts 7:35, except for the insertion of the adverb ("yesterday"), which is missing from the MT, but which is fairly inferrable from v. 13: "And he went out the next day." (*A*) and (*D*)

*b*Acts 7:35

35 Τοῦτον τὸν Μωϋσῆν ὃν ἠρνήσαντο εἰπόντες· τίς σε κατέστησεν ἄρχοντα καὶ δικαστήν⸋; τοῦτον ὁ θεὸς ⸋[καὶ] ἄρχοντα καὶ λυτρωτὴν ἀπέσταλκεν σὺν χειρὶ ἀγγέλου τοῦ ὀφθέντος αὐτῷ ἐν τῇ βάτῳ.

Note that Acts 7:35 is identical in wording to Acts 7:27, "who has constituted you or appointed you a ruler and a judge." The Greek wording is the same and so is the Hebrew in both cases. (*A*)

33: Ex 2:22 | see Gen 15:13–14[14]

34: Ex 3:2

² וַיֵּרָא מַלְאַךְ יְהוָה אֵלָיו בְּלַבַּת־אֵשׁ מִתּוֹךְ הַסְּנֶה וַיַּרְא וְהִנֵּה הַסְּנֶה בֹּעֵר בָּאֵשׁ וְהַסְּנֶה אֵינֶנּוּ אֻכָּל:

² ὤφθη δὲ αὐτῷ ἄγγελος κυρίου ἐν φλογὶ πυρὸς ἐκ τοῦ βάτου, καὶ ὁρᾷ ὅτι ὁ βάτος καίεται πυρί, ὁ δὲ βάτος οὐ κατεκαίετο.

35: Ex 3:5–10

⁵ וַיֹּאמֶר אַל־תִּקְרַב הֲלֹם שַׁל־נְעָלֶיךָ מֵעַל רַגְלֶיךָ כִּי הַמָּקוֹם אֲשֶׁר אַתָּה עוֹמֵד עָלָיו אַדְמַת־קֹדֶשׁ הוּא: ⁶ וַיֹּאמֶר אָנֹכִי אֱלֹהֵי אָבִיךָ אֱלֹהֵי אַבְרָהָם אֱלֹהֵי יִצְחָק וֵאלֹהֵי יַעֲקֹב וַיַּסְתֵּר מֹשֶׁה פָּנָיו כִּי יָרֵא מֵהַבִּיט אֶל־הָאֱלֹהִים: ⁷ וַיֹּאמֶר יְהוָה רָאֹה רָאִיתִי אֶת־עֳנִי עַמִּי אֲשֶׁר בְּמִצְרָיִם וְאֶת־צַעֲקָתָם שָׁמַעְתִּי מִפְּנֵי נֹגְשָׂיו כִּי יָדַעְתִּי אֶת־מַכְאֹבָיו: ⁸ וָאֵרֵד לְהַצִּילוֹ מִיַּד מִצְרַיִם וּלְהַעֲלֹתוֹ מִן־הָאָרֶץ הַהִוא אֶל־אֶרֶץ טוֹבָה וּרְחָבָה אֶל־אֶרֶץ זָבַת חָלָב וּדְבָשׁ אֶל־מְקוֹם הַכְּנַעֲנִי וְהַחִתִּי וְהָאֱמֹרִי וְהַפְּרִזִּי וְהַחִוִּי וְהַיְבוּסִי: ⁹ וְעַתָּה הִנֵּה צַעֲקַת בְּנֵי־יִשְׂרָאֵל בָּאָה אֵלָי וְגַם־רָאִיתִי אֶת־הַלַּחַץ אֲשֶׁר מִצְרַיִם לֹחֲצִים אֹתָם: ¹⁰ וְעַתָּה לְכָה וְאֶשְׁלָחֲךָ אֶל־פַּרְעֹה וְהוֹצֵא אֶת־עַמִּי בְנֵי־יִשְׂרָאֵל מִמִּצְרָיִם:

³ εἶπεν δὲ Μωυσῆς Παρελθὼν ὄψομαι τὸ ὅραμα τὸ μέγα τοῦτο, τί ὅτι οὐ κατακαίεται ὁ βάτος. ⁴ ὡς δὲ εἶδεν κύριος ὅτι προσάγει ἰδεῖν, ἐκάλεσεν αὐτὸν κύριος ἐκ τοῦ βάτου λέγων Μωυσῆ, Μωυσῆ. ὁ δὲ εἶπεν Τί ἐστιν; ⁵ καὶ εἶπεν Μὴ ἐγγίσῃς ὧδε· λῦσαι τὸ ὑπόδημα ἐκ τῶν ποδῶν σου· ὁ γὰρ τόπος, ἐν ᾧ σὺ ἕστηκας, γῆ ἁγία ἐστίν. ⁶ καὶ εἶπεν αὐτῷ Ἐγώ εἰμι ὁ θεὸς τοῦ πατρός σου, θεὸς Αβρααμ καὶ θεὸς Ισαακ καὶ θεὸς Ιακωβ. ἀπέστρεψεν δὲ Μωυσῆς τὸ πρόσωπον αὐτοῦ· εὐλαβεῖτο γὰρ κατεμβλέψαι ἐνώπιον τοῦ θεοῦ. ⁷ εἶπεν δὲ κύριος πρὸς Μωυσῆν Ἰδὼν εἶδον τὴν κάκωσιν τοῦ λαοῦ μου τοῦ ἐν Αἰγύπτῳ καὶ τῆς κραυγῆς αὐτῶν ἀκήκοα ἀπὸ τῶν ἐργοδιωκτῶν· οἶδα γὰρ τὴν ὀδύνην αὐτῶν· ⁸ καὶ κατέβην ἐξελέσθαι αὐτοὺς ἐκ χειρὸς Αἰγυπτίων καὶ ἐξαγαγεῖν αὐτοὺς ἐκ τῆς γῆς ἐκείνης καὶ εἰσαγαγεῖν αὐτοὺς εἰς τὴν ἀγαθὴν καὶ πολλήν, εἰς τὴν ῥέουσαν γάλα καὶ μέλι, εἰς τὸν τόπον τῶν Χαναναίων καὶ Χετταίων καὶ Αμορραίων καὶ Φερεζαίων καὶ Γεργεσαίων καὶ Ευαίων καὶ Ιεβουσαίων. ⁹ καὶ νῦν ἰδοὺ κραυγὴ τῶν υἱῶν Ισραηλ ἥκει πρός με, κἀγὼ ἑώρακα τὸν θλιμμόν, ὃν οἱ Αἰγύπτιοι θλίβουσιν αὐτούς. ¹⁰ καὶ νῦν δεῦρο ἀποστελῶ σε πρὸς Φαραω βασιλέα Αἰγύπτου, καὶ ἐξάξεις τὸν λαόν μου τοὺς υἱοὺς Ισραηλ ἐκ τῆς Αἰγύπτου. —

36: Ex 3:6

⁶ וַיֹּאמֶר אָנֹכִי אֱלֹהֵי אָבִיךָ אֱלֹהֵי אַבְרָהָם אֱלֹהֵי יִצְחָק וֵאלֹהֵי יַעֲקֹב וַיַּסְתֵּר מֹשֶׁה פָּנָיו כִּי יָרֵא מֵהַבִּיט אֶל־הָאֱלֹהִים:

⁶ καὶ εἶπεν αὐτῷ Ἐγώ εἰμι ὁ θεὸς τοῦ πατρός σου, θεὸς Αβρααμ καὶ θεὸς Ισαακ καὶ θεὸς Ιακωβ. ἀπέστρεψεν δὲ Μωυσῆς τὸ πρόσωπον αὐτοῦ· εὐλαβεῖτο γὰρ κατεμβλέψαι ἐνώπιον τοῦ θεοῦ.

Ex 3:15

¹⁵ וַיֹּאמֶר עוֹד אֱלֹהִים אֶל־מֹשֶׁה כֹּה־תֹאמַר אֶל־בְּנֵי יִשְׂרָאֵל יְהוָה אֱלֹהֵי אֲבֹתֵיכֶם אֱלֹהֵי אַבְרָהָם אֱלֹהֵי יִצְחָק וֵאלֹהֵי יַעֲקֹב שְׁלָחַנִי אֲלֵיכֶם זֶה־שְּׁמִי לְעֹלָם וְזֶה זִכְרִי לְדֹר דֹּר:

¹⁵ καὶ εἶπεν ὁ θεὸς πάλιν πρὸς Μωυσῆν Οὕτως ἐρεῖς τοῖς υἱοῖς Ισραηλ Κύριος ὁ θεὸς τῶν πατέρων ὑμῶν, θεὸς Αβρααμ καὶ θεὸς Ισαακ καὶ θεὸς Ιακωβ, ἀπέσταλκέν με πρὸς ὑμᾶς· τοῦτό μού ἐστιν ὄνομα αἰώνιον καὶ μνημόσυνον γενεῶν γενεαῖς.

*a*Acts 7:30

30 Καὶ ⸀πληρωθέντων ἐτῶν⸜ τεσσεράκοντα ὤφθη αὐτῷ ἐν τῇ ἐρήμῳ τοῦ ὄρους Σινᾶ ἄγγελος ᵀ ἐν ⸀φλογὶ πυρὸς⸜ βάτου.

Ex 3:2; MT = LXX, but (1) NT Acts 7:30 omits κυρίου after ἄγγελος, and (2) it defers ἄγγελος seven words after its verb ὤφθη. (Note that בְּ = ἐν both in LXX and NT.) (*A*) and (*D*)

---

*a*Acts 7:33–34

33 ⸀εἶπεν δὲ αὐτῷ ὁ κύρι- ος⸜· λῦσον τὸ ὑπόδημα τῶν ποδῶν σου, ὁ γὰρ τόπος ἐφ' ᾧ ⸀ ἕ- στηκας γῆ ἁγία ἐστίν. 34 ἰδὼν εἶδον τὴν κάκωσιν τοῦ λαοῦ μου τοῦ ἐν Αἰγύπτῳ καὶ τοῦ στεναγμοῦ ⸀αὐτῶν⸜ ἤκουσα, καὶ κατέβην ἐξελέσθαι αὐτούς· καὶ νῦν δεῦρο ⸀¹ἀποστείλω σε εἰς Αἴγυπτον.

Ex 3:5–10; שַׁל (G32<נָשַׁל) = LXX λῦσαι (λῦσον Acts 7:30); נְעָלֶיךָ מֵעַל רַגְלֶיךָ = τὸ ὑπόδημα (sing.!); ἐκ τῶν ποδῶν LXX and NT, neither of which has σου after ὑπόδημα. Ex 3:7; וְאֶת־צַעֲקָתָם = LXX τῆς κραυγῆς αὐτῶν, NT τοῦ στεναγμοῦ αὐτῶν; either is fine for צַעֲקָם. Ex 3:8; לְהַצִּילוֹ = LXX ἐξαγαγεῖν αὐτούς, NT ἐξελέσθαι αὐτούς; either verb is fine for לְהַצִּיל; MT's לְהַצִּילוֹ refers to עַם, which is singular; however, as is usual in the LXX the plural is used in referring to עַם. (*A*) and (*D*)

---

*a*Mt 22:32

32 ἐγώ εἰμι ὁ θεὸς ᾽Αβραὰμ καὶ °ὁ θεὸς ᾽Ισαὰκ καὶ °ὁ θεὸς ᾽Ιακώβ; οὐκ ἔστιν ⸀[ὁ] θεὸς⸜ νεκρῶν ἀλλὰ ζώντων.

Ex 3:6 = Mt 22:32 = LXX and MT as far as it goes. (*A*)

*b*Mk 12:26

26 περὶ δὲ τῶν νεκρῶν ὅτι ἐγείρονται οὐκ ἀνέγνωτε ἐν τῇ βίβλῳ Μωϋσέως ἐπὶ τοῦ βάτου πῶς εἶπεν αὐτῷ ὁ θεὸς λέγων· ἐγὼ °ὁ θεὸς ᾽Αβραὰμ καὶ ⸀¹[ὁ] θεὸς ᾽Ισαὰκ καὶ ⸀¹[ὁ] θεὸς ᾽Ιακώβ;

Ex 3:15 = Mk 12:26, which quotes more fully, adding ὁ θεὸς ᾽Ιακώβ = MT. Ex 3:15 (LXX) ὁ θεὸς τῶν πατέρων ὑμῶν = אֱלֹהֵי אֲבוֹתֵיכֶם. Lk 20:37 comments on this verse, so an accusative is used after λέγει ("He calls [Him] the Lord God of Abraham"), thus κύριον instead of κύριος of Mt and Mk. Acts 7:32 = Mt & Mk.

*c*Acts 3:13

13 ὁ θεὸς ᾽Αβραὰμ καὶ □[ὁ θεὸς]⸜᾽Ισαὰκ καὶ □[ὁ θεὸς]⸜᾽Ιακώβ, ὁ θεὸς τῶν πατέρων ἡμῶν, ἐδόξασεν τὸν παῖδα αὐτοῦ ᾽Ιησοῦν ὃν ὑμεῖς °μὲν παρεδώκατε ᵀ καὶ ἠρνήσασθε κατὰ πρόσωπον Πιλάτου, κρίναντος ἐκείνου ⸀ἀπολύειν·

Acts 3:13 quotes from Ex 3:15 the phrase "the God of Abraham, the God of Isaac, the God of Jacob, the God of your fathers," so this too is identical with Mt 12:26 and its quotation of the same passage. Actually, both passages (Ex 3:6 and 3:15) have substantially the same wording. There is a textual question, though, whether "the God" is repeated before Isaac and Jacob in connection with Acts 3:13.

15

Ex 3:6 (continued)

only Ex 3:6

37: Ex 3:12

see Gen 15:13–14 [14]

38: Ex 3:15

see Ex 3:6 [36]

39: Ex 9:12

see Zech 11:12–13 [307]

40: Ex 9:16

16 וְאוּלָ֗ם
בַּעֲב֥וּר זֹאת֙ הֶעֱמַדְתִּ֔יךָ בַּעֲב֖וּר הַרְאֹתְךָ֣ אֶת־כֹּחִ֑י וּלְמַ֛עַן סַפֵּ֥ר שְׁמִ֖י
בְּכָל־הָאָֽרֶץ׃

16 καὶ ἕνεκεν τούτου διετηρήθης, ἵνα
ἐνδείξωμαι ἐν σοὶ τὴν ἰσχύν μου, καὶ ὅπως διαγγελῇ τὸ ὄνομά
μου ἐν πάσῃ τῇ γῇ.

41: Ex 12:46

46 בְּבַ֤יִת אֶחָד֙ יֵאָכֵ֔ל
לֹא־תוֹצִ֧יא מִן־הַבַּ֛יִת מִן־הַבָּשָׂ֖ר ח֑וּצָה וְעֶ֖צֶם לֹ֥א תִשְׁבְּרוּ־בֽוֹ׃

46 ἐν οἰκίᾳ
μιᾷ βρωθήσεται, καὶ οὐκ ἐξοίσετε ἐκ τῆς οἰκίας τῶν κρεῶν ἔξω·
καὶ ὀστοῦν οὐ συντρίψετε ἀπ' αὐτοῦ.

Num 9:12

12 לֹֽא־יַשְׁאִ֤ירוּ מִמֶּ֙נּוּ֙ עַד־בֹּ֔קֶר
וְעֶ֖צֶם לֹ֣א יִשְׁבְּרוּ־ב֑וֹ כְּכָל־חֻקַּ֥ת הַפֶּ֖סַח יַעֲשׂ֥וּ אֹתֽוֹ׃

12 οὐ καταλεί-
ψουσιν ἀπ' αὐτοῦ εἰς τὸ πρωὶ καὶ ὀστοῦν οὐ συντρίψουσιν ἀπ'
αὐτοῦ· κατὰ τὸν νόμον τοῦ πασχα ποιήσουσιν αὐτό.

Psalm 34:21 (34:20)

(Psalm 33:21)

21 (ש) שֹׁמֵ֥ר כָּל־עַצְמוֹתָ֑יו אַחַ֥ת מֵהֵ֝֗נָּה לֹ֣א נִשְׁבָּֽרָה׃

21 κύριος φυλάσσει πάντα τὰ ὀστᾶ αὐτῶν,
ἓν ἐξ αὐτῶν οὐ συντριβήσεται.

ᵈLk 20:37

37 ὅτι δὲ ἐγεί-
ρονται οἱ νεκροί, καὶ Μωϋσῆς ⌜ἐμήνυσεν ἐπὶ τῆς βάτου,
ὡς λέγει κύριον τὸν θεὸν Ἀβραὰμ καὶ ᵀ θεὸν Ἰσαὰκ ⸆καὶ ᵀ
θεὸν Ἰακώβ⸌·

ᵉActs 7:32

32 ἐγὼ ὁ θεὸς τῶν πατέρων σου, ὁ θεὸς Ἀβραὰμ καὶ ᵀ Ἰσαὰκ καὶ ᵀ Ἰακώβ. ἔντρομος δὲ γενόμενος Μωϋσῆς οὐκ ἐτόλμα κατανοῆσαι.

ᵃRom 9:17

17 λέγει γὰρ ἡ γρα-
φὴ τῷ Φαραὼ ὅτι εἰς αὐτὸ τοῦτο ἐξήγειρά σε ὅπως ἐνδείξωμαι
ἐν σοὶ τὴν δύναμίν μου καὶ ὅπως διαγγελῇ τὸ ὄνομά μου ἐν
πάσῃ τῇ γῇ.

Ex 9:16; בַּעֲבוּר זֹאת הֶעֱמַרְתִּיךָ = Rom 9:17 εἰς αὐτὸ
τοῦτο ἐξήγειρά σε, whereas LXX reads ἕνεκεν τούτου
διετηρήθης, which implies (?) הֶעֳדְתָּ (a passive *hophal*).
Here is a case where NT = MT as against LXX. (*C*)

Note that MT's בַּעֲבוּר הַרְאֹתְךָ means: "in order to show
you," followed by אֶת־כֹּחִי. LXX reads τὴν ἰσχύν μου,
approximately equal to δύναμίν μου in NT. (*Aᵈ* or *D*)

ᵃJn 19:36

36 ἐγένετο γὰρ ταῦτα ἵνα ἡ γραφὴ πληρωθῇ· ὀστοῦν
οὐ συντριβήσεται αὐτοῦ.

Ex 12:46; וְעֶצֶם לֹא תִשְׁבְּרוּ; LXX συντρίψετε vs. Jn 19:36
ὀστοῦν οὐ συντριβηθήσεται, as if from תְּשֻׁבַּר (N21).
Here NT deviates from both. (*Bᵃ*) Note that Num 9:12
gives similar instructions: לֹא יִשְׁבְּרוּ בוֹ = LXX ὀστοῦν
οὐ συντρίψουσιν. Ps 34:21(20) reads: ἓν ἐξ αὐτῶν οὐ
συντριβήσεται.

42: Ex 13:2

² קַדֶּשׁ־לִ֤י כָל־בְּכ֣וֹר פֶּ֣טֶר
כָּל־רֶ֙חֶם֙ בִּבְנֵ֣י יִשְׂרָאֵ֔ל בָּאָדָ֖ם וּבַבְּהֵמָ֑ה לִ֖י הֽוּא׃

² Ἁγίασόν μοι πᾶν πρω-
τότοκον πρωτογενὲς διανοῖγον πᾶσαν μήτραν ἐν τοῖς υἱοῖς Ισραηλ
ἀπὸ ἀνθρώπου ἕως κτήνους· ἐμοί ἐστιν.

43: Ex 13:12

¹² וְהַעֲבַרְתָּ֥ כָל־
פֶּֽטֶר־רֶ֖חֶם לַֽיהֹוָ֑ה וְכָל־פֶּ֣טֶר ׀ שֶׁ֣גֶר בְּהֵמָ֗ה אֲשֶׁ֨ר יִהְיֶ֥ה לְךָ֛ הַזְּכָרִ֖ים לַֽיהֹוָֽה׃

¹² καὶ ἀφελεῖς
πᾶν διανοῖγον μήτραν, τὰ ἀρσενικά, τῷ κυρίῳ· πᾶν διανοῖγον
μήτραν ἐκ τῶν βουκολίων ἢ ἐν τοῖς κτήνεσίν σου, ὅσα ἐὰν γένη-
ταί σοι, τὰ ἀρσενικά, ἁγιάσεις τῷ κυρίῳ.

44: Ex 13:15

¹⁵ וַיְהִ֗י כִּֽי־הִקְשָׁ֣ה פַרְעֹה֮ לְשַׁלְּחֵנוּ֒ וַיַּהֲרֹ֨ג יְהֹוָ֤ה כָּל־
בְּכוֹר֙ בְּאֶ֣רֶץ מִצְרַ֔יִם מִבְּכֹ֥ר אָדָ֖ם וְעַד־בְּכ֣וֹר בְּהֵמָ֑ה עַל־כֵּן֩ אֲנִ֨י
זֹבֵ֜חַ לַֽיהֹוָ֗ה כָּל־פֶּ֤טֶר רֶ֙חֶם֙ הַזְּכָרִ֔ים וְכָל־בְּכ֥וֹר בָּנַ֖י אֶפְדֶּֽה׃

¹⁵ἡνίκα δὲ ἐσκλήρυνεν Φαραω ἐξαποστεῖλαι ἡμᾶς, ἀπέ-
κτεινεν πᾶν πρωτότοκον ἐν γῇ Αἰγύπτῳ ἀπὸ πρωτοτόκων ἀνθρώπων ἕως πρωτοτόκων κτηνῶν· διὰ τοῦτο ἐγὼ θύω τῷ κυρίῳ πᾶν
διανοῖγον μήτραν, τὰ ἀρσενικά, καὶ πᾶν πρωτότοκον τῶν υἱῶν
μου λυτρώσομαι.

45: Ex 16:18

¹⁸ וַיָּמֹ֣דּוּ בָעֹ֔מֶר וְלֹ֤א הֶעְדִּיף֙ הַמַּרְבֶּ֔ה וְהַמַּמְעִ֖יט לֹ֣א
הֶחְסִ֑יר אִ֖ישׁ לְפִֽי־אָכְל֥וֹ לָקָֽטוּ׃

¹⁸ καὶ μετρήσαντες
τῷ γομορ οὐκ ἐπλεόνασεν ὁ τὸ πολύ, καὶ ὁ τὸ ἔλαττον οὐκ ἠλατ-
τόνησεν· ἕκαστος εἰς τοὺς καθήκοντας παρ᾽ ἑαυτῷ συνέλεξαν.

*a*Lk 2:23

23 καθὼς γέγραπται ἐν
νόμῳ κυρίου ὅτι πᾶν ἄρσεν διανοῖγον μήτραν ἅγιον τῷ
κυρίῳ κληθήσεται,

Ex 13:2; כָּל־בְּכוֹר פֶּטֶר = LXX πᾶν πρωτότοκον πρωτογενὲς διανοῖγον. (*B*[a]) The original may have been πρωτότοκον ἢ πρωτογενές, which is almost synonymous.

פֶּטֶר כָּל־רֶחֶם = LXX διανοῖγον πᾶσαν μήτραν. Lk 2:23 seems to be a quotation according to the basic sense rather than a meticulous word-for-word type of quote, or it may draw upon Ex 13:12: וְהַעֲבַרְתָּ כָל־פֶּטֶר רֶחֶם הַזְּכָרִים . . . לַיהוה = πᾶν ἀνοῖγον τὰ ἀρσενικὰ τῷ κυρίῳ: MT: "You shall give over to Yahweh . . . And you shall take away all that opens the womb, the male [offspring—Hebrew does mention gender of the offspring]." Lk 2:23: "every male that opens the womb." (*B*[a])

Ex 13:12; כָּל־פֶּטֶר רֶחֶם "and you shall give over to Yahweh all that opens up the womb"; LXX πᾶν διανοῖγον, τὰ ἀρσενικά, τῷ κυρίῳ "and you shall take away all that opens up the womb, the male [offspring]." Lk 2:23 (see above).

בְּהֵמָה אֲשֶׁר לְךָ הַזְּכָרִים לַיהוה "the males shall be the Lord's," but LXX τὰ ἀρσενικὰ ἁγιάσεις, which can only correspond to וְהַעֲבַרְתָּ and is (*A*[b]) or (*F*) and therefore inaccurate, except as ἁγιάζειν = "set apart [something] for God." NT uses ἅγιον in "every male that opens the womb shall be called *holy* to the Lord," and therefore seems to draw form the ἁγιάσεις of Ex 13:12 (LXX).

Ex 13:15; כָּל־בְּכוֹר בְּאֶרֶץ מִצְרַיִם = LXX πᾶν πρωτότοκον ἐν γῇ Αἰγύπτῳ, which is a verbal element taken up into the LXX but not in NT.

*a*2 Cor 8:15

15 κα-
θὼς γέγραπται· ὁ τὸ πολὺ οὐκ ἐπλεόνασεν, καὶ ὁ τὸ ὀλίγον
οὐκ ἠλαττόνησεν.

Ex 16:18; compare MT וְלֹא הֶעְדִּיף הַמַּרְבֶּה with LXX οὐκ ἐπλεόνασεν ὁ τὸ πολύ = NT except for word order. Compare MT וְהַמַּמְעִיט לֹא הֶחְסִיר with LXX καὶ ὁ τὸ ἔλαττον οὐκ ἐπλεόνασεν with NT καὶ τὸ ὀλίγον οὐκ κτλ., in which either = MT.

MASORETIC TEXT	SEPTUAGINT

46: Ex 19:6

⁶ וְאַתֶּם תִּהְיוּ־לִי מַמְלֶכֶת כֹּהֲנִים וְגוֹי קָדוֹשׁ אֵלֶּה הַדְּבָרִים אֲשֶׁר תְּדַבֵּר אֶל־בְּנֵי יִשְׂרָאֵל׃

⁶ ὑμεῖς δὲ ἔσεσθέ μοι βασίλειον ἱεράτευμα καὶ ἔθνος ἅγιον. ταῦτα τὰ ῥήματα ἐρεῖς τοῖς υἱοῖς Ισραηλ.

Isa 43:20–21

²⁰ תְּכַבְּדֵנִי חַיַּת הַשָּׂדֶה תַּנִּים וּבְנוֹת יַעֲנָה כִּי־נָתַתִּי בַמִּדְבָּר מַיִם נְהָרוֹת בִּישִׁימֹן לְהַשְׁקוֹת עַמִּי בְחִירִי׃ ²¹ עַם־זוּ יָצַרְתִּי לִי תְּהִלָּתִי יְסַפֵּרוּ׃ ס

²⁰ εὐλογήσει με τὰ θηρία τοῦ ἀγροῦ, σειρῆνες καὶ θυγατέρες στρουθῶν, ὅτι ἔδωκα ἐν τῇ ἐρήμῳ ὕδωρ καὶ ποταμοὺς ἐν τῇ ἀνύδρῳ ποτίσαι τὸ γένος μου τὸ ἐκλεκτόν, ²¹ λαόν μου, ὃν περιεποιησάμην τὰς ἀρετάς μου διηγεῖσθαι.

Isa 61:6

⁶ וְאַתֶּם כֹּהֲנֵי יְהוָה תִּקָּרֵאוּ מְשָׁרְתֵי אֱלֹהֵינוּ יֵאָמֵר לָכֶם חֵיל גּוֹיִם תֹּאכֵלוּ וּבִכְבוֹדָם תִּתְיַמָּרוּ׃

⁶ ὑμεῖς δὲ ἱερεῖς κυρίου κληθήσεσθε, λειτουργοὶ θεοῦ· ἰσχὺν ἐθνῶν κατέδεσθε καὶ ἐν τῷ πλούτῳ αὐτῶν θαυμασθήσεσθε.

47: Ex 19:12–13

¹² וְהִגְבַּלְתָּ אֶת־הָעָם סָבִיב לֵאמֹר הִשָּׁמְרוּ לָכֶם עֲלוֹת בָּהָר וּנְגֹעַ בְּקָצֵהוּ כָּל־הַנֹּגֵעַ בָּהָר מוֹת יוּמָת׃ ¹³ לֹא־תִגַּע בּוֹ יָד כִּי־סָקוֹל יִסָּקֵל אוֹ־יָרֹה יִיָּרֶה אִם־בְּהֵמָה אִם־אִישׁ לֹא יִחְיֶה בִּמְשֹׁךְ הַיֹּבֵל הֵמָּה יַעֲלוּ בָהָר׃

¹² καὶ ἀφοριεῖς τὸν λαὸν κύκλῳ λέγων Προσέχετε ἑαυτοῖς τοῦ ἀναβῆναι εἰς τὸ ὄρος καὶ θιγεῖν τι αὐτοῦ· πᾶς ὁ ἁψάμενος τοῦ ὄρους θανάτῳ τελευτήσει. ¹³ οὐχ ἅψεται αὐτοῦ χείρ· ἐν γὰρ λίθοις λιθοβοληθήσεται ἢ βολίδι κατατοξευθήσεται· ἐάν τε κτῆνος ἐάν τε ἄνθρωπος, οὐ ζήσεται. ὅταν αἱ φωναὶ καὶ αἱ σάλπιγγες καὶ ἡ νεφέλη ἀπέλθῃ ἀπὸ τοῦ ὄρους, ἐκεῖνοι ἀναβήσονται ἐπὶ τὸ ὄρος.

48: Ex 20:12–16

¹² כַּבֵּד אֶת־אָבִיךָ וְאֶת־אִמֶּךָ לְמַעַן יַאֲרִכוּן יָמֶיךָ עַל הָאֲדָמָה אֲשֶׁר־יְהוָה אֱלֹהֶיךָ נֹתֵן לָךְ׃ ס ¹³ לֹא תִּרְצָח׃ ס ¹⁴ לֹא תִּנְאָף׃ ¹⁵ לֹא תִּגְנֹב׃ ס ¹⁶ לֹא־תַעֲנֶה בְרֵעֲךָ עֵד שָׁקֶר׃ ס

¹² τίμα τὸν πατέρα σου καὶ τὴν μητέρα, ἵνα εὖ σοι γένηται, καὶ ἵνα μακροχρόνιος γένῃ ἐπὶ τῆς γῆς τῆς ἀγαθῆς, ἧς κύριος ὁ θεός σου δίδωσίν σοι. — ¹³ οὐ μοιχεύσεις. — ¹⁴ οὐ κλέψεις. — ¹⁵ οὐ φονεύσεις. — ¹⁶ οὐ ψευδομαρτυρήσεις κατὰ τοῦ πλησίον σου μαρτυρίαν ψευδῆ. —

Deut 5:16–20

¹⁶ כַּבֵּד אֶת־אָבִיךָ וְאֶת־אִמֶּךָ כַּאֲשֶׁר צִוְּךָ יְהוָה אֱלֹהֶיךָ לְמַעַן יַאֲרִיכֻן יָמֶיךָ וּלְמַעַן יִיטַב לָךְ עַל הָאֲדָמָה אֲשֶׁר־יְהוָה אֱלֹהֶיךָ נֹתֵן לָךְ׃ ס ¹⁷ לֹא תִּרְצָח׃ ס ¹⁸ וְלֹא תִּנְאָף׃ ס ¹⁹ וְלֹא תִּגְנֹב׃ ס ²⁰ וְלֹא־תַעֲנֶה בְרֵעֲךָ עֵד שָׁוְא׃

¹⁶ τίμα τὸν πατέρα σου καὶ τὴν μητέρα σου, ὃν τρόπον ἐνετείλατό σοι κύριος ὁ θεός σου, ἵνα εὖ σοι γένηται, καὶ ἵνα μακροχρόνιος γένῃ ἐπὶ τῆς γῆς, ἧς κύριος ὁ θεός σου δίδωσίν σοι. — ¹⁷ οὐ μοιχεύσεις. — ¹⁸ οὐ φονεύσεις. — ¹⁹ οὐ κλέψεις. — ²⁰ οὐ ψευδομαρτυρήσεις κατὰ τοῦ πλησίον σου μαρτυρίαν ψευδῆ. —

^a1 Pet 2:9

9 ὑμεῖς δὲ γένος ἐκλεκτόν, βασίλει-
ον ἱεράτευμα, ἔθνος ἅγιον, λαὸς εἰς περιποίησιν, ὅπως
τὰς ἀρετὰς ἐξαγγείλητε τοῦ ἐκ σκότους ὑμᾶς καλέσαν-
τος εἰς τὸ θαυμαστὸν °αὐτοῦ φῶς·

Ex 19:6: (1) NT (1 Pet 2:9) inserts γένος ἐκλεκτόν before "a kingdom of priests," whereas MT and LXX omit it here. עַם בְּחִירִי is from Is 43:20 and is therefore a conflate; (2) MT מַמְלֶכֶת כֹּהֲנִים = LXX βασίλειον ἱεράτευμα, where there is a slight difference in phrasing but not in sense. (*A*-)

Is 43:20 contributes only עַמִּי בְּחִירִי as noted under (1).

Is 61:6 has nothing in common with 1 Pet 2:9 except θαυμασθήσεσθε to suggest θαυμαστὸν (αὐτοῦ φῶς). (*A*, although a combined conflate)

---

^aHeb 12:20

20 οὐκ ἔφερον
γὰρ τὸ διαστελλόμενον· κἂν θηρίον θίγῃ τοῦ ὄρους, λι-
θοβοληθήσεται^T·

Ex 19:12–13: (1) כִּי־סָקוֹל יִסָּקֵל = LXX ἐν γὰρ λίθοις λιθο-βοληθήσεται = the final word, λιθοβοληθήσεται, in Heb 12:20 (2) אִם־בְּהֵמָה (לֹא יִהְיֶה) = LXX "Beware of going up to the mountain and touching it"—θίγειν τι αὐτοῦ . . . ἐὰν τὲ κτῆνος (Heb 12:20 κἂν θηρίον θίγῃ). Actually the Heb 12:20 verse seems to be a summary rather than a word-for-word quote. (*A*^d) or (*D*)

---

^aMt 19:18–19 *(see also [68],d)

18 ⌜λέγει αὐτῷ· ποίας;⌝ ὁ δὲ Ἰησοῦς ⌜εἶπεν·⌝
τὸ οὐ φονεύσεις, οὐ μοιχεύσεις, οὐ κλέψεις, οὐ ψευδομαρτυρήσεις, **19** τίμα τὸν πατέρα καὶ τὴν μητέρα, καὶ*ἀγαπήσεις τὸν
πλησίον σου ὡς σεαυτόν.

Ex 20:12-16 uses the same words, but Mt 19:18–19 uses a different order of commandments from the order in the Decalogue.

^bMk 10:19

19 τὰς ἐντολὰς οἶδας· ⌜μὴ φονεύσῃς,
μὴ μοιχεύσῃς⌝, μὴ κλέψῃς, μὴ ψευδομαρτυρήσῃς, □μὴ ἀποστερήσῃς,⌝ τίμα τὸν πατέρα σου καὶ τὴν μητέρα^T.

^cLk 18:20

20 τὰς ἐντολὰς οἶδας· ⌜μὴ μοιχεύσῃς,
μὴ φονεύσῃς, μὴ κλέψῃς, μὴ ψευδομαρτυρήσῃς⌝, τίμα τὸν πατέρα σου καὶ τὴν μητέρα^T.

Deut 5:16–20 = Ex 20:12-16. Mk 10:19 inserts μὴ ἀποστερήσῃς (which suggests a double-up of μὴ κλέψῃς). There is one μὴ ἀποστερήσεις in LXX, namely in Deut 24:14: οὐκ ἀπαδικήσεις (ἀποστερήσεις according to Codex Alexandrinus, Ambrosianus, Coislinianus, and Armenian Cyprian) μισθὸν πένητος = MT לֹא תַעֲשֹׁק שָׂכִיר עָנִי. Christ may have had this in mind, in which case we have a conflate quotation used by Him. (*A*)

48 (continued)

Deut 24:14 (only Mk 10:19)   **only Ex 20:12; Deut 5:16**

¹⁴ לֹא־תַעֲשֹׁק שָׂכִיר עָנִי וְאֶבְיוֹן מֵאַחֶיךָ אוֹ מִגֵּרְךָ אֲשֶׁר בְּאַרְצְךָ בִּשְׁעָרֶיךָ׃

¹⁴Οὐκ ἀπαδικήσεις μισθὸν πένητος καὶ ἐνδεοῦς ἐκ τῶν ἀδελφῶν σου ἢ ἐκ τῶν προσηλύτων τῶν ἐν ταῖς πόλεσίν σου ·

49: Ex 20:13   (Ex 20:15)

¹³ לֹא תִּרְצָח׃

¹⁵οὐ φονεύσεις. —

Deut 5:17   **(Deut 5:18)**

¹⁷ לֹא תִּרְצָח׃

¹⁸οὐ φονεύσεις. —

50: Ex 20:13–17

¹³ לֹא תִּרְצָח׃ ס ¹⁴ לֹא תִּנְאָף׃
¹⁵ לֹא תִּגְנֹב׃ ס ¹⁶ לֹא־תַעֲנֶה בְרֵעֲךָ עֵד שָׁקֶר׃ ס ¹⁷ לֹא
תַחְמֹד בֵּית רֵעֶךָ לֹא־תַחְמֹד אֵשֶׁת רֵעֶךָ וְעַבְדּוֹ וַאֲמָתוֹ וְשׁוֹרוֹ
וַחֲמֹרוֹ וְכֹל אֲשֶׁר לְרֵעֶךָ׃

— ¹³οὐ μοιχεύσεις. — ¹⁴οὐ κλέψεις. — ¹⁵οὐ φονεύσεις. — ¹⁶οὐ
ψευδομαρτυρήσεις κατὰ τοῦ πλησίον σου μαρτυρίαν ψευδῆ. —
¹⁷οὐκ ἐπιθυμήσεις τὴν γυναῖκα τοῦ πλησίον σου. οὐκ ἐπιθυμήσεις
τὴν οἰκίαν τοῦ πλησίον σου οὔτε τὸν ἀγρὸν αὐτοῦ οὔτε τὸν
παῖδα αὐτοῦ οὔτε τὴν παιδίσκην αὐτοῦ οὔτε τοῦ βοὸς αὐτοῦ οὔτε
τοῦ ὑποζυγίου αὐτοῦ οὔτε παντὸς κτήνους αὐτοῦ οὔτε ὅσα τῷ
πλησίον σού ἐστιν.

Lev 19:18 compare with [68]

¹⁸ לֹא־תִקֹּם וְלֹא־תִטֹּר אֶת־בְּנֵי עַמֶּךָ וְאָהַבְתָּ לְרֵעֲךָ כָּמוֹךָ אֲנִי
יְהוָה׃

¹⁸καὶ οὐκ ἐκδικᾶ-
ταί σου ἡ χείρ, καὶ οὐ μηνιεῖς τοῖς υἱοῖς τοῦ λαοῦ σου καὶ ἀγαπήσεις τὸν πλησίον σου ὡς σεαυτόν· ἐγώ εἰμι κύριος.

Deut 5:17–21

¹⁷ לֹא תִּרְצָח׃
¹⁸ וְלֹא תִּנְאָף׃ ס ¹⁹ וְלֹא תִּגְנֹב׃ ס ²⁰ וְלֹא־תַעֲנֶה בְרֵעֲךָ
עֵד שָׁוְא׃ ס ²¹⁽¹⁸⁾ וְלֹא תַחְמֹד אֵשֶׁת רֵעֶךָ ס וְלֹא
תִתְאַוֶּה בֵּית רֵעֶךָ שָׂדֵהוּ וְעַבְדּוֹ וַאֲמָתוֹ שׁוֹרוֹ וַחֲמֹרוֹ וְכֹל אֲשֶׁר
לְרֵעֶךָ׃

¹⁷οὐ μοιχεύ-
σεις. — ¹⁸οὐ φονεύσεις. — ¹⁹οὐ κλέψεις. — ²⁰οὐ ψευδομαρτυρήσεις κατὰ τοῦ πλησίον σου μαρτυρίαν ψευδῆ. — ²¹οὐκ ἐπιθυμήσεις τὴν γυναῖκα τοῦ πλησίον σου. οὐκ ἐπιθυμήσεις τὴν οἰκίαν
τοῦ πλησίον σου οὔτε τὸν ἀγρὸν αὐτοῦ οὔτε τὸν παῖδα αὐτοῦ
οὔτε τὴν παιδίσκην αὐτοῦ οὔτε τοῦ βοὸς αὐτοῦ οὔτε τοῦ ὑποζυγίου αὐτοῦ οὔτε παντὸς κτήνους αὐτοῦ οὔτε ὅσα τῷ πλησίον
σού ἐστιν.

^{d}Mt 15:4 *(see also [53],a)

4 ὁ γὰρ θεὸς ⌐εἶπεν· τίμα τὸν πατέρα ⊤ καὶ τὴν μητέρα ⌐,
καὶ· ὁ κακολογῶν πατέρα ἢ μητέρα θανάτῳ τελευτάτω.
*

^{e}Mk 7:10 *(see also [53],b)

10 Μωϋσῆς γὰρ εἶπεν· τίμα τὸν πατέρα σου καὶ
τὴν μητέρα σου, καὶ· ὁ κακολογῶν πατέρα ἢ μητέρα θανάτῳ
*
τελευτάτω.

^{f}Eph 6:2–3

2 τίμα τὸν πατέρα σου
καὶ τὴν μητέρα, ἥτις ᵒἐστὶν ἐντολὴ πρώτη ἐν ἐπαγγελίᾳ,
3 ἵνα εὖ σοι γένηται καὶ ἔσῃ μακροχρόνιος ἐπὶ τῆς γῆς.

Ex 20:12 = Deut 5:16, which furnishes the basis for
τίμα τὸν πατέρα σου καὶ τὴν μητέρα σου for (1) Lk
18:20, (2) Mt 15:4a, (3) Mk 7:10 (its parallel), and
(4) Eph 6:2–3. (It is Deut 5:16 that contributes לְמַעַן
יִיטַב לָךְ.)

---

^{a}Mt 5:21

21 Ἠκούσατε ὅτι ἐρρέθη τοῖς ἀρχαίοις· οὐ φονεύσεις·
ὃς δ' ἂν φονεύσῃ, ἔνοχος ἔσται τῇ κρίσει.

^{b}Jas 2:11 *(see also [51],b)

11 ὁ γὰρ εἰπών ✱ μὴ ⌐μοιχεύσῃς, εἶπεν
καὶ· ⌐μὴ φονεύσῃς·⌐ εἰ δὲ οὐ μοιχεύεις φονεύεις δέ, ⌐γέ-
γονας ⌐¹παραβάτης νόμου.

Ex 20:13; MT = LXX = Mt 5:21. (*A*). James 2:11
simply repeats "thou shalt not commit adultery" and
"thou shalt not murder" as in Mt 5:21. (*A*)

Deut 5:17. (*A*)

---

^{a}Rom 13:9

9 ⌐τὸ γὰρ
οὐ μοιχεύσεις, οὐ φονεύσεις, οὐ κλέψεις, ⊤ οὐκ ἐπιθυμήσεις,
καὶ εἴ τις ἑτέρα ἐντολή, ἐν ⌐τῷ λόγῳ τούτῳ⌐ ἀνακεφαλαι-
οῦται □[ἐν τῷ]⟍· ἀγαπήσεις τὸν πλησίον σου ὡς ⌐σεαυτόν.

Ex 20:13–17; MT = LXX = Rom 13:9a. (*A*)

Lev 19:18; MT = LXX = Rom 13:9b. (*A*)

Deut 5:17–21 = Ex 20:13–17.

MASORETIC TEXT	SEPTUAGINT
51: Ex 20:14	**(Ex 20:13)**
¹⁴ לֹא תִּנְאָף׃	¹³ οὐ μοιχεύσεις. —
Deut 5:18	**(Deut 5:17)**
¹⁸ וְלֹא תִּנְאָף׃	¹⁷ οὐ μοιχεύ- σεις. —

52: Ex 20:17

¹⁷ לֹא תַחְמֹד בֵּית רֵעֶךָ לֹא־תַחְמֹד אֵשֶׁת רֵעֶךָ וְעַבְדּוֹ וַאֲמָתוֹ וְשׁוֹרוֹ וַחֲמֹרוֹ וְכֹל אֲשֶׁר לְרֵעֶךָ׃

¹⁷ οὐκ ἐπιθυμήσεις τὴν γυναῖκα τοῦ πλησίον σου. οὐκ ἐπιθυμήσεις τὴν οἰκίαν τοῦ πλησίον σου οὔτε τὸν ἀγρὸν αὐτοῦ οὔτε τὸν παῖδα αὐτοῦ οὔτε τὴν παιδίσκην αὐτοῦ οὔτε τοῦ βοὸς αὐτοῦ οὔτε τοῦ ὑποζυγίου αὐτοῦ οὔτε παντὸς κτήνους αὐτοῦ οὔτε ὅσα τῷ πλησίον σού ἐστιν.

Deut 5:21

²¹⁽¹⁸⁾ וְלֹא תַחְמֹד אֵשֶׁת רֵעֶךָ ס וְלֹא תִתְאַוֶּה בֵּית רֵעֶךָ שָׂדֵהוּ וְעַבְדּוֹ וַאֲמָתוֹ שׁוֹרוֹ וַחֲמֹרוֹ וְכֹל אֲשֶׁר לְרֵעֶךָ׃

²¹ οὐκ ἐπιθυμήσεις τὴν γυναῖκα τοῦ πλησίον σου. οὐκ ἐπιθυμήσεις τὴν οἰκίαν τοῦ πλησίον σου οὔτε τὸν ἀγρὸν αὐτοῦ οὔτε τὸν παῖδα αὐτοῦ οὔτε τὴν παιδίσκην αὐτοῦ οὔτε τοῦ βοὸς αὐτοῦ οὔτε τοῦ ὑποζυγίου αὐτοῦ οὔτε παντὸς κτήνους αὐτοῦ οὔτε ὅσα τῷ πλησίον σού ἐστιν.

53: Ex 21:17

¹⁷ וּמְקַלֵּל אָבִיו וְאִמּוֹ מוֹת יוּמָת׃

(Ex 21:16)

¹⁶ ὁ κακολογῶν πατέ- ρα αὐτοῦ ἢ μητέρα αὐτοῦ τελευτήσει θανάτῳ. —

54: Ex 21:24

²⁴ עַיִן תַּחַת עַיִן שֵׁן תַּחַת שֵׁן יָד תַּחַת יָד רֶגֶל תַּחַת רָגֶל׃

²⁴ ὀφθαλμὸν ἀντὶ ὀφθαλμοῦ, ὀδόντα ἀντὶ ὀδόν- τος, χεῖρα ἀντὶ χειρός, πόδα ἀντὶ ποδός,

Deut 19:21

²¹ וְלֹא תָחוֹס עֵינֶךָ נֶפֶשׁ בְּנֶפֶשׁ עַיִן בְּעַיִן שֵׁן בְּשֵׁן יָד בְּיָד רֶגֶל בְּרָגֶל׃

²¹ οὐ φείσεται ὁ ὀφθαλμός σου ἐπ᾽ αὐτῷ· ψυχὴν ἀντὶ ψυχῆς, ὀφθαλμὸν ἀντὶ ὀφθαλμοῦ, ὀδόντα ἀντὶ ὀδόντος, χεῖρα ἀντὶ χειρός, πόδα ἀντὶ ποδός.

55: Ex 22:27 (22:28)

²⁷ אֱלֹהִים לֹא תְקַלֵּל וְנָשִׂיא בְעַמְּךָ לֹא תָאֹר׃

²⁷ θε- οὺς οὐ κακολογήσεις καὶ ἄρχοντας τοῦ λαοῦ σου οὐ κακῶς ἐρεῖς. —

*a*Mt 5:27

27 Ἠκούσατε ὅτι ἐρρέθη ᵀ· οὐ μοιχεύσεις.

Ex 20:14 = Deut 5:18 = LXX = Mt 5:27 οὐ μοιχεύσεις. (*A*)

*b*Jas 2:11   only Ex 20:14   *(see also [49],b)

11 ὁ ⸀γὰρ εἰπών· μὴ ⸀μοιχεύσῃς, εἰπεν
καὶ·⸀*⸀μὴ φονεύσῃς·⸃ εἰ δὲ οὐ μοιχεύεις φονεύεις δέ,ⁿγέ-
γονας ⸀παραβάτης νόμου.

---

*a*Rom 7:7

7 Τί οὖν ἐροῦμεν; ᵀ ὁ νόμος ἁμαρτία; μὴ γένοιτο· ἀλλὰ
τὴν ἁμαρτίαν οὐκ ἔγνων εἰ μὴ διὰ νόμου· τήν τε γὰρ ἐπι-
θυμίαν οὐκ ᾔδειν εἰ μὴ ὁ νόμος ἔλεγεν· οὐκ ἐπιθυμήσεις.

Ex 20:17 = Deut 5:21 = LXX = Rom 7:7c οὐκ ἐπιθυμήσεις. (*A*)

---

*a*Mt 15:4 *(see also [48],d)

4 ὁ γὰρ θεὸς ⸀εἶπεν·*τίμα τὸν πατέρα ᵀ καὶ τὴν μητέρα ᵀ,
καί· ὁ κακολογῶν πατέρα ἢ μητέρα θανάτῳ τελευτάτω.

Ex 21:17 (LXX 21:16). (*A*)

*b*Mk 7:10 *(see also [48],e)

10 Μωϋσῆς γὰρ εἶπεν·*τίμα τὸν πατέρα σου καὶ
τὴν μητέρα σου, καί· ὁ κακολογῶν πατέρα ἢ μητέρα θανάτῳ
τελευτάτω.

---

*a*Mt 5:38 *(see also [70],a)

✷ 38 Ἠκούσατε ὅτι ἐρρέθη·*ὀφθαλμὸν ἀντὶ ὀφθαλμοῦ ᵒκαὶ
ὀδόντα ἀντὶ ὀδόντος.

Ex 21:24 = Deut 19:21 = LXX = Mt 5:38. (*A*)

---

*a*Acts 23:5

5 ἔφη τε ὁ Παῦλος· οὐκ ᾔδειν, ἀδελφοί,
ὅτι ἐστὶν ἀρχιερεύς· γέγραπται γὰρ ὅτι ἄρχοντα τοῦ λαοῦ
σου οὐκ ἐρεῖς κακῶς.

Ex 22:27(28); MT וְנָשִׂיא בְעַמְּךָ לֹא תָאֹר = LXX except for
τοῦ λαοῦ; נָשִׂיא = ἄρχων = Acts 23:5. (*A*)

Masoretic Text	Septuagint
56: Ex 23:20	**see Mal 3:1 [311]**

57:. Ex 24:8

וַיִּקַּח מֹשֶׁה אֶת־הַדָּם וַיִּזְרֹק עַל־הָעָם וַיֹּאמֶר הִנֵּה דַם־
הַבְּרִית אֲשֶׁר כָּרַת יְהוָה עִמָּכֶם עַל כָּל־הַדְּבָרִים הָאֵלֶּה:

⁸λαβὼν δὲ Μωυσῆς τὸ αἷμα κατεσκέδασεν τοῦ λαοῦ
καὶ εἶπεν Ἰδοὺ τὸ αἷμα τῆς διαθήκης, ἧς διέθετο κύριος πρὸς ὑμᾶς
περὶ πάντων τῶν λόγων τούτων.

58: Ex 25:40

⁴⁰וּרְאֵה וַעֲשֵׂה בְּתַבְנִיתָם אֲשֶׁר־אַתָּה מָרְאֶה בָּהָר:

⁴⁰ὅρα ποιή- σεις κατὰ τὸν τύπον τὸν δεδειγμένον σοι ἐν τῷ ὄρει.

59: Ex 32:1

32 ¹וַיַּרְא הָעָם כִּי־בֹשֵׁשׁ מֹשֶׁה לָרֶדֶת מִן־הָהָר וַיִּקָּהֵל הָעָם
עַל־אַהֲרֹן וַיֹּאמְרוּ אֵלָיו קוּם ׀ עֲשֵׂה־לָנוּ אֱלֹהִים אֲשֶׁר יֵלְכוּ לְפָנֵינוּ
כִּי־זֶה ׀ מֹשֶׁה הָאִישׁ אֲשֶׁר הֶעֱלָנוּ מֵאֶרֶץ מִצְרַיִם לֹא יָדַעְנוּ מֶה־הָיָה
לוֹ:

¹Καὶ ἰδὼν ὁ λαὸς ὅτι κεχρόνικεν Μωυσῆς καταβῆναι ἐκ τοῦ
ὄρους, συνέστη ὁ λαὸς ἐπὶ Ααρων καὶ λέγουσιν αὐτῷ Ἀνάστηθι
καὶ ποίησον ἡμῖν θεούς, οἳ προπορεύσονται ἡμῶν· ὁ γὰρ Μωυσῆς
οὗτος ὁ ἄνθρωπος, ὃς ἐξήγαγεν ἡμᾶς ἐξ Αἰγύπτου, οὐκ οἴδαμεν,
τί γέγονεν αὐτῷ.

Ex 32:23

²³וַיֹּאמְרוּ לִי
עֲשֵׂה־לָנוּ אֱלֹהִים אֲשֶׁר יֵלְכוּ לְפָנֵינוּ כִּי־זֶה ׀ מֹשֶׁה הָאִישׁ אֲשֶׁר הֶעֱלָנוּ
מֵאֶרֶץ מִצְרַיִם לֹא יָדַעְנוּ מֶה־הָיָה לוֹ:

²³λέγουσιν γάρ μοι Ποίησον ἡμῖν θεούς, οἳ προπορεύσονται ἡμῶν· ὁ γὰρ Μωυσῆς οὗτος ὁ ἄνθρωπος, ὃς ἐξήγαγεν
ἡμᾶς ἐξ Αἰγύπτου, οὐκ οἴδαμεν, τί γέγονεν αὐτῷ.

60: Ex 32:6

⁶וַיַּשְׁכִּימוּ מִמָּחֳרָת וַיַּעֲלוּ עֹלֹת וַיַּגִּשׁוּ
שְׁלָמִים וַיֵּשֶׁב הָעָם לֶאֱכֹל וְשָׁתוֹ וַיָּקֻמוּ לְצַחֵק:

⁶καὶ ὀρθρίσας τῇ ἐπαύριον ἀνεβίβασεν
ὁλοκαυτώματα καὶ προσήνεγκεν θυσίαν σωτηρίου, καὶ ἐκάθισεν ὁ
λαὸς φαγεῖν καὶ πιεῖν καὶ ἀνέστησαν παίζειν.

61: Ex 32:23	**see Ex 32:1 [59]**

62: Ex 33:19

¹⁹וַיֹּאמֶר אֲנִי
אַעֲבִיר כָּל־טוּבִי עַל־פָּנֶיךָ וְקָרָאתִי בְשֵׁם יְהוָה לְפָנֶיךָ וְחַנֹּתִי אֶת־
אֲשֶׁר אָחֹן וְרִחַמְתִּי אֶת־אֲשֶׁר אֲרַחֵם:

¹⁹καὶ εἶπεν Ἐγὼ παρελεύσομαι πρότερός σου τῇ δόξῃ μου καὶ
καλέσω ἐπὶ τῷ ὀνόματί μου Κύριος ἐναντίον σου· καὶ ἐλεήσω ὃν
ἂν ἐλεῶ, καὶ οἰκτιρήσω ὃν ἂν οἰκτίρω.

NEW TESTAMENT	COMMENTARY
*a*Heb 9:20 20 λέγων· *τοῦτο τὸ αἷμα τῆς διαθήκης ἧς ἐνετείλατο πρὸς ὑμᾶς ὁ* *θεός.*	Heb 9:20 follows LXX and MT of Exod 24:8 quite faithfully, except that it substitutes ἐνετείλατο for διέθετο (i.e., "commanded" instead of "appointed") and θεός for κύριος (MT יהוה). (A-)
*a*Heb 8:5 **5** οἵτινες ὑποδείγματι καὶ σκιᾷ λατρεύουσιν τῶν ἐπουρανίων, καθὼς κεχρημάτισται Μωϋσῆς μέλλων ἐπιτελεῖν τὴν σκηνήν· *ὅρα γάρ φησιν, ποιήσεις πάντα* *κατὰ τὸν τύπον τὸν δειχθέντα σοι ἐν τῷ ὄρει·*	Ex 25:40; MT = LXX = Heb 8:5 (except that Heb inserts πάντα before κατά). (A) or (A*b*)
*a*Acts 7:40 **40** εἰπόντες τῷ Ἀαρών· *ποίησον* *ἡμῖν θεοὺς οἳ προπορεύσονται ἡμῶν· ὁ γὰρ Μωϋσῆς οὗτος,* *ὃς ἐξήγαγεν ἡμᾶς ἐκ γῆς Αἰγύπτου, οὐκ οἴδαμεν τί* ⌐ἐγένετο⌐ *αὐτῷ.*	Ex 32:1; LXX γέγονεν compared to NT Acts 7:40 ἐγένετο. (A*d*) Ex 32:23; LXX identical to 32:1.
*a*1 Cor 10:7 **7** μηδὲ εἰδω- λολάτραι γίνεσθε καθὼς τινες αὐτῶν, ὥσπερ γέγραπται· ἐκάθισεν ὁ λαὸς φαγεῖν καὶ πεῖν καὶ ἀνέστησαν παίζειν.	Ex 32:6. (A)
*a*Rom 9:15 **15** τῷ Μωϋσεῖ γὰρ λέγει· *ἐλεήσω ὃν ἂν ἐλεῶ καὶ οἰκτιρή-* *σω ὃν ἂν οἰκτίρω.* **16** ἄρα οὖν οὐ τοῦ θέλοντος οὐδὲ τοῦ τρέχοντος ἀλλὰ τοῦ ⌐ἐλεῶντος θεοῦ.	Ex 33:19. (A)

27

63: Lev 10:9

יַ֜יִן וְשֵׁכָ֣ר אַל־תֵּ֣שְׁתְּ ׀ אַתָּ֣ה ׀
וּבָנֶ֣יךָ אִתָּ֗ךְ בְּבֹאֲכֶ֛ם אֶל־אֹ֥הֶל מוֹעֵ֖ד וְלֹ֣א תָמֻ֑תוּ חֻקַּ֥ת עוֹלָ֖ם
לְדֹרֹתֵיכֶֽם׃

⁹Οἶνον καὶ σικερα οὐ
πίεσθε, σὺ καὶ οἱ υἱοί σου μετὰ σοῦ, ἡνίκα ἂν εἰσπορεύησθε εἰς
τὴν σκηνὴν τοῦ μαρτυρίου, ἢ προσπορευομένων ὑμῶν πρὸς τὸ
θυσιαστήριον, καὶ οὐ μὴ ἀποθάνητε (νόμιμον αἰώνιον εἰς τὰς γενεὰς ὑμῶν)

Num 6:3

³ מִיַּ֤יִן וְשֵׁכָר֙ יַזִּ֔יר חֹ֥מֶץ יַ֛יִן וְחֹ֥מֶץ שֵׁכָ֖ר לֹ֣א יִשְׁתֶּ֑ה וְכָל־
מִשְׁרַ֤ת עֲנָבִים֙ לֹ֣א יִשְׁתֶּ֔ה וַעֲנָבִ֛ים לַחִ֥ים וִיבֵשִׁ֖ים לֹ֥א יֹאכֵֽל׃

³ἀπὸ οἴνου καὶ σικερα,
ἁγνισθήσεται ἀπὸ οἴνου καὶ ὄξος ἐξ οἴνου καὶ ὄξος ἐκ σικερα οὐ
πίεται καὶ ὅσα κατεργάζεται ἐκ σταφυλῆς οὐ πίεται καὶ σταφυλὴν
πρόσφατον καὶ σταφίδα οὐ φάγεται.

64: Lev 12:8

⁸ וְאִם־לֹ֨א תִמְצָ֣א יָדָהּ֮ דֵּ֣י שֶׂה֒ וְלָֽקְחָ֣ה
שְׁתֵּֽי־תֹרִ֗ים א֤וֹ שְׁנֵי֙ בְּנֵ֣י יוֹנָ֔ה אֶחָ֥ד לְעֹלָ֖ה וְאֶחָ֣ד לְחַטָּ֑את וְכִפֶּ֧ר עָלֶ֛יהָ
הַכֹּהֵ֖ן וְטָהֵֽרָה׃

⁸ἐὰν δὲ μὴ εὑρίσκῃ ἡ χεὶρ αὐτῆς τὸ
ἱκανὸν εἰς ἀμνόν, καὶ λήμψεται δύο τρυγόνας ἢ δύο νεοσσοὺς
περιστερῶν, μίαν εἰς ὁλοκαύτωμα καὶ μίαν περὶ ἁμαρτίας, καὶ ἐξι-
λάσεται περὶ αὐτῆς ὁ ἱερεύς, καὶ καθαρισθήσεται.

65: Lev 18:5

⁵ וּשְׁמַרְתֶּ֤ם אֶת־
חֻקֹּתַי֙ וְאֶת־מִשְׁפָּטַ֔י אֲשֶׁ֨ר יַעֲשֶׂ֥ה אֹתָ֛ם הָאָדָ֖ם וָחַ֣י בָּהֶ֑ם אֲנִ֖י יְהוָֽה׃

⁵καὶ φυλάξεσθε πάντα
τὰ προστάγματά μου καὶ πάντα τὰ κρίματά μου καὶ ποιήσετε αὐτά,
ἃ ποιήσας ἄνθρωπος ζήσεται ἐν αὐτοῖς· ἐγὼ κύριος ὁ θεὸς ὑμῶν.

66: Lev 19:2

² דַּבֵּ֞ר אֶל־כָּל־עֲדַ֧ת בְּנֵֽי־
יִשְׂרָאֵ֛ל וְאָמַרְתָּ֥ אֲלֵהֶ֖ם קְדֹשִׁ֣ים תִּהְי֑וּ כִּ֣י קָד֔וֹשׁ אֲנִ֖י יְהוָ֥ה אֱלֹהֵיכֶֽם׃

²Λάλησον τῇ συνα-
γωγῇ τῶν υἱῶν Ισραηλ καὶ ἐρεῖς πρὸς αὐτούς Ἅγιοι ἔσεσθε, ὅτι
ἐγὼ ἅγιος, κύριος ὁ θεὸς ὑμῶν.

[a] Lk 1:15

15 Ἔσται γὰρ μέγας ἐνώπιον ⸀[τοῦ] κυρίου⸀,
καὶ οἶνον καὶ σίκερα οὐ μὴ πίῃ,
καὶ πνεύματος ἁγίου πλησθήσεται
ἔτι ⸀ἐκ κοιλίας⸀ μητρὸς αὐτοῦ,

Lk 1:15, referring to John the Baptist, picks up allusive language from Lev 10:9 ordaining a prohibition against wine for all officiating priests. In so doing it converts MT's 2nd pers. sing. (addressed to Aaron) into 3rd pers. sing. (*A*) or (*F*)

Num 6:3 gives the ordinance for the order of the Nazarite and indicates that a Nazarite, like the priest, must abstain from wine and strong drink. But in the case of the Nazarite, it is made clear that he has to observe this abstinence only during the duration of his vow. The language of course is a little bit different in Num 6:3 in that it says he shall be sanctified from, that is, so as to abstain from, liquor and strong drink, but the sense is the same.

[a] Lk 2:24

24 καὶ τοῦ δοῦναι θυσίαν κατὰ τὸ εἰρη-μένον ἐν τῷ νόμῳ κυρίου, ζεῦγος τρυγόνων ἢ δύο νοσσοὺς περιστερῶν.

Lev 12:8; MT שְׁתֵּי־תֹרִים = LXX δύο τρυγόνας (Luke 2:24: ζεῦγος τρυγόνων). (*A*[d])

[a] Rom 10:5

5 Μωϋσῆς γὰρ γράφει ⸀τὴν δικαιοσύνην τὴν ἐκ [τοῦ] νόμου ὅτι⸀ ὁ ποιήσας °αὐτὰ °¹ἄνθρωπος ζήσεται ἐν ⸀αὐτοῖς.

Lev 18:5; וְאֶת־מִשְׁפָּטַי אֲשֶׁר יַעֲשֶׂה אֹתָם הָאָדָם = LXX (προστάγματά μου καὶ πάντα τὰ) κρίματά μου καὶ ποιήσετε αὐτά, ἃ ποιήσας ἄνθρωπος ζήσεται ἐν αὐτοῖς. (*B*[a])

[b] Gal 3:12

12 ὁ δὲ νόμος οὐκ ἔστιν ἐκ πίστεως, ἀλλ᾽ ὁ ποιήσας αὐτὰ ⸀ ζή-σεται ἐν αὐτοῖς.

Rom 10:5 ὅτι ὁ ποιήσας αὐτὰ ἄνθρωπος ζήσεται ἐν αὐτοῖς. Gal 3:12 reads virtually the same. Note that the reason for the slight deviation in Rom 10:5 is the stream of the context, which precluded opening with ἃ ποιήσας; yet ἃ is really picked up by the following αὐτά (which is not needed and is therefore not found in the LXX).

[a] 1 Pet 1:16

16 ⸀διό-τι γέγραπται⸀ °[ὅτι] ἅγιοι ⸀ἔσεσθε, ⸀ὅτι ἐγὼ ἅγιός °¹[εἰμι].

Lev 19:2. (*A*)

MASORETIC TEXT	SEPTUAGINT

67: Lev 19:12

וְלֹֽא־תִשָּׁבְע֥וּ בִשְׁמִ֖י לַשָּׁ֑קֶר וְחִלַּלְתָּ֛ אֶת־שֵׁ֥ם אֱלֹהֶ֖יךָ אֲנִ֥י יְהוָֽה׃

¹²καὶ οὐκ ὀμεῖσθε τῷ ὀνόματί μου ἐπ' ἀδίκῳ καὶ οὐ βεβη-
λώσετε τὸ ὄνομα τοῦ θεοῦ ὑμῶν· ἐγώ εἰμι κύριος ὁ θεὸς ὑμῶν.

Num 30:3 (30:2)

³אִישׁ֩ כִּֽי־יִדֹּ֨ר נֶ֜דֶר לַֽיהוָ֗ה אֽוֹ־הִשָּׁ֤בַע שְׁבֻעָה֙
לֶאְסֹ֤ר אִסָּר֙ עַל־נַפְשׁ֔וֹ לֹ֥א יַחֵ֖ל דְּבָר֑וֹ כְּכָל־הַיֹּצֵ֥א מִפִּ֖יו יַעֲשֶֽׂה׃

³ἄνθρωπος ἄνθρωπος,
ὃς ἂν εὔξηται εὐχὴν κυρίῳ ἢ ὀμόσῃ ὅρκον ἢ ὁρίσηται ὁρισμῷ
περὶ τῆς ψυχῆς αὐτοῦ, οὐ βεβηλώσει τὸ ῥῆμα αὐτοῦ· πάντα, ὅσα
ἐὰν ἐξέλθῃ ἐκ τοῦ στόματος αὐτοῦ, ποιήσει.

68: Lev 19:18 (compare with [51])

¹⁸לֹֽא־תִקֹּ֤ם וְלֹֽא־תִטֹּר֙ אֶת־בְּנֵ֣י עַמֶּ֔ךָ וְאָֽהַבְתָּ֥ לְרֵעֲךָ֖ כָּמ֑וֹךָ
אֲנִ֖י יְהוָֽה׃

¹⁸καὶ οὐκ ἐκδικᾶ-
ταί σου ἡ χείρ, καὶ οὐ μηνιεῖς τοῖς υἱοῖς τοῦ λαοῦ σου καὶ ἀγαπήσεις τὸν πλησίον σου ὡς σεαυτόν· ἐγώ εἰμι κύριος.

Deut 6:5

⁵וְאָ֣הַבְתָּ֔ אֵ֖ת יְהוָ֣ה אֱלֹהֶ֑יךָ בְּכָל־לְבָבְךָ֥ וּבְכָל־נַפְשְׁךָ֖
וּבְכָל־מְאֹדֶֽךָ׃

⁵καὶ ἀγα-
πήσεις κύριον τὸν θεόν σου ἐξ ὅλης τῆς καρδίας σου καὶ ἐξ ὅλης
τῆς ψυχῆς σου καὶ ἐξ ὅλης τῆς δυνάμεώς σου.

only Lev 19:18

Josh 22:5

⁵רַ֣ק׀ שִׁמְר֣וּ מְאֹ֗ד לַעֲשׂ֜וֹת
אֶת־הַמִּצְוָ֣ה וְאֶת־הַתּוֹרָ֗ה אֲשֶׁ֨ר צִוָּ֥ה אֶתְכֶ֛ם מֹשֶׁ֥ה עֶֽבֶד־יְהוָה֖ לְאַהֲבָ֞ה
אֶת־יְהוָ֣ה אֱלֹֽהֵיכֶ֗ם וְלָלֶ֤כֶת בְּכָל־דְּרָכָיו֙ וְלִשְׁמֹ֣ר מִצְוֺתָ֔יו וּלְדָבְקָה־
ב֖וֹ וּלְעָבְד֑וֹ בְּכָל־לְבַבְכֶ֖ם וּבְכָל־נַפְשְׁכֶֽם׃

⁵ἀλλὰ
φυλάξασθε ποιεῖν σφόδρα τὰς ἐντολὰς καὶ τὸν νόμον, ὃν ἐνετείλατο ἡμῖν ποιεῖν Μωυσῆς ὁ παῖς κυρίου, ἀγαπᾶν κύριον τὸν θεὸν
ὑμῶν, πορεύεσθαι πάσαις ταῖς ὁδοῖς αὐτοῦ, φυλάξασθαι τὰς ἐντολὰς αὐτοῦ καὶ προσκεῖσθαι αὐτῷ καὶ λατρεύειν αὐτῷ ἐξ ὅλης τῆς
διανοίας ὑμῶν καὶ ἐξ ὅλης τῆς ψυχῆς ὑμῶν.

*a*Mt 5:33

33 Πάλιν ἠκούσατε ὅτι ἐρρέθη ᵒτοῖς ἀρχαίοις⁀· οὐκ ἐπιορκήσεις, ἀποδώσεις δὲ τῷ κυρίῳ τοὺς ὅρκους σου.

Mt 5:33 uses the introductory formula ἐρρέθη τοῖς ἀρχαίοις ("it was said to the ancients," or possibly—since the dative of agent was often used with the aorist passive in Classical Greek—"it was said *by* the ancients." This may not be intended as a quotation from the Torah itself, but rather a summation of the law pertaining to the obligatory fulfillment of oaths. The effect of the two passages cited, Lev 19:12 and Num 30:3(2) is certainly a stern prohibition against perjury, or against the failure to fulfill what has been assumed as an obligation under oath. This summary of the teaching sounds like a pronouncement by a doctor of the Law rather than a quotation from the Mosaic text itself. This was unquestionably the case with Mt 5:43: "You have heard that it was said, 'You shall love your neighbor and hate your enemy.'" Nowhere in the Torah was it ever stated that a true believer was to hate his אֹיֵב or צַר. This could only be a casuistic interpretation by later "lawyers" perhaps those belonging to the Pharisaic school.

*a*Mk 12:33

33 καὶ τὸ ἀγαπᾶν αὐτὸν ἐξ ὅλης ᵒτῆς καρδίας καὶ ἐξ ὅλης τῆς ⌜συνέσεως καὶ ἐξ ὅλης τῆς ⌐ ἰσχύος καὶ τὸ ἀγαπᾶν τὸν πλησίον ὡς ἑαυτὸν περισσότερόν ἐστιν πάντων τῶν ὁλοκαυτωμάτων καὶ ᵀ θυσιῶν.

Lev 19:18*b* (cf. 50); MT = LXX = Mk 12:33*b* = Mt 5:43 = Mt 19:19 = Mt 22:39. (*A*)

*b*Lk 10:27

27 ὁ δὲ ἀποκριθεὶς εἶπεν· ἀγαπήσεις κύριον τὸν θεόν ᵒσου ⌜ἐξ ὅλης [τῆς] καρδίας⌝ σου ᵒ¹καὶ ⌐ἐν ὅλῃ τῇ ψυχῇ⌝ σου ⌐¹καὶ ἐν ὅλῃ τῇ ἰσχύϊ σου⌝ ⌐²καὶ ἐν ὅλῃ τῇ διανοίᾳ σου⌝, καὶ τὸν πλησίον σου ὡς σεαυτόν.

Deut 6:5*a*; Mt = LXX = Mk 12:33 = Lk 10:27 = Mt 22:37.

Compare MT בְּכָל־לְבָבְךָ וּבְכָל־נַפְשְׁךָ וּבְכָל־מְאֹדֶךָ with LXX καρδίας ... ψυχῆς ... δυνάμεως; Lk 10:27 ἐξ ... καρδίας, ἐν ψυχῇ σου ... τῇ διανοίᾳ σου. LXX often translates לֵבָב as διάνοια as well as καρδία. (*B*ᵃ)

*c*Mt 5:43

43 Ἠκούσατε ὅτι ἐρρέθη! ἀγαπήσεις τὸν πλησίον σου καὶ μισήσεις τὸν ἐχθρόν σου.

*d*Mt 19:19 *(see also [48],a)

19*τίμα τὸν πατέρα καὶ τὴν μητέρα, καὶ ἀγαπήσεις τὸν πλησίον σου ὡς σεαυτόν.

*e*Mt 22:39

39 δευτέρα ᵒδὲ ⌜ὁμοία αὐτῇ⌝· ἀγαπήσεις τὸν πλησίον σου ὡς σεαυτόν.

Joshua 22:5 picks up the Deut 6:5 wording on the first and great commandment but limits it only to "from your whole heart and your whole soul and shall serve him." I suppose you would have to say with your whole mind and with your whole soul. Mind, διανοίας of course, does refer to לבב or heart.

Lev 19:18 (continued)

לֹא־תִקֹּם וְלֹא־תִטֹּר אֶת־בְּנֵי עַמֶּךָ וְאָהַבְתָּ לְרֵעֲךָ כָּמוֹךָ 18
אֲנִי יְהוָה:

¹⁸ καὶ οὐκ ἐκδικᾶταί σου ἡ χείρ, καὶ οὐ μηνιεῖς τοῖς υἱοῖς τοῦ λαοῦ σου καὶ ἀγαπήσεις τὸν πλησίον σου ὡς σεαυτόν· ἐγώ εἰμι κύριος.

only Lev 19:18

Deut 6:5

only Deut 6:5

וְאָהַבְתָּ אֵת יְהוָה 5
אֱלֹהֶיךָ בְּכָל־לְבָבְךָ וּבְכָל־נַפְשְׁךָ וּבְכָל־מְאֹדֶךָ:

⁵ καὶ ἀγαπήσεις κύριον τὸν θεόν σου ἐξ ὅλης τῆς καρδίας σου καὶ ἐξ ὅλης τῆς ψυχῆς σου καὶ ἐξ ὅλης τῆς δυνάμεώς σου.

69: Lev 23:29

כִּי כָל־הַנֶּפֶשׁ אֲשֶׁר לֹא־תְעֻנֶּה 29
בְּעֶצֶם הַיּוֹם הַזֶּה וְנִכְרְתָה מֵעַמֶּיהָ:

²⁹ πᾶσα ψυχή, ἥτις μὴ ταπεινωθήσεται ἐν αὐτῇ τῇ ἡμέρᾳ ταύτῃ, ἐξολεθρευθήσεται ἐκ τοῦ λαοῦ αὐτῆς.

Deut 18:19

וְהָיָה הָאִישׁ אֲשֶׁר לֹא־יִשְׁמַע אֶל־דְּבָרַי אֲשֶׁר יְדַבֵּר בִּשְׁמִי אָנֹכִי 19
אֶדְרֹשׁ מֵעִמּוֹ:

¹⁹ καὶ ὁ ἄνθρωπος, ὃς ἐὰν μὴ ἀκούσῃ ὅσα ἐὰν λαλήσῃ ὁ προφήτης ἐπὶ τῷ ὀνόματί μου, ἐγὼ ἐκδικήσω ἐξ αὐτοῦ.

70: Lev 24:20

שֶׁבֶר תַּחַת שֶׁבֶר עַיִן תַּחַת עַיִן שֵׁן תַּחַת שֵׁן כַּאֲשֶׁר 20
יִתֵּן מוּם בָּאָדָם כֵּן יִנָּתֶן בּוֹ:

²⁰ σύντριμμα ἀντὶ συντρίμματος, ὀφθαλμὸν ἀντὶ ὀφθαλμοῦ, ὀδόντα ἀντὶ ὀδόντος· καθότι ἂν δῷ μῶμον τῷ ἀνθρώπῳ, οὕτως δοθήσεται αὐτῷ.

71: Lev 26:12

וְהִתְהַלַּכְתִּי 12
בְּתוֹכְכֶם וְהָיִיתִי לָכֶם לֵאלֹהִים וְאַתֶּם תִּהְיוּ־לִי לְעָם:

¹² καὶ ἐμπεριπατήσω ἐν ὑμῖν καὶ ἔσομαι ὑμῶν θεός, καὶ ὑμεῖς ἔσεσθέ μου λαός.

Ezek 37:27

וְהָיָה מִשְׁכָּנִי עֲלֵיהֶם וְהָיִיתִי לָהֶם לֵאלֹהִים וְהֵמָּה יִהְיוּ־ 27
לִי לְעָם:

²⁷ καὶ ἔσται ἡ κατασκήνωσις μου ἐν αὐτοῖς, καὶ ἔσομαι αὐτοῖς θεός, καὶ αὐτοί μου ἔσονται λαός.

*f*Mk 12:31

31 ⸀δευτέρα αὕτη⸀· ἀγαπήσεις τὸν
πλησίον σου ὡς σεαυτόν. μείζων τούτων ἄλλη ἐντολὴ οὐκ
ἔστιν.

*g*Gal 5:14

14 ὁ γὰρ πᾶς νόμος ἐν
⸀ἑνὶ λόγῳ⸀ ⸀πεπλήρωται, ἐν τῷ· ἀγαπήσεις τὸν πλησίον
σου ὡς σεαυτόν.

*h*Jas 2:8

8 Εἰ μέντοι ⸀νόμον τελεῖτε βασιλικὸν⸀ ⸀κατὰ τὴν
γραφήν⸀· ἀγαπήσεις τὸν πλησίον σου ὡς σεαυτόν, καλῶς
ποιεῖτε·

*i*Mt 22:37

37 ⸀ὁ δὲ ἔφη αὐτῷ⸀· ἀγα-
πήσεις κύριον τὸν θεόν σου ἐν ὅλῃ °τῇ καρδίᾳ σου καὶ ἐν ὅλῃ
°¹τῇ ψυχῇ σου καὶ ἐν ὅλῃ τῇ ⸀διανοίᾳ σου·

---

*a*Acts 3:23

23 ἔσται δὲ πᾶσα ψυχὴ
ἥτις ἐὰν μὴ ἀκούσῃ τοῦ προφήτου ἐκείνου ἐξολεθρευθήσεται ἐκ τοῦ λαοῦ.

Lev 23:29 contributes וְנִכְרְתָה מֵעַמֶּיהָ = Acts 3:23b =
LXX ἐξολεθρευθήσεται ἐκ τοῦ λαοῦ αὐτῆς (except
that Acts 3:23b omits αὐτῆς).

Deut 18:19 contributes הָאִישׁ אֲשֶׁר לֹא־יִשְׁמַע אֶל־דְּבָרַי
אֲשֶׁר יְדַבֵּר toward Acts 3:23a: ἔσται δὲ πᾶσα ψυχὴ ἥτις
ἐὰν μὴ ἀκούσῃ τοῦ προφήτου ἐκείνου. Those two
passages are combined into a conflate. (*A*) and (*B*ᵃ)

---

*a*Mt 5:38 *(see also [54],a)

38 Ἠκούσατε ὅτι ἐρρέθη· ὀφθαλμὸν ἀντὶ ὀφθαλμοῦ °καὶ
ὀδόντα ἀντὶ ὀδόντος.

Lev 24:20. (*A*)

---

*a*2 Cor 6:16

16 τίς δὲ συγκατάθε-
σις ναῷ θεοῦ μετὰ εἰδώλων; ⸀ἡμεῖς γὰρ ναὸς θεοῦ ἐσμεν⸀
ζῶντος, καθὼς εἶπεν ὁ θεὸς ὅτι
ἐνοικήσω ἐν αὐτοῖς καὶ ἐμπεριπατήσω
καὶ ἔσομαι αὐτῶν θεὸς καὶ αὐτοὶ ἔσονταί ⸀μου λαός.

Lev 26:12 contributes to 2 Cor 6:16 (*B*ᵃ) except for
ἐνοικήσω ἐν αὐτοῖς, which is paraphrased from Ezek
37:27 (LXX) καὶ ἔσται ἡ κατασκήνωσίς μου ἐν αὐτοῖς
κτλ.; 2 Cor 6:16 ἐνοικήσω ἐν αὐτοῖς (very close in
wording!). (*A*-)

72: Num 6:3

see Lev 10:9 [63]

73: Num 9:12

see Ex 12:46 [41]

74: Num 16:5

⁵ וַיְדַבֵּר אֶל־קֹרַח וְאֶל־כָּל־עֲדָתוֹ
לֵאמֹר בֹּקֶר וְיֹדַע יְהֹוָה אֶת־אֲשֶׁר־לוֹ וְאֶת־הַקָּדוֹשׁ וְהִקְרִיב
אֵלָיו וְאֵת אֲשֶׁר יִבְחַר־בּוֹ יַקְרִיב אֵלָיו:

⁵καὶ ἐλάλησεν πρὸς Κορε καὶ πρὸς
πᾶσαν αὐτοῦ τὴν συναγωγὴν λέγων Ἐπέσκεπται καὶ ἔγνω ὁ θεὸς
τοὺς ὄντας αὐτοῦ καὶ τοὺς ἁγίους καὶ προσηγάγετο πρὸς ἑαυτόν,
καὶ οὓς ἐξελέξατο ἑαυτῷ, προσηγάγετο πρὸς ἑαυτόν.

Isa 26:13

¹³ יְהֹוָה אֱלֹהֵינוּ בְּעָלוּנוּ אֲדֹנִים זוּלָתֶךָ לְבַד־בְּךָ נַזְכִּיר שְׁמֶךָ:

¹³κύριε ὁ θεὸς ἡμῶν, κτῆσαι ἡμᾶς · κύριε, ἐκτὸς σοῦ ἄλλον οὐκ οἴδαμεν, τὸ ὄνομά σου ὀνομάζομεν.

75: Num 27:17

¹⁷ אֲשֶׁר־יֵצֵא לִפְנֵיהֶם וַאֲשֶׁר יָבֹא לִפְנֵיהֶם וַאֲשֶׁר יוֹצִיאֵם וַאֲשֶׁר
יְבִיאֵם וְלֹא תִהְיֶה עֲדַת יְהֹוָה כַּצֹּאן אֲשֶׁר אֵין־לָהֶם רֹעֶה:

¹⁷ὅστις ἐξελεύσεται πρὸ
προσώπου αὐτῶν καὶ ὅστις εἰσελεύσεται πρὸ προσώπου αὐτῶν
καὶ ὅστις ἐξάξει αὐτοὺς καὶ ὅστις εἰσάξει αὐτούς, καὶ οὐκ ἔσται
ἡ συναγωγὴ κυρίου ὡσεὶ πρόβατα, οἷς οὐκ ἔστιν ποιμήν.

2 Chron 18:16

¹⁶ וַיֹּאמֶר
רָאִיתִי אֶת־כָּל־יִשְׂרָאֵל נְפוֹצִים עַל־הֶהָרִים כַּצֹּאן אֲשֶׁר אֵין־לָהֶן
רֹעֶה וַיֹּאמֶר יְהֹוָה לֹא־אֲדֹנִים לָאֵלֶּה יָשׁוּבוּ אִישׁ־לְבֵיתוֹ בְּשָׁלוֹם:

¹⁶καὶ εἶπεν Εἶδον τὸν Ισραηλ διεσπαρ-
μένους ἐν τοῖς ὄρεσιν ὡς πρόβατα οἷς οὐκ ἔστιν ποιμήν, καὶ εἶπεν
κύριος Οὐκ ἔχουσιν ἡγούμενον, ἀναστρεφέτωσαν ἕκαστος εἰς τὸν
οἶκον αὐτοῦ ἐν εἰρήνῃ.

76: Num 30:3 (30:2)

see Lev 19:12 [67]

77: Deut 4:24

²⁴ כִּי יְהֹוָה אֱלֹהֶיךָ אֵשׁ אֹכְלָה הוּא אֵל קַנָּא:

²⁴ὅτι κύριος
ὁ θεός σου πῦρ καταναλίσκον ἐστίν, θεὸς Ζηλωτής.

Deut 9:3

³ וְיָדַעְתָּ הַיּוֹם כִּי יְהֹוָה אֱלֹהֶיךָ הוּא־הָעֹבֵר לְפָנֶיךָ אֵשׁ אֹכְלָה
הוּא יַשְׁמִידֵם וְהוּא יַכְנִיעֵם לְפָנֶיךָ וְהוֹרַשְׁתָּם וְהַאֲבַדְתָּם מַהֵר כַּאֲשֶׁר
דִּבֶּר יְהֹוָה לָךְ:

³καὶ γνώσῃ σήμερον
ὅτι κύριος ὁ θεός σου, οὗτος προπορεύεται πρὸ προσώπου σου·
πῦρ καταναλίσκον ἐστίν· οὗτος ἐξολεθρεύσει αὐτούς, καὶ οὗτος
ἀποστρέψει αὐτοὺς ἀπὸ προσώπου σου, καὶ ἀπολεῖς αὐτούς, καθ-
άπερ εἶπέν σοι κύριος.

*a*2 Tim 2:19

19 ὁ μέντοι
στερεὸς θεμέλιος τοῦ θεοῦ ἔστηκεν, ἔχων τὴν σφρα-
γῖδα ταύτην· ἔγνω κύριος ⌃ τοὺς ὄντας αὐτοῦ, καί· ἀπο-
στήτω ἀπὸ ἀδικίας πᾶς ὁ ὀνομάζων τὸ ὄνομα κυρίου.

Num 16:5 = LXX ὁ θεός = 2 Tim 2:19 ὁ θεός (*A*); but
one part of 2 Tim 2:19*b* seems to have no other source
except for *Sirach 35:3* εὐδοκία κυρίου ἀποστῆναι ἀπὸ
πονηρίας, although the πᾶς ὁ ὀνομάζων τὸ ὄνομα
κυρίου is from Is 26:13 שְׁמֶךָ נַזְכִּיר לְבַד־בְּךָ . . . יהוה
(LXX κύριε . . . τὸ ὄνομά σου ὀνομάζομεν). So this is
a conflate quotation from at least two or probably three
sources. Note, though, that Job 36:10 (LXX) καὶ εἶπεν
ὅτι ἐπιστραφήσονται ἐξ ἀδικίας is quite close as well.
(*A*[d])

---

*a*Mt 9:36

36 Ἰδὼν δὲ τοὺς ὄχλους ⌃ ἐσπλαγχνίσθη περὶ αὐτῶν, ὅτι
ἦσαν ⌜ἐσκυλμένοι καὶ ἐρριμμένοι ὡσεὶ πρόβατα μὴ ἔχοντα
ποιμένα.

Num 27:17; MT כַּצֹּאן אֲשֶׁר אֵין־לָהֶם רֹעֶה = LXX οἷς οὐκ
ἔστιν ποιμήν; Mt 9:36 (πρόβατα) μὴ ἔχοντα ποιμένα.

*b*Mk 6:34

34 Καὶ ἐξελθὼν εἶδεν πολὺν ὄχλον καὶ ἐσπλαγχνίσθη
⌜ἐπ' αὐτούς⌝, ὅτι ἦσαν ☐ὡς πρόβατα⟍ μὴ ἔχοντα ποιμένα,
καὶ ἤρξατο διδάσκειν αὐτοὺς πολλά.

2 Chron 18:16; כַּצֹּאן אֲשֶׁר אֵין־לָהֶן רֹעֶה, LXX ὡς πρόβατα οἷς οὐκ ἔστιν ποιμήν. (*F*)

Mk 6:34 is simply the synoptic parallel to Mt 9:36 and
includes the phrase "as sheep not having a shepherd"
which verbally differs from the Septuagint rendering but
is really quite identical in meaning.

---

*a*Heb 12:29

29 ⌜καὶ γὰρ ὁ θεὸς ἡμῶν πῦρ καταναλίσκον.

Heb 12:29 lacks any formula of quotation, but it seems
to adopt the key phrase of Deut 4:24 as a very authoritative pronouncement concerning the judicial severity of
God. The Greek rendering in the LXX is identical with
the form of the quotation in Heb 12:29 and is an
accurate rendering of the MT. (*A*)

Deut 9:3 contains the same essential element of consum-
ing fire אֵשׁ אֹכְלָה, with the same wording in the Greek
whether Lev 24, Deut 9:3, or Heb 12:29, that is πῦρ
καταναλίσκον.

78: Deut 4:35

³⁵ אַתָּה֙ הָרְאֵ֣תָ לָדַ֔עַת כִּ֥י יְהוָ֖ה ה֣וּא הָאֱלֹהִ֑ים אֵ֥ין ע֖וֹד מִלְבַדּֽוֹ׃

³⁵ ὥστε εἰδῆσαί σε ὅτι κύριος ὁ θεός σου, οὗτος θεός ἐστιν, καὶ οὐκ ἔστιν ἔτι πλὴν αὐτοῦ.

Deut 6:4

⁴ שְׁמַ֖ע יִשְׂרָאֵ֑ל יְהוָ֥ה אֱלֹהֵ֖ינוּ יְהוָ֥ה ׀ אֶחָֽד׃

⁴ Καὶ ταῦτα τὰ δικαιώματα καὶ τὰ κρίματα, ὅσα ἐνετείλατο κύριος τοῖς υἱοῖς Ισραηλ ἐν τῇ ἐρήμῳ ἐξελθόντων αὐτῶν ἐκ γῆς Αἰγύπτου Ἄκουε, Ισραηλ· κύριος ὁ θεὸς ἡμῶν κύριος εἷς ἐστιν·

Isa 45:21

²¹ הַגִּ֣ידוּ וְהַגִּ֔ישׁוּ אַ֥ף יִֽוָּעֲצ֖וּ יַחְדָּ֑ו
מִ֣י הִשְׁמִ֣יעַ זֹאת֩ מִקֶּ֨דֶם מֵאָ֜ז הִגִּידָ֗הּ
הֲלֽוֹא־אֲנִ֤י יְהוָה֙ וְאֵֽין־ע֤וֹד אֱלֹהִים֙ מִבַּלְעָדַ֔י
אֵֽל־צַדִּ֣יק וּמוֹשִׁ֔יעַ אַ֖יִן זוּלָתִֽי׃

²¹ εἰ ἀναγγελοῦσιν,
ἐγγισάτωσαν, ἵνα γνῶσιν ἅμα τίς ἀκουστὰ ἐποίησεν ταῦτα ἀπ' ἀρχῆς. τότε ἀνηγγέλη ὑμῖν Ἐγὼ ὁ θεός, καὶ οὐκ ἔστιν ἄλλος πλὴν ἐμοῦ· δίκαιος καὶ σωτὴρ οὐκ ἔστιν πάρεξ ἐμοῦ.

| 79: Deut 5:16 | see Ex 20:12 [48] |

| 80: Deut 5:16–20 | see Ex 20:12–16 [48] |

| 81: Deut 5:17–21 | see Ex 20:13–17 [50] |

| 82: Deut 5:18 | see Ex 20:13 [49] |

| 83: Deut 5:18 | see Ex 20:14 [51] |

| 84: Deut 5:21 | see Ex 20:17 [52] |

| 85: Deut 6:4 | see Deut 4:35 [78] |

86: Deut 6:4–5

⁴ שְׁמַ֖ע יִשְׂרָאֵ֑ל יְהוָ֥ה אֱלֹהֵ֖ינוּ יְהוָ֥ה ׀ אֶחָֽד׃ ⁵ וְאָ֣הַבְתָּ֔ אֵ֖ת יְהוָ֣ה אֱלֹהֶ֑יךָ בְּכָל־לְבָבְךָ֥ וּבְכָל־נַפְשְׁךָ֖ וּבְכָל־מְאֹדֶֽךָ׃

⁴ Καὶ ταῦτα τὰ δικαιώματα καὶ τὰ κρίματα, ὅσα ἐνετείλατο κύριος τοῖς υἱοῖς Ισραηλ ἐν τῇ ἐρήμῳ ἐξελθόντων αὐτῶν ἐκ γῆς Αἰγύπτου Ἄκουε, Ισραηλ· κύριος ὁ θεὸς ἡμῶν κύριος εἷς ἐστιν· ⁵ καὶ ἀγαπήσεις κύριον τὸν θεόν σου ἐξ ὅλης τῆς καρδίας σου καὶ ἐξ ὅλης τῆς ψυχῆς σου καὶ ἐξ ὅλης τῆς δυνάμεώς σου.

*a*Mk 12:32

32 ⁰καὶ εἶπεν αὐτῷ ὁ γραμματεύς· καλῶς, δι-δάσκαλε, ἐπ' ἀληθείας εἶπες ὅτι *εἷς ἐστιν καὶ οὐκ ἔστιν ἄλλος πλὴν αὐτοῦ·*

Deut 4:35; MT lacks εἷς before ἐστιν, הוּא הָאֱלֹהִים אֵין עוֹד מִלְבַדּוֹ as compared to Mk 12:32 εἷς ἐστιν καὶ οὐκ ἔστιν ἄλλος πλὴν αὐτοῦ. (*B*ᵃ)

Deut 6:4; MT אֱלֹהֵינוּ יהוה אֶחָד = LXX κύριος εἷς ἐστιν (Mk 12:32 εἷς ἐστιν, "God" understood from previous context). (*A*)

Is 45:21; LXX Ἐγὼ ὁ θεὸς καὶ, οὐκ ἔστιν ἄλλος πλὴν ἐμοῦ (probably derived from Deut 4:35 with which it is identical).

*a*Mk 12:29–30

29 ⌐ἀπεκρίθη ὁ Ἰησοῦς⌐ ⌐ὅτι πρώτη ἐστίν⌐· ἄκουε, Ἰσρα-ήλ, κύριος ὁ θεὸς ἡμῶν κύριος εἷς ἐστιν, **30** καὶ ἀγαπήσεις κύριον τὸν θεόν σου ἐξ ὅλης ⁰τῆς καρδίας σου καὶ ἐξ ὅλης ⁰¹τῆς ψυχῆς σου ⌐καὶ ἐξ ὅλης ⁰¹τῆς διανοίας σου⌐ καὶ ἐξ

The *shᵉmaᶜ* of Deut 6:4–5 is translated with literal accuracy in the LXX, and the LXX wording is faithfully followed in Mk 12:29–30 except for one insertion. That is, between "with all your soul" and "with all your strength" (which followed immediately after the first phrase in the MT) there appears "and with all your mind" (ὅλης τῆς διανοίας σου). Since διάνοια is a frequent equivalent for the Heb. לֵבָב, it is possible that διάνοια, as a term interpretive of לֵבָב = καρδία was adopted as a legitimate and helpful expansion in the *shᵉmaᶜ* by Jesus' day. (*D*) or (*A*ᵈ)

Masoretic Text	Septuagint
87: Deut 6:5	**see Lev 19:18 [68]**

88: Deut 6:13	¹³ κύριον τὸν θεόν σου φοβηθήσῃ καὶ αὐτῷ λατρεύσεις καὶ πρὸς αὐτὸν κολληθήσῃ καὶ τῷ ὀνόματι αὐτοῦ ὀμῇ.
¹³ אֶת־יְהוָ֤ה אֱלֹהֶ֙יךָ֙ תִּירָ֔א וְאֹת֖וֹ תַעֲבֹ֑ד וּבִשְׁמ֖וֹ תִּשָּׁבֵֽעַ:	

89: Deut 6:16	¹⁶ Οὐκ ἐκπειράσεις κύριον τὸν θεόν σου, ὃν τρόπον ἐξεπειράσασθε ἐν τῷ Πειρασμῷ.
¹⁶ לֹ֣א תְנַסּ֔וּ אֶת־יְהוָ֖ה אֱלֹהֵיכֶ֑ם כַּאֲשֶׁ֥ר נִסִּיתֶ֖ם בַּמַּסָּֽה:	

90: Deut 8:3	³ καὶ ἐκάκωσέν σε καὶ ἐλιμαγχόνησέν σε καὶ ἐψώμισέν σε τὸ μαννα, ὃ οὐκ εἴδησαν οἱ πατέρες σου, ἵνα ἀναγγείλῃ σοι ὅτι οὐκ ἐπ' ἄρτῳ μόνῳ ζήσεται ὁ ἄνθρωπος, ἀλλ' ἐπὶ παντὶ ῥήματι τῷ ἐκπορευομένῳ διὰ στόματος θεοῦ ζήσεται ὁ ἄνθρωπος.
³ וַֽיְעַנְּךָ֮ וַיַּרְעִבֶךָ֒ וַיַּֽאֲכִֽלְךָ֤ אֶת־הַמָּן֙ אֲשֶׁ֣ר לֹא־יָדַ֔עְתָּ וְלֹ֥א יָדְע֖וּן אֲבֹתֶ֑יךָ לְמַ֣עַן הוֹדִֽיעֲךָ֗ כִּ֠י לֹ֣א עַל־הַלֶּ֤חֶם לְבַדּוֹ֙ יִחְיֶ֣ה הָֽאָדָ֔ם כִּ֛י עַל־כָּל־מוֹצָ֥א פִֽי־יְהוָ֖ה יִחְיֶ֥ה הָאָדָֽם:	

91: Deut 9:3	**see Deut 4:24 [77]**

92: Deut 9:4	⁴ μὴ εἴπῃς ἐν τῇ καρδίᾳ σου ἐν τῷ ἐξαναλῶσαι κύριον τὸν θεόν σου τὰ ἔθνη ταῦτα ἀπὸ προσώπου σου λέγων Διὰ τὰς δικαιοσύνας μου εἰσήγαγέν με κύριος κληρονομῆσαι τὴν γῆν τὴν ἀγαθὴν ταύτην· ἀλλὰ διὰ τὴν ἀσέβειαν τῶν ἐθνῶν τούτων κύριος ἐξολεθρεύσει αὐτοὺς πρὸ προσώπου σου.
⁴ אַל־תֹּאמַ֣ר בִּלְבָבְךָ֗ בַּהֲדֹ֣ף יְהוָה֩ אֱלֹהֶ֙יךָ אֹתָ֥ם ׀ מִלְּפָנֶ֘יךָ֙ לֵאמֹר֒ בְּצִדְקָתִי֙ הֱבִיאַ֣נִי יְהוָ֔ה לָרֶ֖שֶׁת אֶת־הָאָ֣רֶץ הַזֹּ֑את וּבְרִשְׁעַת֙ הַגּוֹיִ֣ם הָאֵ֔לֶּה יְהוָ֖ה מוֹרִישָׁ֥ם מִפָּנֶֽיךָ:	

[a]Mt 4:10

10 τότε λέγει
αὐτῷ ὁ Ἰησοῦς· ὕπαγε[T], σατανᾶ· γέγραπται γάρ· *κύριον*
τὸν θεόν σου προσκυνήσεις καὶ αὐτῷ μόνῳ λατρεύσεις.

[b]Lk 4:8

8 καὶ ἀποκριθεὶς [F]ὁ Ἰησοῦς εἶπεν
αὐτῷ⌐· [T] γέγραπται· ⌐[1]*κύριον τὸν θεόν σου προσκυνήσεις*[L1]
καὶ αὐτῷ μόνῳ λατρεύσεις.

Deut 6:13 lacks תִּשְׁתַּחֲוֶה = NT προσκυνήσεις (Lk 4:8
and Mt 4:10). Likewise, the LXX lacks it and inserts
καὶ πρὸς αὐτὸν κολληθήσῃ, which is missing in MT
and NT. Neither MT nor LXX has Lk 4:8 or Mk 4:10's
μόνῳ after αὐτῷ. All three deviate from each other. ([B][a])

---

[a]Mt 4:7

7 ἔφη αὐτῷ ὁ Ἰησοῦς· πάλιν γέγραπται· ⌐*οὐκ ἐκπειράσεις*⌐
κύριον τὸν θεόν σου.

[b]Lk 4:12

12 καὶ ἀποκριθεὶς εἶπεν αὐτῷ ὁ Ἰησοῦς ⌐[1]*ὅτι εἴρηται*⌐·
οὐκ ἐκπειράσεις κύριον τὸν θεόν σου.[L]

Deut 6:16; MT = LXX = Mt 4:7 = Lk 4:12. (*A*)

---

[a]Mt 4:4

4 ὁ δὲ ἀποκριθεὶς εἶπεν· γέγραπται· *οὐκ*
ἐπ' ἄρτῳ μόνῳ ζήσεται ὁ ἄνθρωπος, ἀλλ' ⌐*ἐπὶ παντὶ ῥήματι*
[□]*ἐκπορευομένῳ διὰ στόματος*⌐ *θεοῦ:*

[b]Lk 4:4

4 καὶ ἀπεκρίθη πρὸς αὐτὸν ὁ Ἰησοῦς·
γέγραπται ὅτι *οὐκ ἐπ' ἄρτῳ μόνῳ ζήσεται ὁ ἄνθρωπος*[T].

Deut 8:3. (*A*, except word order)

---

[a]Rom 10:6a   Only Deut 9:4

6 ἡ δὲ ἐκ πίστεως δικαιοσύνη οὕτως λέγει· *μὴ*
εἴπῃς ἐν τῇ καρδίᾳ σου· τίς ἀναβήσεται εἰς τὸν οὐρανόν;
τοῦτ' ἔστιν Χριστὸν καταγαγεῖν·

Deut 9:4. (*A*; a mere phrase borrowed—no evident
quotation)

92 (continued)

Deut 30:12–14

¹² לֹ֥א בַשָּׁמַ֖יִם הִ֑וא לֵאמֹ֗ר מִ֣י יַעֲלֶה־לָּ֤נוּ הַשָּׁמַ֙יְמָה֙
וְיִקָּחֶ֣הָ לָּ֔נוּ וְיַשְׁמִעֵ֥נוּ אֹתָ֖הּ וְנַעֲשֶֽׂנָּה: ¹³ וְלֹא־מֵעֵ֥בֶר לַיָּ֖ם הִ֑וא לֵאמֹ֗ר
מִ֣י יַעֲבָר־לָ֜נוּ אֶל־עֵ֤בֶר הַיָּם֙ וְיִקָּחֶ֣הָ לָּ֔נוּ וְיַשְׁמִעֵ֥נוּ אֹתָ֖הּ וְנַעֲשֶֽׂנָּה:
¹⁴ כִּֽי־קָר֥וֹב אֵלֶ֛יךָ הַדָּבָ֖ר מְאֹ֑ד בְּפִ֥יךָ וּבִֽלְבָבְךָ֖ לַעֲשֹׂתֽוֹ: ס

¹²οὐκ ἐν τῷ οὐρανῷ ἄνω
ἐστὶν λέγων Τίς ἀναβήσεται ἡμῖν εἰς τὸν οὐρανὸν καὶ λήμψεται
αὐτὴν ἡμῖν; καὶ ἀκούσαντες αὐτὴν ποιήσομεν. ¹³οὐδὲ πέραν τῆς
θαλάσσης ἐστὶν λέγων Τίς διαπεράσει ἡμῖν εἰς τὸ πέραν τῆς θαλάσσης καὶ λήμψεται ἡμῖν αὐτήν; καὶ ἀκουστὴν ἡμῖν ποιήσει αὐτήν, καὶ ποιήσομεν. ¹⁴ἔστιν σου ἐγγὺς τὸ ῥῆμα σφόδρα ἐν τῷ
στόματί σου καὶ ἐν τῇ καρδίᾳ σου καὶ ἐν ταῖς χερσίν σου αὐτὸ
ποιεῖν.

Psalm 107:26

²⁶ יַעֲל֣וּ שָׁ֭מַיִם יֵרְד֣וּ תְהוֹמ֑וֹת נַ֝פְשָׁ֗ם בְּרָעָ֥ה תִתְמוֹגָֽג:

²⁶ἀναβαίνουσιν ἕως τῶν οὐρανῶν
καὶ καταβαίνουσιν ἕως τῶν ἀβύσσων,
ἡ ψυχὴ αὐτῶν ἐν κακοῖς ἐτήκετο,

93: Deut 9:19

¹⁹ כִּ֣י
יָגֹ֗רְתִּי מִפְּנֵ֤י הָאַף֙ וְהַ֣חֵמָ֔ה אֲשֶׁ֨ר קָצַ֧ף יְהוָ֛ה עֲלֵיכֶ֖ם לְהַשְׁמִ֣יד אֶתְכֶ֑ם
וַיִּשְׁמַ֤ע יְהוָה֙ אֵלַ֔י גַּ֖ם בַּפַּ֥עַם הַהִֽוא:

¹⁹καὶ ἔκφοβός εἰμι διὰ τὴν ὀργὴν καὶ
τὸν θυμόν, ὅτι παρωξύνθη κύριος ἐφ' ὑμῖν ἐξολεθρεῦσαι ὑμᾶς· καὶ
εἰσήκουσεν κύριος ἐμοῦ καὶ ἐν τῷ καιρῷ τούτῳ.

94: Deut 17:7

⁷ יַ֣ד הָעֵדִ֞ים תִּֽהְיֶה־בּ֤וֹ בָרִֽאשֹׁנָה֙ לַהֲמִית֔וֹ וְיַ֥ד כָּל־הָעָ֖ם
בָּאַחֲרֹנָ֑ה וּבִֽעַרְתָּ֥ הָרָ֖ע מִקִּרְבֶּֽךָ:

⁷καὶ ἡ χεὶρ τῶν μαρτύρων ἔσται ἐπ'
αὐτῷ ἐν πρώτοις θανατῶσαι αὐτόν, καὶ ἡ χεὶρ παντὸς τοῦ λαοῦ
ἐπ' ἐσχάτων· καὶ ἐξαρεῖς τὸν πονηρὸν ἐξ ὑμῶν αὐτῶν.

Deut 19:19

¹⁹ וַעֲשִׂ֣יתֶם ל֔וֹ כַּאֲשֶׁ֥ר זָמַ֖ם לַעֲשֹׂ֣ות לְאָחִ֑יו וּבִֽעַרְתָּ֥ הָרָ֖ע
מִקִּרְבֶּֽךָ:

¹⁹καὶ ποιήσετε αὐτῷ ὃν τρόπον ἐπονηρεύσατο ποιῆσαι
κατὰ τοῦ ἀδελφοῦ αὐτοῦ, καὶ ἐξαρεῖς τὸν πονηρὸν ἐξ ὑμῶν αὐτῶν.

Deut 22:21

²¹ וְהוֹצִ֜יאוּ אֶת־הַֽנַּעֲרָ֣ אֶל־
פֶּ֣תַח בֵּית־אָבִ֗יהָ וּסְקָל֩וּהָ֩ אַנְשֵׁ֨י עִירָ֤הּ בָּֽאֲבָנִים֙ וָמֵ֔תָה כִּֽי־עָשְׂתָ֤ה
נְבָלָה֙ בְּיִשְׂרָאֵ֔ל לִזְנ֖וֹת בֵּ֣ית אָבִ֑יהָ וּבִֽעַרְתָּ֥ הָרָ֖ע מִקִּרְבֶּֽךָ:

²¹καὶ ἐξάξουσιν τὴν
νεᾶνιν ἐπὶ τὰς θύρας οἴκου πατρὸς αὐτῆς, καὶ λιθοβολήσουσιν
αὐτὴν οἱ ἄνδρες τῆς πόλεως αὐτῆς ἐν λίθοις, καὶ ἀποθανεῖται, ὅτι
ἐποίησεν ἀφροσύνην ἐν υἱοῖς Ισραηλ ἐκπορνεῦσαι τὸν οἶκον τοῦ
πατρὸς αὐτῆς· καὶ ἐξαρεῖς τὸν πονηρὸν ἐξ ὑμῶν αὐτῶν.

Deut 22:24

²⁴ וְהוֹצֵאתֶ֣ם אֶת־שְׁנֵיהֶ֗ם אֶל־שַׁ֜עַר ׀ הָעִ֣יר הַהִוא֮ וּסְקַלְתֶּ֣ם
אֹתָם֮ בָּאֲבָנִים֮ וָמֵ֒תוּ֒ אֶת־הַֽנַּעֲרָ֗ עַל־דְּבַר֙ אֲשֶׁ֣ר לֹא־צָעֲקָ֣ה בָעִ֔יר
וְאֶ֨ת־הָאִ֔ישׁ עַל־דְּבַ֥ר אֲשֶׁר־עִנָּ֖ה אֶת־אֵ֣שֶׁת רֵעֵ֑הוּ וּבִֽעַרְתָּ֥ הָרָ֖ע
מִקִּרְבֶּֽךָ:

²⁴ἐξάξετε ἀμφοτέρους
ἐπὶ τὴν πύλην τῆς πόλεως αὐτῶν, καὶ λιθοβοληθήσονται ἐν λίθοις
καὶ ἀποθανοῦνται· τὴν νεᾶνιν, ὅτι οὐκ ἐβόησεν ἐν τῇ πόλει, καὶ
τὸν ἄνθρωπον, ὅτι ἐταπείνωσεν τὴν γυναῖκα τοῦ πλησίον· καὶ ἐξαρεῖς τὸν πονηρὸν ἐξ ὑμῶν αὐτῶν. —

Deut 24:7

⁷ כִּֽי־יִמָּצֵ֣א אִ֗ישׁ גֹּנֵ֨ב נֶ֤פֶשׁ מֵאֶחָיו֙ מִבְּנֵ֣י יִשְׂרָאֵ֔ל וְהִתְעַמֶּר־בּ֖וֹ
וּמְכָר֑וֹ וּמֵת֙ הַגַּנָּ֣ב הַה֔וּא וּבִֽעַרְתָּ֥ הָרָ֖ע מִקִּרְבֶּֽךָ:

⁷Ἐὰν δὲ ἁλῷ ἄνθρωπος κλέπτων ψυχὴν τῶν ἀδελφῶν αὐτοῦ
τῶν υἱῶν Ισραηλ καὶ καταδυναστεύσας αὐτὸν ἀποδῶται, ἀποθανεῖται ὁ κλέπτης ἐκεῖνος· καὶ ἐξαρεῖς τὸν πονηρὸν ἐξ ὑμῶν αὐτῶν.

*b*Rom 10:6–8   only Deut 30:12–14

6 ἡ δὲ ἐκ πίστεως δικαιοσύνη οὕτως λέγει· μὴ εἴπῃς ἐν τῇ καρδίᾳ σου· τίς ἀναβήσεται εἰς τὸν οὐρανόν; τοῦτ' ἔστιν Χριστὸν καταγαγεῖν· 7 ἤ· τίς καταβήσεται εἰς τὴν ἄβυσσον; τοῦτ' ἔστιν Χριστὸν ἐκ νεκρῶν ἀναγαγεῖν. 8 ἀλλὰ τί λέγει⌐; ἐγγύς σου τὸ ῥῆμά ἐστιν ἐν τῷ στόματί σου καὶ ἐν τῇ καρδίᾳ σου, τοῦτ' ἔστιν τὸ ῥῆμα τῆς πίστεως ὃ κηρύσσομεν.

Deut 30:12 (*A*). Rom 12:6 picks up "Do not say in thy heart" from Deut 9:4 but the rest of it, that is, "who shall ascend up into heaven," is taken from Deut 30:12, and we find that this is repeated or picked up in Psalm 107:26, "who shall ascend into heaven," but then followed by, "they shall descend into the depths" תהמות which is picked up by Rom 10:6 as "who shall descend into the deep," the singular τὴν ἄβυσσον rather than the plural of the LXX. But in Rom 10:8 the word is nye "in thy mouth or in thy heart" is taken from Deut 30:14, "the word is very near in thy mouth or in thy heart" which corresponds perfectly with the Hebrew. (*A*)

*a*Heb 12:21

21 καί, οὕτω φοβερὸν ἦν τὸ φανταζόμενον, Μωϋσῆς εἶπεν· ἔκφοβός εἰμι καὶ ⌐ἔντρομος.

Deut 9:19; Compare MT כִּי יָגֹרְתִּי with LXX καὶ ἔκφοβός and NT Heb 12:21 ἔκφοβός εἰμι. (*A*)

*a*1 Cor 5:13

13 τοὺς δὲ ἔξω ὁ θεὸς ⌐κρινεῖ. ⌐ἐξάρατε τὸν πονηρὸν ἐξ ὑμῶν αὐτῶν.

Deut 17:7. (*A*)

Deut 24:7 = Deut 17:7 מִקִּרְבֶּךָ . . . וּבִעַרְתָּ = LXX = 1 Cor 5:13. (*A*)

Deut 19:19; same as above.

Deut 22:21; like the other two quotations preceding, it also attests the phrase "Thou shalt cast out the wicked one from your midsts" but it contributes nothing distinctive or new.

Deut 22:24; same as above.

95: Deut 18:15–16

נָבִ֨יא מִקִּרְבְּךָ֤ מֵאַחֶ֙יךָ֙ כָּמֹ֔נִי יָקִ֥ים לְךָ֖ יְהוָ֣ה אֱלֹהֶ֑יךָ אֵלָ֖יו תִּשְׁמָעֽוּן׃ [15]

כְּכֹ֨ל אֲשֶׁר־שָׁאַ֜לְתָּ מֵעִ֨ם יְהוָ֤ה אֱלֹהֶ֙יךָ֙ בְּחֹרֵ֔ב בְּי֥וֹם הַקָּהָ֖ל לֵאמֹ֑ר לֹ֣א אֹסֵ֗ף לִשְׁמֹ֙עַ֙ אֶת־קוֹל֙ יְהוָ֣ה אֱלֹהָ֔י וְאֶת־הָאֵ֨שׁ הַגְּדֹלָ֤ה הַזֹּאת֙ לֹֽא־אֶרְאֶ֣ה ע֔וֹד וְלֹ֖א אָמֽוּת׃ [16]

[15] προφήτην ἐκ τῶν ἀδελφῶν σου ὡς ἐμὲ ἀναστήσει σοι κύριος ὁ θεός σου, αὐτοῦ ἀκούσεσθε

[16] κατὰ πάντα, ὅσα ᾐτήσω παρὰ κυρίου τοῦ θεοῦ σου ἐν Χωρηβ τῇ ἡμέρᾳ τῆς ἐκκλησίας λέγοντες Οὐ προσθήσομεν ἀκοῦσαι τὴν φωνὴν κυρίου τοῦ θεοῦ ἡμῶν καὶ τὸ πῦρ τὸ μέγα τοῦτο οὐκ ὀψόμεθα ἔτι οὐδὲ μὴ ἀποθάνωμεν,

---

96: Deut 18:19

see Lev 23:29 [69]

97: Deut 19:15

לֹא־יָקוּם֩ [15]
עֵ֨ד אֶחָ֜ד בְּאִ֗ישׁ לְכָל־עָוֹן֙ וּלְכָל־חַטָּ֔את בְּכָל־חֵ֖טְא אֲשֶׁ֣ר יֶחֱטָ֑א עַל־פִּ֣י ׀ שְׁנֵ֣י עֵדִ֗ים א֚וֹ עַל־פִּ֣י שְׁלֹשָֽׁה־עֵדִ֖ים יָק֥וּם דָּבָֽר׃

[15] Οὐκ ἐμμενεῖ μάρτυς εἷς μαρτυρῆσαι κατὰ ἀνθρώπου κατὰ πᾶσαν ἀδικίαν καὶ κατὰ πᾶν ἁμάρτημα καὶ κατὰ πᾶσαν ἁμαρτίαν, ἣν ἂν ἁμάρτῃ· ἐπὶ στόματος δύο μαρτύρων καὶ ἐπὶ στόματος τριῶν μαρτύρων σταθήσεται πᾶν ῥῆμα.

98: Deut 19:19

see Deut 17:7 [94]

99: Deut 19:21

see Ex 21:24 [54]

100: Deut 21:23

לֹא־תָלִ֨ין נִבְלָת֜וֹ עַל־ [23]
הָעֵ֗ץ כִּֽי־קָב֤וֹר תִּקְבְּרֶ֙נּוּ֙ בַּיּ֣וֹם הַה֔וּא כִּֽי־קִלְלַ֥ת אֱלֹהִ֖ים תָּל֑וּי וְלֹ֤א תְטַמֵּא֙ אֶת־אַדְמָ֣תְךָ֔ אֲשֶׁר֙ יְהוָ֣ה אֱלֹהֶ֔יךָ נֹתֵ֥ן לְךָ֖ נַחֲלָֽה׃

[23] οὐκ ἐπικοιμηθήσεται τὸ σῶμα αὐτοῦ ἐπὶ τοῦ ξύλου, ἀλλὰ ταφῇ θάψετε αὐτὸν ἐν τῇ ἡμέρᾳ ἐκείνῃ, ὅτι κεκατηραμένος ὑπὸ θεοῦ πᾶς κρεμάμενος ἐπὶ ξύλου· καὶ οὐ μιανεῖτε τὴν γῆν, ἣν κύριος ὁ θεός σου δίδωσίν σοι ἐν κλήρῳ.

101: Deut 22:21

see Deut 17:7 [94]

102: Deut 22:24

see Deut 17:7 [94]

---

[a]Acts 7:37

37 οὗτός ἐστιν °ὁ Μωϋσῆς ὁ εἴπας τοῖς υἱοῖς Ἰσραήλ· *προφήτην ὑμῖν ἀναστήσει ὁ θεὸς ἐκ τῶν ἀδελφῶν ὑμῶν ὡς ἐμέ* ᵀ.

[b]Acts 3:22

22 Μωϋσῆς μὲν ⌐εἴπεν ὅτι *προφήτην ὑμῖν ἀναστήσει κύριος ὁ θεὸς* ᶠὑμῶν *ἐκ τῶν ἀδελφῶν ὑμῶν ὡς ἐμέ· αὐτοῦ ἀκούσεσθε κατὰ πάντα ὅσα ἂν* ⌐¹λαλήσῃ *πρὸς ὑμᾶς.*

Deut 18:15; MT = LXX = Acts 7:37 except for word order and omission of κύριος before θεὸς. Acts 7:37 = Acts 3:22 except that it inserts κύριος. (A) or (A-)

Deut 18:16; LXX κατὰ πάντα . . . ᾐτήσω. Acts 3:22 adds αὐτοῦ ἀκούσεσθε (+ κατὰ πάντα ὅσα ἂν λαλήσῃ). (Aᵈ)

[a]Mt 18:16

16 ἐὰν δὲ μὴ ἀκούσῃ, παράλαβε ⌐μετὰ σοῦ ἔτι ἕνα ἢ δύο⌐, ἵνα *ἐπὶ στόματος* ᶠ*δύο μαρτύρων ἢ τριῶν*⌐ *σταθῇ πᾶν ῥῆμα·*

[b]2 Cor 13:1

13 Τρίτον τοῦτο ⌐ἔρχομαι πρὸς ὑμᾶς· *ἐπὶ στόματος δύο μαρτύρων καὶ τριῶν σταθήσεται πᾶν ῥῆμα.*

Deut 19:15: (1) MT has עַל-פִּי also before שְׁלֹשָׁה (as well as before שְׁנֵי). Otherwise, LXX = MT, repeating ἐπὶ στόματος; Mt 18:16 omits the second ἐπὶ στόματος; (2) MT has no כָּל before the final דָּבָר; LXX and Mt 18:16 have πᾶν before ῥῆμα. (Aᵈ)

Note that 2 Cor 13:1 also contains the phrase "At the mouth of two or three witnesses, every word shall be established." The difference in the Greek wording is minimal. Both the σταθῇ of Mt 18:16 and the σταθήσεται of 2 Cor 13:1 are equally legitimate translations of יָקוּם, the second-to-last word in Deut 19:15.

[a]Gal 3:13

13 Χριστὸς ἡμᾶς ἐξηγόρασεν ἐκ τῆς κατάρας τοῦ νόμου γενόμενος ὑπὲρ ἡμῶν κατάρα, ὅτι γέγραπται· *ἐπικατάρατος πᾶς ὁ κρεμάμενος ἐπὶ ξύλου,*

Deut 21:23; MT = LXX with אֱלֹהִים after קְלָלַת and ὑπὸ θεοῦ after κεκατηραμένος. Gal 3:13 omits (ὑπὸ) θεοῦ. It also has ἐπικατάρατος instead of LXX κεκατηραμένος. (Aᵈ)

43

103: Deut 24:1, 3

24 ¹ כִּי־יִקַּח אִישׁ אִשָּׁה וּבְעָלָהּ וְהָיָה אִם־לֹא תִמְצָא־חֵן בְּעֵינָיו כִּי־מָצָא בָהּ עֶרְוַת דָּבָר וְכָתַב לָהּ סֵפֶר כְּרִיתֻת וְנָתַן בְּיָדָהּ וְשִׁלְּחָהּ מִבֵּיתוֹ:

¹ Ἐὰν δέ τις λάβῃ γυναῖκα καὶ συνοικήσῃ αὐτῇ, καὶ ἔσται ἐὰν μὴ εὕρῃ χάριν ἐναντίον αὐτοῦ, ὅτι εὗρεν ἐν αὐτῇ ἄσχημον πρᾶγμα, καὶ γράψει αὐτῇ βιβλίον ἀποστασίου καὶ δώσει εἰς τὰς χεῖρας αὐτῆς καὶ ἐξαποστελεῖ αὐτὴν ἐκ τῆς οἰκίας αὐτοῦ,

³ וּשְׂנֵאָהּ הָאִישׁ הָאַחֲרוֹן וְכָתַב לָהּ סֵפֶר כְּרִיתֻת וְנָתַן בְּיָדָהּ וְשִׁלְּחָהּ מִבֵּיתוֹ אוֹ כִי יָמוּת הָאִישׁ הָאַחֲרוֹן אֲשֶׁר־לְקָחָהּ לוֹ לְאִשָּׁה:

³ καὶ μισήσῃ αὐτὴν ὁ ἀνὴρ ὁ ἔσχατος καὶ γράψει αὐτῇ βιβλίον ἀποστασίου καὶ δώσει εἰς τὰς χεῖρας αὐτῆς καὶ ἐξαποστελεῖ αὐτὴν ἐκ τῆς οἰκίας αὐτοῦ, ἢ ἀποθάνῃ ὁ ἀνὴρ ὁ ἔσχατος, ὃς ἔλαβεν αὐτὴν ἑαυτῷ γυναῖκα,

104: Deut 24:7

see Deut 17:7 [94]

105: Deut 24:14

see Ex 20:12–16 [48]

106: Deut 25:4

⁴ לֹא־תַחְסֹם שׁוֹר בְּדִישׁוֹ:

⁴ Οὐ φιμώσεις βοῦν ἀλοῶντα.

107: Deut 25:5, 7

⁵ כִּי־יֵשְׁבוּ אַחִים יַחְדָּו וּמֵת אַחַד מֵהֶם וּבֵן אֵין־לוֹ לֹא־תִהְיֶה אֵשֶׁת־הַמֵּת הַחוּצָה לְאִישׁ זָר יְבָמָהּ יָבֹא עָלֶיהָ וּלְקָחָהּ לוֹ לְאִשָּׁה וְיִבְּמָהּ:

⁵ Ἐὰν δὲ κατοικῶσιν ἀδελφοὶ ἐπὶ τὸ αὐτὸ καὶ ἀποθάνῃ εἷς ἐξ αὐτῶν, σπέρμα δὲ μὴ ᾖ αὐτῷ, οὐκ ἔσται ἡ γυνὴ τοῦ τεθνηκότος ἔξω ἀνδρὶ μὴ ἐγγίζοντι· ὁ ἀδελφὸς τοῦ ἀνδρὸς αὐτῆς εἰσελεύσεται πρὸς αὐτὴν καὶ λήμψεται αὐτὴν ἑαυτῷ γυναῖκα καὶ συνοικήσει αὐτῇ.

⁷ וְאִם־לֹא יַחְפֹּץ הָאִישׁ לָקַחַת אֶת־יְבִמְתּוֹ וְעָלְתָה יְבִמְתּוֹ הַשַּׁעְרָה אֶל־הַזְּקֵנִים וְאָמְרָה מֵאֵין יְבָמִי לְהָקִים לְאָחִיו שֵׁם בְּיִשְׂרָאֵל לֹא אָבָה יַבְּמִי:

⁷ ἐὰν δὲ μὴ βούληται ὁ ἄνθρωπος λαβεῖν τὴν γυναῖκα τοῦ ἀδελφοῦ αὐτοῦ, καὶ ἀναβήσεται ἡ γυνὴ ἐπὶ τὴν πύλην ἐπὶ τὴν γερουσίαν καὶ ἐρεῖ Οὐ θέλει ὁ ἀδελφὸς τοῦ ἀνδρός μου ἀναστῆσαι τὸ ὄνομα τοῦ ἀδελφοῦ αὐτοῦ ἐν Ισραηλ, οὐκ ἠθέλησεν ὁ ἀδελφὸς τοῦ ἀνδρός μου.

*a*Mt 5:31   only Deut 24:1

31 Ἐρρέθη δέ· ὃς ἂν ἀπολύσῃ τὴν γυναῖκα αὐτοῦ, δότω αὐτῇ ἀποστάσιον.

*b*Mt 19:7   only Deut 24:1

7 λέγουσιν αὐτῷ· τί οὖν Μωϋ-
σῆς ἐνετείλατο δοῦναι βιβλίον ἀποστασίου καὶ ἀπολῦσαι °[αὐτήν];

*c*Mk 10:4

4 οἱ δὲ εἶπαν· ⸀ἐπέτρεψεν Μωϋσῆς⸀ βιβλίον ἀποστασίου
γράψαι καὶ ἀπολῦσαι.

Deut 24:1, 3: (1) MT has וְשִׁלְּחָהּ (24:1) = LXX καὶ
ἐξαποστελεῖ αὐτήν. Mt 5:31 summarizes, using ὃς ἂν
ἀπολύσῃ τὴν γυναῖκα. The Ἐρρέθη is not necessarily a
direct quote from Scripture, but rather seems to be a
summarizing statement by the teachers of the Law (*D*ᵃ
or *F*); (2) וְנָתַן בְּיָדָהּ = LXX καὶ δώσει εἰς τὰς χεῖρας
αὐτῆς (*D*ᵃ or *A*ᵈ); Mt 5:31 summarizes and simplifies
by δότω αὐτῇ; (3) סֵפֶר כְּרִיתֻת = LXX βιβλίον ἀποσταίου;
Mt 5:31 has simply ἀποστάσιον (*D*ᵃ or *A*ᵈ; again, this
reflects an *A*ᵈ intention to summarize rather than to
quote verbatim. The summary is both adequate and
accurate).

Deut 24:3 is identical with verse 1 (LXX) in the wording
of the pertinent phrase εἰς τὰς χεῖρας αὐτῆς and ἐξαποστελεῖ instead of the NT's αὐτῇ and ἀπολῦσαι,
which is followed also by Mt 19:7 and Mk 10:4. Mk is
closer to the MT than the LXX, but uses ἀπολῦσαι as
opposed to LXX's ἐξαποστελεῖ. (*A*ᵈ)

*a*1 Cor 9:9

9 ⸀ἐν γὰρ τῷ Μωϋσέως νόμῳ γέγραπται⸀· οὐ ⸀κημώσεις
βοῦν ἀλοῶντα. μὴ τῶν βοῶν μέλει τῷ θεῷ

*b*1 Tim 5:18

18 λέγει γὰρ ἡ γραφή· ⸀βοῦν ἀλοῶντα οὐ
φιμώσεις⸀, καί· ἄξιος ὁ ἐργάτης ⸀τοῦ μισθοῦ⸀ αὐτοῦ.

Deut 25:4; לֹא־תַחְסֹם = LXX οὐ φιμώσεις = 1 Cor 9:9
Οὐ κημώσεις (which, however, is a doubtful reading,
since p⁴⁶, A, B², C, and D¹ read φιμώσεις, *A*), and
1 Tim 5:18 uses φιμώσεις (*A*). Note that καί· ἄξιος ὁ
ἐργάτης τοῦ μισθοῦ αὐτοῦ may not be intended as part
of the OT quote (λέγει ἡ γραφή, which introduces βοῦν
ἀλοῶντα), but may be an inferential comment deduced
by tradition as having a bearing on human relationships. Therefore the GK text should not be in italics for
ἄξιος ... αὐτοῦ). (*A*-)

*a*Mt 22:24

24 λέγοντες· διδάσκαλε, Μωϋσῆς εἶπεν· ἐάν τις ἀποθάνῃ
μὴ ἔχων τέκνα, ἐπιγαμβρεύσει ὁ ἀδελφὸς αὐτοῦ □τὴν γυναῖκα
αὐτοῦ⸀ καὶ ἀναστήσει σπέρμα τῷ ἀδελφῷ αὐτοῦ.

*b*Mk 12:19

19 διδάσκαλε, Μωϋσῆς ἔγραψεν ἡμῖν ὅτι ἐάν τινος
ἀδελφὸς ἀποθάνῃ καὶ καταλίπῃ γυναῖκα καὶ ⸀μὴ ἀφῇ
τέκνον⸀, ἵνα λάβῃ ὁ ἀδελφὸς αὐτοῦ τὴν γυναῖκα ᵀ καὶ ἐξαναστήσῃ σπέρμα τῷ ἀδελφῷ αὐτοῦ.

Mt 22:24 gives a different wording from that of Mk
12:19 and Lk 20:28 as they make reference to the
ordinance of Deut 25:5, 7. Matthew quotes the Saddu-
cees as summarizing the passage in a way that accurately conveys the intent, though it does not follow the
LXX wording as carefully as Mark and Luke do. The
differences are as follows: (a) Mt 22 puts it quite
simply: "If anyone dies, not having children"; Mk and
Lk make it: "If anyone's brother dies"—as compared

107 (continued)

Gen 38:8

8 וַיֹּאמֶר יְהוּדָה לְאוֹנָן בֹּא אֶל־אֵשֶׁת אָחִיךָ וְיַבֵּם אֹתָהּ וְהָקֵם
זֶרַע לְאָחִיךָ:

8εἶπεν δὲ Ιουδας τῷ Αυναν Εἴσελθε
πρὸς τὴν γυναῖκα τοῦ ἀδελφοῦ σου καὶ γάμβρευσαι αὐτὴν καὶ
ἀνάστησον σπέρμα τῷ ἀδελφῷ σου.

108: Deut 27:26

26 אָרוּר אֲשֶׁר לֹא־יָקִים אֶת־דִּבְרֵי הַתּוֹרָה־
הַזֹּאת לַעֲשׂוֹת אוֹתָם וְאָמַר כָּל־הָעָם אָמֵן:

26Ἐπικατάρατος πᾶς ἄνθρωπος, ὃς οὐκ ἐμμενεῖ ἐν πᾶσιν τοῖς
λόγοις τοῦ νόμου τούτου τοῦ ποιῆσαι αὐτούς· καὶ ἐροῦσιν πᾶς
ὁ λαός Γένοιτο.

109: Deut 29:3 (29:4)

3 וְלֹא־נָתַן יְהוָה לָכֶם לֵב לָדַעַת וְעֵינַיִם
לִרְאוֹת וְאָזְנַיִם לִשְׁמֹעַ עַד הַיּוֹם הַזֶּה:

3καὶ οὐκ ἔδωκεν κύριος ὁ θεὸς ὑμῖν καρδίαν εἰδέναι καὶ ὀ-
φθαλμοὺς βλέπειν καὶ ὦτα ἀκούειν ἕως τῆς ἡμέρας ταύτης.

Isa 29:10

10 כִּי־נָסַךְ עֲלֵיכֶם יְהוָה רוּחַ תַּרְדֵּמָה | פְּסֶה:
וַיְעַצֵּם אֶת־עֵינֵיכֶם אֶת־הַנְּבִיאִים וְאֶת־רָאשֵׁיכֶם הַחֹזִים

10ὅτι πεπότικεν ὑμᾶς κύριος πνεύματι κατανύξεως καὶ καμμύσει
τοὺς ὀφθαλμοὺς αὐτῶν καὶ τῶν προφητῶν αὐτῶν καὶ τῶν ἀρχόν-
των αὐτῶν, οἱ ὁρῶντες τὰ κρυπτά.

110: Deut 30:12–14

see Deut 9:4 [92]

^cLk 20:28

28 λέ-
γοντες· διδάσκαλε, Μωϋσῆς ἔγραψεν ἡμῖν, ἐάν τινος
ἀδελφὸς ἀποθάνῃ ⸂ ἔχων γυναῖκα, καὶ οὗτος ἄτεκνος ⸀ ᾖ ⸃, ἵνα
λάβῃ ὁ ἀδελφὸς αὐτοῦ τὴν γυναῖκα καὶ ἐξαναστήσῃ σπέρμα
τῷ ἀδελφῷ αὐτοῦ.

with MT ("If brothers live together and one of them dies"), which is somewhat closer to Mk and Lk than it is to Mt, even though they also are somewhat abbreviated ("if someone's brother dies"); (b) Mt follows up with "not having children," as compared with Mk's "and does not leave a child" and Lk's "and he is childless"; the MT reads "and there is no son to him," for which LXX has: "and there is no offspring to him." All five differ slightly in wording, but not in sense; (c) Mt continues: "His brother shall perform levirate marriage (ἐπιγαμβρεύσει) to his wife (a technical term for which Delitzsch uses יְיַבֵּם in his Hebrew NT); Mk puts it: "that his brother take the wife" (Alexandrinus and Bezae supply "his" before "wife"); Lk reads the same as Mk. Mt words it: "her brother-in-law shall take her to wife for himself." Here again the three evangelists slightly differ from each other and from the LXX (Deut 25:5) as well (which uses the middle λήμψεται instead of the active λάβῃ and also uses no "his"—αὐτοῦ—after γυναῖκα); (d) The final clause in Mt 22:24 is taken from Deut 25:7, and differs from MT only by using σπέρμα ("seed") instead of שֵׁם ("a name"); Mk and Lk do the same, whereas LXX adheres quite literally to MT with τὸ ὄνομα (although needlessly making it articular). To sum up, it is fair to say that none of the evangelists has borrowed directly from the LXX, and all have abbreviated or paraphrased slightly the Heb. text. As far as Gen 38:8 is concerned, it has no verbal resemblance to the NT quotations. (D)

^aGal 3:10

10 Ὅσοι γὰρ ἐξ ἔργων νόμου εἰσίν, ὑπὸ κατάραν εἰ-
σίν· γέγραπται γὰρ ὅτι ἐπικατάρατος πᾶς ὃς οὐκ ἐμμένει ⸀
πᾶσιν τοῖς γεγραμμένοις ἐν τῷ βιβλίῳ τοῦ νόμου τοῦ ποιῆσαι αὐτά.

Deut 27:26; MT has "cursed is the one who does not confirm (לֹא יָקִים 'establish') the words of this Law," whereas the LXX has "who does not abide in all (οὐκ ἐμμενεῖ ἐν πᾶσιν) the words of this Law" = Gal 3:10. It is possible that LXX read יָקוּם instead of כָּל־יָקִים in V^{G Ken 84} 4MSS (not Hexapla). (B)

^aRom 11:8

8 ⸀καθὼς γέγραπται·
ἔδωκεν αὐτοῖς ὁ θεὸς πνεῦμα κατανύξεως,
ὀφθαλμοὺς τοῦ μὴ βλέπειν καὶ ὦτα τοῦ μὴ ἀκούειν,
ἕως τῆς σήμερον ἡμέρας.

Rom 11:8 is a conflate of Isa 29:10 which contributes the phrase "the spirit of stupor." The rest of the quotation is taken from Deut 29:3(4), so we have in Rom 11:8 a conflate quotation, but really (A).

111: Deut 31:6, 8

⁶חִזְקוּ וְאִמְצוּ אַל־תִּירְאוּ וְאַל־תַּעַרְצוּ מִפְּנֵיהֶם
כִּי ׀ יְהוָה אֱלֹהֶיךָ הוּא הַהֹלֵךְ עִמָּךְ לֹא יַרְפְּךָ וְלֹא יַעַזְבֶךָּ:

⁸וַיהוָה הוּא ׀ הַהֹלֵךְ לְפָנֶיךָ
הוּא יִהְיֶה עִמָּךְ לֹא יַרְפְּךָ וְלֹא יַעַזְבֶךָּ לֹא תִירָא וְלֹא תֵחָת:

⁶ἀνδρίζου καὶ ἴσχυε,
μὴ φοβοῦ μηδὲ δειλία μηδὲ πτοηθῇς ἀπὸ προσώπου αὐτῶν, ὅτι
κύριος ὁ θεός σου ὁ προπορευόμενος μεθ' ὑμῶν ἐν ὑμῖν οὐ μή
σε ἀνῇ οὔτε μή σε ἐγκαταλίπῃ.

⁸καὶ κύριος ὁ συμπορευόμενος μετὰ σοῦ οὐκ ἀνήσει σε οὐδὲ μὴ
ἐγκαταλίπῃ σε · μὴ φοβοῦ μηδὲ δειλία.

112: Deut 32:4

see Psalm 111:2 [187]

113: Deut 32:21

²¹הֵם קִנְאוּנִי בְלֹא־אֵל כִּעֲסוּנִי בְּהַבְלֵיהֶם
וַאֲנִי אַקְנִיאֵם בְּלֹא־עָם בְּגוֹי נָבָל אַכְעִיסֵם:

²¹αὐτοὶ παρεζήλωσάν με ἐπ' οὐ θεῷ,
παρώργισάν με ἐν τοῖς εἰδώλοις αὐτῶν ·
κἀγὼ παραζηλώσω αὐτοὺς ἐπ' οὐκ ἔθνει,
ἐπ' ἔθνει ἀσυνέτῳ παροργιῶ αὐτούς.

114: Deut 32:35–36

³⁵לִי נָקָם וְשִׁלֵּם לְעֵת תָּמוּט רַגְלָם
כִּי קָרוֹב יוֹם אֵידָם וְחָשׁ עֲתִדֹת לָמוֹ:
³⁶כִּי־יָדִין יְהוָה עַמּוֹ וְעַל־עֲבָדָיו יִתְנֶחָם
כִּי יִרְאֶה כִּי־אָזְלַת יָד וְאֶפֶס עָצוּר וְעָזוּב:

³⁵ἐν ἡμέρᾳ ἐκδικήσεως ἀνταποδώσω,
ἐν καιρῷ, ὅταν σφαλῇ ὁ πούς αὐτῶν ·
ὅτι ἐγγὺς ἡμέρα ἀπωλείας αὐτῶν,
καὶ πάρεστιν ἕτοιμα ὑμῖν.
³⁶ὅτι κρινεῖ κύριος τὸν λαὸν αὐτοῦ
καὶ ἐπὶ τοῖς δούλοις αὐτοῦ παρακληθήσεται ·
εἶδεν γὰρ παραλελυμένους αὐτοὺς
καὶ ἐκλελοιπότας ἐν ἐπαγωγῇ καὶ παρειμένους.

Psalm 135:14

¹⁴כִּי־יָדִין יְהוָה עַמּוֹ וְעַל־עֲבָדָיו יִתְנֶחָם:

(Psalm 134:14)

14 ὅτι κρινεῖ κύριος τὸν λαὸν αὐτοῦ
καὶ ἐπὶ τοῖς δούλοις αὐτοῦ παρακληθήσεται.

115: Deut 32:43

⁴³הַרְנִינוּ גוֹיִם עַמּוֹ כִּי דַם־עֲבָדָיו יִקּוֹם
וְנָקָם יָשִׁיב לְצָרָיו וְכִפֶּר אַדְמָתוֹ עַמּוֹ:

⁴³εὐφράνθητε, οὐρανοί, ἅμα αὐτῷ,
καὶ προσκυνησάτωσαν αὐτῷ πάντες υἱοὶ θεοῦ ·
εὐφράνθητε, ἔθνη, μετὰ τοῦ λαοῦ αὐτοῦ,
καὶ ἐνισχυσάτωσαν αὐτῷ πάντες ἄγγελοι θεοῦ ·
ὅτι τὸ αἷμα τῶν υἱῶν αὐτοῦ ἐκδικᾶται,
καὶ ἐκδικήσει καὶ ἀνταποδώσει δίκην τοῖς ἐχθροῖς
καὶ τοῖς μισοῦσιν ἀνταποδώσει,
καὶ ἐκκαθαριεῖ κύριος τὴν γῆν τοῦ λαοῦ αὐτοῦ.

*a*Heb 13:5

5 Ἀφιλάργυρος
ὁ τρόπος, ⌜ἀρκούμενοι τοῖς παροῦσιν. αὐτὸς γὰρ εἴρη-
κεν· *οὐ μή σε ἀνῶ οὐδ' οὐ μή σε* ⌜ἐγκαταλίπω,

Deut 31:6, 8 = Heb 13:5. (*A*)

Deut 32:4, adapted in Rev 15:3 as a new Song of Moses (cf. 187). (*F*)

---

*a*Rom 10:19

19 ἀλλὰ λέγω, μὴ Ἰσραὴλ οὐκ ἔγνω; πρῶτος Μωϋσῆς
λέγει·
    ἐγὼ παραζηλώσω ὑμᾶς ἐπ' οὐκ ἔθνει,
    ἐπ' ἔθνει ἀσυνέτῳ παροργιῶ ὑμᾶς.

Deut 32:21; MT varies with Rom 10:19 only by contextually adapting to ὑμᾶς (for the sake of greater vividness) the αὐτούς of LXX (= אַקְנִיאֵם), as if to address a reproach to unbelieving Israel in Paul's own day. (*A-*)

---

*a*Rom 12:19   only Deut 32:35

19 μὴ ἑαυτοὺς ἐκδικοῦντες, ἀγα-
πητοί, ἀλλὰ δότε τόπον τῇ ὀργῇ, γέγραπται γάρ· *ἐμοὶ ἐκδίκησις, ἐγὼ ἀνταποδώσω, λέγει κύριος.·*

Deut 32:35–36: (1) Rom 12:19; here NT = MT as against the LXX ἐμοὶ ἐκδίκησις = לִי נָקָם (*C*), whereas LXX ἐν ἡμέρᾳ ἐκδικήσεως, implying לְיוֹם נָקָם (so Samaritan also!). As for the MT לִי נָקָם וְשִׁלֵּם "Vengeance is Mine and He/he will requite/recompense at the time when their foot totters," perhaps amend to שִׁלֵּם as D65 = וְשִׁלַּמְתִּי or וַאֲשַׁלֵּם. LXX "In the day of vengeance I will requite, at the time when their foot slips"; (2) Heb 10:30*a* = Rom 12:19, but Heb 10:30*b* = Psalm 135:14, כִּי יָדִין יהוה עַמּוֹ. LXX reads in Psalm 134:14 ὅτι κρινεῖ κύριος τὸν λαὸν αὐτοῦ, which = Heb 10:30*b* κρινεῖ κύριος τὸν λαὸν αὐτοῦ. (*A*)/(*A-*)

*b*Heb 10:30

30 οἴδαμεν γὰρ τὸν εἰπόντα·
    *ἐμοὶ ἐκδίκησις, ἐγὼ ἀνταποδώσω*ᵀ.
καὶ πάλιν·ᵀ
    ˢ*κρινεῖ κύριος*ᶻ *τὸν λαὸν αὐτοῦ.*

---

*a*Rom 15:10

10 καὶ πάλιν λέγει·
    εὐφράνθητε, ἔθνη, μετὰ τοῦ λαοῦ αὐτοῦ.

Deut 32:43 lacks the portion containing LXX's εὐφράν-θητε, ἔθνη, μετὰ τοῦ λαοῦ αὐτοῦ, a clause that appears in Rom 15:10. 4Qᴰᵗ reads: הַרְנִינוּ שָׁמַיִם עַמּוֹ [וְהִשְׁתַּחֲוּוּ לוֹ בְּנֵי אֱלֹהִים וְהָבוּ עֹז לוֹ כָּל־בְּנֵי אֱלֹהִים וְהַרְנִינוּ גוֹיִם אֶת־עַמּוֹ וְחִזְּקוּ לוֹ כָּל־ מַלְאֲכֵי אֵל כִּי] דַּם בָּנָיו יִקּוֹם וְנָקָם יָשִׁיב לְצָרָיו [וְלִמְשַׂנְאָיו יְשַׁלֵּם וְכִפֶּר אַדְמַת עַמּוֹ]. This reconstruction is given by Albright, "New Light on Early Recensions of the Hebrew Bible," *BASOR* 140 (1955), 32–33. All the

115 (continued)

Psalm 95:7

⁷ יֵבֹ֤שׁוּ ׀ כָּל־עֹ֬בְדֵי פֶ֗סֶל הַמִּֽתְהַלְלִ֥ים בָּאֱלִילִ֑ים הִשְׁתַּחֲווּ־ל֝וֹ כָּל־אֱלֹהִֽים׃

7 αἰσχυνθήτωσαν πάντες οἱ προσκυνοῦντες τοῖς γλυπτοῖς οἱ ἐγκαυχώμενοι ἐν τοῖς εἰδώλοις αὐτῶν · προσκυνήσατε αὐτῷ, πάντες οἱ ἄγγελοι αὐτοῦ.

116: Josh 22:5

see Lev 19:18 [68]

117: 1 Sam 12:22

²² כִּ֠י לֹֽא־יִטֹּ֤שׁ יְהוָה֙ אֶת־עַמּ֔וֹ בַּעֲב֖וּר שְׁמ֣וֹ הַגָּד֑וֹל כִּ֚י הוֹאִ֣יל יְהוָ֔ה לַעֲשׂ֥וֹת אֶתְכֶ֛ם ל֖וֹ לְעָֽם׃

²² ὅτι οὐκ ἀπώσεται κύριος τὸν λαὸν αὐτοῦ διὰ τὸ ὄνομα αὐτοῦ τὸ μέγα, ὅτι ἐπιεικέως κύριος προσελάβετο ὑμᾶς αὐτῷ εἰς λαόν.

Psalm 94:14

(Psalm 93:14)

¹⁴ כִּ֤י ׀ לֹא־יִטֹּ֣שׁ יְהוָ֣ה עַמּ֑וֹ וְ֝נַחֲלָת֗וֹ לֹ֣א יַעֲזֹֽב׃

14 ὅτι οὐκ ἀπώσεται κύριος τὸν λαὸν αὐτοῦ καὶ τὴν κληρονομίαν αὐτοῦ οὐκ ἐγκαταλείψει,

---

118: 1 Sam 13:14

¹⁴ וְעַתָּ֖ה מַמְלַכְתְּךָ֣ לֹא־תָק֑וּם בִּקֵּשׁ֩ יְהוָ֨ה ל֜וֹ אִ֣ישׁ כִּלְבָב֗וֹ וַיְצַוֵּ֨הוּ יְהוָ֤ה לְנָגִיד֙ עַל־עַמּ֔וֹ כִּ֚י לֹ֣א שָׁמַ֔רְתָּ אֵ֥ת אֲשֶֽׁר־צִוְּךָ֖ יְהוָֽה׃

¹⁴ καὶ νῦν ἡ βασιλεία σου οὐ στήσεται, καὶ ζητήσει κύριος ἑαυτῷ ἄνθρωπον κατὰ τὴν καρδίαν αὐτοῦ, καὶ ἐντελεῖται κύριος αὐτῷ εἰς ἄρχοντα ἐπὶ τὸν λαὸν αὐτοῦ, ὅτι οὐκ ἐφύλαξας ὅσα ἐνετείλατό σοι κύριος.

Psalm 89:21

(Psalm 88:21)

²¹ מָ֭צָאתִי דָּוִ֣ד עַבְדִּ֑י בְּשֶׁ֖מֶן קָדְשִׁ֣י מְשַׁחְתִּֽיו׃

21 εὗρον Δαυιδ τὸν δοῦλόν μου, ἐν ἐλαίῳ ἁγίῳ μου ἔχρισα αὐτόν.

Isa 44:28

²⁸ הָאֹמֵ֤ר לְכ֙וֹרֶשׁ֙ רֹעִ֔י וְכָל־חֶפְצִ֖י יַשְׁלִ֑ם וְלֵאמֹ֤ר לִירוּשָׁלִַ֙ם֙ תִּבָּנֶ֔ה וְהֵיכָ֖ל תִּוָּסֵֽד׃

²⁸ ὁ λέγων Κύρῳ φρονεῖν, καὶ Πάντα τὰ θελήματά μου ποιήσει · ὁ λέγων Ιερουσαλημ Οἰκοδομηθήσῃ, καὶ τὸν οἶκον τὸν ἅγιόν μου θεμελιώσω.

underlined clauses are in the LXX but not in the MT (which may have suffered from homoeoteleuton!). (Either A or Bª, depending upon the trustworthiness of the *Vorlage* of the LXX in this passage.)

*b*Heb 1:6

6 ὅταν δὲ πάλιν εἰσαγάγῃ τὸν πρωτότοκον εἰς τὴν οἰκου-
μένην, λέγει·
καὶ προσκυνησάτωσαν αὐτῷ πάντες ἄγγελοι θεοῦ.

Psalm 95:7 contributes the wording of Heb 1:6, "Worship him all you his angels." Although it is a slight ifference in that Heb 1:6 says "Let all the angels of God worship him," essentially it is the same thing. The inserted material of Deut 32:43 is not needed to serve as a basis for the quote in Heb 1:6, because it is there even in Psalm 95:7.

*a*Rom 11:2

2 *οὐκ ἀπώσατο ὁ θεὸς τὸν*
λαὸν αὐτοῦ ὃν προέγνω. ἢ οὐκ οἴδατε ἐν Ἠλίᾳ τί λέγει ἡ
γραφή, ὡς ἐντυγχάνει τῷ θεῷ κατὰ τοῦ Ἰσραήλ ᵀ;

The opening clause in 1 Sam 12:22 is accurately rendered in the Septuagintal form as the first clause of Rom 11:2, though it is not technically a quotation as such. Yet it faithfully reproduces the Samuel passage, and is therefore (F) or (A).

Note that Psalm 94:14 also has the same expression as 1 Sam 12:22, "The Lord will not reject His people," which is the part quoted in Rom 11:2.

*a*Acts 13:22

22 καὶ μεταστήσας αὐτὸν ἤγειρεν
ˢτὸν Δαυὶδ αὐτοῖςᶻ εἰς βασιλέα ᾧ καὶ εἶπεν μαρτυρήσας·
εὗρον Δαυὶδ τὸν τοῦ Ἰεσσαί, °ἄνδρα κατὰ τὴν καρδίαν
μου, ὃς ποιήσει πάντα τὰ θελήματά μου.

1 Sam 13:14; MT בִּקֵּשׁ יהוה לוֹ אִישׁ כִּלְבָבוֹ = LXX καὶ ζητήσει κύριος ἑαυτῷ ἄνθρωπον κατὰ τὴν καρδίαν αὐτοῦ = NT Acts 13:22 εὗρον Δαυὶδ τὸν τοῦ Ἰεσσαί, ἄνδρα κατὰ τὴν καρδίαν μου. (A)

Psalm 89:21; LXX (88:21) εὗρον Δαυὶδ τὸν δοῦλόν μου + "anointed him with oil." (A)

Isa 44:28; compare the MT הָאֹמֵר לְכוֹרֶשׁ רֹעִי וְכָל־חֶפְצִי יַשְׁלִם and LXX ὁ λέγων Κύρῳ φρονεῖν and LXX καὶ Πάντα τὰ θελήματά μου ποιήσει. Same words, but different subject. Said of Cyrus as a type of liberator of God's people, but not said of David; however, as Cyrus is a type of Christ as liberator of the captivity of Israel, and because Christ is both descendant and antitype of David, there is a sense in which this refers back to David because of "David's greater Son." (E)

119: 2 Sam 5:2   see Mic 5:1 [299]

120: 2 Sam 7:8

‏8 וְעַתָּה כֹּה־תֹאמַר לְעַבְדִּי לְדָוִד כֹּה אָמַר יְהוָה צְבָאוֹת אֲנִי לְקַחְתִּיךָ מִן־הַנָּוֶה מֵאַחַר הַצֹּאן לִהְיוֹת נָגִיד עַל־עַמִּי עַל־ יִשְׂרָאֵל:‏

⁸καὶ νῦν τάδε ἐρεῖς
τῷ δούλῳ μου Δαυιδ Τάδε λέγει κύριος παντοκράτωρ Ἔλαβόν σε ἐκ τῆς μάνδρας τῶν προβάτων τοῦ εἶναί σε εἰς ἡγούμενον ἐπὶ τὸν λαόν μου ἐπὶ τὸν Ισραηλ

121: 2 Sam 7:14

‏14 אֲנִי אֶהְיֶה־לּוֹ לְאָב וְהוּא יִהְיֶה־לִּי לְבֵן אֲשֶׁר בְּהַעֲוֹתוֹ וְהֹכַחְתִּיו בְּשֵׁבֶט אֲנָשִׁים וּבְנִגְעֵי בְּנֵי אָדָם:‏

¹⁴ἐγὼ ἔσομαι αὐτῷ εἰς πατέρα, καὶ αὐτὸς ἔσται
μοι εἰς υἱόν· καὶ ἐὰν ἔλθῃ ἡ ἀδικία αὐτοῦ, καὶ ἐλέγξω αὐτὸν ἐν ῥάβδῳ ἀνδρῶν καὶ ἐν ἁφαῖς υἱῶν ἀνθρώπων·

only 2 Sam 7:14 ◁

1 Chron 17:13

‏13 אֲנִי אֶהְיֶה־לּוֹ לְאָב וְהוּא יִהְיֶה־לִּי לְבֵן וְחַסְדִּי לֹא־אָסִיר מֵעִמּוֹ כַּאֲשֶׁר הֲסִירוֹתִי מֵאֲשֶׁר הָיָה לְפָנֶיךָ:‏

¹³ἐγὼ ἔσομαι
αὐτῷ εἰς πατέρα, καὶ αὐτὸς ἔσται μοι εἰς υἱόν· καὶ τὸ ἔλεός μου οὐκ ἀποστήσω ἀπ' αὐτοῦ ὡς ἀπέστησα ἀπὸ τῶν ὄντων ἔμπροσθέν σου.

122: 2 Sam 22:3   see Isa 8:17–18 [210]

123: 2 Sam 22:50

‏50 עַל־כֵּן אוֹדְךָ יְהוָה בַּגּוֹיִם וּלְשִׁמְךָ אֲזַמֵּר:‏

⁵⁰διὰ τοῦτο ἐξομολογήσομαί σοι, κύριε, ἐν τοῖς ἔθνεσιν
καὶ ἐν τῷ ὀνόματί σου ψαλῶ,

Psalm 18:50 (18:49)

‏50 עַל־כֵּן אוֹדְךָ בַגּוֹיִם יְהוָה וּלְשִׁמְךָ אֲזַמֵּרָה:‏

(Psalm 17:50)

50 διὰ τοῦτο ἐξομολογήσομαί σοι ἐν ἔθνεσιν, κύριε,
καὶ τῷ ὀνόματί σου ψαλῶ,

124: 1 Kings 19:10, 14

‏10 וַיֹּאמֶר קַנֹּא קִנֵּאתִי לַיהוָה אֱלֹהֵי צְבָאוֹת כִּי־עָזְבוּ בְרִיתְךָ בְּנֵי יִשְׂרָאֵל אֶת־מִזְבְּחֹתֶיךָ הָרָסוּ וְאֶת־נְבִיאֶיךָ הָרְגוּ בֶחָרֶב וָאִוָּתֵר אֲנִי לְבַדִּי וַיְבַקְשׁוּ אֶת־נַפְשִׁי לְקַחְתָּהּ:‏

¹⁰καὶ εἶπεν Ηλιου Ζηλῶν ἐζήλωκα
τῷ κυρίῳ παντοκράτορι, ὅτι ἐγκατέλιπόν σε οἱ υἱοὶ Ἰσραηλ· τὰ θυσιαστήριά σου κατέσκαψαν καὶ τοὺς προφήτας σου ἀπέκτειναν ἐν ῥομφαίᾳ, καὶ ὑπολέλειμμαι ἐγὼ μονώτατος, καὶ ζητοῦσι τὴν ψυχήν μου λαβεῖν αὐτήν.

‏14 וַיֹּאמֶר קַנֹּא קִנֵּאתִי לַיהוָה אֱלֹהֵי צְבָאוֹת כִּי־עָזְבוּ בְרִיתְךָ בְּנֵי יִשְׂרָאֵל אֶת־מִזְבְּחֹתֶיךָ הָרָסוּ וְאֶת־נְבִיאֶיךָ הָרְגוּ בֶחָרֶב וָאִוָּתֵר אֲנִי לְבַדִּי וַיְבַקְשׁוּ אֶת־נַפְשִׁי לְקַחְתָּהּ:‏

¹⁴καὶ εἶπεν Ηλιου Ζηλῶν ἐζήλωκα τῷ κυρίῳ παντοκράτορι,
ὅτι ἐγκατέλιπον τὴν διαθήκην σου οἱ υἱοὶ Ισραηλ· τὰ θυσιαστήριά σου καθεῖλαν καὶ τοὺς προφήτας σου ἀπέκτειναν ἐν ῥομφαίᾳ, καὶ ὑπολέλειμμαι ἐγὼ μονώτατος, καὶ ζητοῦσι τὴν ψυχήν μου λαβεῖν αὐτήν.

*a*2 Cor 6:18

18 καὶ ἔσομαι ὑμῖν εἰς πατέρα
  καὶ ὑμεῖς ἔσεσθέ μοι εἰς υἱοὺς καὶ θυγατέρας,
λέγει κύριος παντοκράτωρ.

2 Sam 7:8; MT כֹּה אָמַר יהוה צְבָאוֹת = LXX λέγει κύριος παντοκράτωρ = 2 Cor 6:18. (*A*, and *E*, see Summary and Conclusions).

*b*Heb 1:5   (see also [133],b)

5 Τίνι γὰρ εἶπέν ποτε τῶν ἀγγέλων·
  υἱός μου εἶ σύ,
    ἐγὼ σήμερον γεγέννηκά σε;
καὶ πάλιν·
    ἐγὼ ἔσομαι αὐτῷ εἰς πατέρα,
    καὶ αὐτὸς ἔσται μοι εἰς υἱόν;

2 Sam 7:14; MT = LXX = Heb 1:5*b*. (*A*)

Compare Heb 1:5*a* with Psalm 2:7*b* and ἐγὼ σήμερον γεγέννηκά σε . . . הַיּוֹם יְלִדְתִּיךָ (133 = Psalm 2:7*b*), which indicates a conflate of three passages.

*c*Rev 21:7

7 ὁ νικῶν ⌐κληρονομήσει ταῦτα καὶ
ἔσομαι ⌐αὐτῷ θεὸς καὶ ⌐αὐτὸς ἔσται μοι υἱός⌐.

*a*Rom 15:9

9 τὰ
δὲ ἔθνη ὑπὲρ ἐλέους δοξάσαι τὸν θεόν, καθὼς γέγραπται·
    διὰ τοῦτο ἐξομολογήσομαί σοι ἐν ἔθνεσιν ᵀ
    καὶ τῷ ὀνόματί σου ψαλῶ.

2 Sam 22:50 = Rom 15:9. (*A*)

Psalm 18:50(49) is the parallel passage to 2 Sam 22:50. (*A*)

*a*Rom 11:3

3 κύριε,
τοὺς προφήτας σου ἀπέκτειναν, τὰ θυσιαστήριά σου κατέσκαψαν, κἀγὼ ὑπελείφθην μόνος καὶ ζητοῦσιν τὴν ψυχήν μου.

1 Kings 19:10 = Rom 11:3, except in the order of the last two clauses, in which NT reverses the order followed in MT and LXX (*B*ᵃ). However, note that Rom 11:3 differs in wording from LXX, though not in meaning; LXX καὶ ὑπολέλειμμαι (perfect passive), Rom 11:3 κἀγὼ ὑπελείφθην μόνος. (*C*).

1 Kings 19:10 (cont.); וַיְבַקְשׁוּ אֶת־נַפְשִׁי (לְקַחְתָּהּ) = LXX = NT. (*A*)

125: 1 Kings 19:18

¹⁸ וְהִשְׁאַרְתִּי בְיִשְׂרָאֵל
שִׁבְעַת אֲלָפִים כָּל־הַבִּרְכַּיִם אֲשֶׁר לֹא־כָרְעוּ לַבַּעַל וְכָל־הַפֶּה אֲשֶׁר
לֹא־נָשַׁק לוֹ:

¹⁸ καὶ καταλείψεις ἐν Ισραηλ
ἑπτὰ χιλιάδας ἀνδρῶν, πάντα γόνατα, ἃ οὐκ ὤκλασαν γόνυ τῷ
Βααλ, καὶ πᾶν στόμα, ὃ οὐ προσεκύνησεν αὐτῷ.

126: 2 Kings 1:10, 12

¹⁰ וַיַּעֲנֶה אֵלִיָּהוּ
וַיְדַבֵּר אֶל־שַׂר הַחֲמִשִּׁים וְאִם־אִישׁ אֱלֹהִים אָנִי תֵּרֶד אֵשׁ מִן־הַשָּׁמַיִם
וְתֹאכַל אֹתְךָ וְאֶת־חֲמִשֶּׁיךָ וַתֵּרֶד אֵשׁ מִן־הַשָּׁמַיִם וַתֹּאכַל אֹתוֹ וְאֶת־
חֲמִשָּׁיו:

¹⁰ καὶ ἀπεκρίθη Ηλιου καὶ
εἶπεν πρὸς τὸν πεντηκόνταρχον Καὶ εἰ ἄνθρωπος τοῦ θεοῦ ἐγώ,
καταβήσεται πῦρ ἐκ τοῦ οὐρανοῦ καὶ καταφάγεταί σε καὶ τοὺς
πεντήκοντά σου · καὶ κατέβη πῦρ ἐκ τοῦ οὐρανοῦ καὶ κατέφαγεν
αὐτὸν καὶ τοὺς πεντήκοντα αὐτοῦ.

¹² וַיַּעַן אֵלִיָּה
וַיְדַבֵּר אֲלֵיהֶם אִם־אִישׁ הָאֱלֹהִים אָנִי תֵּרֶד אֵשׁ מִן־הַשָּׁמַיִם וְתֹאכַל
אֹתְךָ וְאֶת־חֲמִשֶּׁיךָ וַתֵּרֶד אֵשׁ־אֱלֹהִים מִן־הַשָּׁמַיִם וַתֹּאכַל אֹתוֹ וְאֶת־
חֲמִשָּׁיו:

¹² καὶ ἀπεκρίθη Ηλιου καὶ ἐλάλησεν πρὸς αὐτὸν καὶ εἶπεν
Εἰ ἄνθρωπος τοῦ θεοῦ ἐγώ εἰμι, καταβήσεται πῦρ ἐκ τοῦ οὐρανοῦ
καὶ καταφάγεταί σε καὶ τοὺς πεντήκοντά σου · καὶ κατέβη πῦρ ἐκ
τοῦ οὐρανοῦ καὶ κατέφαγεν αὐτὸν καὶ τοὺς πεντήκοντα αὐτοῦ.

127: 1 Chron 17:13

see 2 Sam 7:14 [121]

128: 2 Chron 18:16

see Num 27:17 [75]

129: Job 5:13

¹³ לֹכֵד חֲכָמִים בְּעָרְמָם   וַעֲצַת נִפְתָּלִים נִמְהָרָה:

13 ὁ καταλαμβάνων σοφοὺς ἐν τῇ φρονήσει,
βουλὴν δὲ πολυπλόκων ἐξέστησεν ·

130: Job 16:19

¹⁹ גַּם־עַתָּה הִנֵּה־בַשָּׁמַיִם עֵדִי   וְשָׂהֲדִי בַּמְּרוֹמִים:

19 καὶ νῦν ἰδοὺ ἐν οὐρανοῖς ὁ μάρτυς μου,
ὁ δὲ συνίστωρ μου ἐν ὑψίστοις.

Psalm 118:25

²⁵ אָנָּא יְהוָה הוֹשִׁיעָה נָּא   אָנָּא יְהוָה הַצְלִיחָה נָּא:

25 ὦ κύριε, σῶσον δή,
ὦ κύριε, εὐόδωσον δή.

Psalm 148:1

¹ הַלְלוּ יָהּ
הַלְלוּ אֶת־יְהוָה מִן־הַשָּׁמַיִם   הַלְלוּהוּ בַּמְּרוֹמִים:

1   Αλληλουια · Αγγαιου καὶ Ζαχαριου.
Αἰνεῖτε τὸν κύριον ἐκ τῶν οὐρανῶν,
αἰνεῖτε αὐτὸν ἐν τοῖς ὑψίστοις.

NEW TESTAMENT	COMMENTARY
[a]Rom 11:4	
4 ἀλλὰ τί λέγει αὐτῷ ὁ χρηματισμός; ⌜κατέλιπον ἐμαυτῷ ἑπτακισχιλίους ἄνδρας, οἵτινες οὐκ ἔκαμψαν γόνυ τῇ Βάαλ.	1 Kings 19:18 = Rom 11:4. (*A*)
[a]Lk 9:54	
54 ἰδόντες δὲ οἱ μαθηταὶ ⌐ Ἰάκωβος καὶ Ἰωάννης εἶπαν· κύριε, θέλεις εἴπωμεν *πῦρ καταβῆναι ἀπὸ τοῦ οὐρανοῦ καὶ ἀναλῶσαι αὐτούς*⌐;	2 Kings 1:10, 12—Lk 9:54. (*F*)
[b]Rev 20:9	
9 καὶ ἀνέβησαν ἐπὶ τὸ πλάτος τῆς γῆς καὶ ⌜ἐκύκλευσαν τὴν παρεμβολὴν τῶν ἁγίων ⌐ καὶ τὴν πόλιν τὴν ἠγαπημένην, καὶ κατέβη πῦρ ⌐ἐκ τοῦ οὐρανοῦ⌐ καὶ κατέφαγεν αὐτούς.	Note that Rev 20:9 has essentially the same wording as Lk 9:54 in that it says "that fire came down from heaven and devoured them" which is very close to Lk 9:54 "Do you want fire to come down from heaven and destroy them?" However, these are not really quotations but allusions. (*F*)
[a]1 Cor 3:19	
19 ἡ γὰρ σοφία τοῦ κόσμου τούτου μωρία παρὰ τῷ θεῷ ἐστιν. γέγραπται γάρ· ὁ δρασσόμενος τοὺς σοφοὺς ἐν τῇ πανουργίᾳ αὐτῶν·	Job 5:13 is more accurately rendered in 1 Cor 3:19 than in the LXX so far as the term בְּעָרְמָם "in their craftiness" (1 Cor 3:19; ἐν τῇ πανουργίᾳ αὐτῶν) is concerned. The LXX uses ἐν τῇ φρονήσει ("in prudence/understanding") rather than the sly and crafty form of wisdom implied by עֹרֶם. As for לָכֵד, the LXX καταλαμβάνων and the NT δρασσόμενος are about equally good, although they have slightly different connotations in Greek. (*C*)
[a]Mk 11:10	
10 εὐλογημένη ἡ ἐρχομένη βασιλεία τοῦ πατρὸς ἡμῶν Δαυίδ· ⌜ὡσαννὰ ἐν τοῖς ὑψίστοις.	Job 16:19 and Psalm 148:1 = Mk 11:10. (*A*)
	Psalm 118:25; Hosannah is to be translated into Greek as "saved please" or "save I pray" or "Oh Lord give prosperity." So that while Mk 1:10 retains a transcription of the Hebrew as *Hosannah*, the LXX for Psalm 118:25 does translate the Hebrew into Greek.

131: Job 41:3 (41:11)

3 מִי הִקְדִּימַנִי וַאֲשַׁלֵּם   תַּחַת כָּל־הַשָּׁמַיִם לִי־הוּא:

3 ἢ τίς ἀντιστήσεταί μοι καὶ ὑπομενεῖ,
εἰ πᾶσα ἡ ὑπ᾽ οὐρανὸν ἐμή ἐστιν;

132: Psalm 2:1–2

1 לָמָּה רָגְשׁוּ גוֹיִם   וּלְאֻמִּים יֶהְגּוּ־רִיק:
2 יִתְיַצְּבוּ מַלְכֵי־אֶרֶץ   וְרוֹזְנִים נוֹסְדוּ־יָחַד
עַל־יְהוָה וְעַל־מְשִׁיחוֹ:

1 Ἵνα τί ἐφρύαξαν ἔθνη
καὶ λαοὶ ἐμελέτησαν κενά;
2 παρέστησαν οἱ βασιλεῖς τῆς γῆς,
καὶ οἱ ἄρχοντες συνήχθησαν ἐπὶ τὸ αὐτὸ
κατὰ τοῦ κυρίου καὶ κατὰ τοῦ χριστοῦ αὐτοῦ
διάψαλμα

133: Psalm 2:7

7 אֲסַפְּרָה אֶל חֹק   יְהוָה
אָמַר אֵלַי בְּנִי אַתָּה   אֲנִי הַיּוֹם יְלִדְתִּיךָ:

7 διαγγέλλων τὸ πρόσταγμα κυρίου
Κύριος εἶπεν πρός με Υἱός μου εἶ σύ,
ἐγὼ σήμερον γεγέννηκά σε·

134: Psalm 2:9

9 תְּרֹעֵם בְּשֵׁבֶט בַּרְזֶל   כִּכְלִי יוֹצֵר תְּנַפְּצֵם:

9 ποιμανεῖς αὐτοὺς ἐν ῥάβδῳ σιδηρᾷ,
ὡς σκεῦος κεραμέως συντρίψεις αὐτούς.

*a*Rom 11:35

35 ἢ τίς προέδωκεν αὐτῷ,
   καὶ ἀνταποδοθήσεται αὐτῷ;

Job 41:3(41:11) is very accurately rendered in Rom 11:35, except that God is speaking in the first person in the Job passage, whereas He is talked about in the third person in Rom 11:35. The LXX rendering of this clause mistakes הִקְדִּים as a word for "rise up against" or "rise up in opposition," rather than "to do first" or "to anticipate" or "to give to someone first." Hence Paul's προέδωκεν αὐτῷ is much better than LXX's ἀντιστήσεταί μοι. As for the second verb, וַאֲשַׁלֵּם, Rom 11:35 furnishes a perfect equivalent in ἀνταποδοθήσεται, whereas LXX is very wide of the mark in καὶ ὑπομενεῖ ("and shall patiently endure"). (*C*)

*a*Acts 4:25–26

25 ʳὁ τοῦ πατρὸς ἡμῶν διὰ πνεύματος ἁγίου στόματος Δαυὶδ παιδός σου εἰπώνʱ·
   ἱνατί ἐφρύαξαν ἔθνη
     καὶ λαοὶ ἐμελέτησαν κενά;
26 παρέστησαν οἱ βασιλεῖς τῆς γῆς
   καὶ οἱ ἄρχοντες συνήχθησαν ἐπὶ τὸ αὐτὸ
   κατὰ τοῦ κυρίου καὶ κατὰ τοῦ χριστοῦ αὐτοῦ.

Psalm 2:1–2; MT = LXX = Acts 4:25–26. (*A*)

*a*Acts 13:33

33 ὅτι ταύτην ὁ θεὸς
ἐκπεπλήρωκεν ʳτοῖς τέκνοις [αὐτῶν] ἡμῖνʱ ἀναστήσας
ʳἸησοῦν ʳὡς καὶ ʱ ἐν ʳ¹τῷ ψαλμῷ γέγραπται τῷ δευτέρῳʱ·
   υἱός μου εἶ σύ,
   ἐγὼ σήμερον γεγέννηκά σεᵀ.

*b*Heb 1:5 *(see also [120],a)

5 Τίνι γὰρ εἶπέν ποτε τῶν ἀγγέλων·
υἱός μου εἶ σύ,
   ἐγὼ σήμερον γεγέννηκά σε;
καὶ πάλιν·
★ἐγὼ ἔσομαι αὐτῷ εἰς πατέρα,
   καὶ αὐτὸς ἔσται μοι εἰς υἱόν;

*c*Heb 5:5

5 Οὕτως καὶ ὁ Χριστὸς οὐχ ἑαυτὸν ἐδόξασεν γενηθῆναι ἀρχιερέα ἀλλ' ὁ λαλήσας πρὸς αὐτόν·
   υἱός μου εἶ σύ, ἐγὼ σήμερον γεγέννηκά σε·

Psalm 2:7; MT = LXX = Acts 13:13 = Heb 1:5*a* (*A*). Also, Heb 5:5: "Thou art my Son, today I have begotten Thee" is an accurate translation of Psalm 2:7, even as Acts 13:33 is. See also #121, 2 Sam 7:14. (*A*)

*a*Rev 2:26–27

26 Καὶ ὁ νικῶν καὶ ὁ τηρῶν ἄχρι τέλους τὰ ἔργα μου, δώσω αὐτῷ ἐξουσίαν ἐπὶ τῶν ἐθνῶν 27 καὶ *ποιμανεῖ αὐτοὺς ἐν ῥάβδῳ σιδηρᾷ ὡς τὰ σκεύη τὰ κεραμικὰ* ʳσυν*τρίβεται,*

Psalm 2:9 has תְּרֹעֵם בְּשֵׁבֶט בַּרְזֶל, Rev 2:27 has ποιμανεῖ. Note that תְּרֹעֵם is from רָעָה, not רָעַע (= רָצַץ). (*A*)/(*A-*)

135: Psalm 4:5 (4:4)

5 רִגְזוּ וְאַל־תֶּחֱטָאוּ אִמְרוּ בִלְבַבְכֶם עַל־מִשְׁכַּבְכֶם וְדֹמּוּ [סֶלָה:

5 ὀργίζεσθε καὶ μὴ ἁμαρτάνετε ·
λέγετε ἐν ταῖς καρδίαις ὑμῶν
καὶ ἐπὶ ταῖς κοίταις ὑμῶν κατανύγητε.
διάψαλμα.

136: Psalm 5:10 (5:9)

10 כִּי אֵין בְּפִיהוּ נְכוֹנָה קִרְבָּם הַוּוֹת
קֶבֶר־פָּתוּחַ גְּרוֹנָם לְשׁוֹנָם יַחֲלִיקוּן:

Psalm 140:4

4 שָׁנְנוּ לְשׁוֹנָם כְּמוֹ־נָחָשׁ חֲמַת עַכְשׁוּב תַּחַת שְׂפָתֵימוֹ סֶלָה:

(Psalm 139:4)

10 ὅτι οὐκ ἔστιν ἐν τῷ στόματι αὐτῶν ἀλήθεια,
ἡ καρδία αὐτῶν ματαία ·
τάφος ἀνεῳγμένος ὁ λάρυγξ αὐτῶν,
ταῖς γλώσσαις αὐτῶν ἐδολιοῦσαν.

4 ἠκόνησαν γλῶσσαν αὐτῶν ὡσεὶ ὄφεως,
ἰὸς ἀσπίδων ὑπὸ τὰ χείλη αὐτῶν.
διάψαλμα.

137: Psalm 6:9 (6:8)

9 סוּרוּ מִמֶּנִּי כָּל־פֹּעֲלֵי אָוֶן כִּי־שָׁמַע יְהוָה קוֹל בִּכְיִי:

9 ἀπόστητε ἀπ' ἐμοῦ, πάντες οἱ ἐργαζόμενοι τὴν ἀνομίαν,
ὅτι εἰσήκουσεν κύριος τῆς φωνῆς τοῦ κλαυθμοῦ μου ·

138: Psalm 8:3 (8:2)

3 מִפִּי עוֹלְלִים וְיֹנְקִים יִסַּדְתָּ עֹז
לְמַעַן צוֹרְרֶיךָ לְהַשְׁבִּית אוֹיֵב וּמִתְנַקֵּם:

3 ἐκ στόματος νηπίων καὶ θηλαζόντων κατηρτίσω αἶνον
ἕνεκα τῶν ἐχθρῶν σου
τοῦ καταλῦσαι ἐχθρὸν καὶ ἐκδικητήν.

139: Psalm 8:5-7 (8:4-6)

5 מָה־אֱנוֹשׁ כִּי־תִזְכְּרֶנּוּ וּבֶן־אָדָם כִּי תִפְקְדֶנּוּ:
6 וַתְּחַסְּרֵהוּ מְּעַט מֵאֱלֹהִים וְכָבוֹד וְהָדָר תְּעַטְּרֵהוּ:
7 תַּמְשִׁילֵהוּ בְּמַעֲשֵׂי יָדֶיךָ כֹּל שַׁתָּה תַחַת־רַגְלָיו:

5 τί ἐστιν ἄνθρωπος, ὅτι μιμνήσκῃ αὐτοῦ,
ἢ υἱὸς ἀνθρώπου, ὅτι ἐπισκέπτῃ αὐτόν;
6 ἠλάττωσας αὐτὸν βραχύ τι παρ' ἀγγέλους,
δόξῃ καὶ τιμῇ ἐστεφάνωσας αὐτόν ·
7 καὶ κατέστησας αὐτὸν ἐπὶ τὰ ἔργα τῶν χειρῶν σου,
πάντα ὑπέταξας ὑποκάτω τῶν ποδῶν αὐτοῦ,

*a*Eph 4:26

26 ὀργίζεσθε καὶ μὴ ἁμαρτάνετε· ὁ ἥλιος μὴ ἐπιδυέ-
τω ἐπὶ °[τῷ] παροργισμῷ ὑμῶν,

Psalm 4:5(4); MT = LXX = Eph 4:26. (*A*)

---

*a*Rom 3:13

13 τάφος ἀνεῳγμένος ὁ λάρυγξ αὐτῶν,
   ταῖς γλώσσαις αὐτῶν ἐδολιοῦσαν,
   ἰὸς ἀσπίδων ὑπὸ τὰ χείλη αὐτῶν·

Psalm 5:10(9); קֶבֶר־פָּתוּחַ גְּרוֹנָם לְשׁוֹנָם יַחֲלִיקוּן = τάφος
. . . ἐδολιοῦσαν (Psalm 139:4). LXX = Rom 3:13*a*+*b*.
MT הֶחֱלִיק = LXX δολιόω: "flatter" = "deceive," (only
here in LXX) "act deceptively." (*A*)

---

*a*Mt 7:23

23 καὶ τότε ὁμολογήσω αὐτοῖς ὅτι οὐδέποτε ἔγνων ὑμᾶς·
┌ἀποχωρεῖτε ἀπ' ἐμοῦ ᵀ οἱ ἐργαζόμενοι τὴν ἀνομίαν.

Psalm 6:9(8); MT = Mt 7:23. LXX ἀπόστητε = Mt 7:23
ἀποχωρεῖτε. (*A*-) or (*F*)

---

*a*Mt 21:16

16 καὶ εἶπαν αὐτῷ· ἀκούεις τί οὗ-
τοι λέγουσιν; ὁ δὲ Ἰησοῦς λέγει αὐτοῖς· ναί. οὐδέποτε
ἀνέγνωτε °ὅτι
   ἐκ στόματος νηπίων καὶ θηλαζόντων κατηρτίσω αἶνον;

Psalm 8:3(2); MT = LXX = Mt 21:16. (*A*)

---

*a*Heb 2:6–8

6 διεμαρτύρατο δέ πού τις λέγων·
   ┌τί ἐστιν ἄνθρωπος ὅτι μιμνήσκῃ αὐτοῦ,
    ἢ υἱὸς ἀνθρώπου ὅτι ἐπισκέπτῃ αὐτόν;
7 ἠλάττωσας αὐτὸν βραχύ τι παρ' ἀγγέλους,
   δόξῃ καὶ τιμῇ ἐστεφάνωσας αὐτόν, ᵀ
8 πάντα ὑπέταξας ὑποκάτω τῶν ποδῶν αὐτοῦ.
ἐν ┌τῷ γὰρ┐ ὑποτάξαι °[αὐτῷ] τὰ πάντα οὐδὲν ἀφῆκεν
αὐτῷ ἀνυπότακτον. Νῦν δὲ οὔπω ὁρῶμεν αὐτῷ τὰ πάντα
ὑποτεταγμένα·

Psalm 8:5–7(4–6); MT = LXX = Heb 2:6–7 (*A*). Note
that ἀγγέλους is used in LXX and NT for אֱלֹהִים, for
often בְּנֵי אֱלֹהִים is used in the sense of angels: Deut
32:43 (4Q Dtᵃ); Job 1:6, 2:1; Psalm 29:1; 89:6. אֱלֹהִים
alone is used for angels: Psalm 97:7; 138:1. "A little
lower than God" is totally unacceptable (despite NASB,
NIV: "the heavenly beings") in view of the transcen-
dence of God taught in the OT. (*A*-)

*b*1 Cor 15:27   only Psalm 8:6

27 πάντα γὰρ ὑπέταξεν ὑπὸ τοὺς πόδας αὐτοῦ. ὅταν δὲ
εἴπῃ °ὅτι πάντα ὑποτέτακται, δῆλον ὅτι ἐκτὸς τοῦ ὑπο-
τάξαντος αὐτῷ τὰ πάντα.

1 Cor 15:27 quotes from Psalm 8:6, "for he has sub-
jected all things under his feet" is accurate since Paul is
speaking about the psalmist at this point and therefore
referring to the Lord in the Psalm; therefore he refers to
him in the third person. (*A*)

140: Psalm 10:7

(Psalm 9:28)

אָלָה' פִּיהוּ מָלֵא וּמִרְמוֹת' וָתֹךְ תַּחַת לְשׁוֹנוֹ עָמָל וָאָוֶן:

28 οὗ ἀρᾶς τὸ στόμα αὐτοῦ γέμει καὶ πικρίας καὶ δόλου,
ὑπὸ τὴν γλῶσσαν αὐτοῦ κόπος καὶ πόνος.

141: Psalm 14:1–3

(Psalm 13:1–3)

¹ לַמְנַצֵּחַ' לְדָוִד
אָמַר נָבָל בְּלִבּוֹ אֵין אֱלֹהִים
הִשְׁחִיתוּ הִתְעִיבוּ' עֲלִילָה' אֵין עֹשֵׂה־טוֹב'
² יְהֹוָה' מִשָּׁמַיִם' הִשְׁקִיף עַל־בְּנֵי־אָדָם
לִרְאוֹת הֲיֵשׁ מַשְׂכִּיל' דֹּרֵשׁ' אֶת־אֱלֹהִים:
³ הַכֹּל סָר' יַחְדָּו נֶאֱלָחוּ
אֵין' עֹשֵׂה־טוֹב אֵין גַּם־אֶחָד:

1   Εἰς τὸ τέλος · ψαλμὸς τῷ Δαυιδ.
Εἶπεν ἄφρων ἐν καρδίᾳ αὐτοῦ Οὐκ ἔστιν θεός ·
διέφθειραν καὶ ἐβδελύχθησαν ἐν ἐπιτηδεύμασιν,
οὐκ ἔστιν ποιῶν χρηστότητα, οὐκ ἔστιν ἕως ἑνός.
2 κύριος ἐκ τοῦ οὐρανοῦ διέκυψεν ἐπὶ τοὺς υἱοὺς τῶν ἀνθρώπων
τοῦ ἰδεῖν εἰ ἔστιν συνίων ἢ ἐκζητῶν τὸν θεόν.
3 πάντες ἐξέκλιναν, ἅμα ἠχρεώθησαν,
οὐκ ἔστιν ποιῶν χρηστότητα, οὐκ ἔστιν ἕως ἑνός.
[τάφος ἀνεῳγμένος ὁ λάρυγξ αὐτῶν,
ταῖς γλώσσαις αὐτῶν ἐδολιοῦσαν ·
ἰὸς ἀσπίδων ὑπὸ τὰ χείλη αὐτῶν,
ὧν τὸ στόμα ἀρᾶς καὶ πικρίας γέμει ·
ὀξεῖς οἱ πόδες αὐτῶν ἐκχέαι αἷμα ·
σύντριμμα καὶ ταλαιπωρία ἐν ταῖς ὁδοῖς αὐτῶν,
καὶ ὁδὸν εἰρήνης οὐκ ἔγνωσαν ·
οὐκ ἔστιν φόβος θεοῦ ἀπέναντι τῶν ὀφθαλμῶν αὐτῶν.]

Psalm 53:1–3

(Psalm 52:1–3)

¹ לַמְנַצֵּחַ עַל־מָחֲלַת' מַשְׂכִּיל לְדָוִד:
² אָמַר נָבָל בְּלִבּוֹ אֵין אֱלֹהִים
הִשְׁחִיתוּ וְהִתְעִיבוּ' עָוֶל' אֵין עֹשֵׂה־טוֹב:
³ אֱלֹהִים מִשָּׁמַיִם' הִשְׁקִיף עַל־בְּנֵי אָדָם
לִרְאוֹת הֲיֵשׁ מַשְׂכִּיל' דֹּרֵשׁ אֶת־אֱלֹהִים:

1   Εἰς τὸ τέλος, ὑπὲρ μαελεθ · συνέσεως τῷ Δαυιδ.
2 Εἶπεν ἄφρων ἐν καρδίᾳ αὐτοῦ Οὐκ ἔστιν θεός.
διεφθάρησαν καὶ ἐβδελύχθησαν ἐν ἀνομίαις,
οὐκ ἔστιν ποιῶν ἀγαθόν.
3 ὁ θεὸς ἐκ τοῦ οὐρανοῦ διέκυψεν ἐπὶ τοὺς υἱοὺς τῶν ἀνθρώπων
τοῦ ἰδεῖν εἰ ἔστιν συνίων ἢ ἐκζητῶν τὸν θεόν.

^aRom 3:14

14 ὧν τὸ στόμα ^T ἀρᾶς καὶ πικρίας γέμει,

Psalm 10:7; מִרְמוֹת = LXX δόλου (οὗ ἀρᾶς τὸ στόμα αὐτοῦ γέμει καὶ πικρίας καὶ δόλου . . .), but not included in Rom 3:14 (ὧν τὸ στόμα ἀρᾶς καὶ πικρίας γέμει). Thus only the first three words appear in all three: אָלָה פִּיהוּ מָלֵא (B^d). Note that תֹּךְ ("oppression, tyranny") is misrendered as πικρίας in LXX and NT. Apparently Schleusner (p. 763) takes πικρία as a rendering of מִרְמָה as if there were a confusion with מרר or מרה (instead of רָמָה, the actual root of מִרְמָה). Yet on p. 630, he identifies תֹּךְ with δόλος as one possibility. Then, on p. 631 he connects תֹּךְ with δόλος as if it could also mean a deception (*fraus*), which Zorell (p. 898) defines as "the violent harrassment of the poor." Rom 3:14 adapts the singular pronoun פִּיהוּ (LXX οὗ . . . τὸ στόμα αὐτοῦ) to the general context, which has been referring to mankind in general. The word order of Rom 3 differs slightly from that of LXX. (*A*-)

---

^aRom 3:10–12

10 καθὼς γέγραπται ὅτι
οὐκ ἔστιν δίκαιος οὐδὲ εἷς.
11 οὐκ ἔστιν ^Oὁ συνίων,
οὐκ ἔστιν ^{O1}ὁ ^Γἐκζητῶν τὸν θεόν.
12 πάντες ἐξέκλιναν ἅμα ἠχρεώθησαν·
οὐκ ἔστιν ^Oὁ ποιῶν χρηστότητα,
[□][οὐκ ἔστιν]`` ἕως ἑνός.

Psalm 14:1–3; 14:1b: אָמַר נָבָל בְּלִבּוֹ אֵין אֱלֹהִים = nothing in LXX or NT.

Psalm 14:2; MT ("Yahweh looked down from heaven upon the sons of men, to see if there was anyone of understanding/who understands (לִרְאוֹת הֲיֵשׁ מַשְׂכִּיל), one seeking God (דֹּרֵשׁ אֶת־אֱלֹהִים)." Compare Rom 3:11: "There is no one who understands," and Rom 3:11b: οὐκ ἔστιν ὁ ἐκζητῶν τὸν θεόν. NT draws the inference and question from MT. (*A*^d)

Psalm 14:3; הַכֹּל סָר יַחְדָּו נֶאֱלָחוּ = LXX πάντες ἐξέκλιναν, ἅμα ἠχρεώθησαν = NT. (*A*)

MT אֵין עֹשֵׂה־טוֹב אֵין גַּם־אֶחָד = LXX οὐκ ἔστιν ποιῶν χρηστότητα, οὐκ ἔστιν ἕως ἑνός. Compare with NT: . . . δίκαιος . . . οὐδὲ . . . εἷς (*A*^d) or (*C*). Note that this is an independent translation in Rom 3:10, in some ways closer to the MT but for the most part more idiomatic and simpler Greek; equivalent in meaning though not in literalness. In the Psalm 53 (LXX 52:2b) parallel, ἀγαθόν is used instead of χρηστότητα (but LXX does not use the δίκαιος of Rom 3:10).

142: Psalm 16:8–11

(Psalm 15:8–11)

8 שִׁוִּיתִי יְהוָה לְנֶגְדִּי תָמִיד   כִּי מִימִינִי בַּל־אֶמּוֹט:

9 לָכֵן ׀ שָׂמַח לִבִּי וַיָּגֶל כְּבוֹדִי   אַף־בְּשָׂרִי יִשְׁכֹּן לָבֶטַח:

10 כִּי ׀ לֹא־תַעֲזֹב נַפְשִׁי לִשְׁאוֹל   לֹא־תִתֵּן חֲסִידְךָ לִרְאוֹת שָׁחַת:

11 תּוֹדִיעֵנִי אֹרַח חַיִּים

שֹׂבַע שְׂמָחוֹת אֶת־פָּנֶיךָ   נְעִמוֹת בִּימִינְךָ נֶצַח:

8 προωρώμην τὸν κύριον ἐνώπιόν μου διὰ παντός,
ὅτι ἐκ δεξιῶν μού ἐστιν, ἵνα μὴ σαλευθῶ.

9 διὰ τοῦτο ηὐφράνθη ἡ καρδία μου,
καὶ ἠγαλλιάσατο ἡ γλῶσσά μου,
ἔτι δὲ καὶ ἡ σάρξ μου κατασκηνώσει ἐπ' ἐλπίδι,

10 ὅτι οὐκ ἐγκαταλείψεις τὴν ψυχήν μου εἰς ᾅδην
οὐδὲ δώσεις τὸν ὅσιόν σου ἰδεῖν διαφθοράν.

11 ἐγνώρισάς μοι ὁδοὺς ζωῆς ·
πληρώσεις με εὐφροσύνης μετὰ τοῦ προσώπου σου,
τερπνότητες ἐν τῇ δεξιᾷ σου εἰς τέλος.

143: Psalm 18:50 (18:49)

see 2 Sam 22:50 [123]

*a*Acts 2:25–28

25 Δαυὶδ γὰρ λέγει εἰς αὐτόν·
προορώμην τὸν κύριον ᵀ ἐνώπιόν μου διὰ παντός,
ὅτι ἐκ δεξιῶν μού ἐστιν ἵνα μὴ σαλευθῶ.
26 διὰ τοῦτο ηὐφράνθη ˢ ἡ καρδία μου ᶻ
καὶ ἠγαλλιάσατο ἡ γλῶσσά μου,

ἔτι δὲ καὶ ἡ σάρξ μου κατασκηνώσει ἐπ᾽ ἐλπίδι,
27 ὅτι οὐκ ἐγκαταλείψεις τὴν ψυχήν μου εἰς ᾅδην
οὐδὲ δώσεις τὸν ὅσιόν σου ἰδεῖν διαφθοράν.
28 ἐγνώρισάς μοι ὁδοὺς ζωῆς,
πληρώσεις με εὐφροσύνης μετὰ τοῦ προσώπου σου.

*b*Acts 2:31   only Psalm 16:10

31 ⸆προϊδὼν ἐλάλησεν
περὶ τῆς ἀναστάσεως τοῦ Χριστοῦ ὅτι οὔτε ἐγκατελείφθη
ᵀ εἰς ⸆ᾅδην ⸀¹οὔτε ἡ σὰρξ αὐτοῦ εἶδεν διαφθοράν.

*c*Acts 13:35   only Psalm 16:10

35 ⸆διότι καὶ ⸀ἐν ἑτέρῳ⸩ λέγει·
οὐ δώσεις τὸν ὅσιόν σου ἰδεῖν διαφθοράν.

Psalm 16:8–11 (line 1, first colon); MT = LXX = NT (Acts 2:25–28) except שִׁוִּיתִי, where LXX = NT προωρώμην (line 1, second colon); MT = LXX = NT except בַּל־אֶמּוֹט where LXX = NT ἵνα μὴ σαλευθῶ, which is probably a standard equivalence: בַּל = ἵνα μή. (*A*)

Psalm 16:9; MT = LXX 15:9 = Acts 2:26. (*A*)

Psalm 16:10 (first colon); MT = LXX = Acts 2:27*a* (*A*); (second colon) MT = LXX = Acts 2:27*b* except that שַׁחַת (from שׁוּחַ?) may = "the pit" (of the grave), which the LXX rendered διαφθορά, as if from שָׁחַת. This is central to Peter's application of the verse to Christ's body, which did not decay in the grave. Yet Zorell (p. 836) defines שַׁחַת as: (1) *perditio, pernicies, interitus* (rather than pit); (2) *corruptio, putrefactio* (the putrefaction of a moldering corpse in Job 17:14, in parallel with worms). Therefore, לִרְאוֹת שַׁחַת = *experiri corruptionem*. Thus the idea of "pit" was probably not maintained in the mind of David and his contemporaries, for "pit" would be expressed by שׁוּחָה, בּוֹר, בְּאֵר, פַּחַת, or שִׁיחָה. (But שַׁחַת does occur as *Fallgrube* for wild animals in Psalm 94:13; Prov 26:27; cf. also Psalm 7:16; 9:16; 35:7; Ez 19:4, 8; Job 9:31, where the reference is to a pit with slimy and miry contents.) The great majority of its occurrences refer to the grave or to the netherworld, *Sheol* (so G-B 821A). G-B comments that LXX occasionally treated שַׁחַת as if from שָׁחַת, hence διαφθορά in Sir 9:9; 48:6; (51:2 uses ἀπώλεια); many claim this for Job 17:14 also, though "unwahrscheinlich." (*A*ᵈ / *B*ᵃ)

Psalm 16:11; MT = LXX = Acts 2:28 except: (1) אֹרַח became plural ὁδούς in both; (2) שֹׂבַע שְׂמָחוֹת becomes verb πληρώσεις με εὐφροσύνης. It probably was understood as *piel* inf. שָׂבַע, though not quite equivalent to πληρόω.

Acts 2:31 refers to God in the third person, but otherwise accurately quotes from Psalm 16:10, "His soul (the Messiah) is not left unto Hades, nor did his flesh see corruption" (which is accurate for "Thou wilt not leave my soul unto Hades, nor wilt thou give thy holy one to see corruption"). But this is an accurate quotation even though it may leave out a word or two. Acts 13:35, "Thou will not give thy holy one or godly one to see corruption" is accurate for the second part of Psalm 16:10. (*A*)

144: Psalm 19:5 (19:4)

בְּכָל־הָאָרֶץ ׀ יָצָא קַוָּם וּבִקְצֵה תֵבֵל מִלֵּיהֶם 5
לַשֶּׁמֶשׁ שָׂם־אֹהֶל בָּהֶם :

(Psalm 18:5)

5 εἰς πᾶσαν τὴν γῆν ἐξῆλθεν ὁ φθόγγος αὐτῶν
καὶ εἰς τὰ πέρατα τῆς οἰκουμένης τὰ ῥήματα αὐτῶν.
ἐν τῷ ἡλίῳ ἔθετο τὸ σκήνωμα αὐτοῦ ·

145: Psalm 22:2 (22:1)

אֵלִי אֵלִי לָמָה עֲזַבְתָּנִי רָחוֹק מִישׁוּעָתִי דִּבְרֵי שַׁאֲגָתִי : 2

(Psalm 21:2)

2 Ὁ θεὸς ὁ θεός μου, πρόσχες μοι · ἵνα τί ἐγκατέλιπές με ;
μακρὰν ἀπὸ τῆς σωτηρίας μου οἱ λόγοι τῶν παραπτωμά-
των μου.

146: Psalm 22:19 (22:18)

יְחַלְּקוּ בְגָדַי לָהֶם וְעַל־לְבוּשִׁי יַפִּילוּ גוֹרָל : 19

(Psalm 21:19)

19 διεμερίσαντο τὰ ἱμάτιά μου ἑαυτοῖς
καὶ ἐπὶ τὸν ἱματισμόν μου ἔβαλον κλῆρον.

*a*Rom 10:18

18 ἀλλὰ λέγω, μὴ οὐκ
ἤκουσαν; μενοῦνγε·
  εἰς πᾶσαν τὴν γῆν ἐξῆλθεν ὁ φθόγγος αὐτῶν
  καὶ εἰς τὰ πέρατα τῆς οἰκουμένης τὰ ῥήματα αὐτῶν.

Psalm 19:5(4), first colon; MT בְּכָל־הָאָרֶץ יָצָא קַוָּם compared with LXX ὁ φθόγγος αὐτῶν (perhaps קַוָּם was read as קוֹלָם; קַו is a little unexpected here, and is in a context of expressed testimony rather than of space measurement) = NT Rom 10:18 (*B*). But קַו might = a chord in a musical instrument (φθόγγος).

Second colon: MT וּבִקְצֵה תֵבֵל מִלֵּיהֶם = LXX καὶ εἰς τὰ πέρατα τῆς οἰκουμένης τὰ ῥήματα αὐτῶν = Rom 10:18*b*. (*A*)

---

*a*Mt 27:46

46 περὶ δὲ τὴν ἐνάτην ὥραν ⌜ἀν-
εβόησεν ὁ Ἰησοῦς φωνῇ μεγάλῃ λέγων·
  ⌜ηλι ηλι⌝ ⌜λεμα σαβαχθανι⌝;
τοῦτ' ἔστιν· θεέ μου θεέ μου, ἱνατί με ἐγκατέλιπες;

*b*Mk 15:34

34 καὶ τῇ ⌜ἐνάτῃ ὥρᾳ⌝ ἐβόησεν □ὁ Ἰησοῦς⌝ φωνῇ μεγάλῃ·
  ⌜ελωι ⌜ελωι ⌜λεμα σαβαχθανι⌝;
ὅ ἐστιν μεθερμηνευόμενον· ὁ θεός °μου □1ὁ θεός μου⌝,
εἰς τί ⌜1ἐγκατέλιπές με⌝;

Psalm 22:2(1); LXX inserts πρόσχες μοι, perhaps suggesting an inserted הַקְשִׁיבָה לִי as *BH* apparently suggests. But NT does not follow LXX at all here, but adopts an Aramaic paraphrase, לְמָא שְׁבַקְתַּנִי, which Matthew directly transliterates and then translates using a vocative inflection, Θεέ. Compare Mk 15:34 ἐλωί ἐλωί . . . ὁ θεός μου ὁ θεός μου; cf. with LXX ὁ Θεός μου, ὁ Θεός μου, πρόσχες μου, ἵνα τί ἐγκατέλιπές με. (*C*)

---

*a*Jn 19:24

24 εἶπαν
οὖν πρὸς ἀλλήλους· μὴ σχίσωμεν αὐτόν, ἀλλὰ λάχω-
μεν περὶ αὐτοῦ τίνος ἔσται· ἵνα ἡ γραφὴ πληρωθῇ
□[ἡ λέγουσα]⌝·
  διεμερίσαντο τὰ ἱμάτιά μου ἑαυτοῖς
  καὶ ἐπὶ τὸν ἱματισμόν μου ἔβαλον κλῆρον.
Οἱ μὲν οὖν στρατιῶται ταῦτα ἐποίησαν.

*b*Mt 27:35

35 **Σταυρώσαντες δὲ αὐτὸν διεμερίσαντο τὰ ἱμάτια αὐτοῦ** ⌜βάλλοντες κλῆρον⌝,

*c*Mk 15:24

24 Καὶ ⌜σταυροῦσιν αὐτὸν καὶ⌝ διαμερίζονται τὰ ἱμάτια αὐτοῦ, βάλλοντες κλῆρον ἐπ' αὐτὰ □τίς τί ἄρῃ⌝.

*d*Lk 23:24

34 □[[ὁ δὲ Ἰησοῦς ἔλε-
γεν· πάτερ, ἄφες αὐτοῖς, οὐ γὰρ οἴδασιν τί ποιοῦσιν.]]⌝
⌜διαμεριζόμενοι δὲ τὰ ἱμάτια αὐτοῦ ⌜ἔβαλον ⌜1κλήρους.

Psalm 22:19(18); MT = LXX = John 19:24*b*. (*A*)

Mk 15:24 is really a synoptic parallel of Mt 27:35 and so also is Lk 23:24, but of course since they are talking about the fulfillment of the prophetic type set forth in Psalm 22:19(18), the imperfect tense of the Hebrew is not preserved but put into the aorist—"they parted his garments." That, of course, conforms to the Septuagint rendering even of Psalm 22:19, but Lk 23:24, has a participle—"parting." "They cast lots" with the aorist ἔβαλον, is of course more accurate. Mk 15 uses the present tense, "they," that is the historical present, "they part his garments, casting a lot." Lk 23:24 uses "parting his garments, they cast lots," which is almost the same although the Hebrew uses the singular word for lot, so this is a very minor verbal deviation.

147: Psalm 22:23 (22:22)

23 אֲסַפְּרָה שִׁמְךָ לְאֶחָי   בְּתוֹךְ קָהָל אֲהַלְלֶךָּ:

(Psalm 21:23)

23 διηγήσομαι τὸ ὄνομά σου τοῖς ἀδελφοῖς μου,
ἐν μέσῳ ἐκκλησίας ὑμνήσω σε

148: Psalm 24:1

1 לְדָוִד מִזְמוֹר
לַיהוָה הָאָרֶץ וּמְלוֹאָהּ   תֵּבֵל וְיֹשְׁבֵי בָהּ:

(Psalm 23:1)

1 Ψαλμὸς τῷ Δαυιδ · τῆς μιᾶς σαββάτων.
Τοῦ κυρίου ἡ γῆ καὶ τὸ πλήρωμα αὐτῆς,
ἡ οἰκουμένη καὶ πάντες οἱ κατοικοῦντες ἐν αὐτῇ ·

149: Psalm 31:6 (31:5)

6 בְּיָדְךָ אַפְקִיד רוּחִי   פָּדִיתָה אוֹתִי יְהוָה אֵל אֱמֶת:

(Psalm 30:6)

6 εἰς χεῖράς σου παραθήσομαι τὸ πνεῦμά μου ·
ἐλυτρώσω με, κύριε ὁ θεὸς τῆς ἀληθείας.

150: Psalm 32:1–2

1 לְדָוִד מַשְׂכִּיל
אַשְׁרֵי נְשׂוּי־פֶּשַׁע   כְּסוּי חֲטָאָה:
2 אַשְׁרֵי אָדָם לֹא יַחְשֹׁב   יְהוָה לוֹ עָוֹן
וְאֵין בְּרוּחוֹ רְמִיָּה:

(Psalm 31:1–2)

1 Τῷ Δαυιδ · συνέσεως.
Μακάριοι ὧν ἀφέθησαν αἱ ἀνομίαι
καὶ ὧν ἐπεκαλύφθησαν αἱ ἁμαρτίαι ·
2 μακάριος ἀνήρ, οὗ οὐ μὴ λογίσηται κύριος ἁμαρτίαν,
οὐδὲ ἔστιν ἐν τῷ στόματι αὐτοῦ δόλος.

151: Psalm 34:9 (34:8)

9 (ט) טַעֲמוּ וּרְאוּ כִּי־טוֹב יְהוָה   אַשְׁרֵי הַגֶּבֶר יֶחֱסֶה־בּוֹ:

(Psalm 33:9)

9 γεύσασθε καὶ ἴδετε ὅτι χρηστὸς ὁ κύριος ·
μακάριος ἀνήρ, ὃς ἐλπίζει ἐπ' αὐτόν.

152: Psalm 34:13–17 (34:12-16)

13 (מ) מִי־הָאִישׁ הֶחָפֵץ חַיִּים   אֹהֵב יָמִים לִרְאוֹת טוֹב:
14 (נ) נְצֹר לְשׁוֹנְךָ מֵרָע   וּשְׂפָתֶיךָ מִדַּבֵּר מִרְמָה:
15 (ס) סוּר מֵרָע וַעֲשֵׂה־טוֹב   בַּקֵּשׁ שָׁלוֹם וְרָדְפֵהוּ:
16 (ע) עֵינֵי יְהוָה אֶל־צַדִּיקִים   וְאָזְנָיו אֶל־שַׁוְעָתָם:
17 (פ) פְּנֵי יְהוָה בְּעֹשֵׂי רָע   לְהַכְרִית מֵאֶרֶץ זִכְרָם:

(Psalm 33:13–17)

13 τίς ἐστιν ἄνθρωπος ὁ θέλων ζωὴν
ἀγαπῶν ἡμέρας ἰδεῖν ἀγαθάς;
14 παῦσον τὴν γλῶσσάν σου ἀπὸ κακοῦ
καὶ χείλη σου τοῦ μὴ λαλῆσαι δόλον.
15 ἔκκλινον ἀπὸ κακοῦ καὶ ποίησον ἀγαθόν,
ζήτησον εἰρήνην καὶ δίωξον αὐτήν ·
16 ὀφθαλμοὶ κυρίου ἐπὶ δικαίους,
καὶ ὦτα αὐτοῦ εἰς δέησιν αὐτῶν ·
17 πρόσωπον δὲ κυρίου ἐπὶ ποιοῦντας κακὰ
τοῦ ἐξολεθρεῦσαι ἐκ γῆς τὸ μνημόσυνον αὐτῶν.

153: Psalm 34:21

see Ex 12:46 [41]

^aHeb 2:12

12 λέγων·
ἀπαγγελῶ τὸ ὄνομά σου τοῖς ἀδελφοῖς μου,
ἐν μέσῳ ἐκκλησίας ὑμνήσω σε,

Psalm 22:23(22); MT = LXX = Heb 2:12 except LXX renders אֲסַפְּרָה as διηγήσομαι and Heb 2:12 as ἀπαγγελῶ. (A^d)

---

^a1 Cor 10:26

26 τοῦ κυρίου γὰρ ἡ γῆ καὶ τὸ πλήρωμα αὐτῆς.

Psalm 24:1; MT = LXX (except that πάντες is inserted before οἱ κατοικοῦντες. That is not the part quoted in 1 Cor 10:26). (A)

---

^aLk 23:46

46 καὶ φωνήσας φωνῇ μεγάλῃ ὁ Ἰησοῦς εἶπεν· πάτερ, εἰς χεῖράς σου ⌜παρατίθεμαι τὸ πνεῦμά μου. τοῦτο δὲ εἰπὼν ἐξέπνευσεν. ^T

Psalm 31:6 is not really quoted to prove a point, but there is a simple borrowing of traditional language: MT בְּיָדְךָ אַפְקִיד רוּחִי LXX εἰς χεῖράς σου παραθήσομαι τὸ πνεῦμά μου = Lk 23:46 except παρατίθεμαι (present instead of future). (A) or (F)

---

^aRom 4:7–8

7 μακάριοι ὧν ἀφέθησαν αἱ ἀνομίαι
καὶ ὧν ἐπεκαλύφθησαν αἱ ἁμαρτίαι·
8 μακάριος ἀνὴρ ⌜οὗ οὐ μὴ λογίσηται κύριος ἁμαρτίαν.

Psalm 32:1–2; MT = LXX = Rom 4:7–8 except that פֶּשַׁע (singular) נְשׂוּי = ὧν (plural) ἀφέθησαν αἱ ἀνομίαι (plural for singular: similarly ὧν ἐπεκαλύφθησαν αἱ ἁμαρτίαι) = Rom 4:8. (A/A-)

---

^a1 Pet 2:3

3 ⌜εἰ ἐγεύσασθε ^T ὅτι ⌜χρηστὸς ὁ κύριος.

Psalm 34:9 = 1 Pet 2:3. (A)

---

^a1 Pet 3:10–12

10 ὁ γὰρ θέλων ζωὴν ἀγαπᾶν
καὶ ἰδεῖν ἡμέρας ἀγαθὰς
παυσάτω τὴν γλῶσσαν ^T ἀπὸ κακοῦ
καὶ χείλη ^T τοῦ μὴ ⌜λαλῆσαι δόλον,
11 ἐκκλινάτω °δὲ ἀπὸ κακοῦ καὶ ποιησάτω ἀγαθόν,
ζητησάτω εἰρήνην καὶ διωξάτω αὐτήν·
12 ὅτι ὀφθαλμοὶ κυρίου ἐπὶ δικαίους
καὶ ὦτα αὐτοῦ εἰς δέησιν αὐτῶν,
πρόσωπον δὲ κυρίου ἐπὶ ποιοῦντας κακά ^T.

Psalm 34:13–17(12–16); v. 13, MT = LXX = 1 Pet 3:10. (A)

v. 14 MT = LXX (except second person singular imperative of נְצֹר & LXX παῦσον becomes third person παυσάτω) = NT (except that Nestle text lacks σου after γλῶσσάν and after χείλη). (A^d)

v. 15, MT = LXX = NT except third person singular imperative ἐκκλινάτω for LXX's ἔκκλινον. (A^d)

v. 16, MT = LXX = NT 1 Pet 3:12a. (A)

v. 17a, MT = LXX = NT 1 Pet 3:12b. (A)

MASORETIC TEXT	SEPTUAGINT

154: Psalm 34:21

Psalm 34:21:

19 אַל־יִשְׂמְחוּ־לִ֥י אֹיְבַ֣י שֶׁ֑קֶר שֹׂנְאַ֥י חִ֝נָּ֗ם יִקְרְצוּ־עָֽיִן׃

(Psalm 34:19)

19 μὴ ἐπιχαρείησάν μοι οἱ ἐχθραίνοντές μοι ἀδίκως,
οἱ μισοῦντές με δωρεὰν καὶ διανεύοντες ὀφθαλμοῖς.

Psalm 69:5

5 רַבּ֤וּ ׀ מִשַּׂעֲר֣וֹת רֹאשִׁי֮ שֹׂנְאַ֪י חִ֫נָּ֥ם
עָצְמ֣וּ מַ֭צְמִיתַי אֹיְבַ֣י שֶׁ֑קֶר
אֲשֶׁ֥ר לֹא־גָ֝זַ֗לְתִּי אָ֣ז אָשִֽׁיב׃

(Psalm 68:5)

5 ἐπληθύνθησαν ὑπὲρ τὰς τρίχας τῆς κεφαλῆς μου οἱ μισοῦντές με δωρεάν,
ἐκραταιώθησαν οἱ ἐχθροί μου οἱ ἐκδιώκοντές με ἀδίκως·
ἃ οὐχ ἥρπασα, τότε ἀπετίννυον.

155: Psalm 36:2 (36:1)

2 נְאֻם־פֶּ֣שַׁע לָ֭רָשָׁע בְּקֶ֣רֶב לִבִּ֑י
אֵֽין־פַּ֥חַד אֱ֝לֹהִ֗ים לְנֶ֣גֶד עֵינָֽיו׃

(Psalm 35:2)

2 Φησὶν ὁ παράνομος τοῦ ἁμαρτάνειν ἐν ἑαυτῷ,
οὐκ ἔστιν φόβος θεοῦ ἀπέναντι τῶν ὀφθαλμῶν αὐτοῦ·

156: Psalm 40:7–9 (40:6–8)

7 זֶ֤בַח וּמִנְחָ֨ה ׀ לֹֽא־חָפַ֗צְתָּ אָ֭זְנַיִם כָּרִ֣יתָ לִּ֑י עוֹלָ֥ה וַ֝חֲטָאָ֗ה לֹ֣א
8 שָׁאָֽלְתָּ׃ אָ֣ז אָ֭מַרְתִּי הִנֵּה־בָ֑אתִי
בִּמְגִלַּת־סֵ֝֗פֶר כָּת֥וּב עָלָֽי׃
9 לַֽעֲשֽׂוֹת־רְצוֹנְךָ֣ אֱלֹהַ֣י חָפָ֑צְתִּי וְ֝תֽוֹרָתְךָ֗ בְּת֣וֹךְ מֵעָֽי׃

(Psalm 39:7–9)

7 θυσίαν καὶ προσφορὰν οὐκ ἠθέλησας,
ὠτία δὲ κατηρτίσω μοι·
ὁλοκαύτωμα καὶ περὶ ἁμαρτίας οὐκ ᾔτησας
8 τότε εἶπον Ἰδοὺ ἥκω,
ἐν κεφαλίδι βιβλίου γέγραπται περὶ ἐμοῦ·
9 τοῦ ποιῆσαι τὸ θέλημά σου, ὁ θεός μου, ἐβουλήθην
καὶ τὸν νόμον σου ἐν μέσῳ τῆς κοιλίας μου.

157: Psalm 41:10 (41:9)

10 גַּם־אִ֤ישׁ שְׁלוֹמִ֨י ׀ אֲשֶׁר־בָּטַ֣חְתִּי ב֑וֹ אוֹכֵ֥ל לַ֝חְמִ֗י הִגְדִּ֖יל עָלַ֣י
עָקֵֽב׃

(Psalm 40:10)

10 καὶ γὰρ ὁ ἄνθρωπος τῆς εἰρήνης μου, ἐφ' ὃν ἤλπισα,
ὁ ἐσθίων ἄρτους μου, ἐμεγάλυνεν ἐπ' ἐμὲ πτερνισμόν·

158: Psalm 42:6, 12 (42:5, 11)

6 מַה־תִּשְׁתּוֹחֲחִ֨י ׀ נַפְשִׁי֮ וַתֶּהֱמִ֪י עָ֫לָ֥י
הוֹחִ֣ילִי לֵֽ֭אלֹהִים כִּי־ע֣וֹד אוֹדֶ֑נּוּ יְשׁוּע֥וֹת פָּנָֽיו׃

12 מַה־תִּשְׁתּוֹחֲחִ֨י ׀ נַפְשִׁי֮ וּֽמַה־תֶּהֱמִ֪י עָ֫לָ֥י
הוֹחִ֣ילִי לֵֽ֭אלֹהִים כִּי־ע֣וֹד אוֹדֶ֑נּוּ יְשׁוּעֹ֥ת פָּ֝נַ֗י וֵֽאלֹהָֽי׃

(Psalm 41:6, 12)

6 ἵνα τί περίλυπος εἶ, ψυχή, καὶ ἵνα τί συνταράσσεις με;
ἔλπισον ἐπὶ τὸν θεόν, ὅτι ἐξομολογήσομαι αὐτῷ·
σωτήριον τοῦ προσώπου μου ὁ θεός μου.

12 ἵνα τί περίλυπος εἶ, ψυχή, καὶ ἵνα τί συνταράσσεις με;
ἔλπισον ἐπὶ τὸν θεόν, ὅτι ἐξομολογήσομαι αὐτῷ·
ἡ σωτηρία τοῦ προσώπου μου ὁ θεός μου.

NEW TESTAMENT	COMMENTARY
ᵃJn 15:25 **25** ἀλλ᾽ ἵνα πληρωθῇ ὁ λόγος ὁ ⸀ἐν τῷ νόμῳ αὐτῶν γεγραμμένος⸀ ὅτι ἐμίσησάν με δωρεάν.	Psalm 35:19b; MT שֹׂנְאַי חִנָּם ("those who hate me without cause") = LXX (οἱ ἐχθραίνοντές μοι ἀδίκως) οἱ μισοῦντές με δωρεάν = John 15:25 . . . ἐμίσησάν με δωρεάν. (Aᵈ) Jn 15:25 has the simple statement—"They hated me without cause," which appears in Psalm 69:5 as "those who hate me without cause," using the participle as Psalm 35:19 did. The way this is quoted in Jn 15 fits in better with its own context and is really quite accurate to the Hebrew.
ᵃRom 3:18 **18** οὐκ ἔστιν φόβος θεοῦ ἀπέναντι τῶν ὀφθαλμῶν αὐτῶν.	Psalm 36:2(1); MT = LXX = Rom 3:18. (A)

ᵃHeb 10:5–7
 	
5 Διὸ εἰσερχό-
μενος εἰς τὸν κόσμον λέγει·
    θυσίαν καὶ προσφορὰν οὐκ ἠθέλησας,
        σῶμα δὲ κατηρτίσω μοι·
6 ⸀ὁλοκαυτώματα καὶ περὶ ἁμαρτίας οὐκ εὐδόκησας.
7 τότε εἶπον· ἰδοὺ ἥκω,
    ἐν κεφαλίδι βιβλίου γέγραπται ᵀ περὶ ἐμοῦ,
        τοῦ ποιῆσαι ὁ θεὸς τὸ θέλημά σου.
	Psalm 40:7–9(6–8); v. 7a MT = LXX; NT Heb 10:5 has σῶμα instead of ὠτία (אָזְנַיִם). Here we observe that LXX is more faithful to the Hebrew. NT uses synecdoche (the whole for the part); the ears represent the entire body of the servant of Yahweh, listening and attentive to the voice of God's command. (Dᵃ)
	
	v. 7b MT = LXX = Heb 10:6. (A)
	
	v. 8–9a MT = LXX = Heb 10:7. (A)

ᵃJn 13:18 **18** Οὐ περὶ πάντων ὑμῶν λέγω· ἐγὼ οἶδα ⸀τίνας ἐξελε- ξάμην· ἀλλ᾽ ἵνα ἡ γραφὴ πληρωθῇ· ὁ τρώγων ⸀μου τὸν ἄρτον ⸀¹ἐπῆρεν ᵒἐπ᾽ ἐμὲ τὴν πτέρναν αὐτοῦ.	Psalm 41:10(9); MT: אֹכֵל לַחְמִי הִגְדִּיל עָלַי עָקֵב—LXX ὁ ἐσθίων ἄρτους μου, ἐμεγάλυνεν ἐπ᾽ ἐμὲ πτερνισνόν, (*supplantatio, deceptio, dolus, fraus*; Schleusner, p. 914) renders: "has formed geat plots = *insidias* = against me"). NT John 3:18 ὁ τρώγων μου τὸν ἄρτον ἐπῆρεν ἐπ᾽ ἐμὲ τὴν πτέρναν αὐτοῦ. Note that the LXX is more literal in ἐμεγάλυνεν for הִגְדִּיל (to the confusion of the Greek reader), but interpretive in equating עָקֵב ("heel") with πτερνισμός. (D) + (C)
ᵃMt 26:38 only Psalm 42:6, 12 **38** τότε λέγει αὐτοῖς· περίλυπός ἐστιν ἡ ψυχή μου ἕως θανάτου· μείνατε ᵀ ὧδε καὶ γρηγορεῖ- τε μετ᾽ ἐμοῦ.	Psalm 42:6, 12; Mt 26:38 and Mk 14:34 (F). This is not a quotation, but is very close in wording as Jesus applies it to Himself (hence μου); in Psalm 42:12 He addressed Himself, using נַפְשִׁי. LXX leaves out μου after ψυχή; therefore NT is closer to MT than LXX is. (F)

MASORETIC TEXT	SEPTUAGINT
159: Psalm 43:5	**(Psalm 42:5)**

5 מַה־תִּשְׁתּוֹחֲחִי ׀ נַפְשִׁי וּמַה־תֶּהֱמִי עָלָי
הוֹחִילִי לֵאלֹהִים כִּי־עוֹד אוֹדֶנּוּ יְשׁוּעֹת פָּנַי וֵאלֹהָי׃

5 ἵνα τί περίλυπος εἶ, ψυχή, καὶ ἵνα τί συνταράσσεις με;
ἔλπισον ἐπὶ τὸν θεόν, ὅτι ἐξομολογήσομαι αὐτῷ ·
σωτήριον τοῦ προσώπου μου ὁ θεός μου.

160: Psalm 44:23 (44:22)	**(Psalm 43:23)**

23 כִּי־עָלֶיךָ הֹרַגְנוּ כָל־הַיּוֹם נֶחְשַׁבְנוּ כְּצֹאן טִבְחָה׃

23 ὅτι ἕνεκα σοῦ θανατούμεθα ὅλην τὴν ἡμέραν,
ἐλογίσθημεν ὡς πρόβατα σφαγῆς.

161: Psalm 45:7–8 (45:6–7)	**(Psalm 44:7–8)**

7 כִּסְאֲךָ אֱלֹהִים עוֹלָם וָעֶד שֵׁבֶט מִישֹׁר שֵׁבֶט מַלְכוּתֶךָ׃
8 אָהַבְתָּ צֶּדֶק וַתִּשְׂנָא רֶשַׁע
עַל־כֵּן ׀ מְשָׁחֲךָ אֱלֹהִים אֱלֹהֶיךָ שֶׁמֶן שָׂשׂוֹן מֵחֲבֵרֶיךָ׃

7 ὁ θρόνος σου, ὁ θεός, εἰς τὸν αἰῶνα τοῦ αἰῶνος,
ῥάβδος εὐθύτητος ἡ ῥάβδος τῆς βασιλείας σου.
8 ἠγάπησας δικαιοσύνην καὶ ἐμίσησας ἀνομίαν ·
διὰ τοῦτο ἔχρισέν σε ὁ θεὸς ὁ θεός σου
ἔλαιον ἀγαλλιάσεως παρὰ τοὺς μετόχους σου.

162: Psalm 51:6 (51:4)	**(Psalm 50:6)**

6 לְךָ לְבַדְּךָ ׀ חָטָאתִי וְהָרַע בְּעֵינֶיךָ עָשִׂיתִי
לְמַעַן תִּצְדַּק בְּדָבְרֶךָ תִּזְכֶּה בְשָׁפְטֶךָ׃

6 σοὶ μόνῳ ἥμαρτον
καὶ τὸ πονηρὸν ἐνώπιόν σου ἐποίησα,
ὅπως ἂν δικαιωθῇς ἐν τοῖς λόγοις σου
καὶ νικήσῃς ἐν τῷ κρίνεσθαί σε.

163: Psalm 53:2–4 (53:1–3)	**see Psalm 14:1–3 [141]**

164: Psalm 62:13 (62:12)	**(Psalm 61:13)**

13 וּלְךָ־אֲדֹנָי חָסֶד כִּי־אַתָּה תְשַׁלֵּם לְאִישׁ כְּמַעֲשֵׂהוּ׃

13 ὅτι τὸ κράτος τοῦ θεοῦ, καὶ σοί, κύριε, τὸ ἔλεος,
ὅτι σὺ ἀποδώσεις ἑκάστῳ κατὰ τὰ ἔργα αὐτοῦ.

Prov 24:12

12 כִּי־תֹאמַר הֵן לֹא־יָדַעְנוּ זֶה הֲלֹא־תֹכֵן לִבּוֹת ׀ הוּא־יָבִין
וְנֹצֵר נַפְשְׁךָ הוּא יֵדָע וְהֵשִׁיב לְאָדָם כְּפָעֳלוֹ׃

12 ἐὰν δὲ εἴπῃς Οὐκ οἶδα τοῦτον,
γίνωσκε ὅτι κύριος καρδίας πάντων γινώσκει,
καὶ ὁ πλάσας πνοὴν πᾶσιν αὐτὸς οἶδεν πάντα,
ὃς ἀποδίδωσιν ἑκάστῳ κατὰ τὰ ἔργα αὐτοῦ.

*b*Mk 14:34

34 καὶ λέγει αὐτοῖς · περίλυπός ἐστιν
ἡ ψυχή μου ἕως θανάτου · μείνατε ὧδε καὶ γρηγορεῖτε.

Psalm 43:5 also uses the expression "Why art thou cast down my soul, O my soul," which is rendered in the LXX as "Why art thou very grieved (περίλυπος)." In Mk 13:34 Jesus says to them "My soul is very grieved unto death," which is substantially what Mt 26:38 says also.

---

*a*Rom 8:36

36 καθὼς γέγραπται ὅτι
ἕνεκεν σοῦ θανατούμεθα ὅλην τὴν ἡμέραν,
ἐλογίσθημεν ὡς πρόβατα σφαγῆς.

Psalm 44:23(22); MT = LXX (43:23) = Rom 8:36. (*A*)

---

*a*Heb 1:8–9

8 πρὸς δὲ τὸν υἱόν ·
ὁ θρόνος σου ὁ θεὸς εἰς τὸν αἰῶνα □τοῦ αἰῶνος`,

□καὶ ⌐ἡ ῥάβδος τῆς εὐθύτητος` ῥάβδος τῆς βασιλείας ⌐σου.
9 ἠγάπησας δικαιοσύνην καὶ ἐμίσησας ⌐ἀνομίαν ·
διὰ τοῦτο ἔχρισέν σε ὁ θεὸς ὁ θεός σου
ἔλαιον ἀγαλλιάσεως παρὰ τοὺς μετόχους σου.

Psalm 45:7–8(6–7); v. 7 MT = LXX (44:7–8) = Heb 1:8–9 (word for word). (*A*)

---

*a*Rom 3:4

4 μὴ γένοιτο · ⌐γινέσθω δὲ ὁ θεὸς ἀλη-
θής, πᾶς δὲ ἄνθρωπος ψεύστης, ⌐καθὼς γέγραπται ·
ὅπως ἂν δικαιωθῇς ἐν τοῖς λόγοις σου
καὶ ⌐[1]νικήσεις ἐν τῷ κρίνεσθαί σε.

Psalm 51:6; MT = LXX = Rom 3:4*b* (word for word) except that בְּדָבְרֶךָ ("in Thy speaking") is pointed בְּדָבְרֶךָ, which is perfectly reasonable. (*A-*)

---

*a*Mt 16:27

27 μέλλει γὰρ ὁ υἱὸς
τοῦ ἀνθρώπου ἔρχεσθαι ἐν τῇ δόξῃ τοῦ πατρὸς αὐτοῦ
μετὰ τῶν ἀγγέλων αὐτοῦ, καὶ τότε ἀποδώσει ἑκάστῳ κατὰ
⌐τὴν πρᾶξιν` αὐτοῦ.

*b*Rom 2:6

6 ὃς ἀποδώσει ἑκάστῳ κατὰ
τὰ ἔργα αὐτοῦ ·

Mt 16:27 does not present Ps 62:13(12) or Prov 24:12 as formal quotations, but it adopts their verbiage in an allusive way. Yet the wording of this passage conforms closely to Ps 62:13*b* and Prov 24:12*d*, both in LXX and Mt 16:27 and Rom 2:6. Interestingly enough, Mt 16 furnishes a rendering of כְּמַעֲשֵׂהוּ ("according to his work") in closer conformity (i.e. τὴν πρᾶξιν αὐτοῦ) than LXX does with its plur. ἔργα ("according to his deeds"). It actually is truer to the consonants and vowel-pointing of מַעֲשֵׂהוּ than the plural ἔργα (which, however appears as τὰ ἔργα αὐτοῦ in Rom 2:6. As for Prov 24:12, it uses וְהֵשִׁיב rather than תְּשַׁלֵּם ("and He will render" instead of "Thou wilt requite") and employs the term כְּפָעֳלוֹ ("according to his activity" rather than Ps 62's ("according to his work"). (*F*)

165: Psalm 68:19 (68:18)

(Psalm 67:19)

יּ עָלִיתָ לַמָּרוֹם ׀ שָׁבִיתָ שֶּׁבִי לָקַחְתָּ מַתָּנוֹת בָּאָדָם
וְאַף סוֹרְרִים לִשְׁכֹּן יָהּ אֱלֹהִים׃

19 ἀνέβης εἰς ὕψος, ᾐχμαλώτευσας αἰχμαλωσίαν,
ἔλαβες δόματα ἐν ἀνθρώπῳ,
καὶ γὰρ ἀπειθοῦντες τοῦ κατασκηνῶσαι.
κύριος ὁ θεὸς εὐλογητός,

166: Psalm 69:5 (69:4)

see Psalm 35:19 [154]

167: Psalm 69:10 (69:9)

(Psalm 68:10)

10 כִּי־קִנְאַת בֵּיתְךָ אֲכָלָתְנִי וְחֶרְפּוֹת חוֹרְפֶיךָ נָפְלוּ עָלָי׃

10 ὅτι ὁ ζῆλος τοῦ οἴκου σου κατέφαγέν με,
καὶ οἱ ὀνειδισμοὶ τῶν ὀνειδιζόντων σε ἐπέπεσαν ἐπ' ἐμέ.

168: Psalm 69:23–24 (69:22–23)

(Psalm 68:23–24)

23 יְהִי־שֻׁלְחָנָם לִפְנֵיהֶם לְפָח וְלִשְׁלוֹמִים לְמוֹקֵשׁ׃
24 תֶּחְשַׁכְנָה עֵינֵיהֶם מֵרְאוֹת וּמָתְנֵיהֶם תָּמִיד הַמְעַד׃

23 γενηθήτω ἡ τράπεζα αὐτῶν ἐνώπιον αὐτῶν εἰς παγίδα
καὶ εἰς ἀνταπόδοσιν καὶ εἰς σκάνδαλον·
24 σκοτισθήτωσαν οἱ ὀφθαλμοὶ αὐτῶν τοῦ μὴ βλέπειν,
καὶ τὸν νῶτον αὐτῶν διὰ παντὸς σύγκαμψον·

*a*Eph 4:8

8 διὸ λέγει·
ἀναβὰς εἰς ὕψος ᾐχμαλώτευσεν αἰχμαλωσίαν,
ᵀ ἔδωκεν δόματα ⌈τοῖς ἀνθρώποις.

Psalm 68:19*a*; MT עָלִיתָ לַמָּרוֹם שָׁבִיתָ שֶּׁבִי = LXX ἀνέβης εἰς ὕψος, ᾐχμαλώτευσας αἰχμαλωσίαν = Eph 4:8 ἀναβὰς εἰς ὕψος ᾐχμαλώτευσεν. (*A*ᵈ)

68:19*b*; MT לָקַחְתָּ מַתָּנוֹת בָּאָדָם = LXX ἔλαβες δόματα ἐν ἀνθρώπῳ (very literal!) but Eph 4:8*b* ἔδωκεν δόματα τοῖς ἀνθρώποις. Note that instead of ἐν we have dative τοῖς ἀνθρώποις in which the deviation is the main point of the quotation!(*E*). But since God does not require gifts from men for His own sake, the Targum (which reads as follows: מְלֶקֶת לִרְקִיע שְׁבִיתָא שְׁבִיתָא אַלְפְתָּא פִּתְגָּמֵי אוֹרַיְתָא לְהוֹן יְהַבְתָּא לְהוֹן מַתָּנָן לִבְנֵי נָשָׁא: "Thou hast ascended to the firmament: Thou has led captivity captive; Thou has taught them the words of the law: Thou hast given gifts to the children of men") has rightly derived the inference that God has received or taken gifts in hand in order to distribute them among (בָּאָדָם) men, rather than His having received gifts "consisting of" (בְּ) men or "among" men. Who could have given Him men whom He did not already have under His sovereign rule? Therefore, Paul has followed the inferential interpretation that was later found written down when the Targum received a stable written form but which had existed for centuries in oral form. God received/took those gifts for distribution among men (בָּאָדָם-) and specifically those men and women who were in covenant relationship with Him.

---

*a*Jn 2:17

17 ⌈ἐμνήσθησαν οἱ μαθηταὶ αὐτοῦ ὅτι γεγραμμένον ἐστίν· ᵀ ὁ ζῆλος τοῦ οἴκου σου καταφάγεταί με.

*b*Rom 15:3

3 καὶ γὰρ ὁ Χριστὸς οὐχ ἑαυτῷ ἤρεσεν, ἀλ-λὰ καθὼς γέγραπται· οἱ ὀνειδισμοὶ τῶν ὀνειδιζόντων σε ἐπέπεσαν ἐπ' ἐμέ.

Psalm 69:10*a*(9); MT כִּי־קִנְאַת בֵּיתְךָ אֲכָלָתְנִי = LXX ὅτι ὁ ζῆλος τοῦ οἴκου σου κατέφαγέν με (aorist!).

John 2:17 = LXX except καταφάγεται "consumes/will consume me" (?), which could be an interpretation of אָכְלָה as a prophetic perfect. (*A*ᵈ)

69:10*b*; MT וְחֶרְפּוֹת חוֹרְפֶיךָ נָפְלוּ עָלָי = LXX exactly (ἔπεσαν) = Rom 15:3*b*. (*A*)

---

*a*Rom 11:9–10

9 καὶ Δαυὶδ λέγει·
γενηθήτω ἡ τράπεζα αὐτῶν εἰς παγίδα καὶ εἰς θήραν
καὶ εἰς σκάνδαλον καὶ εἰς ἀνταπόδομα αὐτοῖς,
10 σκοτισθήτωσαν οἱ ὀφθαλμοὶ αὐτῶν τοῦ μὴ βλέπειν
καὶ τὸν νῶτον αὐτῶν διὰ παντὸς σύγκαμψον.

Psalm 69:23–24(22–23); v. 23*a* MT יְהִי . . . לְפָח = LXX (68:23a) exactly, including ἐνώπιον αὐτῶν = לִפְנֵיהֶם.

Rom 11:9*a* = LXX (68:23) except (1) ἐνώπιον αὐτῶν (actually superfluous) is omitted, and (2) after εἰς παγίδα is added καὶ εἰς θήραν (not italicized); or else it

168 (continued)

169: Psalm 69:26 (69:25)

²⁶ תְּהִי־טִירָתָם נְשַׁמָּה בְּאָהֳלֵיהֶם אַל־יְהִי יֹשֵׁב:

(Psalm 68:26)

26 γενηθήτω ἡ ἔπαυλις αὐτῶν ἠρημωμένη,
καὶ ἐν τοῖς σκηνώμασιν αὐτῶν μὴ ἔστω ὁ κατοικῶν·

Psalm 109:8

⁸ יִהְיוּ־יָמָיו מְעַטִּים פְּקֻדָּתוֹ יִקַּח אַחֵר:

(Psalm 108:8)

8 γενηθήτωσαν αἱ ἡμέραι αὐτοῦ ὀλίγαι,
καὶ τὴν ἐπισκοπὴν αὐτοῦ λάβοι ἕτερος·

170: Psalm 78:2

² אֶפְתְּחָה בְמָשָׁל פִּי אַבִּיעָה חִידוֹת מִנִּי־קֶדֶם:

(Psalm 77:2)

2 ἀνοίξω ἐν παραβολαῖς τὸ στόμα μου,
φθέγξομαι προβλήματα ἀπ᾽ ἀρχῆς.

171: Psalm 78:24

²⁴ וַיַּמְטֵר עֲלֵיהֶם מָן לֶאֱכֹל וּדְגַן־שָׁמַיִם נָתַן לָמוֹ:

(Psalm 77:24)

24 καὶ ἔβρεξεν αὐτοῖς μαννα φαγεῖν
καὶ ἄρτον οὐρανοῦ ἔδωκεν αὐτοῖς·

paraphrases MT's וְלִשְׁלוֹמִים לְמוֹקֵשׁ, a phrase supported by 'A, E, Θ, and Jerome's Hebrew Psalter, but by the Peshitta pointed as וְשִׁלּוּחָם, which is really much more appropriate to the context: "for their retribution and their share" = θήραν. But since that is equivalent to καὶ (וְ before שְׁלוֹמִים) and θήρα = מוֹקֵשׁ, that cannot really be classed as a deviation. (A^d)

v. 24 MT הַמְעַד (*Hiphil* imper. from מָעַד "slip"; H "cause to shake/totter") = LXX σκοτισθήτωσαν . . . σύγκαμψον = Rom 11:10 exactly. (A)

^{a}Acts 1:20

20 γέγραπται
γαρ ἐν βίβλῳ ψαλμῶν·
    γενηθήτω ἡ ἔπαυλις ⌜αὐτοῦ ἔρημος
    καὶ μὴ ἔστω ὁ κατοικῶν ἐν αὐτῇ,
καί·
    τὴν ἐπισκοπὴν αὐτοῦ λαβέτω ἕτερος.

Psalm 69:26(25); MT = LXX (68:26) exactly, with ἠρημωμένη (perfect passive participle), which Acts 1:20 gives as an adjective (ἔρημος), and αὐτῶν (plural) instead of Acts 1:20 αὐτοῦ. Here Peter is applying the general malediction upon the enemies of God and of the psalmist to Judas Iscariot as an individual (αὐτοῦ). (A^d) or (A)

Also, LXX = MT in ἐν τοῖς σκηνώμασιν αὐτῶν (בְּאָהֳלֵיהֶם), whereas Acts 1:20*b* shortens it to ἐν αὐτῇ after ὁ κατοικῶν (= LXX; MT singular יֹשֵׁב) referring to ἡ ἔπαυλις αὐτῶν as an antecedent. That shortening or simplification flows better with the context of Peter's remarks, and constitutes no alteration of sense whatever (A^d). Psalm 109:8 is the source of the last part of Acts 1:20, which is a perfectly accurate translation, "let another take his bishopric (office)."

^{a}Mt 13:35

35 ὅπως πληρωθῇ
τὸ ῥηθὲν διὰ ⌜ τοῦ προφήτου λέγοντος·
    ἀνοίξω ἐν παραβολαῖς τὸ στόμα μου,
    ἐρεύξομαι κεκρυμμένα ἀπὸ καταβολῆς °[κόσμου].

Psalm 78:2*a*; MT פִּי . . . אֶפְתְּחָה = LXX (77:2) = Mt 13:35*b* (which perfectly renders ἀνοίξω . . . στόμα μου), but 78:2*b* חִידוֹת is poorly rendered in LXX as προβλήματα, (though Schleusner [p. 859] interprets πρόβλημα as capable of meaning *obscurior questio quae ad solvendum proponitur* "a rather obscure question which is set forth to be solved"). Mt 13:35*c* is much closer to חִידוֹת with κεκρυμμένα, which is closer also to Theodotion. ($C^θ$)

^{a}Jn 6:31

31 οἱ πατέρες ἡμῶν
τὸ μάννα ἔφαγον ἐν τῇ ἐρήμῳ, καθώς ἐστιν γεγραμμένον·
ἄρτον ἐκ τοῦ οὐρανοῦ ⌜ἔδωκεν αὐτοῖς φαγεῖν.

Psalm 78:24; MT = LXX (77:24) = John 6:31 except that φαγεῖν is at the end rather than the beginning. (A)

172: Psalm 82:6	**(Psalm 81:6)**
6 אֲנִי־אָמַרְתִּי אֱלֹהִים אַתֶּם וּבְנֵי עֶלְיוֹן כֻּלְּכֶם:	6 ἐγὼ εἶπα Θεοί ἐστε καὶ υἱοὶ ὑψίστου πάντες ·
173: Psalm 86:9	**(Psalm 85:9)**
9 כָּל־גּוֹיִם ׀ אֲשֶׁר עָשִׂיתָ יָבוֹאוּ ׀ וְיִשְׁתַּחֲווּ לְפָנֶיךָ אֲדֹנָי וִיכַבְּדוּ לִשְׁמֶךָ:	9 πάντα τὰ ἔθνη, ὅσα ἐποίησας, ἥξουσιν καὶ προσκυνήσουσιν ἐνώπιόν σου, κύριε, καὶ δοξάσουσιν τὸ ὄνομά σου,
Jer 10:6–7	
6 מֵאֵין כָּמוֹךָ יְהוָה גָּדוֹל אַתָּה וְגָדוֹל שִׁמְךָ בִּגְבוּרָה: 7 מִי לֹא יִרָאֲךָ מֶלֶךְ הַגּוֹיִם כִּי לְךָ יָאָתָה כִּי בְכָל־חַכְמֵי הַגּוֹיִם וּבְכָל־מַלְכוּתָם מֵאֵין כָּמוֹךָ:	
174: Psalm 89:21	see 1 Sam 13:14 [118]
175: Psalm 91:11–12	**(Psalm 90:11–12)**
11 כִּי מַלְאָכָיו יְצַוֶּה־לָּךְ לִשְׁמָרְךָ בְּכָל־דְּרָכֶיךָ: 12 עַל־כַּפַּיִם יִשָּׂאוּנְךָ פֶּן־תִּגֹּף בָּאֶבֶן רַגְלֶךָ:	11 ὅτι τοῖς ἀγγέλοις αὐτοῦ ἐντελεῖται περὶ σοῦ τοῦ διαφυλάξαι σε ἐν πάσαις ταῖς ὁδοῖς σου · 12 ἐπὶ χειρῶν ἀροῦσίν σε, μήποτε προσκόψῃς πρὸς λίθον τὸν πόδα σου ·
176: Psalm 94:11	**(Psalm 93:11)**
11 יְהוָה יֹדֵעַ מַחְשְׁבוֹת אָדָם כִּי־הֵמָּה הָבֶל:	11 κύριος γινώσκει τοὺς διαλογισμοὺς τῶν ἀνθρώπων ὅτι εἰ- σὶν μάταιοι.
177: Psalm 94:14	see 1 Sam 12:22 [117]

*a*Jn 10:34

34 ἀπεκρίθη ⸀αὐτοῖς [ὁ] ᾽Ιησοῦς⸀· οὐκ ἔστιν γεγραμμένον ἐν τῷ νόμῳ °ὑμῶν ὅτι ἐγὼ εἶπα· θεοί ἐστε;

Psalm 82:6; MT = LXX (81:6) = John 10:34. (*A*)

---

*a*Rev 15:4   (see also [187])

4 τίς ⸆ οὐ °μὴ φοβηθῇ, κύριε,
    καὶ ⸀δοξάσει τὸ ὄνομά σου;
ὅτι μόνος ⸀ὅσιος,
    ὅτι ⸀πάντα τὰ ἔθνη⸀ ἥξουσιν
    καὶ προσκυνήσουσιν ἐνώπιόν σου,
ὅτι τὰ δικαιώματά ⸆ σου ἐφανερώθησαν.

This song of the angels and saints as set forth in Rev 15:4 is not presented as a quotation, but it alludes to portions of Psalm 86:9 and Jer 10:6–7. That is to say, it starts off with the first clause of Jer 6:7 (מִי לֹא יְרָאֲךָ, "Who will not fear Thee?") then follows with the last clause of Psalm 86:9 (אֲדֹנָי וִיכַבְּדוּ לִשְׁמֶךָ "O Lord, and they will glorify Thy name"). Then come the first two clauses of Psalm 86:9 in reverse order. That is, "and they shall glorify Thy name" comes before "all the nations will come," followed by "and they shall worship before Thee." (*F*)

---

*a*Mt 4:6

6 καὶ λέγει αὐτῷ· εἰ υἱὸς εἶ τοῦ θεοῦ, βάλε σεαυτὸν ⸆ κά-τω· γέγραπται γὰρ ὅτι
    τοῖς ἀγγέλοις αὐτοῦ ἐντελεῖται περὶ σοῦ
    καὶ ἐπὶ χειρῶν ἀροῦσίν σε,
    μήποτε προσκόψῃς πρὸς λίθον τὸν πόδα σου.

Psalm 91:11–12; MT = LXX (90:11–12) = Mt 4:6 except that it omits the second colon of v. 11. (*A*)

*b*Lk 4:10–11

10 γέγραπται γὰρ ὅτι
    τοῖς ἀγγέλοις αὐτοῦ ἐντελεῖται περὶ σοῦ
    τοῦ διαφυλάξαι σε
11 καὶ °¹ὅτι
    ἐπὶ χειρῶν ἀροῦσίν σε,
    μήποτε προσκόψῃς πρὸς λίθον τὸν πόδα σου.

Psalm 91:11; MT = LXX (90:11) = Lk 4:10*b*—that has part of the second colon missing in Mt 4:6, i.e., τοῦ διαφυλάξαι σε (but omitting LXX ἐν πάσαις ταῖς ὁδοῖς σου).
(*A*)

---

*a*1 Cor 3:20

20 καὶ πάλιν· κύριος γι-νώσκει τοὺς διαλογισμοὺς τῶν ⸀σοφῶν ὅτι εἰσὶν μάταιοι.

Psalm 94:11; MT מַחְשְׁבוֹת = LXX διαλογισμοὺς τῶν ἀνθρώπων, for which 1 Cor 3:20 has σοφῶν but 33.630.1506 has some Vulgate MSS and Bohairic MSS read ἀνθρώπων; but not so in my edition, which reads ⲚⲚⲒⲘⲞⲕⲘⲉⲕ ⲚⲦⲉ ⲚⲓⲤⲁⲃⲉⲩ "the meditations of the wise". (*A*ᵈ)

178: Psalm 95:7–11

(Psalm 94:7–11)

7 כִּי הוּא אֱלֹהֵינוּ וַאֲנַחְנוּ עַם מַרְעִיתוֹ וְצֹאן
יָדוֹ הַיּוֹם אִם־בְּקֹלוֹ תִשְׁמָעוּ:

8 אַל־תַּקְשׁוּ לְבַבְכֶם כִּמְרִיבָה כְּיוֹם מַסָּה בַּמִּדְבָּר:

9 אֲשֶׁר נִסּוּנִי אֲבוֹתֵיכֶם בְּחָנוּנִי גַּם־רָאוּ פָעֳלִי:

10 אַרְבָּעִים שָׁנָה אָקוּט בְּדוֹר וָאֹמַר עַם תֹּעֵי לֵבָב הֵם
וְהֵם לֹא־יָדְעוּ דְרָכָי:

11 אֲשֶׁר־נִשְׁבַּעְתִּי בְאַפִּי אִם־יְבֹאוּן אֶל־מְנוּחָתִי:

7 ὅτι αὐτός ἐστιν ὁ θεὸς ἡμῶν,
καὶ ἡμεῖς λαὸς νομῆς αὐτοῦ
καὶ πρόβατα χειρὸς αὐτοῦ.
σήμερον, ἐὰν τῆς φωνῆς αὐτοῦ ἀκούσητε,

8 μὴ σκληρύνητε τὰς καρδίας ὑμῶν ὡς ἐν τῷ παραπικρασμῷ
κατὰ τὴν ἡμέραν τοῦ πειρασμοῦ ἐν τῇ ἐρήμῳ,

9 οὗ ἐπείρασαν οἱ πατέρες ὑμῶν,
ἐδοκίμασαν καὶ εἴδοσαν τὰ ἔργα μου.

10 τεσσαράκοντα ἔτη προσώχθισα τῇ γενεᾷ ἐκείνῃ
καὶ εἶπα Ἀεὶ πλανῶνται τῇ καρδίᾳ
καὶ αὐτοὶ οὐκ ἔγνωσαν τὰς ὁδούς μου,

11 ὡς ὤμοσα ἐν τῇ ὀργῇ μου
Εἰ εἰσελεύσονται εἰς τὴν κατάπαυσίν μου.

only Psalm 95:7–8

only Psalm 95:11

179: Psalm 97:7

see Deut 32:43 [115]

180: Psalm 102:26–28 (102:25–27)   see also [130]

(Psalm 101:26–28)

26 לְפָנִים הָאָרֶץ יָסַדְתָּ וּמַעֲשֵׂה יָדֶיךָ שָׁמָיִם:

27 הֵמָּה יֹאבֵדוּ וְאַתָּה תַעֲמֹד וְכֻלָּם כַּבֶּגֶד יִבְלוּ [יַחֲמוֹ]
כַּלְּבוּשׁ תַּחֲלִיפֵם וְיַחֲלֹפוּ: 28 וְאַתָּה־הוּא וּשְׁנוֹתֶיךָ לֹא

26 κατ' ἀρχὰς σύ, κύριε, τὴν γῆν ἐθεμελίωσας,
καὶ ἔργα τῶν χειρῶν σού εἰσιν οἱ οὐρανοί·

27 αὐτοὶ ἀπολοῦνται, σὺ δὲ διαμενεῖς,
καὶ πάντες ὡς ἱμάτιον παλαιωθήσονται,
καὶ ὡσεὶ περιβόλαιον ἀλλάξεις αὐτούς, καὶ ἀλλαγήσονται·

28 σὺ δὲ ὁ αὐτὸς εἶ, καὶ τὰ ἔτη σου οὐκ ἐκλείψουσιν.

*a*Heb 3:7–11

7 Διό, καθὼς λέγει τὸ πνεῦμα τὸ ἅγιον·
   σήμερον ἐὰν τῆς φωνῆς αὐτοῦ ἀκούσητε,
 8 μὴ σκληρύνητε τὰς καρδίας ὑμῶν ὡς ἐν τῷ παραπικρασμῷ
   κατὰ τὴν ἡμέραν τοῦ πειρασμοῦ ἐν τῇ ἐρήμῳ,
 9 οὗ ἐπείρασαν ⊤ οἱ πατέρες ὑμῶν ⌐ἐν δοκιμασίᾳ⌐
   καὶ εἶδον τὰ ἔργα μου 10 τεσσεράκοντα ἔτη·
 διὸ προσώχθισα τῇ γενεᾷ ⌐ταύτῃ
   καὶ εἶπον· ἀεὶ πλανῶνται ⌐τῇ καρδίᾳ,
 αὐτοὶ δὲ⌐ οὐκ ἔγνωσαν τὰς ὁδούς μου,
   11 ὡς ὤμοσα ἐν τῇ ὀργῇ μου·
 εἰ εἰσελεύσονται εἰς τὴν κατάπαυσίν μου.

Psalm 95:7–11; v. 7d MT = LXX (94:7d) = Heb 3:7b (A)

v. 8 MT = LXX = Heb 3:8.

v. 9a MT = LXX = Heb 3:9a. (A)

v. 9b MT בְּחָנוּנִי גַּם־רָאוּ פָעֳלִי = LXX ἐδοκίμασαν (without με) καὶ εἴδοσαν τὰ ἔργα μου (plural!); Heb 3:9b ἐν δοκιμασίᾳ ("by the way of testing"—no με object!) καὶ εἶδον τὰ ἔργα μου. There may have been a textual error in the LXX tradition, yet ἐν δοκιμασίᾳ is not as close to בְּחָנוּנִי as is ἐδοκίμασαν. (Bᵃ)

v. 10a MT almost = LXX except that it has no demonstrative with τῇ γενεᾷ (בְּדוֹר alone in LXX = Heb 3:10a with its ταύτῃ after γενεᾷ). (B)

v. 10b MT = LXX = Heb 3:10b. (A)

v. 10c MT = LXX = Heb 3:10c. (A)

v. 11 MT = LXX = Heb 3:10d. (A)

*b*Heb 3:15

15 ἐν τῷ λέγεσθαι·
   σήμερον ἐὰν τῆς φωνῆς αὐτοῦ ἀκούσητε,

Note that Heb 3:15 contains only Psalm 95:7b but is (A).

*c*Heb 4:7

7 πάλιν τινὰ ὁρίζει ἡμέραν, σή-
μερον, ἐν Δαυὶδ λέγων μετὰ τοσοῦτον χρόνον, καθὼς
⌐προείρηται·
   σήμερον ἐὰν τῆς φωνῆς αὐτοῦ ἀκούσητε,
   μὴ σκληρύνητε τὰς καρδίας ὑμῶν.

Also, Heb 4:7 contains only Psalm 95:7b–8a but is (A).

*d*Heb 4:3, 5

3 ⌐Εἰσερχόμεθα ⌐γὰρ εἰς ᵒ[τὴν] κατάπαυσιν οἱ
πιστεύσαντες, καθὼς εἴρηκεν·
   ὡς ὤμοσα ἐν τῇ ὀργῇ μου·
   ᵒ¹εἰ εἰσελεύσονται εἰς τὴν κατάπαυσίν μου,
καίτοι τῶν ἔργων ἀπὸ καταβολῆς κόσμου γενηθέντων.
5 καὶ ἐν τούτῳ πάλιν· ⌐εἰ εἰσελεύσονται εἰς
   τὴν κατάπαυσίν μου.

*a*Heb 1:10–12

10 καί·
   σὺ κατ' ἀρχάς, κύριε, τὴν γῆν ἐθεμελίωσας,
   καὶ ἔργα τῶν χειρῶν σού εἰσιν οἱ οὐρανοί·
 11 αὐτοὶ ἀπολοῦνται, σὺ δὲ ⌐διαμένεις,
   καὶ πάντες ὡς ἱμάτιον παλαιωθήσονται,

Psalm 102:26–28 (25–27); v. 26a MT = LXX (101:26a) except that LXX inserts κύριε, as does Heb 1:10a. (A)

v. 26b MT = LXX except that LXX uses plural ἔργα for MT's מַעֲשֵׂה יָדֶיךָ. (A)

180 (continued)

181: Psalm 104:4

‏׃י עֹשֶׂה מַלְאָכָיו רוּחֹות   מְשָׁרְתָיו אֵשׁ לֹהֵט

(Psalm 103:4)

4 ὁ ποιῶν τοὺς ἀγγέλους αὐτοῦ πνεύματα
καὶ τοὺς λειτουργοὺς αὐτοῦ πῦρ φλέγον.

182: Psalm 104:12

‏׃יב עֲלֵיהֶם עֹוף־הַשָּׁמַיִם יִשְׁכֹּון   מִבֵּין עֳפָאיִם יִתְּנוּ־קֹול

(Psalm 103:12)

12 ἐπ' αὐτὰ τὰ πετεινὰ τοῦ οὐρανοῦ κατασκηνώσει,
ἐκ μέσου τῶν πετρῶν δώσουσιν φωνήν.

183: Psalm 107:26

see Deut 9:4 [92]

184: Psalm 109:8

see Psalm 69:26 [169]

Heb 1:10–12 (continued)

12 καὶ ὡσεὶ περιβόλαιον ⌐ἑλίξεις αὐτούς,
□ὡς ἱμάτιον⌐ καὶ ἀλλαγήσονται·
σὺ δὲ ὁ αὐτὸς εἶ καὶ τὰ ἔτη σου οὐκ ἐκλείψουσιν.

v. 27a MT = LXX = NT except that the editor has pointed the LXX future (διαμενεῖς) and Heb 1:11a is διαμένεις, but accents are of late origin! (*A*)

v. 27b MT = LXX except that יִבְלוּ = "wear out/away," and παλαιωθήσονται = "will wax old" = Heb 1:11b. (*A*ᵈ) or (*B*)

v. 27c MT = LXX (תַּחֲלִיפֵם = ἀλλάξεις αὐτούς), but Heb 1:12 has deviated from LXX as follows: LXX ἀλλάξεις ("wilt change them"), NT ἑλίξεις ("roll them up"). Note that ἑλίξεις could have been a scribal auditory error for ἀλλάξεις, but since ℵ* D* read ἀλλάξεις (and likewise Vulg.ᶜˡᵉᵐ·) the original reading in Heb 1:12 is debatable. (*B*ᵃ)

v. 27c (cont.); the rest of Heb 1:12b = LXX = MT. (*A*)

v. 28 MT = LXX = Heb 1:12c. Note יִתָּמּוּ = ἐκλείψουσιν "shall come to an end"/"will fail/be lacking/peter out"). (*A*)

ᵃHeb 1:7

7 καὶ πρὸς μὲν τοὺς ἀγγέλους ⌐ λέγει·
ὁ ποιῶν τοὺς ἀγγέλους αὐτοῦ ⌐πνεύματα
καὶ τοὺς λειτουργοὺς αὐτοῦ πυρὸς φλόγα,

Psalm 104:4; MT אֵשׁ לֹהֵט = LXX (103:4) πῦρ φλέγνον = Heb 1:7 πυρὸς φλόγα, which is a close paraphrase. (*A*ᵈ)

ᵃMt 13:32

32 ὃ μικρότε-
ρον μέν ἐστιν πάντων τῶν σπερμάτων, ὅταν δὲ ⌐αὐξηθῇ
μεῖζον τῶν λαχάνων ἐστὶν καὶ γίνεται δένδρον, ὥστε ἐλθεῖν τὰ πετεινὰ τοῦ οὐρανοῦ καὶ κατασκηνοῦν ἐν τοῖς κλάδοις αὐτοῦ.

Psalm 104:12-Mt 13:32; Mk 4:32; Lk 13:19; LXX's (103:12) πετρῶν is wrong for עֳפָאִים, but NT correctly renders it as κλάδους. (*F*/*C*)

ᵇMk 4:32

32 καὶ ὅταν
σπαρῇ, ἀναβαίνει καὶ γίνεται ⌐μεῖζον πάντων τῶν λαχά-
νων⌐ καὶ ποιεῖ κλάδους μεγάλους, ὥστε δύνασθαι ὑπὸ
τὴν σκιὰν αὐτοῦ τὰ πετεινὰ τοῦ οὐρανοῦ κατασκηνοῦν.

ᶜLk 13:19

19 ὁμοία ἐστὶν κόκκῳ σινάπεως,
ὃν λαβὼν ἄνθρωπος ἔβαλεν εἰς ⌐ κῆπον ⌐ἑαυτοῦ, καὶ ηὔ-
ξησεν καὶ ἐγένετο εἰς δένδρονᵀ, καὶ τὰ πετεινὰ τοῦ οὐρανοῦ κατεσκήνωσεν ἐν τοῖς κλάδοις αὐτοῦ.

185: Psalm 110:1 (see also Dan 7:13 [284],f–k)

(Psalm 109:1)

ᵃ לְדָוִ֗ד מִ֫זְמ֥וֹר

נְאֻ֤ם יְהֹוָ֨ה ׀ לַֽאדֹנִ֗י שֵׁ֥ב לִֽימִינִ֑י

עַד־אָשִׁ֥ית אֹ֝יְבֶ֗יךָ הֲדֹ֣ם לְרַגְלֶֽיךָ׃

1   Τῷ Δαυιδ ψαλμός.
Εἶπεν ὁ κύριος τῷ κυρίῳ μου Κάθου ἐκ δεξιῶν μου,
ἕως ἂν θῶ τοὺς ἐχθρούς σου ὑποπόδιον τῶν ποδῶν **σου.**

𝕾

¹³ ἐθεώρουν ἐν ὁράματι τῆς νυκτὸς καὶ ἰδοὺ
ἐπὶ τῶν νεφελῶν τοῦ οὐρανοῦ ὡς υἱὸς ἀνθρώπου ἤρχετο, καὶ ὡς
παλαιὸς ἡμερῶν παρῆν, καὶ οἱ παρεστηκότες παρῆσαν αὐτῷ.

θ´

¹³ ἐθε-
ώρουν ἐν ὁράματι τῆς νυκτὸς καὶ ἰδοὺ μετὰ τῶν νεφελῶν τοῦ
οὐρανοῦ ὡς υἱὸς ἀνθρώπου ἐρχόμενος ἦν καὶ ἕως τοῦ παλαιοῦ
τῶν ἡμερῶν ἔφθασεν καὶ ἐνώπιον αὐτοῦ προσηνέχθη.

186: Psalm 110:4

(Psalm 109:4)

⁴ נִשְׁבַּ֤ע יְהֹוָ֨ה ׀ וְלֹ֥א יִנָּחֵ֗ם

אַתָּֽה־כֹהֵ֥ן לְעוֹלָ֑ם עַל־דִּ֝בְרָתִ֗י מַלְכִּי־צֶֽדֶק׃

4 ὤμοσεν κύριος καὶ οὐ μεταμεληθήσεται
Σὺ εἶ ἱερεὺς εἰς τὸν αἰῶνα κατὰ τὴν τάξιν Μελχισεδεκ.

*a*Mt 22:44

44 εἶπεν ⊤ κύριος τῷ κυρίῳ μου·
κάθου ἐκ δεξιῶν μου,
ἕως ἂν θῶ τοὺς ἐχθρούς σου
⌜ὑποκάτω τῶν ποδῶν σου⌝;

*b*Mk 12:36

36 αὐτὸς ⊤ Δαυὶδ εἶπεν ἐν τῷ πνεύματι
τῷ ἁγίῳ·
εἶπεν ⊤ κύριος τῷ κυρίῳ μου·
⌜κάθου ἐκ δεξιῶν μου,
ἕως ἂν θῶ τοὺς ἐχθρούς σου
⌜ὑποκάτω τῶν ποδῶν σου.

*c*Lk 20:42–43

42 ⌜αὐτὸς γὰρ⌝ Δαυὶδ λέγει ἐν ⌜βίβλῳ
ψαλμῶν·
⌜εἶπεν ⊤ κύριος τῷ κυρίῳ μου·
κάθου ἐκ δεξιῶν μου,
43 ἕως ἂν θῶ τοὺς ἐχθρούς σου
⌜ὑποπόδιον τῶν ποδῶν σου.

*d*Acts 2:34–35

34 οὐ
γὰρ Δαυὶδ ἀνέβη εἰς τοὺς οὐρανούς, λέγει δὲ αὐτός·
εἶπεν ᵒ[ὁ] κύριος τῷ κυρίῳ μου· κάθου ἐκ δεξιῶν μου,
35 ἕως ἂν θῶ τοὺς ἐχθρούς σου ὑποπόδιον τῶν ποδῶν σου.

*e*Heb 1:13

13 πρὸς τίνα δὲ τῶν ἀγγέλων εἴρηκέν ποτε·
κάθου ἐκ δεξιῶν μου,
ἕως ἂν θῶ τοὺς ἐχθρούς σου ὑποπόδιον τῶν ποδῶν σου;

Psalm 110:1; MT = LXX (109:1) = Mt 22:44 and Mk 12:36 except that NT uses ὑποκάτω for LXX's ὑποπόδιον = הֲדֹם; W + 0102^Athos vii cent. read ὑποπόδιον. (*A*^d)

---

*a*Heb 5:6, 10

6 καθὼς καὶ ἐν ἑτέρῳ λέγει·
σὺ ⊤ ἱερεὺς εἰς τὸν αἰῶνα κατὰ τὴν τάξιν Μελχισέδεκ,

10 προσαγορευθεὶς ὑπὸ τοῦ θεοῦ ἀρχιερεὺς κατὰ τὴν τάξιν Μελχισέδεκ.

*b*Heb 7:17, 21

17 ⌜μαρτυρεῖται γὰρ ὅτι
σὺ ⊤ ἱερεὺς εἰς τὸν αἰῶνα κατὰ τὴν τάξιν Μελχισέδεκ.

21 ὁ δὲ μετὰ
ὁρκωμοσίας διὰ τοῦ λέγοντος πρὸς αὐτόν·
ὤμοσεν κύριος καὶ οὐ μεταμεληθήσεται·
σὺ ⊤ ἱερεὺς εἰς τὸν αἰῶνα ⊤.

Psalm 110:4a; MT = LXX (109:4a) = Heb 7:21 (*A*). Note that דִּבְרָה = (1) cause, reason, (2) manner = τάξιν, which is reasonably equivalent and meaningful. (*A*-)

Psalm 110:4b; MT = LXX = Heb 5:6 = Heb 7:17. (*A*)

187: Psalm 111:2

(Psalm 110:2)

(ג) ² גְּדֹלִים מַעֲשֵׂי יְהוָה

(ד) דְּרוּשִׁים לְכָל־חֶפְצֵיהֶם׃

2 μεγάλα τὰ ἔργα κυρίου,
ἐξεζητημένα εἰς πάντα τὰ θελήματα αὐτοῦ·

Deut 32:4

⁴ הַצּוּר תָּמִים פָּעֳלוֹ   כִּי כָל־דְּרָכָיו מִשְׁפָּט

אֵל אֱמוּנָה וְאֵין עָוֶל   צַדִּיק וְיָשָׁר הוּא׃

⁴ θεός, ἀληθινὰ τὰ ἔργα αὐτοῦ,
καὶ πᾶσαι αἱ ὁδοὶ αὐτοῦ κρίσεις·
θεὸς πιστός, καὶ οὐκ ἔστιν ἀδικία,
δίκαιος καὶ ὅσιος κύριος.

Jer 10:6

⁶ מֵאֵין כָּמוֹךָ יְהוָה   גָּדוֹל אַתָּה

וְגָדוֹל שִׁמְךָ בִּגְבוּרָה׃

Psalm 145:17

(Psalm 144:17)

(צ) ¹⁷ צַדִּיק יְהוָה בְּכָל־דְּרָכָיו   וְחָסִיד בְּכָל־מַעֲשָׂיו׃

17 δίκαιος κύριος ἐν πάσαις ταῖς ὁδοῖς αὐτοῦ
καὶ ὅσιος ἐν πᾶσιν τοῖς ἔργοις αὐτοῦ.

Amos 3:13

(Amos 4:13)

¹³ שִׁמְעוּ וְהָעִידוּ בְּבֵית יַעֲקֹב נְאֻם־אֲדֹנָי יְהוִה אֱלֹהֵי הַצְּבָאוֹת׃

¹³ διότι ἰδοὺ ἐγὼ στερεῶν βροντὴν καὶ κτίζων πνεῦμα καὶ ἀπαγγέλλων εἰς ἀνθρώπους τὸν χριστὸν αὐτοῦ, ποιῶν ὄρθρον καὶ ὁμίχλην καὶ ἐπιβαίνων ἐπὶ τὰ ὕψη τῆς γῆς· κύριος ὁ θεὸς ὁ παντοκράτωρ ὄνομα αὐτῷ.

188: Psalm 112:9

(Psalm 111:9)

(פ) ⁹ פִּזַּר נָתַן לָאֶבְיוֹנִים

(צ) צִדְקָתוֹ עֹמֶדֶת לָעַד

(ק) קַרְנוֹ תָּרוּם בְּכָבוֹד׃

9 ἐσκόρπισεν, ἔδωκεν τοῖς πένησιν·
ἡ δικαιοσύνη αὐτοῦ μένει εἰς τὸν αἰῶνα τοῦ αἰῶνος,
τὸ κέρας αὐτοῦ ὑψωθήσεται ἐν δόξῃ.

189: Psalm 116:10

(Psalm 115:1)

¹⁰ הֶאֱמַנְתִּי כִּי אֲדַבֵּר   אֲנִי עָנִיתִי מְאֹד׃

1   Αλληλουια.
Ἐπίστευσα, διὸ ἐλάλησα·
ἐγὼ δὲ ἐταπεινώθην σφόδρα.

190: Psalm 117:1

(Psalm 116:1)

¹ הַלְלוּ אֶת־יְהוָה כָּל־גּוֹיִם   שַׁבְּחוּהוּ כָּל־הָאֻמִּים׃

1   Αλληλουια.
Αἰνεῖτε τὸν κύριον, πάντα τὰ ἔθνη,
ἐπαινέσατε αὐτόν, πάντες οἱ λαοί,

191: Psalm 118:6

(Psalm 117:6)

⁶ יְהוָה לִי לֹא אִירָא   מַה־יַּעֲשֶׂה לִי אָדָם׃

6 κύριος ἐμοὶ βοηθός,
οὐ φοβηθήσομαι τί ποιήσει μοι ἄνθρωπος.

*a*Rev 15:3–4   (see also [173])

3 καὶ ⌜ᾄδουσιν τὴν ᾠδὴν Μωϋσέως ᵒτοῦ
δούλου τοῦ θεοῦ καὶ τὴν ᾠδὴν τοῦ ἀρνίου λέγοντες·
  μεγάλα καὶ θαυμαστὰ τὰ ἔργα σου,
  κύριε ὁ θεὸς ὁ παντοκράτωρ·
  δίκαιαι καὶ ἀληθιναὶ αἱ ὁδοί σου,
  ⌜ὁ βασιλεὺς⌝ τῶν ⌜ἐθνῶν·
  4 τίς ᵀ οὐ ᵒμὴ φοβηθῇ, κύριε,
  καὶ ⌜δοξάσει τὸ ὄνομά σου;
  ὅτι μόνος ⌜ὅσιος,
  ὅτι ⌜πάντα τὰ ἔθνη⌝ ἥξουσιν
  καὶ προσκυνήσουσιν ἐνώπιόν σου,
  ὅτι τὰ δικαιώματά ᵀ σου ἐφανερώθησαν.

Psalm 111:2 contributes to Rev 15:3 μεγάλα τὰ ἔργα σου.

Jer 10:6 contributes ὁ βασιλεὺς τῶν ἐθνῶν (MT: מֶלֶךְ הַגּוֹיִם). (*F*)

Psalm 145:17 contributes δίκαιος ἐν ταῖς ὁδοῖς αὐτοῦ (δίκαιαι οἱ ὁδοί σου);

Amos 3:13 contributes the phrase "The Lord God, the Almighty," which begins the second line in Rev 15:3, expressed as a vocative: "O Lord, God, the Almighty."

---

*a*2 Cor 9:9

9 καθὼς γέγραπται·
  ἐσκόρπισεν, ἔδωκεν τοῖς πένησιν,
  ἡ δικαιοσύνη αὐτοῦ μένει εἰς τὸν αἰῶναᵀ.

Psalm 112:9; MT = LXX (111:9, with the addition of τοῦ αἰῶνος) = 2 Cor 9:9 (without τοῦ αἰῶνος). (*C*)

---

*a*2 Cor 4:13

13 Ἔχοντες δὲ τὸ αὐτὸ πνεῦμα τῆς πίστεως κατὰ
τὸ γεγραμμένον· ἐπίστευσα, διὸ ᵀ ἐλάλησα, καὶ ἡμεῖς πι-
στεύομεν, διὸ καὶ λαλοῦμεν,

Psalm 116:10; MT (with כִּי before אֲדַבֵּר) = LXX (115:1) (כִּי = διό) = 2 Cor 4:13 (also διό; in this case כִּי must be asseverative "Surely . . . ." But it is reasonable for the LXX to pick up a causal equivalent here, since the speaking surely ensues from the believing). (*A*ᵈ)

---

*a*Rom 15:11

11 καὶ πάλινᵀ·
  αἰνεῖτε, πάντα τὰ ἔθνη, τὸν κύριον
  καὶ ⌜ἐπαινεσάτωσαν αὐτὸν πάντες οἱ λαοί.

Psalm 117:1; MT = LXX (116:1) = Rom 15:11 except that the third plural imperative ἐπαινεσάτωσαν is used instead of second plural imperative αἰνεῖτε. (*A*ᵈ)

---

*a*Heb 13:6

6 ὥστε θαρ-
ροῦντας ἡμᾶς λέγειν·
  κύριος ἐμοὶ βοηθός, ᵒ[καὶ] οὐ φοβηθήσομαι,
  τί ποιήσει μοι ἄνθρωπος;

Psalm 118:6; MT has merely יהוה לִי ("Yahweh is for me"). LXX (117:6) brings out a more specific role for God: ἐμοὶ βοηθός ("a *Helper* to me"). Heb 13:6 follows LXX in this βοηθός. *BH* notes that the Peshitta also implies בְּעֹזְרִי. (*B*)

192: Psalm 118:22–23

(Psalm 117:22–23)

²² אֶבֶן מָאֲסוּ הַבּוֹנִים הָיְתָה לְרֹאשׁ פִּנָּה:
²³ מֵאֵת יְהוָה הָיְתָה זֹּאת הִיא נִפְלָאת בְּעֵינֵינוּ:

22 λίθον, ὃν ἀπεδοκίμασαν οἱ οἰκοδομοῦντες,
   οὗτος ἐγενήθη εἰς κεφαλὴν γωνίας·
23 παρὰ κυρίου ἐγένετο αὕτη
   καὶ ἔστιν θαυμαστὴ ἐν ὀφθαλμοῖς ἡμῶν.

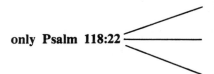

only Psalm 118:22

193: Psalm 118:25–26   (see also [130])

(Psalm 117:25–26)

²⁵ אָנָּא יְהוָה הוֹשִׁיעָה נָּא אָנָּא יְהוָה הַצְלִיחָה נָּא:
²⁶ בָּרוּךְ הַבָּא בְּשֵׁם יְהוָה בֵּרַכְנוּכֶם מִבֵּית יְהוָה:

25 ὦ κύριε, σῶσον δή,
   ὦ κύριε, εὐόδωσον δή.
26 εὐλογημένος ὁ ἐρχόμενος ἐν ὀνόματι κυρίου·
   εὐλογήκαμεν ὑμᾶς ἐξ οἴκου κυρίου.

ᵃMt 21:42

42 Λέγει αὐτοῖς ὁ Ἰησοῦς· οὐδέποτε ἀνέγνωτε ἐν ταῖς γραφαῖς·
> λίθον ὃν ἀπεδοκίμασαν οἱ οἰκοδομοῦντες,
> οὗτος ἐγενήθη εἰς κεφαλὴν γωνίας·
> παρὰ κυρίου ἐγένετο αὕτη
> καὶ ἔστιν θαυμαστὴ ἐν ὀφθαλμοῖς ⌐ἡμῶν;

ᵇMk 12:10–11

10 οὐδὲ τὴν γραφὴν ταύτην ἀνέγνωτε·
> λίθον ὃν ἀπεδοκίμασαν οἱ οἰκοδομοῦντες,
> οὗτος ἐγενήθη εἰς κεφαλὴν γωνίας·
11 παρὰ κυρίου ἐγένετο αὕτη
> καὶ ἔστιν θαυμαστὴ ἐν ὀφθαλμοῖς ἡμῶν;

ᶜLk 20:17

17 ὁ δὲ ἐμβλέψας
αὐτοῖς εἶπεν· τί οὖν ἐστιν τὸ γεγραμμένον τοῦτο·
> λίθον ὃν ἀπεδοκίμασαν οἱ οἰκοδομοῦντες,
> οὗτος ἐγενήθη εἰς κεφαλὴν γωνίας;

ᵈActs 4:11

11 οὗτός
ἐστιν ὁ λίθος, ὁ ἐξουθενηθεὶς ὑφ' ὑμῶν τῶν οἰκοδόμων,
ὁ γενόμενος εἰς κεφαλὴν γωνίας.

ᵉ1 Pet 2:7

7 ὑμῖν οὖν ἡ τιμὴ τοῖς πιστεύουσιν, ⌐ἀπιστοῦσιν δὲ ⌐λίθος
ὃν ἀπεδοκίμασαν οἱ οἰκοδομοῦντες, οὗτος ἐγενήθη εἰς κεφαλὴν γωνίας

Psalm 118:22–23; MT = LXX (117:22–23) = (1) Mt 21:42, (2) Mk 12:10–11, (3) Lk 20:17 (quotes only 118:22 but is identical in wording), (4) Acts 4:11 (likewise), and (5) 1 Pet 2:7 (likewise). (*A*)

ᵃMt 21:9

9 οἱ δὲ ὄχλοι οἱ προ-
άγοντες ᵒαὐτὸν καὶ οἱ ἀκολουθοῦντες ἔκραζον λέγοντες·
> ὡσαννὰ τῷ υἱῷ Δαυίδ·
> εὐλογημένος ὁ ἐρχόμενος ἐν ὀνόματι κυρίου·
> ὡσαννὰ ἐν τοῖς ὑψίστοις.ᵀ

ᵇMk 11:9–10

9 καὶ οἱ προάγοντες καὶ οἱ ἀκολουθοῦντες ἔκραζον· ᵀ
> ⌐ὡσαννά·
> εὐλογημένος ὁ ἐρχόμενος ἐν ὀνόματι κυρίου·
10 εὐλογημένη ἡ ἐρχομένη βασιλεία τοῦ πατρὸς ἡ-
μῶν Δαυίδ·
> ⌐ὡσαννὰ ἐν τοῖς ὑψίστοις.

Psalm 118:25–26; v. 25a אָנָּא יהוה הוֹשִׁיעָה נָּא; LXX (117:25a) ὦ κύριε, σῶσον δή; Mt 21:9 ὡσαννὰ (τῷ υἱῷ Δαυίδ), which is simply transcribing what the crowd called out in Hebrew.

v. 25b; אָנָּא יהוה הַצְלִיחָה נָּא; LXX ὦ κύριε, εὐόδωσον δή.

v. 26a; בָּרוּךְ הַבָּא בְּשֵׁם יהוה = LXX εὐλογημένος ὁ ἐρχόμενος ἐν ὀνόματι κυρίου + ἐν ὑψίστοις. (1) Mt 21:9 (same as LXX followed by ὡσαννά); (2) Mk 11:9 has the same ὡσαννά . . . κυρίου + ὡσαννά; (3) John 12:13 has the same ὡσαννά + βασιλεὺς τοῦ Ἰσραήλ, which is not part of the quotation. (*A*)

193 (continued)

only Psalm 118:26

194: Psalm 132:11

11 נִשְׁבַּע־יְהוָה ׀ לְדָוִד אֱמֶת֘ לֹֽא־יָשׁ֢וּב מִמֶּ֥נָּה
מִפְּרִ֥י בִטְנְךָ֑ אָ֝שִׁ֗ית לְכִסֵּא־לָֽךְ׃

(Psalm 131:11)

11 ὤμοσεν κύριος τῷ Δαυιδ ἀλήθειαν καὶ οὐ μὴ ἀθετήσει αὐτήν
Ἐκ καρποῦ τῆς κοιλίας σου θήσομαι ἐπὶ τὸν θρόνον σου·

195: Psalm 135:14

see Deut 32:35–36 [114]

196: Psalm 140:4 (140:3)

see Psalm 5:10 [136]

197: Psalm 145:17

see Psalm 111:2 [187]

198: Psalm 148:1

see Job 16:19 [130]

*c*Jn 12:13

13 Ἔλαβον τὰ βαΐα τῶν φοινίκων καὶ ἐξῆλθον εἰς ὑπάντη-
σιν αὐτῷ καὶ ⌜ἐκραύγαζον⌝·
ὡσαννά·
εὐλογημένος ὁ ἐρχόμενος ἐν ὀνόματι κυρίου,
⌜[καὶ] ὁ⌝ βασιλεὺς τοῦ Ἰσραήλ.

*d*Mt 23:39

39 λέγω γὰρ ὑμῖν, οὐ μή με ἴδητε ἀπ'
ἄρτι ἕως ἂν εἴπητε·
εὐλογημένος ὁ ἐρχόμενος ἐν ὀνόματι κυρίου.

*e*Lk 13:35

35 ἰδοὺ ἀφίεται ὑμῖν ὁ οἶκος ὑμῶν⌐. λέγω
○[δὲ] ὑμῖν, ⌐ οὐ μὴ ⌐ἴδητέ με⌐ ἕως ⌜[ἥξει ὅτε]⌝ εἴπητε·
εὐλογημένος ὁ ἐρχόμενος ἐν ὀνόματι κυρίου.

*f*Lk 19:38

38 λέγοντες·
εὐλογημένος ὁ ⌜ἐρχόμενος,
ὁ βασιλεὺς⌝ ἐν ὀνόματι κυρίου⌐·
⌐ἐν οὐρανῷ εἰρήνη⌐
καὶ δόξα ἐν ὑψίστοις.

Three additional NT passages also have only εὐλογημένος . . . κυρίου, all (*A*): Mt 23:39; Lk 13:35; 19:38,
which inserts ὁ βασιλεύς after ἐρχόμενος and before
ἐν ὀνόματι, thus confirming the John 12:13 report that
Jesus was actually hailed as messianic King by the
welcoming throng on Palm Sunday.

---

*a*Acts 2:30

30 προφήτης οὖν ὑπάρχων καὶ εἰδὼς ὅτι
ὅρκῳ ὤμοσεν αὐτῷ ὁ θεὸς ἐκ καρποῦ τῆς ⌜ὀσφύος αὐτοῦ⌐
καθίσαι ἐπὶ τὸν θρόνον αὐτοῦ,

Psalm 132:11; MT נִשְׁבַּע־יהוה לְדָוִד . . . מִפְּרִי בִטְנְךָ אָשִׁית
לְכִסֵּא־לָךְ; Acts 2:30 ὤμοσεν αὐτῷ ὁ θεὸς ἐκ καρποῦ τῆς
ὀσφύος αὐτοῦ καθίσαι ἐπὶ τὸν θρόνον αὐτοῦ. (*F*)

The NT puts into third person singular what the MT
has in second person singular masculine. That does not
purport to be a direct quotation, but a summary of the
substance of Psalm 132:11 and 2 Sam 7:13. Yet allusive
or summary as it is, the words used are quite close.
Θεός refers to יהוה and ὀσφύς is used for בֶּטֶן, perhaps
because κοιλία sounded a bit strange in the minds of
the Greeks as a term for the seat of man's generative
power.

199: Prov 3:11–12

‏11 מוּסַ֣ר יְהוָה בְּנִ֣י אַל־תִּמְאָ֑ס וְאַל־תָּ֝קֹ֗ץ בְּתוֹכַחְתּֽוֹ׃
‏12 כִּ֤י אֶ֥ת אֲשֶׁ֣ר יֶאֱהַ֣ב יְהוָ֣ה יוֹכִ֑יחַ וּ֝כְאָ֗ב אֶת־בֵּ֥ן יִרְצֶֽה׃

11 Υἱέ, μὴ ὀλιγώρει παιδείας κυρίου
    μηδὲ ἐκλύου ὑπ' αὐτοῦ ἐλεγχόμενος·
12 ὃν γὰρ ἀγαπᾷ κύριος παιδεύει,
    μαστιγοῖ δὲ πάντα υἱὸν ὃν παραδέχεται.

200: Prov 3:34

‏34 אִם־לַלֵּצִ֥ים הֽוּא־יָלִ֑יץ וְ֝לַעֲנָיִ֗ים יִתֶּן־חֵֽן׃

34 κύριος ὑπερηφάνοις ἀντιτάσσεται,
    ταπεινοῖς δὲ δίδωσιν χάριν.

201: Prov 11:31

‏31 הֵ֤ן צַדִּ֣יק בָּאָ֣רֶץ יְשֻׁלָּ֑ם אַ֝ף כִּי־רָשָׁ֥ע וְחוֹטֵֽא׃

31 εἰ ὁ μὲν δίκαιος μόλις σῴζεται,
    ὁ ἀσεβὴς καὶ ἁμαρτωλὸς ποῦ φανεῖται;

NEW TESTAMENT	COMMENTARY
^aHeb 12:5–6	

^aHeb 12:5–6

5 καὶ ἐκλέλησθε τῆς παρα-
κλήσεως, ἥτις ὑμῖν ὡς υἱοῖς διαλέγεται·
  υἱέ ^ομου, μὴ ὀλιγώρει παιδείας κυρίου
  ⌐μηδὲ ἐκλύου ὑπ᾽ αὐτοῦ ἐλεγχόμενος·
6 ὃν γὰρ ἀγαπᾷ κύριος παιδεύει,
  μαστιγοῖ δὲ πάντα υἱὸν ὃν παραδέχεται.

Prov 3:11–12; MT תָּקֹץ (G42) from קוּץ "feel a loathing/ abhorrence" for which ἐκλύεσθαι is not too accurate; this is the only time קוּץ is so rendered in the LXX (cf. Schl., 718A). MT is treated a bit freely by LXX; MT: (1) אַל־תָּקֹץ "do not abhor" = μηδὲ ἐκλύου "don't be disheartened"; (2) παιδεύει "chastens, educates" = יוֹכִיחַ "rebukes"; (3) וּכְאָב is read as וְכָאַב (Dc 10, from כָּאַב "disciplines, trains"—"be in pain")), which, however, has no *Piel* in Biblical Hebrew, but only *Hiphil*. Thus MT's "even like a father" becomes "and he pains/hurts/ grieves" (μαστιγοῖ "flogs"). The principal variation from MT rests upon a possible (though unlikely) vowel pointing. (*B*)

^aJas 4:6

6 μείζονα δὲ δί-
δωσιν χάριν; διὸ λέγει·
  ὁ θεὸς ὑπερηφάνοις ἀντιτάσσεται,
  ταπεινοῖς δὲ δίδωσιν χάριν.

^b1 Pet 5:5

5 Ὁμοίως [⊤],
νεώτεροι, ὑποτάγητε πρεσβυτέροις· πάντες δὲ ⌐ἀλλή-
λοις⌐ τὴν ταπεινοφροσύνην ἐγκομβώσασθε, ὅτι ^ο[ὁ] θεὸς
ὑπερηφάνοις ἀντιτάσσεται, ταπεινοῖς δὲ δίδωσιν χάριν.

Prov 3:34; MT = LXX except that: (1) לֵצִים is "scoffers/ cynics" rather than ὑπερηφάνοις "the proud" (also in Isa 29:20). Schl. (332A) comments: *Causam pro effectu posuerunt:* (2) יָלִיץ becomes ἀντιτάσσεται; i.e., "God mocks" or "opposes," which is hardly correct of justified.

Jas 4:6 and 1 Pet 5:5 follow LXX except that they use θεός rather than LXX's κύριος (for יהוה). (*B*)

^a1 Pet 4:18

18 καὶ εἰ ὁ [⊤] δίκαιος μόλις σῴζεται, ὁ ⌐ἀσεβὴς καὶ ἁμαρτωλός⌐ ποῦ φανεῖται;

Prov 11:31; v. 31a MT הֵן צַדִּיק בָּאָרֶץ יְשֻׁלָּם, LXX: (1) εἰ (rather than ἰδού) ὁ μὲν δίκαιος μόλις σῴζεται: (2) μόλις seems to replace בארץ (rather than ἐν τῇ χώρᾳ): (3) σῴζεται is wrong for יְשֻׁלָּם "meets retribution/ is requited" (LXX thought שֻׁלָּם could mean "bring into peace/safety"; only in Job 8:6 does it mean "make safe" [*BDB*, 1022B], and that is clearly not the thought involved in this context). Here is a case of a poorly rendered LXX passage adopted without change in NT (1 Pet 4:18). (*B*)

v. 31b MT אַף כִּי־רָשָׁע וְחוֹטֵא ("How much rather the ungodly and the sinner?"); LXX (= NT) ὁ ἀσεβὴς καὶ ἁμαρτωλὸς ποῦ φανεῖται "Where shall the ungodly and the sinners appear?" This deviation is hardly justifiable, but the basic thrust of the verse remains the same—the certainty of God's judgment on the wicked and un- believing, though He holds even sincere believers ac- countable for their comparatively minor offenses—an *a minori* argument that fits in perfectly with the context of 1 Pet 4:18. (*E*)

202: Prov 24:12

see Psalm 62:13 [164]

203: Prov 25:21–22

²¹ אִם־רָעֵב שֹׂנַאֲךָ הַאֲכִלֵהוּ לָחֶם ˣ וְאִם־צָמֵא הַשְׁקֵהוּ מָיִם ᵇ :

²² כִּי גֶחָלִים אַתָּה חֹתֶה עַל־רֹאשׁוֹ ᵇ וַיהוָה יְשַׁלֶּם־לָךְ :

21 ἐὰν πεινᾷ ὁ ἐχθρός σου, τρέφε αὐτόν,
   ἐὰν διψᾷ, πότιζε αὐτόν ·

22 τοῦτο γὰρ ποιῶν ἄνθρακας πυρὸς σωρεύσεις ἐπὶ τὴν
   κεφαλὴν αὐτοῦ,
   ὁ δὲ κύριος ἀνταποδώσει σοι ἀγαθά.

204: Prov 26:11

¹¹ כְּכֶלֶב שָׁב עַל־קֵאוֹ כְּסִיל שׁוֹנֶה בְאִוַּלְתּוֹ :

11 ὥσπερ κύων ὅταν ἐπέλθῃ ἐπὶ τὸν ἑαυτοῦ ἔμετον καὶ μισητὸς γένηται,
   οὕτως ἄφρων τῇ ἑαυτοῦ κακίᾳ ἀναστρέψας ἐπὶ τὴν
   ἑαυτοῦ ἁμαρτίαν.

11a ἔστιν αἰσχύνη ἐπάγουσα ἁμαρτίαν,
   καὶ ἔστιν αἰσχύνη δόξα καὶ χάρις.

205: Isa 1:9

⁹ לוּלֵי יְהוָה צְבָאוֹת הוֹתִיר לָנוּ שָׂרִיד כִּמְעָט ˣ

כִּסְדֹם הָיִינוּ לַעֲמֹרָה דָּמִינוּ :

9 καὶ εἰ μὴ κύριος
σαβαωθ ἐγκατέλιπεν ἡμῖν σπέρμα, ὡς Σοδομα ἂν ἐγενήθημεν καὶ
ὡς Γομορρα ἂν ὡμοιώθημεν.

206: Isa 6:9–10

⁹ וַיֹּאמֶר לֵךְ וְאָמַרְתָּ לָעָם הַזֶּה

שִׁמְעוּ שָׁמוֹעַ וְאַל־תָּבִינוּ וּרְאוּ רָאוֹ וְאַל־תֵּדָעוּ :

¹⁰ הַשְׁמֵן לֵב־הָעָם הַזֶּה וְאָזְנָיו הַכְבֵּד וְעֵינָיו הָשַׁע

פֶּן־יִרְאֶה בְעֵינָיו וּבְאָזְנָיו יִשְׁמָע וּלְבָבוֹ יָבִין וָשָׁב וְרָפָא לוֹ :

9 καὶ εἶπεν Πορεύθητι
καὶ εἶπον τῷ λαῷ τούτῳ Ἀκοῇ ἀκούσετε καὶ οὐ μὴ συνῆτε καὶ
βλέποντες βλέψετε καὶ οὐ μὴ ἴδητε · 10 ἐπαχύνθη γὰρ ἡ καρδία τοῦ
λαοῦ τούτου, καὶ τοῖς ὠσὶν αὐτῶν βαρέως ἤκουσαν καὶ τοὺς
ὀφθαλμοὺς αὐτῶν ἐκάμμυσαν, μήποτε ἴδωσιν τοῖς ὀφθαλμοῖς καὶ
τοῖς ὠσὶν ἀκούσωσιν καὶ τῇ καρδίᾳ συνῶσιν καὶ ἐπιστρέψωσιν
11 καὶ ἰάσομαι αὐτούς.

*a*Rom 12:20

20 ⌜ἀλλὰ ἐὰν⌝
πεινᾷ ὁ ἐχθρός σου, ψώμιζε αὐτόν· ⌜ἐὰν διψᾷ, πότιζε αὐτόν·
τοῦτο γὰρ ποιῶν ἄνθρακας πυρὸς σωρεύσεις ἐπὶ ⌜τὴν κεφα-
λὴν⌝ αὐτοῦ.

Prov 25:21–22; MT = LXX = Rom 12:20 except that:
(1) MT's הַאֲכִלֵהוּ לֶחֶם is closer to ψώμιζε than LXX's
τρέφε; (2) τοῦτο γὰρ ποιῶν is inserted before כִּי גֶחָלִים
to help the reader understand that the mandate of v. 21
in the previous clause has been adopted/followed by
the agent in v. 22. It is remarkable that Paul so closely
follows LXX in this passage, especially since he does
not introduce it as a quote from earlier Scripture. (*A*[d])
or (*F*)

*a*2 Pet 2:22

22 συμβέβηκεν ᵀ αὐ-
τοῖς τὸ τῆς ἀληθοῦς ⌜παροιμίας· κύων ἐπιστρέψας ἐπὶ
τὸ ἴδιον ἐξέραμα, καί· ὗς λουσαμένη εἰς ⌜κυλισμὸν
βορβόρου.

Prov 26:11; MT = NT but not LXX; MT כְּכֶלֶב שָׁב
עַל־קֵאוֹ, LXX ὥσπερ κύων ὅταν ἐπέλθῃ ἐπὶ τὸν
ἑαυτοῦ ἔμετον (adding καὶ μισητὸς γένηται), 2 Pet 2:22
κύων ἐπιστρέψας ἐπὶ τὸ ἴδιον ἐξέραμα. It looks as if
Peter was translating directly from the MT here, dis-
regarding LXX altogether. His ἐπιστρέψας is much
closer to שָׁב than LXX's ἐπέληθη. (His following statement concerning a washed swine going back to her
wallow has no OT origin at all. It does parallel very
closely the previous statement concerning the dog,
though it may have been only a popular proverb then
current in the Near East.) (*C*)

*a*Rom 9:29

29 καὶ καθὼς προείρηκεν Ἡσαΐας·
εἰ μὴ κύριος σαβαὼθ ἐγκατέλιπεν ἡμῖν σπέρμα,
ὡς Σόδομα ἂν ἐγενήθημεν καὶ ὡς Γόμορρα ἂν ὡ-
μοιώθημεν.

Isa 1:9; MT = LXX = Rom 9:29 except that: (1) שָׂרִיד
"escaped remnant" is represented by σπέρμα only here
in the entire LXX, although פְּלֵיטָה "preserved remnant"
does appear as σπέρμα in Isa 15:9; (2) כִּמְעָט is omitted
altogether in LXX & NT, unless perhaps "seed" is
intended to convey the idea of a very small remainder
(שָׂרִיד כִּמְעָט). (*B*)

*a*Mt 13:14–15

14 καὶ ⌜ἀνα-
πληροῦται αὐτοῖς ἡ προφητεία Ἡσαΐου ἡ λέγουσα·
ᵀ ἀκοῇ ἀκούσετε καὶ οὐ μὴ συνῆτε,
καὶ βλέποντες βλέψετε καὶ οὐ μὴ ἴδητε.

15 ἐπαχύνθη γὰρ ἡ καρδία τοῦ λαοῦ τούτου,
καὶ τοῖς ὠσὶν ᵀ βαρέως ἤκουσαν
καὶ τοὺς ὀφθαλμοὺς αὐτῶν ἐκάμμυσαν,
μήποτε ἴδωσιν τοῖς ὀφθαλμοῖς
καὶ τοῖς ὠσὶν ἀκούσωσιν
καὶ τῇ καρδίᾳ συνῶσιν
καὶ ἐπιστρέψωσιν καὶ ἰάσομαι αὐτούς.

Isa 6:9–10; v. 9*b* MT = LXX = Mt 13:14 except: (1) the
last word οὐ μὴ ἴδητε for אַל־תֵּדָעוּ should be μὴ γνῶτε/
εἰδῆτε subj.). Also Mk 4:12 = Acts 28:26 (but neither
Lk 8:10 nor John 12:40 have v. 9, only v. 10).

v. 10*a*: (1) MT's הַשְׁמֵן → ἐπαχύνθη (as if vocalized
Hp10 הֻשְׁמַן), LXX = Mt 13:15*a* and Acts 28:27*a*;
(2) הַכְבֵּד = βαρέως ἤκουσεν (i.e., הֻכְבַּד H10), LXX =
Mt 13:15*b* and Acts 28:27*b*; (3) הָשַׁע = ἐκάμμυσαν (i.e.,
הֻשַׁע H10 rather than impv.), LXX = Mt 13:15*c* and
Acts 28:27*c*; (4) וְרָפָא לוֹ is an impersonal idiomatic

206 (continued)

207: Isa 7:14

¹⁴ לָכֵ֞ן יִתֵּ֙ן אֲדֹנָ֥י ה֛וּא לָכֶ֖ם
אֹ֑ות הִנֵּ֣ה הָעַלְמָ֗ה הָרָה֙ וְיֹלֶ֣דֶת בֵּ֔ן וְקָרָ֥את שְׁמֹ֖ו עִמָּ֥נוּ אֵֽל׃

¹⁴ διὰ τοῦτο δώσει κύ-
ριος αὐτὸς ὑμῖν σημεῖον · ἰδοὺ ἡ παρθένος ἐν γαστρὶ ἕξει καὶ τέξεται υἱόν, καὶ καλέσεις τὸ ὄνομα αὐτοῦ Εμμανουηλ ·

(Isa 8:8, 10)

⁸ καὶ ἀφελεῖ ἀπὸ τῆς Ιουδαίας ἄνθρω-
πον ὃς δυνήσεται κεφαλὴν ἆραι ἢ δυνατὸν συντελέσασθαί τι, καὶ
ἔσται ἡ παρεμβολὴ αὐτοῦ ὥστε πληρῶσαι τὸ πλάτος τῆς χώρας
σου · μεθ' ἡμῶν ὁ θεός.

¹⁰ καὶ ἣν ἂν βουλεύσησθε βουλήν, διασκεδάσει
κύριος, καὶ λόγον ὃν ἐὰν λαλήσητε, οὐ μὴ ἐμμείνῃ ὑμῖν, ὅτι μεθ'
ἡμῶν κύριος ὁ θεός.

208: Isa 8:12–13

¹² לֹא־תֹאמְר֣וּן קֶ֔שֶׁר לְכֹ֧ל אֲשֶׁר־יֹאמַ֛ר הָעָ֥ם הַזֶּ֖ה קָ֑שֶׁר
וְאֶת־מֹורָאֹ֥ו לֹֽא־תִֽירְא֖וּ וְלֹ֥א תַעֲרִֽיצוּ׃
¹³ אֶת־יְהוָ֥ה צְבָאֹ֖ות אֹתֹ֣ו תַקְדִּ֑ישׁוּ וְה֥וּא מֹורַאֲכֶ֖ם וְה֥וּא מַֽעֲרִֽצְכֶֽם׃

¹² Μήποτε εἴπητε σκληρόν · πᾶν
γάρ, ὃ ἐὰν εἴπῃ ὁ λαὸς οὗτος, σκληρόν ἐστιν · τὸν δὲ φόβον αὐτοῦ
οὐ μὴ φοβηθῆτε οὐδὲ μὴ ταραχθῆτε · ¹³ κύριον αὐτὸν ἁγιάσατε,
καὶ αὐτὸς ἔσται σου φόβος.

*b*Mk 4:12

12 ἵνα βλέποντες βλέπωσιν καὶ μὴ ἴδωσιν,
καὶ ἀκούοντες ἀκούωσιν καὶ μὴ συνιῶσιν,
μήποτε ἐπιστρέψωσιν καὶ ⌜ἀφεθῇ αὐτοῖς⌝ᵀ.

*c*Acts 28:26–27

26 λέγων·
πορεύθητι πρὸς τὸν λαὸν τοῦτον καὶ εἰπόν·
ἀκοῇ ἀκούσετε καὶ οὐ μὴ συνῆτε
καὶ βλέποντες βλέψετε καὶ οὐ μὴ ⌜ἴδητε·
27 ⌜ἐπαχύνθη γὰρ ἡ καρδία τοῦ λαοῦ τούτου
καὶ τοῖς ὠσὶν βαρέως ἤκουσαν
καὶ τοὺς ὀφθαλμοὺς αὐτῶν ἐκάμμυσαν·
μήποτε ἴδωσιν τοῖς ὀφθαλμοῖς
καὶ τοῖς ὠσὶν ἀκούσωσιν
καὶ τῇ καρδίᾳ συνῶσιν
καὶ ⌜ἐπιστρέψωσιν, καὶ ⌜¹ἰάσομαι αὐτούς.

*d*Lk 8:10   only Isa 6:9

10 ὁ δὲ εἶπεν· ὑμῖν δέδοται γνῶναι τὰ μυ-
στήρια ⸆τῆς βασιλείας⸅ τοῦ θεοῦ, * τοῖς δὲ λοιποῖς ἐν παραβολαῖς, ἵνα
βλέποντες μὴ ⌜βλέπωσιν
καὶ ἀκούοντες μὴ συνιῶσιν.

*e*Jn 12:40   only Isa 6:10

40 τετύφλωκεν αὐτῶν ⸆τοὺς ὀφθαλμοὺς
καὶ ⌜ἐπώρωσεν αὐτῶν⸅ τὴν καρδίαν,
ἵνα μὴ ἴδωσιν τοῖς ὀφθαλμοῖς
καὶ ⸆ νοήσωσιν τῇ καρδίᾳ
καὶ ⌜στραφῶσιν, καὶ ἰάσομαι αὐτούς.

---

expression requiring a bit of recasting to be intelligible to the Greeks (καὶ ἰαθησεται or better ἰαθῇ—as a passive—would have been closer than καὶ ἰάσομαι αὐτούς) (*B*). However, note that this voweling of the Sopherim consonantal text may reflect a theological preference. That is, sinful, disobedient Judah has hardened itself in willful rejection of God's mandates; the emphasis is laid on human guilt rather than upon that judicial blinding by which God confirms the wicked in their unbelief, making them ripe for the coming judgment. But in the case of John, the approach is quite different: (1) John 12:40*a* τετύφλωκεν is God's judicial blinding inferred from Isa 6:10 הָשַׁע (H32) commanded to Isaiah, or else John read הֵשַׁע (H10) with יהוה as an implied subject (*C*); (2) John 12:40*b* puts Isa 6:10*a* after 10*b* and renders הַכְבֵּד H32 as הֻכְבַּד; (3) John 12:40*c* uses ἵνα μή + subjunctive for פֶּן־; LXX's μήποτε is equivalent, but a little more dramatic; (4) John 12:40*d* uses νοήσωσιν for יָבִין, rather than LXX's συνῶσιν; and 40*e* is στραφῶσιν rather than LXX's ἐπιστρέψωσιν (for וְשָׁב). Clearly, John 12:40 is not following the LXX at all; probably it renders from the Hebrew consonantal text directly.

---

*a*Mt 1:23

23 ἰδοὺ ἡ παρθένος ἐν γαστρὶ ἕξει καὶ τέξεται υἱόν,
καὶ ⌜καλέσουσιν τὸ ὄνομα αὐτοῦ Ἐμμανουήλ,
ὅ ἐστιν μεθερμηνευόμενον μεθ' ἡμῶν ὁ θεός.

Isa 7:14; MT = LXX = Mt 1:23 except (1) וְקָרָאת (Gc13) is καλέσεις ("thou shalt call") in LXX. In Mt 1:23 it appears as καλέσουσιν; *BH* apparatus: several MSS point as קָרָאת, LXX in Vaticanus & Alexandrinus reads καλέσεις; so also Aquila, Symmachus, and Theodotion; LXX Sinaiticus = καλέσει ("she shall call") Marchalianus, O. Lat *vocabitis*, Syriac, Vulgate *vocabitur*. קָרָאת וְ may be a textual variant of קָרְאָה or even with שְׁמוֹ as subject rather than object. The καλέσουσιν is an Aramaic-type third person plural, equivalent to a passive. Isa 8:8, 10 MT עִמָּנוּ־אֵל = LXX μεθ' ἡμῶν ὁ θεός or μεθ' ἡμῶν κύριος ὁ θεός (v. 10). (*A*)

---

*a*1 Pet 3:14–15

14 ἀλλ' εἰ καὶ πάσχοιτε διὰ δικαιοσύνην,
μακάριοι⸆. τὸν δὲ φόβον αὐτῶν μὴ φοβηθῆτε ⸂μηδὲ ταραχθῆτε⸃, **15** κύριον δὲ τὸν ⌜Χριστὸν ἁγιάσατε ἐν ταῖς καρδίαις ὑμῶν, ἕτοιμοι ⌜ἀεὶ πρὸς ἀπολογίαν παντὶ τῷ ⌜¹αἰτοῦντι ὑμᾶς λόγον περὶ τῆς ἐν ὑμῖν ἐλπίδος,

---

Isa 8:12–13; v. 12 MT וְאֶת־מוֹרָאוֹ לֹא־תִירָאוּ וְלֹא תַעֲרִיצוּ = LXX τὸν δὲ φόβον αὐτοῦ οὐ μὴ φοβηθῆτε οὐδὲ μὴ ταραχθῆτε = 1 Pet 3:14 τὸν δὲ φόβον αὐτῶν, etc. since the antecedent of מוראו is plural in sense—הָעָם הַזֶּה. (*A*ᵈ)

v. 13 MT אֶת־יהוה צְבָאוֹת אֹתוֹ תַקְדִּישׁוּ = LXX κύριον αὐτὸν ἁγιάσατε = 1 Pet 3:15 κύριον δὲ τὸν Χριστὸν (instead of αὐτόν or צְבָאוֹת) ἁγιάσατε. (*A*ᵈ)

209: Isa 8:14

¹⁴ וְהָיָה לְמִקְדָּשׁ וּלְאֶבֶן נֶגֶף וּלְצוּר מִכְשׁוֹל
לִשְׁנֵי בָתֵּי יִשְׂרָאֵל לְפַח וּלְמוֹקֵשׁ לְיוֹשֵׁב יְרוּשָׁלָ͏ִם׃

Isa 28:16

¹⁶ לָכֵן כֹּה אָמַר אֲדֹנָי יְהוִה
הִנְנִי יִסַּד בְּצִיּוֹן אָבֶן אֶבֶן בֹּחַן
פִּנַּת יִקְרַת מוּסָד מוּסָּד הַמַּאֲמִין לֹא יָחִישׁ׃

¹⁴καὶ ἐὰν ἐπ' αὐτῷ πεποιθὼς ᾖς, ἔσται
σοι εἰς ἁγίασμα, καὶ οὐχ ὡς λίθου προσκόμματι συναντήσεσθε
αὐτῷ οὐδὲ ὡς πέτρας πτώματι · ὁ δὲ οἶκος Ιακωβ ἐν παγίδι, καὶ
ἐν κοιλάσματι ἐγκαθήμενοι ἐν Ιερουσαλημ.

¹⁶διὰ τοῦτο οὕτως λέγει κύριος 'Ιδοὺ ἐγὼ ἐμβαλῶ εἰς τὰ θεμέλια
Σιων λίθον πολυτελῆ ἐκλεκτὸν ἀκρογωνιαῖον ἔντιμον εἰς τὰ θεμέλια
αὐτῆς, καὶ ὁ πιστεύων ἐπ' αὐτῷ οὐ μὴ καταισχυνθῇ.

only Isa 28:16 ⎯⎯⎯⎯

210: Isa 8:17–18

¹⁷ וְחִכִּיתִי לַיהוָה הַמַּסְתִּיר פָּנָיו מִבֵּית יַעֲקֹב וְקִוֵּיתִי־לוֹ׃
¹⁸ הִנֵּה אָנֹכִי וְהַיְלָדִים אֲשֶׁר נָתַן־לִי יְהוָה לְאֹתוֹת וּלְמוֹפְתִים
מֵעִם יְהוָה צְבָאוֹת הַשֹּׁכֵן בְּהַר צִיּוֹן׃ ס   [בְּיִשְׂרָאֵל

2 Sam 22:3

³ אֱלֹהֵי צוּרִי אֶחֱסֶה־בּוֹ
מָגִנִּי וְקֶרֶן יִשְׁעִי מִשְׂגַּבִּי וּמְנוּסִי מֹשִׁעִי מֵחָמָס תֹּשִׁעֵנִי׃

Isa 12:2

² הִנֵּה אֵל יְשׁוּעָתִי אֶבְטַח וְלֹא אֶפְחָד
כִּי־עָזִּי וְזִמְרָת יָהּ יְהוָה וַיְהִי־לִי לִישׁוּעָה׃

¹⁷καὶ ἐρεῖ Μενῶ τὸν θεὸν τὸν ἀποστρέψαντα τὸ πρόσωπον
αὐτοῦ ἀπὸ τοῦ οἴκου Ιακωβ καὶ πεποιθὼς ἔσομαι ἐπ' αὐτῷ. ¹⁸ἰδοὺ
ἐγὼ καὶ τὰ παιδία, ἅ μοι ἔδωκεν ὁ θεός, καὶ ἔσται εἰς σημεῖα καὶ
τέρατα ἐν τῷ οἴκῳ Ισραηλ παρὰ κυρίου σαβαωθ, ὃς κατοικεῖ ἐν
τῷ ὄρει Σιων.

³ὁ θεός μου φύλαξ ἔσται μου, πεποιθὼς ἔσομαι ἐπ' αὐτῷ,
ὑπερασπιστής μου καὶ κέρας σωτηρίας μου,
ἀντιλήμπτωρ μου καὶ καταφυγή μου σωτηρίας μου,
ἐξ ἀδίκου σώσεις με.

²ἰδοὺ
ὁ θεός μου σωτήρ μου κύριος, πεποιθὼς ἔσομαι ἐπ' αὐτῷ καὶ
σωθήσομαι ἐν αὐτῷ καὶ οὐ φοβηθήσομαι, διότι ἡ δόξα μου καὶ ἡ
αἴνεσίς μου κύριος καὶ ἐγένετό μοι εἰς σωτηρίαν.

*a*Rom 9:33

33 καθὼς γέγραπται·
   ἰδοὺ τίθημι ἐν Σιὼν λίθον προσκόμματος καὶ πέτραν σκανδάλου,
   καὶ ᵀ ὁ πιστεύων ἐπ' αὐτῷ οὐ ⸀καταισχυνθήσεται.

Isa 8:14; MT וְהָיָה לְמִקְדָּשׁ וּלְאֶבֶן נֶגֶף וּלְצוּר מִכְשׁוֹל; LXX εἰς ἁγίασμα, καὶ οὐχ ὡς λίθου προσκόμματι συναντήσεσθε αὐτῷ οὐδὲ ὡς πέτρας πτώματι; Rom 9:33 ἰδοὺ τίθημι ἐν Σιὼν λίθον προσκόμματος καὶ πέτραν σκανδάλου. Note that LXX has λίθου and προσκόμματι (as object of συναντήσεσθε αὐτῷ). Here the NT rendering is completely independent of LXX and corresponds almost perfectly to the MT, as if translated directly from it (*C*). Note that Rom 10:11 has the same wording as Rom 9:33, which faithfully renders Isa 28:16. Isa 28:16—1 Pet 2:6. (*A*)

*b*Rom 10:11

11 λέγει γὰρ ἡ γραφή· ᵀ πᾶς ὁ πιστεύων ἐπ' αὐτῷ οὐ καταισχυνθήσεται.

*c*1 Pet 2:6

6 διότι περι-
ἰδοὺ τίθημι ἐν Σιὼν λίθον ⸀ἀκρογωνιαῖον ἐκλεκτὸν ἔντιμον⸀
καὶ ὁ πιστεύων ἐπ' αὐτῷ οὐ μὴ καταισχυνθῇ.

---

*a*Heb 2:13

13 καὶ πάλιν·
   ἐγὼ ἔσομαι πεποιθὼς ἐπ' αὐτῷ,
καὶ πάλιν·
   ἰδοὺ ἐγὼ καὶ τὰ παιδία ἅ μοι ἔδωκεν ὁ θεός.

Isa 8:17–18; v. 17 MT: וְקִוֵּיתִי לוֹ = LXX καὶ πεποιθὼς ἔσομαι ἐπ' αὐτῷ = Heb 2:13*a* ἐγὼ ἔσομαι πεποιθὼς ἐπ' αὐτῷ. (*A*)

v. 18 MT הִנֵּה אָנֹכִי וְהַיְלָדִים אֲשֶׁר נָתַן־לִי יהוה = LXX ἰδοὺ ἐγὼ καὶ τὰ παιδία, ἅ μοι ἔδωκέν ὁ θεός = Heb 2:13*b*. (*A*)

Isa 12:2; MT הִנֵּה אֵל יְשׁוּעָתִי אֶבְטַח וְלֹא אֶפְחָד; LXX πεποιθὼς ἔσομαι ἐπ' αὐτῷ καὶ σωθήσομαι ἐν αὐτῷ; Heb 2:13*a* ἐγὼ ἔσομαι πεποιθὼς ἐπ' αὐτῷ. Since ἐπ' αὐτῷ does not find a basis in the MT, it is much more likely that Heb 2 had only Isa 8:17 in mind—especially if it ties in directly with the next verse (Isa 8:18) in the Heb 2:13 quotation of it. (*A*ᵈ)

Apart from word order, 2 Sam 22:3 has the same text as Isa 8:17; these both furnish the basis for the quotation in Heb 2:13*a*. Isa 12:2 also contains the identical expression.

211: Isa 8:23–9:1 (9:1–2)

²³ כִּי לֹא מוּעָף לַאֲשֶׁר מוּצָק לָהּ

כָּעֵת הָרִאשׁוֹן הֵקַל

אַרְצָה זְבֻלוּן וְאַרְצָה נַפְתָּלִי

וְהָאַחֲרוֹן הִכְבִּיד דֶּרֶךְ הַיָּם

עֵבֶר הַיַּרְדֵּן גְּלִיל הַגּוֹיִם:

9 ¹ הָעָם הַהֹלְכִים בַּחֹשֶׁךְ רָאוּ אוֹר גָּדוֹל

יֹשְׁבֵי בְּאֶרֶץ צַלְמָוֶת אוֹר נָגַהּ עֲלֵיהֶם:

²³ καὶ οὐκ
ἀπορηθήσεται ὁ ἐν στενοχωρίᾳ ὢν ἕως καιροῦ.

Τοῦτο πρῶτον ποίει, ταχὺ ποίει, χώρα Ζαβουλων, ἡ γῆ Νεφθαλιμ ὁδὸν θαλάσσης καὶ οἱ λοιποὶ οἱ τὴν παραλίαν κατοικοῦντες καὶ πέραν τοῦ Ιορδάνου, Γαλιλαία τῶν ἐθνῶν, τὰ μέρη τῆς Ιουδαίας. ¹ ὁ λαὸς ὁ πορευόμενος ἐν σκότει, ἴδετε φῶς μέγα· οἱ κατοικοῦντες ἐν χώρᾳ καὶ σκιᾷ θανάτου, φῶς λάμψει ἐφ' ὑμᾶς.

212: Isa 10:22–23

see Hos 2:3, 25 [288–289]

213: Isa 11:10

¹⁰ וְהָיָה בַּיּוֹם הַהוּא שֹׁרֶשׁ יִשַׁי אֲשֶׁר עֹמֵד לְנֵס עַמִּים
אֵלָיו גּוֹיִם יִדְרֹשׁוּ וְהָיְתָה מְנֻחָתוֹ כָּבוֹד:

¹⁰ Καὶ ἔσται ἐν τῇ ἡμέρᾳ ἐκείνῃ ἡ ῥίζα τοῦ Ιεσσαι καὶ ὁ ἀνιστάμενος ἄρχειν ἐθνῶν, ἐπ' αὐτῷ ἔθνη ἐλπιοῦσιν, καὶ ἔσται ἡ ἀνάπαυσις αὐτοῦ τιμή.

214: Isa 12:2

see Isa 8:17–18 [210]

215: Isa 13:10

¹⁰ כִּי־כוֹכְבֵי הַשָּׁמַיִם וּכְסִילֵיהֶם לֹא יָהֵלּוּ אוֹרָם
חָשַׁךְ הַשֶּׁמֶשׁ בְּצֵאתוֹ וְיָרֵחַ לֹא־יַגִּיהַּ אוֹרוֹ:

¹⁰ οἱ γὰρ ἀστέρες τοῦ οὐρανοῦ καὶ ὁ Ὠρίων καὶ πᾶς ὁ κόσμος τοῦ οὐρανοῦ τὸ φῶς οὐ δώσουσιν, καὶ σκοτισθήσεται τοῦ ἡλίου ἀνατέλλοντος, καὶ ἡ σελήνη οὐ δώσει τὸ φῶς αὐτῆς.

*a*Mt 4:15–16

15 γῆ Ζαβουλὼν καὶ γῆ Νεφθαλίμ,
ὁδὸν θαλάσσης·, πέραν τοῦ Ἰορδάνου,
Γαλιλαία τῶν ἐθνῶν, :1
16 ὁ λαὸς ὁ καθήμενος ἐν ⌜σκότει
φῶς εἶδεν μέγα,

Isa 8:23–9:1 (9:1–2); MT = LXX = Mt 4:15–16, except that: (1) אַרְצָה = LXX χώρα =Mt 4:15 γῆ before Ζαβουλών (both have γῆ before Νεφθαλίμ = MT's אַרְצָה); (2) both LXX and NT omit entirely the phrase וְהָאַחֲרוֹן הִכְבִּיד coming before דֶּרֶךְ הַיָּם (ὁδὸν θαλάσσης); (3) Isa 9:1 has הָעָם הַהֹלְכִים = LXX ὁ λαὸς ὁ πορευόμενος, but Mt 4:16 has ὁ λαὸς ὁ καθήμενος (*E*); (4) Isa 9:1 has רָאוּ אוֹר גָּדוֹל, which LXX makes G37 ἴδετε φῶς μέγα but Mt 4:16 correctly has φῶς εἶδεν μέγα. Note that LXX carries through with second person plural in the final words: φῶς λάμψει ἐφ᾿ ὑμᾶς, which is not included in the NT quote, but the MT has אוֹר נָגַהּ עֲלֵיהֶם. (*C*)

*a*Rom 15:12

12 καὶ πάλιν Ἡσαΐας λέγει·
ἔσται ἡ ῥίζα τοῦ Ἰεσσαὶ
καὶ ὁ ἀνιστάμενος ἄρχειν ἐθνῶν,
ἐπ᾿ αὐτῷ ἔθνη ἐλπιοῦσιν.

Isa 11:10; MT וְהָיָה . . . שֹׁרֶשׁ יִשַׁי אֲשֶׁר עֹמֵד לְנֵס עַמִּים; LXX Καὶ ἔσται . . . ἡ ῥίζα τοῦ Ἰεσσαι καὶ ὁ ἀνιστάμενος ἄρχειν ἐθνῶν = Rom 15:12. (*B*)

Note that: (1) MT gives no real support for either καὶ or ὁ before ἀνιστάμενος, although no definite article is required in Hebrew poetic style. MT probably means: "The root of Jesse will be standing/rising up" as a standard for the Gentiles; (2) לְנֵס is wrongly rendered as ἄρχειν. Schl. (368A) suggests *Vexillum superioritatis et dominii signum est* ("a banner is a symbol of superiority and sovereignty"). Bootius, however, suggested that the LXX may have read לְנֵס as לְנָשִׂיא (very unlikely). But the reason for getting ἄρχειν out of לְנֵס remains obscure). A regimental or imperial banner can hardly be rendered "to rule over."

a Mt 24:29

29 Εὐθέως δὲ μετὰ τὴν θλῖψιν τῶν ἡμερῶν ἐκείνων
ὁ ἥλιος σκοτισθήσεται,
καὶ ἡ σελήνη οὐ δώσει τὸ φέγγος αὐτῆς,
καὶ οἱ ἀστέρες πεσοῦνται ⌜ἀπὸ τοῦ οὐρανοῦ,
καὶ αἱ δυνάμεις τῶν οὐρανῶν σαλευθήσονται.

Isa 13:10; It is not clear that the second half of this verse is a true quotation; it merely picks up allusions. v. 10*b* MT חָשַׁךְ . . . אוֹר = LXX καὶ σκοτισθήσεται τοῦ ἡλίου ἀνατέλλοντος, καὶ ἡ σελήνη οὐ δώσει τὸ φῶς αὐτῆς; Mt 24:29 has ὁ ἥλιος σκοτισθήσεται (= חָשַׁךְ הַשֶּׁמֶשׁ); (*C*), more accurate than the LXX and independent of it; καὶ ἡ σελήνη οὐ δώσει τὸ φέγγος (LXX has φῶς) αὐτῆς (φέγγος is equally good for אוֹר). (*A*)

215 (continued)

Isa 34:4

וְנָמַ֙קּוּ֙ כָּל־צְבָ֣א הַשָּׁמַ֔יִם
וְנָגֹ֤לּוּ כַסֵּ֙פֶר֙ הַשָּׁמָ֔יִם וְכָל־צְבָאָ֖ם יִבּ֑וֹל
כִּנְבֹ֤ל עָלֶה֙ מִגֶּ֔פֶן וּכְנֹבֶ֖לֶת מִתְּאֵנָֽה׃

⁴ καὶ ἑλιγή-
σεται ὁ οὐρανὸς ὡς βιβλίον, καὶ πάντα τὰ ἄστρα πεσεῖται ὡς
φύλλα ἐξ ἀμπέλου καὶ ὡς πίπτει φύλλα ἀπὸ συκῆς.

216: Isa 22:13

וְהִנֵּ֣ה ׀ שָׂשׂ֣וֹן וְשִׂמְחָ֗ה הָרֹ֤ג ׀ בָּקָר֙ וְשָׁחֹ֣ט צֹ֔אן
אָכֹ֥ל בָּשָׂ֖ר וְשָׁת֣וֹת יָ֑יִן אָכ֣וֹל וְשָׁת֔וֹ כִּ֥י מָחָ֖ר נָמֽוּת׃

¹³ αὐτοὶ δὲ
ἐποιήσαντο εὐφροσύνην καὶ ἀγαλλίαμα σφάζοντες μόσχους καὶ
θύοντες πρόβατα ὥστε φαγεῖν κρέα καὶ πιεῖν οἶνον λέγοντες Φάγωμεν καὶ πίωμεν, αὔριον γὰρ ἀποθνήσκομεν.

217: Isa 25:8

בִּלַּ֤ע הַמָּ֙וֶת֙ לָנֶ֔צַח
וּמָחָ֙ה אֲדֹנָ֧י יְהוִ֛ה דִּמְעָ֖ה מֵעַ֣ל כָּל־פָּנִ֑ים
וְחֶרְפַּ֣ת עַמּ֗וֹ יָסִיר֙ מֵעַ֣ל כָּל־הָאָ֔רֶץ כִּ֥י יְהוָ֖ה דִּבֵּֽר׃

⁸ κατέπιεν ὁ θάνατος ἰσχύσας, καὶ πάλιν ἀφεῖλεν ὁ
θεὸς πᾶν δάκρυον ἀπὸ παντὸς προσώπου· τὸ ὄνειδος τοῦ λαοῦ
ἀφεῖλεν ἀπὸ πάσης τῆς γῆς, τὸ γὰρ στόμα κυρίου ἐλάλησεν.

*b*Mk 13:24–25

24 Ἀλλὰ ἐν ἐκείναις ταῖς ἡμέραις μετὰ τὴν θλῖψιν ἐκείνην

  ὁ ἥλιος σκοτισθήσεται,

    καὶ ἡ σελήνη οὐ δώσει τὸ φέγγος αὐτῆς,

  25 καὶ οἱ ἀστέρες ⌐ἔσονται ἐκ τοῦ οὐρανοῦ πίπτοντες⌐,

    καὶ αἱ δυνάμεις αἱ ἐν τοῖς οὐρανοῖς σαλευθήσονται.

*c*Lk 21:26   only Isa 34:4

26 ἀποψυχόντων ἀνθρώπων ἀπὸ φόβου καὶ προσδοκίας τῶν ἐπερχομένων τῇ οἰκουμένῃ, αἱ γὰρ δυνάμεις ⌐τῶν οὐρανῶν⌐ σαλευθήσονται.

v. 10*a* MT . . . כִּי־כוֹכְבֵי הַשָּׁמַיִם = LXX οἱ γὰρ ἀστέρας τοῦ οὐρανοῦ "will not give her light"; Mt 24:29*c* καὶ οἱ ἀστέρας πεσοῦνται (which does not appear either in the MT or LXX).

Isa 34:4; MT יְבוֹל כִּנְבֹל עָלֶה מִגֶּפֶן; LXX καὶ πάντα τὰ ἄστρα πεσεῖται (wrong for נָבַל). MT וְנָגֹלוּ כַסֵּפֶר הַשָּׁמַיִם; LXX ὡς φύλλα ἐξ ἀμπέλου . . . . Note that: (1) כָּל־צְבָאָם is rendered τὰ ἄστρα; (2) MT יְבוֹל is omitted altogether and כִּנְבֹל is treated like יִפֹּלוּ (without αὐτοῦ).

As for Mt 24:29, it appears as καὶ οἱ ἀστέρες πεσοῦνται, (*F*). But for the last line, καὶ αἱ δυνάμεις τῶν οὐρανῶν σαλευθήσονται, there is really no source in LXX or in MT. But refer to Job 9:6: MT הַמַּרְגִּיז אֶרֶץ מִמְּקוֹמָהּ; LXX ὁ σείων τὴν ὑπ᾽ οὐρανόν ἐκ θεμελίων. Note that σείων is very close to σαλεύων in meaning. Conceivably, there was a reminiscence of this passage in Matthew's σαλευθήσονται, with the נָגֹלוּ כַסֵּפֶר הַשָּׁמַיִם in Isa 34:4. On the whole, however, it seems better to deny all quotation status to Mt 24:29*d*, since it finds no clear source either in the MT or LXX and is not even introduced as a quotation. (*F*)

*a*1 Cor 15:32

32 εἰ κατὰ ἄνθρωπον ἐθηριομάχησα ἐν Ἐφέσῳ, τί μοι τὸ ὄφελος; εἰ νεκροὶ οὐκ ἐγείρονται, *φάγωμεν καὶ πίωμεν, αὔριον γὰρ ἀποθνῄσκομεν.*

Isa 22:13; MT = LXX = 1 Cor 15:32. (*A*)

*a*1 Cor 15:54

54 ὅταν δὲ ⌐τὸ φθαρτὸν τοῦτο ἐνδύσηται⌐ ἀφθαρσίαν καὶ τὸ θνητὸν τοῦτο ἐνδύσηται ⊤ ἀθανασίαν⌐, τότε γενήσεται ὁ λόγος ὁ γεγραμμένος·

  κατεπόθη ὁ θάνατος εἰς ⌐νῖκος.

*b*Rev 7:17

17 ὅτι τὸ ἀρνίον τὸ ἀνὰ μέσον τοῦ θρόνου ⌐ποιμανεῖ⌐ αὐτούς

  καὶ ⌐ὁδηγήσει αὐτοὺς ἐπὶ ⌐ζωῆς πηγὰς ὑδάτων,

  καὶ ἐξαλείψει ὁ θεὸς πᾶν δάκρυον ⌐¹ ἐκ τῶν ὀφθαλμῶν αὐτῶν.

Isa 25:8; MT בִּלַּע הַמָּוֶת לָנֶצַח (note that הַמָּוֶת is object of the verb); LXX κατέπιεν ὁ θάνατος ἰσχύσας; 1 Cor 15:54 κατεπόθη ὁ θάνατος εἰς νῖκος. Theodotion and Peshitta also read κατεπόθη = בִּלַּע. Note that: (1) 1 Cor 15 has expressed in the passive what the MT and LXX put in the active voice; κατεπόθη "death has been swallowed" (as if בֻּלַּע) versus the LXX's "death has swallowed up" (with no expressed object!); (2) לָנֶצַח probably means "forever," yet נֶצַח basically means "pre-eminence" either in rank/glory or in time (endurance,

217 (continued)

218: Isa 26:13

see Num 16:5 [74]

219: Isa 26:19

¹⁹ יִחְיוּ מֵתֶיךָ נְבֵלָתִי יְקוּמוּן הָקִיצוּ וְרַנְּנוּ שֹׁכְנֵי עָפָר
כִּי טַל אוֹרֹת טַלֶּךָ וָאָרֶץ רְפָאִים תַּפִּיל׃

Isa 35:5–6

⁵ אָז תִּפָּקַחְנָה עֵינֵי עִוְרִים וְאָזְנֵי חֵרְשִׁים תִּפָּתַחְנָה׃
⁶ אָז יְדַלֵּג כָּאַיָּל פִּסֵּחַ וְתָרֹן לְשׁוֹן אִלֵּם
כִּי־נִבְקְעוּ בַמִּדְבָּר מַיִם וּנְחָלִים בָּעֲרָבָה׃

Isa 42:18

¹⁸ הַחֵרְשִׁים שְׁמָעוּ וְהַעִוְרִים הַבִּיטוּ לִרְאוֹת׃

Isa 61:1

¹ רוּחַ אֲדֹנָי יְהוִה עָלָי יַעַן מָשַׁח יְהוָה אֹתִי
לְבַשֵּׂר עֲנָוִים שְׁלָחַנִי לַחֲבֹשׁ לְנִשְׁבְּרֵי־לֵב
לִקְרֹא לִשְׁבוּיִם דְּרוֹר וְלַאֲסוּרִים פְּקַח־קוֹחַ׃

¹⁹ἀναστήσονται οἱ νεκροί, καὶ ἐγερθήσον-
ται οἱ ἐν τοῖς μνημείοις, καὶ εὐφρανθήσονται οἱ ἐν τῇ τῇ · ἡ γὰρ
δρόσος ἡ παρὰ σοῦ ἴαμα αὐτοῖς ἐστιν, ἡ δὲ τῇ τῶν ἀσεβῶν πεσεῖται.

⁵τότε ἀνοιχθήσονται ὀφθαλμοὶ τυφλῶν, καὶ ὦτα κωφῶν
ἀκούσονται. ⁶τότε ἁλεῖται ὡς ἔλαφος ὁ χωλός, καὶ τρανὴ ἔσται
γλῶσσα μογιλάλων, ὅτι ἐρράγη ἐν τῇ ἐρήμῳ ὕδωρ καὶ φάραγξ ἐν
τῇ διψώσῃ,

¹⁸Οἱ κωφοί, ἀκούσατε, καὶ οἱ τυφλοί, ἀναβλέψατε ἰδεῖν.

¹Πνεῦμα κυρίου ἐπ' ἐμέ, οὗ εἵνεκεν ἔχρισέν με · εὐαγγελίσασθαι
πτωχοῖς ἀπέσταλκέν με, ἰάσασθαι τοὺς συντετριμμένους τῇ καρδίᾳ,
κηρύξαι αἰχμαλώτοις ἄφεσιν καὶ τυφλοῖς ἀνάβλεψιν,

perpetuity). But in postbiblical Hebrew נָצַח = "be victorious, win, prevail" (Jastrow, 928A) and נֶצַח = "success" (as well as endurance, forever) so (A^d). LXX's ἰσχύσας ("having prevailed") probably shows that this force of the verb was current in Septuagintal times (this is also the Theodotion rendering). Note that in modern Hebrew נָצַח = "conquer" and in Aramaic נַצַּח (pael) = "succeed, be victorious." Hence εἰς νῖκος; the Targum of Jonathan, though Aramaic, somewhat favors the MT in its interpretation of נֶצַח; יְתְנַשּׁוֹן מוֹתָא לְעָלְמִין "they will forget death forever." The Vulgate renders it *praecipitabit mortem in sempiternum* ("He will cast down death forever"). The Peshitta renders as "Death has been swallowed up in victory forever." Rev 7:17 ἐξαλείψει is closer to מָחָה than LXX's ἀφεῖλεν (C); ἐκ τῶν ὀφξαλμῶν (LXX: ἀπὸ παντὸς προσώπου).

---

^a**Mt 11:5**

5 τυφλοὶ ἀναβλέπου-
σιν ⌜καὶ χωλοὶ περιπατοῦσιν⌝, λεπροὶ καθαρίζονται καὶ *κωφοὶ ἀκούουσιν*, καὶ ⌜νεκροὶ ἐγείρονται καὶ πτωχοὶ εὐαγ-
γελίζονται⌝·

^b**Lk 7:22**

22 καὶ ἀποκριθεὶς εἶπεν αὐτοῖς· πορευθέντες ⌜ἀπαγ-
γείλατε Ἰωάννῃ ἃ εἴδετε καὶ ἠκούσατε⌝·

⌑ τυφλοὶ ἀναβλέπουσιν, ⌑ χωλοὶ περιπατοῦσιν,
λεπροὶ καθαρίζονται, °καὶ *κωφοὶ ἀκούουσιν*,
νεκροὶ ἐγείρονται, πτωχοὶ εὐαγγελίζονται·

Isa 26:19: MT יִחְיוּ מֵתֶיךָ נְבֵלָתִי יְקוּמוּן הָקִיצוּ וְרַנְּנוּ שֹׁכְנֵי עָפָר; LXX ἀναστήσονται οἱ νεκροί, καὶ ἐγερθήσονται οἱ ἐν τοῖς μνημείοις καὶ εὐφρανθήσονται οἱ ἐν τῇ γῇ. This is not presented as a quotation, but only as a series of miracles given in the OT to certify the Messiah: Mt 11:5 and Lk 7:22 νεκροὶ ἐγείρονται (F). Note that MT makes those resurrected or resuscitated dead specifically those who will be the Lord's people: "Thy dead ones, My corpses." LXX generalizes to the dead, "those in the graves."

Isa 35:5–6 refers to the opening of the eyes of the blind (ὀφθαλμοὶ τυφλῶν), but Isa 42:18 is closer (see below); at least it has οἱ τυφλοί as the subject, and the same verb in the imperative aorist (ἀναβλέψατε) that occurs as a present ἀναβλέπουσιν in Mt 11:5 and Lk 7:22. MT for this is likewise imperative: הַחֵרְשִׁים שְׁמָעוּ וְהַעִוְרִים הַבִּיטוּ לִרְאוֹת, a verse that also supplies the basis for τυφλοὶ ἀναβλέπουσιν (שְׁמָעוּ is a pausal form of the imperative plural). But for Mt 11:5's χωλοὶ περιπατοῦ-σιν Isa 35:6 comes the closest: ἁλεῖται ὡς ἔλαφος ὁ χωλός ("the lame will leap like a deer"). As for Mt's κωφοὶ ἀκούουσιν Isa 35:6 comes close with ὦτα κωφῶν ἀκούσονται, but Isa 42:18 is closer yet with Οἱ κωφοί, ἀκούσατε (הַחֵרְשִׁים שְׁמָעוּ). Mt's πτωχοὶ εὐαγγελίζονται clearly points to Isa 61:1: לְבַשֵּׂר עֲנָוִים (LXX εὐαγγελί-σασθαι πτωχοῖς).

MASORETIC TEXT	SEPTUAGINT

220: Isa 26:20

²⁰ לֵךְ עַמִּי בֹּא בַחֲדָרֶיךָ וּסְגֹר דְּלָתְיךָ בַּעֲדֶךָ חֲבִי כִמְעַט־רֶגַע עַד־יַעֲבָור־זָעַם׃

²⁰ βάδιζε, λαός μου, εἴσελθε εἰς τὰ ταμίειά σου, ἀπόκλεισον τὴν θύραν σου, ἀποκρύβηθι μικρὸν ὅσον ὅσον, ἕως ἂν παρέλθῃ ἡ ὀργὴ κυρίου·

Hab 2:3–4

³ כִּי עֹוד חָזֹון לַמֹּועֵד וְיָפֵחַ לַקֵּץ וְלֹא יְכַזֵּב אִם־יִתְמַהְמָהּ חַכֵּה־לֹו כִּי־בֹא יָבֹא לֹא יְאַחֵר׃
⁴ הִנֵּה עֻפְּלָה לֹא־יָשְׁרָה נַפְשֹׁו בֹּו וְצַדִּיק בֶּאֱמוּנָתֹו יִחְיֶה׃

³ διότι ἔτι ὅρασις εἰς καιρὸν καὶ ἀνατελεῖ εἰς πέρας καὶ οὐκ εἰς κενόν· ἐὰν ὑστερήσῃ, ὑπόμεινον αὐτόν, ὅτι ἐρχόμενος ἥξει καὶ οὐ μὴ χρονίσῃ. ⁴ ἐὰν ὑποστείληται, οὐκ εὐδοκεῖ ἡ ψυχή μου ἐν αὐτῷ· ὁ δὲ δίκαιος ἐκ πίστεώς μου ζήσεται.

only Hab 2:4 <

221: Isa 27:9

see Isa 59:20–21 [259]

^aHeb 10:37–38

37 ἔτι °γὰρ μικρὸν ὅσον ὅσον,
  ὁ ἐρχόμενος ἥξει καὶ οὐ χρονίσει·
38 ὁ δὲ δίκαιός ⌐μου ἐκ πίστεως⌐ ζήσεται,
  καὶ ἐὰν ὑποστείληται, οὐκ εὐδοκεῖ ⌐ἡ ψυχή μου⌐
  ἐν αὐτῷ.

^bRom 1:17

17 δικαιοσύνη γὰρ θεοῦ ἐν
αὐτῷ ἀποκαλύπτεται ἐκ πίστεως εἰς πίστιν, καθὼς γέ-
γραπται· ὁ δὲ δίκαιος ⊤ ἐκ πίστεως ζήσεται.

^cGal 3:11

11 ὅτι´ δὲ ἐν νόμῳ οὐδεὶς δικαιοῦται παρὰ
τῷ θεῷ δῆλον, ὅτι ὁ δίκαιος ἐκ πίστεως ζήσεται·

Isa 26:20; the phrase μικρὸν ὅσον ὅσον is not being quoted from in Heb 10:37, but Isa 26:20 happens to use it in a totally different connection.

Hab 2:3; MT כִּי־בֹא יָבֹא לֹא יְאַחֵר = LXX ἐρχόμενος ἥξει καὶ οὐ μὴ χρονίσῃ, which = Heb 10:37 except for the ὁ in front of ἐρχόμενος. (A)

Hab 2:4a; MT הִנֵּה עֻפְּלָה becomes in LXX ἐὰν ὑποστείληται, which is a dubious rendering of עֻפְּלָה, a *hapax* probably meaning "has been puffed up (with pride)" from the root עפל, connoting "a swelling, tumor, or mound." Another good possibility is that the correct derivation is from another עפל, = غَفَلَ, "be heedless, be neglectful." The *Hiphil* characteristic from this root (appearing only in Num 14:44) would then mean "show heedlessness," which is not too remote from ὑποστέλλεσθαι "draw back from, shrink from, avoid." This suggests that the proper rendering of Hab 2:4 is: "Behold it (the soul) has become heedless/neglectful." Or if we amend the vocalization to הַנֶּעְפָּלָה (a deponent *Niphal* participle feminine) then: "That (soul) which is heedless/neglectful." The ἐὰν in the LXX might be inferrable from this definite article. Hence this portion of the verse is only moderately free in its rendering; LXX = Heb 10:38b. (E)

Hab 2:4b; MT לֹא־יָשְׁרָה נַפְאוֹ בּוֹ ("His soul is not upright in him") appears in LXX as οὐκ εὐδοκεῖ ἡ ψυχή μου ἐν αὐτῷ. This implies a reading נַפְשִׁי ("my soul") instead of נַפְשׁוֹ. After the introduction of the "square" Hebrew Alphabet, *yod* and *waw* were often confused by the copyists, especially in the Qumran Scrolls. It is therefore quite possible that the original reading of the Hebrew was נַפְשִׁי, and that the verb really should be translated: "My soul is not right in his case (lit. in him)," indicating nonapproval or rejection of the sham believer. For this the LXX gives a justifiable paraphrastic rendering that is followed in Heb 10:38.

Hab 2:4; MT וְצַדִּיק בֶּאֱמוּנָתוֹ יִחְיֶה; LXX ὁ δὲ δίκαιος ἐκ πίστεώς μου ζήσεται = Rom 1:17 except for the μου; (Gal 3:11 likewise omits μου). Here the NT is closer to the MT than LXX, for it implies the πίστις of the righteous man himself, even though there is no αὐτοῦ or ἑαυτοῦ appended to the πίστεως. As for the implications of πίστις, it is true that אֱמוּנָה in the OT usually connotes "faithfulness," but it also serves as the OT word for faith in the sense of a true adherence to God and to His Word (*G-B* Lex. 47B), or of faithfulness in belief and trust (cf. Zorrell *Lex.* 63A).

222: Isa 28:11–12

¹¹ כִּי בְּלַעֲגֵי שָׂפָה וּבְלָשׁוֹן אַחֶרֶת יְדַבֵּר אֶל־הָעָם הַזֶּה:
¹² אֲשֶׁר ׀ אָמַר אֲלֵיהֶם זֹאת הַמְּנוּחָה הָנִיחוּ לֶעָיֵף וְזֹאת הַמַּרְגֵּעָה וְלֹא אָבוּא שְׁמוֹעַ:

¹¹ διὰ φαυλισμὸν χειλέων διὰ γλώσσης ἑτέρας,
ὅτι λαλήσουσιν τῷ λαῷ τούτῳ ¹²λέγοντες αὐτῷ Τοῦτο τὸ ἀνάπαυμα
τῷ πεινῶντι καὶ τοῦτο τὸ σύντριμμα, καὶ οὐκ ἠθέλησαν ἀκούειν.

223: Isa 28:16

see Isa 8:14 [209]

224: Isa 29:10

see Deut 29:3 [109]

225: Isa 29:13

¹³ וַיֹּאמֶר אֲדֹנָי יַעַן כִּי נִגַּשׁ הָעָם הַזֶּה בְּפִיו
וּבִשְׂפָתָיו כִּבְּדוּנִי וְלִבּוֹ רִחַק מִמֶּנִּי
וַתְּהִי יִרְאָתָם אֹתִי מִצְוַת אֲנָשִׁים מְלֻמָּדָה:

¹³ Καὶ εἶπεν κύριος Ἐγγίζει μοι ὁ λαὸς οὗτος τοῖς χείλεσιν αὐτῶν
τιμῶσίν με, ἡ δὲ καρδία αὐτῶν πόρρω ἀπέχει ἀπ᾽ ἐμοῦ, μάτην δὲ
σέβονταί με διδάσκοντες ἐντάλματα ἀνθρώπων καὶ διδασκαλίας.

*a*1 Cor 14:21

21 ἐν
τῷ νόμῳ γέγραπται ὅτι
⌜ἐν ἑτερογλώσσοις καὶ ἐν χείλεσιν ⌜ἑτέρων λαλήσω τῷ
λαῷ τούτῳ
καὶ οὐδ' οὕτως εἰσακούσονταί μου, λέγει κύριος.

Isa 28:11–12; v. 11 MT: כִּי בְּלַעֲגֵי שָׂפָה וּבְלָשׁוֹן אַחֶרֶת יְדַבֵּר אֶל־הָעָם הַזֶּה, "For by the jabbering of a foreign language and by another language He will speak . . ."; (1) The LXX διὰ φαυλισμὸν χειλέων διὰ γλώσσης ἑτέρας ὅτι λαλήσουσιν τῷ λαῷ = 1 Cor 14:21 ἐν ἑτερογλώσσοις καὶ ἐν χείλεσιν ἑτέρων λαλήσω τῷ λαῷ τούτῳ (φαυλισμός =φαύλισμα "disparagement, contempt" only in the LXX according to *L&S*, 1919B), so (*D*); (2) LXX renders לַעֲגֵי שָׂפָה by "contempt in speech." NT omits בְּלַעֲגֵי שָׂפָה altogether and modifies or combines ἐν χείλεσιν ἑτέρων from = לָשׁוֹן אַחֶרֶת = LXX's διὰ γλώσσης ἑτέρας, which of course has about the same meaning, "a foreign language"; (3) MT יְדַבֵּר "He will speak"; LXX "They will speak"; 1 Cor 14:21 "I will speak." All three differ in this matter of who will do the speaking אדבר, ידברו, ידבר. (*B*[d])

(4) MT וְלֹא אָבוּא שְׁמוֹעַ = LXX καὶ οὐκ ἠθέλησαν ἀκούειν; NT καὶ οὐδ' οὕτως εἰσακούσονταί μου. The וְ before אָבוּא may be legitimately translated: "Yet"; if so, then it justifies the οὐδέ of 1 Cor 14:21. And since from context the person who is to be listened to is God Himself, the μου is perfectly warranted. The NT wording heightens the meaning in the light of Israel's opposition to God's Word, and yet that Word found acceptance and faith among Gentiles speaking foreign languages— of which Pentecostal glossalalia was a reminder.

*a*Mt 15:8–9

8 ⌜ὁ λαὸς οὗτος⌝ τοῖς χείλεσίν με τιμᾷ,
ἡ δὲ καρδία αὐτῶν πόρρω ⌜ἀπέχει ἀπ' ἐμοῦ·
9 μάτην δὲ σέβονταί με
διδάσκοντες διδασκαλίας ἐντάλματα ἀνθρώπων.

*b*Mk 7:6–7

6 Ὁ δὲ ⊤ εἶπεν αὐτοῖς· ⊤ καλῶς ἐπροφήτευσεν Ἡσαΐας
περὶ ὑμῶν τῶν ὑποκριτῶν, ὡς γέγραπται ○[ὅτι]
⌜οὗτος ὁ λαὸς⌝ τοῖς χείλεσίν με ⌜τιμᾷ,
ἡ δὲ καρδία αὐτῶν πόρρω ἀπέχει ἀπ' ἐμοῦ·
7 μάτην δὲ σέβονταί με
διδάσκοντες διδασκαλίας ⊤ ἐντάλματα ἀνθρώπων.

Isa 29:13; v. 13a MT יַעַן כִּי נִגַּשׁ הָעָם הַזֶּה בְּפִיו וּבִשְׂפָתָיו כִּבְּדוּנִי; LXX Ἐγγίζοι μοι ὁ λαὸς οὗτος τοῖς χείλεσιν αὐτῶν τιμῶσίν με; (2) MT וְלִבּוֹ רִחַק מִמֶּנִּי; LXX ἡ δὲ καρδία αὐτῶν πόρρω ἀπέχι ἀπ' ἐμοῦ. LXX has (a) omitted בפיו altogether, (b) pointed רִחַק (D10) as רָחַק (G10). Mt 15:8–9 and Mk 7:6–7 omit ἐγγίζει, use singular τιμᾷ rather than plural τιμῶσι, and follow LXX in rendering as רָחַק rather than רִחַק, which may very well be correct, rather than the *piel* of the MT; (3) MT וַתְּהִי יִרְאָתָם אֹתִי מִצְוַת אֲנָשִׁים מְלֻמָּדָה; LXX μάτην δὲ σέβονταί με διδάσκοντες ἐντάλματα ἀνθρώπων καὶ διδασκαλίας; NT has the same μάτην . . . με, but different word order in the next colon: διδάσκοντες διδασκαλίας ἐντάλματα ἀνθρώπων. Here the LXX follows MT word order, but understands מְלֻמָּדָה- as a

226: Isa 29:14

¹⁴ לָכֵן הִנְנִי יוֹסִף◦ לְהַפְלִיא◦◦ אֶת־הָעָם־הַזֶּה◦◦ הַפְלֵא וָפֶלֶא
וְאָבְדָה◦ חָכְמַת חֲכָמָיו וּבִינַת נְבֹנָיו תִּסְתַּתָּר :

¹⁴ διὰ τοῦτο ἰδοὺ ἐγὼ προσθήσω τοῦ μεταθεῖναι τὸν λαὸν τοῦτον καὶ μεταθήσω αὐτοὺς καὶ ἀπολῶ τὴν σοφίαν τῶν σοφῶν καὶ τὴν σύνεσιν τῶν συνετῶν κρύψω.

227: Isa 29:16

¹⁶ הַפְכְּכֶם◦ אִם־כְּחֹמֶר הַיֹּצֵר יֵחָשֵׁב
כִּי־יֹאמַר מַעֲשֶׂה לְעֹשֵׂהוּ◦ לֹא עָשָׂנִי
וְיֵצֶר אָמַר לְיוֹצְרוֹ לֹא הֵבִין :

¹⁶ οὐχ ὡς ὁ πηλὸς τοῦ κερα-
μέως λογισθήσεσθε; μὴ ἐρεῖ τὸ πλάσμα τῷ πλάσαντι Οὐ σύ με ἔπλασας; ἢ τὸ ποίημα τῷ ποιήσαντι Οὐ συνετῶς με ἐποίησας;

collective ("things taught") rather than the MT's singular ("that which is taught"), modifying מִצְוָה. In other words, LXX inserts a καί, making the clause read: "teaching commandments and doctrines of men." This would serve as an acceptable expansion of the MT's "and their fear/reverence of Me has become a (mere) commandment of men which is to be taught" (construing the *pual* participle as a gerundive). The NT reads "teaching (as) doctrines (the) commandments of men." The sense in the MT wording is well preserved here, and the expression of it is a bit smoother for the Greek-speaking audience. The NT quote avoids inserting καί, and is therefore not completely dependent on the LXX (B^d). The μάτην ("vainly") in the LXX and MT seems to be an inference from the context, rather than a לַשָּׁוְא appearing in the supposed *Vorlage* used by the LXX.

---

[a]1 Cor 1:19

19 γέγραπται γάρ·
ἀπολῶ τὴν σοφίαν τῶν σοφῶν
καὶ τὴν σύνεσιν τῶν συνετῶν ἀθετήσω.

Isa 29:14: (1) MT וְאָבְדָה חָכְמַת חֲכָמָיו (Gc 11 from אָבַד); LXX ἀπολῶ points the consonants as וְאַבְדָה (wG44 from אבד), which is just as justifiable as the MT's אָבְדָה so far as syntax and context are concerned; LXX = NT Mk 7:6–7; (2) MT's וּבִינַת נְבֹנָיו תִּסְתַּתָּר ("and the understanding of his prudent ones shall be hidden") is changed by LXX into κρύψω "I will hide," probably to harmonize better with the אבדה of the preceding clause. Here, however, there is no possibility of justifying the LXX as a different and viable vowel pointing; the consonants permit only third person fem. singular (or second masc. singular, which would hardly fit here). The NT follows MT in shifting the verb to first person singular, but uses a different verb, ἀθετήσω. (B^d)

---

[a]Rom 9:20

20 ᾽ὦ ἄνθρωπε, μεν-
οῦνγε᾽ σὺ τίς εἶ ὁ ἀνταποκρινόμενος τῷ θεῷ; μὴ ἐρεῖ τὸ πλάσμα τῷ πλάσαντι· τί με ᾽ἐποίησας οὕτως;

Isa 29:16*b*; MT כִּי־יֹאמַר מַעֲשֶׂה לְעֹשֵׂהוּ לֹא עָשָׂנִי; LXX μὴ ἐρεῖ τὸ πλάσμα τῷ πλάσμα Οὐ σύ με ἔπλασας; note that the LXX here takes כִּי as asseverative ("Indeed"), introducing an interrogative sentence, rather than as a continuative result clause (as MT has it: "shall the potter be considered as equal with the clay, *that* what is made should say . . . ?"). Hence LXX uses μή—interrogative (= Latin *num*?). This is followed by Rom 9:20 μὴ ἐρεῖ . . . πλάσαντι. But note that Rom inserts an interrogative τί ("why?") in place of LXX's negative οὐ before ἔπλασας (which in turn corresponds to MT's לֹא before עָשָׂנִי). It may be that Paul read לְמָא instead of לֹא in his Hebrew Bible (D^a). In any event, the general

227 (continued)

228: Isa 34:4

see Isa 13:10 [215]

229: Isa 35:4

see Isa 62:11 [262]

230: Isa 35:5–6

see Isa 26:19 [219]

231: Isa 40:3

³ קוֹל קוֹרֵא
בַּמִּדְבָּר פַּנּוּ דֶּרֶךְ יְהוָה
יַשְּׁרוּ בָּעֲרָבָה מְסִלָּה לֵאלֹהֵינוּ׃

³ φωνὴ βοῶν-
τος ἐν τῇ ἐρήμῳ Ἑτοιμάσατε τὴν ὁδὸν κυρίου, εὐθείας ποιεῖτε
τὰς τρίβους τοῦ θεοῦ ἡμῶν·

232: Isa 40:6–8

⁶ קוֹל אֹמֵר קְרָא וְאָמַר מָה אֶקְרָא
כָּל־הַבָּשָׂר חָצִיר וְכָל־חַסְדּוֹ כְּצִיץ הַשָּׂדֶה׃ | הָעָם׃
⁷ יָבֵשׁ חָצִיר נָבֵל צִיץ כִּי רוּחַ יְהוָה נָשְׁבָה בּוֹ אָכֵן חָצִיר
⁸ יָבֵשׁ חָצִיר נָבֵל צִיץ וּדְבַר־אֱלֹהֵינוּ יָקוּם לְעוֹלָם׃

⁶ φωνὴ λέγοντος Βόησον· καὶ εἶπα Τί βοήσω; Πᾶσα
σὰρξ χόρτος, καὶ πᾶσα δόξα ἀνθρώπου ὡς ἄνθος χόρτου· ⁷ ἐξηράνθη ὁ χόρτος, καὶ τὸ ἄνθος ἐξέπεσεν, ⁸ τὸ δὲ ῥῆμα τοῦ θεοῦ
ἡμῶν μένει εἰς τὸν αἰῶνα.

meaning of the sentence remains unaffected; the creature is imprudently challenging the sovereign prerogatives of his Creator. However, Paul does pitch the question of the rebel more in the direction of why God made him the way he is, rather than questioning whether God really created him in the first place. Thus he brings out more sharply his meaning by adding an οὕτως which is not found in the ending of Isa 29:16 either in MT or LXX.

---

*a*Mt 3:3

3 οὗτος γάρ ἐστιν ὁ ῥηθεὶς διὰ Ἡσαΐου τοῦ προφήτου λέγοντος·
  □φωνὴ βοῶντος ἐν τῇ ἐρήμῳ· ↘
  ἐτοιμάσατε τὴν ὁδὸν κυρίου,
    □1εὐθείας ποιεῖτε τὰς τρίβους αὐτοῦ.↘

*b*Mk 1:3

3 φωνὴ βοῶντος ἐν τῇ ἐρήμῳ·
  ἐτοιμάσατε τὴν ὁδὸν κυρίου,
  εὐθείας ποιεῖτε τὰς τρίβους ⌐αὐτοῦ⌐1,T1↘

*c*Jn 1:23

23 ἔφη· ἐγὼ φωνὴ βοῶντος ἐν τῇ ἐρήμῳ·
    εὐθύνατε τὴν ὁδὸν κυρίου,
  καθὼς εἶπεν Ἡσαΐας ὁ προφήτης.

Isa 40:3: (1) MT קוֹל . . . דֶּרֶךְ יהוה = LXX = Mt 3:3 and Mk 1:3. Note, however, that קוֹרֵא after קוֹל is usually understood as periphrastic: "A voice is crying out." But it could also indicate a construct pair: "the voice of one who cries out"), which is the way the LXX took it; likewise the NT: φωνὴ βοῶντος (rather than βοῶσα); (2) MT יַשְּׁרוּ בָּעֲרָבָה מְסִלָּה לֵאלֹהֵינוּ; LXX εὐθείας ποιεῖτε τὰς τρίβους "Prepare in the wilderness a highway for Him (αὐτοῦ); Make the paths of our God straight." Note that the LXX degrades מְסִלָּה ("highway") to mere pathways (τρίβους) and shortens "for our God" to merely "His paths"—a difference in wording, but the same in meaning.

In John 1:23 we find φωνὴ . . . ἐρήμῳ as in the Synoptics, but in the second line we find εὐθύνατε τὴν ὁδὸν κυρίου ("Make straight the way/road of the Lord"), with ὁδὸν closer to מְסִלָּה than τρίβους was. John seems to be quite dependent on the LXX in this second line, although just as close to the MT as LXX is. (A^d)

---

*a*1 Pet 1:24–25

24 ⌐διότι
  πᾶσα σὰρξ ○ὡς χόρτος
  καὶ πᾶσα δόξα ⌐αὐτῆς ὡς ἄνθος ○1χόρτου·
  ἐξηράνθη ὁ χόρτος καὶ τὸ ἄνθος T ἐξέπεσεν·
    25 τὸ δὲ ῥῆμα κυρίου μένει εἰς τὸν αἰῶνα.

Isa 40:6–8; MT = LXX = 1 Pet 1:24–25 except that: (1) neither MT nor LXX has a ὡς before χόρτος, but Peter's ὡς makes the thought a bit clearer; (2) for חֶסֶד ("grace, loveliness") LXX (followed by NT) uses a meaning that NIV adopts in "and all their *glory* is like the flowers of the field"; (3) נָבֵל צִיץ ("the flower withers away") is rendered ἐξέπεσεν ("has fallen off") in LXX and NT—possibly because ἐξηράνθη has already been used for יָבֵשׁ. (A^d)

233: Isa 40:13

¹³ מִי־תִכֵּן אֶת־רוּחַ יְהוָה וְאִישׁ עֲצָתוֹ יוֹדִיעֶנּוּ:

¹³τίς ἔγνω νοῦν κυρίου, καὶ τίς αὐτοῦ σύμβουλος ἐγένετο, ὃς συμβιβᾷ αὐτόν;

234: Isa 42:1-4

¹ הֵן עַבְדִּי אֶתְמָךְ־בּוֹ בְּחִירִי רָצְתָה נַפְשִׁי
נָתַתִּי רוּחִי עָלָיו מִשְׁפָּט לַגּוֹיִם יוֹצִיא:
² לֹא יִצְעַק וְלֹא יִשָּׂא וְלֹא־יַשְׁמִיעַ בַּחוּץ קוֹלוֹ:
³ קָנֶה רָצוּץ לֹא יִשְׁבּוֹר וּפִשְׁתָּה כֵהָה לֹא יְכַבֶּנָּה
לֶאֱמֶת יוֹצִיא מִשְׁפָּט: ⁴ לֹא יִכְהֶה וְלֹא יָרוּץ
עַד־יָשִׂים בָּאָרֶץ מִשְׁפָּט וּלְתוֹרָתוֹ אִיִּים יְיַחֵילוּ:

¹Ιακωβ ὁ παῖς μου, ἀντιλήμψομαι αὐτοῦ· Ισραηλ ὁ ἐκλεκτός μου, προσεδέξατο αὐτὸν ἡ ψυχή μου· ἔδωκα τὸ πνεῦμά μου ἐπ' αὐτόν, κρίσιν τοῖς ἔθνεσιν ἐξοίσει. ²οὐ κεκράξεται οὐδὲ ἀνήσει, οὐδὲ ἀκουσθήσεται ἔξω ἡ φωνὴ αὐτοῦ. ³κάλαμον τεθλασμένον οὐ συντρίψει καὶ λίνον καπνιζόμενον οὐ σβέσει, ἀλλὰ εἰς ἀλήθειαν ἐξοίσει κρίσιν. ⁴ἀναλάμψει καὶ οὐ θραυσθήσεται, ἕως ἂν θῇ ἐπὶ τῆς γῆς κρίσιν· καὶ ἐπὶ τῷ ὀνόματι αὐτοῦ ἔθνη ἐλπιοῦσιν.

*a*Rom 11:34

34 τίς γὰρ ἔγνω νοῦν κυρίου;
ἢ τίς σύμβουλος αὐτοῦ ἐγένετο;

*b*1 Cor 2:16

16 τίς γὰρ ἔγνω νοῦν
κυρίου, ὃς συμβιβάσει αὐτόν; ἡμεῖς δὲ νοῦν ⌐Χριστοῦ
ἔχομεν.

Isa 40:13: (1) MT is substantially equivalent to LXX and Rom 11:34 except that (1) תִּכֵּן "measured/directed" (the Spirit of Yahweh) becomes ἔγνω in LXX (a very undistinctive rendering!) and NT (*B*), and (b) MT וְאִישׁ עֲצָתוֹ יוֹדִיעֶנּוּ = "... or as His couselor," a rather approximate rendering, since ἐγένετο hardly does justice to יוֹדִיעֶנּוּ; (2) 1 Cor 2:16 conforms to the LXX in the first clause (τίς γὰρ ἔγνω νοῦν κυρίου), but shows an independent rendition of יוֹדִיעֶנּוּ as συμβιβάσει ("I will instruct"), which is quite accurate. Paul does not follow the LXX here. (*C*)

---

*a*Mt 12:18–21

18 ἰδοὺ ὁ παῖς μου ⊤ ὃν ᾑρέτισα,
ὁ ἀγαπητός μου ⌐εἰς ὃν⌐ εὐδόκησεν ἡ ψυχή μου·
θήσω τὸ πνεῦμά μου ἐπ' αὐτόν,
καὶ κρίσιν τοῖς ἔθνεσιν ἀπαγγελεῖ.
19 οὐκ ἐρίσει οὐδὲ κραυγάσει,
οὐδὲ ἀκούσει τις ἐν ταῖς πλατείαις τὴν φωνὴν αὐτοῦ.
20 □κάλαμον συντετριμμένον↘ οὐ κατεάξει
καὶ λίνον τυφόμενον οὐ σβέσει,
ἕως ἂν ἐκβάλῃ εἰς νῖκος τὴν κρίσιν⊤.
21 καὶ ⊤ τῷ ὀνόματι αὐτοῦ ἔθνη ἐλπιοῦσιν.

Isa 42:1–4; this is a classic case of the independence of the LXX on Matthew's part. Isa 42:1 MT הֵן עַבְדִּי אֶתְמָךְ־בּוֹ; LXX 'Ιακωβ ὁ παῖς μου, ἀντιλήμψομαι αὐτοῦ; Mt 12:18 ἰδοὺ ὁ παῖς μου ὃν ᾑρέτισα; (1) Matthew closely renders MT as "Behold, My Servant," whereas LXX inserts the name Jacob in an interpretive way, dropping out "Behold" in the process (*C*); (2) Isa 42:1*b* MT בְּחִירִי רָצְתָה נַפְשִׁי; LXX Ισραηλ ὁ ἐκλεκτός μου, προσδέξατο αὐτὸν ἡ ψυχή μου; NT Mt 12:18*b* ὁ ἀγαπητός μου εἰς ὃν εὐδόκησεν ἡ ψυχή μου, where "in whom my soul is well pleased" is a good alternative rendering for רָצְתָה, along with LXX's "My soul has received/accepted him" (*C*); (3) 42:1*c* MT נָתַתִּי רוּחִי עָלָיו; LXX ἔδωκα τὸ πνεῦμά μου ἐπ' αὐτόν; Mt 12:18*b* θήσω τὸ πνεῦμά μου, κτλ. Matthew construes נָתַתִּי as a prophetic perfect (hence future θήσω), whereas LXX uses the aorist (*A*[d]); (4) 42:1*d* MT מִשְׁפָּט לַגּוֹיִם יוֹצִיא; LXX κρίσιν τοῖς ἔθνεσιν ἐξοίσει; NT καὶ κρίσιν τοῖς ἔθνεσιν ἀπαγγελεῖ. Here the LXX is more literal (ἐξοίσει = יוֹצִיא), but Matthew conveys the concept more clearly ("He will proclaim judgment") (*A*[d]); (5) 42:2 MT לֹא יִצְעַק וְלֹא יִשָּׂא וְלֹא־יַשְׁמִיעַ בַּחוּץ קוֹלוֹ: (יִשָּׂא also governs קוֹלוֹ); LXX οὐ κεκράξεται οὐδὲ ἀνήσει, οὐδὲ ἀκουσθήσεται ἔξω ἡ φωνὴ αὐτοῦ. The ἀνήσει "give up, desist" is incorrect for יִשָּׂא ... קוֹל. The passive ἀκουσθήσεται is wrong for יַשְׁמִיעַ, although close enough in sense. Mt 12:19 οὐκ ἐρίσει οὐδὲ κραυγάσει, οὐδὲ ἀκούσει τις ἐν ταῖς πλατείαις τὴν φωνὴν αὐτοῦ: (i) ἐρίσει ("will contend/argue contentiously") is a bit paraphrastic for יִצְעַק ("will cry aloud"); (ii) κραυγάσει is much more accurate for יִשָּׂא ... קוֹלוֹ than LXX's ἀνήσει ("will desist"), which is definitely wrong; (iii) ἀκούσει τις is not accurate for יַשְׁמִיעַ, although it is closer in meaning perhaps than LXX's ἀκούσει (which seems to suggest that the messianic Servant is the one who will not hear) (*C*); (6) 42:3 MT קָנֶה רָצוּץ לֹא יִשְׁבּוֹר

113

234 (continued)

235: Isa 42:18

see Isa 26:19 [219]

236: Isa 43:20–21

see Ex 19:6 [46]

237: Isa 44:28

see 1 Sam 13:14 [118]

238: Isa 45:21

see Deut 4:35 [78]

239: Isa 45:23

²³ בִּי נִשְׁבַּעְתִּי

יָצָא מִפִּי צְדָקָה   דָּבָר וְלֹא יָשׁוּב

כִּי־לִי תִּכְרַע כָּל־בֶּרֶךְ   תִּשָּׁבַע כָּל־לָשׁוֹן:

²³κατ' ἐμαυτοῦ ὀμνύω Ἦ μὴν ἐξελεύσεται ἐκ
τοῦ στόματός μου δικαιοσύνη, οἱ λόγοι μου οὐκ ἀποστραφήσονται
ὅτι ἐμοὶ κάμψει πᾶν γόνυ καὶ ἐξομολογήσεται πᾶσα γλῶσσα τῷ
θεῷ

Isa 49:18

¹⁸ שְׂאִי־סָבִיב עֵינַיִךְ וּרְאִי   כֻּלָּם נִקְבְּצוּ בָאוּ־לָךְ | כְּכַלָּה:

חַי־אָנִי נְאֻם־יְהוָה   כִּי כֻלָּם כָּעֲדִי תִלְבָּשִׁי   וּתְקַשְּׁרִים׳

¹⁸ἆρον κύκλῳ τοὺς ὀφθαλμούς σου καὶ ἰδὲ πάν-
τας, ἰδοὺ συνήχθησαν καὶ ἤλθοσαν πρὸς σέ· ζῶ ἐγώ, λέγει κύριος,
ὅτι πάντας αὐτοὺς ἐνδύσῃ καὶ περιθήσῃ αὐτοὺς ὡς κόσμον νύμφης.

וּפִשְׁתָּה כֵהָה לֹא יְכַבֶּנָּה, for which LXX has a good, accurate rendering. Mt 12:20 is likewise accurate, but (i) it uses συντετριμμένον (for רָצוּץ) rather than τεθλασμένον, (A); (ii) uses οὐ κατεάξει ("he will not break/crush") for לֹא יִשְׁבּוֹר rather than LXX's οὐ συντρίψει; (iii) uses τυφόμενον ("smoldering") rather than LXX's καπνιζόμενον ("smoking") for כֵהָה. Then Mt 12:20b skips over the rest of Isa 42:3 and the first part of verse 4; (7) 42:4b reads עַד־יָשִׂים בָּאָרֶץ מִשְׁפָּט וּלְתוֹרָתוֹ אִיִּים יְיַחֵילוּ. For this line the LXX gives an accurate, trouble-free translation, but Mt 12:20c deviates as follows: "Until He puts forth judgment unto victory." That is, Matthew uses ἐκβάλῃ for שִׂים, with κρίσιν = מִשְׁפָּט as its object. This gives a more dynamic force to the action than does the LXX's θῇ ("sets/lays down"). As for εἰς νῖκος, that is impossible for בָּאָרֶץ, which the LXX well renders by ἐπὶ τῆς γῆς. Nestle does not print it in italics, but it is still framed by the context in Isa 42:4. Conceivably the establishment of God's perfect justice on earth is to be understood as involving a conquest or subduing of mankind in order to render them obedient to the Lord's judgment. If so rendered, then εἰς νῖκος brings out explicitly what is implicit in the phraseology of the original. (D)

---

^aRom 14:11

11 γέ- γραπται γάρ·
    ζῶ ἐγώ, λέγει κύριος, ⌜ὅτι ἐμοὶ κάμψει πᾶν γόνυ καὶ πᾶσα γλῶσσα ἐξομολογήσεται τῷ θεῷ.

Is 45:23; MT is quite closely followed by the LXX and NT (Rom 14:11) except that: (1) Paul's introductory ζῶ ἐγώ, λέγει κύριος is picked up from general usage elsewhere in the OT, such as in Isa 49:18, Ezek 5:11 and Jer 22:24 (also quoted in column 1). All of these have חַי־אָנִי נְאֻם יהוה. So also Num 14:28, which introduces God's judgment of forty years' wandering upon the rebels of Kadesh Barnea. (A-)

239 (continued)

Ezek 5:11

‎¹¹לָכֵן֩ חַי־אָ֨נִי נְאֻ֜ם אֲדֹנָ֣י יְהוִ֗ה אִם־לֹ֠א יַ֣עַן אֶת־מִקְדָּשִׁ֞י טִמֵּ֤את בְּכָל־ שִׁקּוּצַ֙יִךְ֙ וּבְכָל־תּוֹעֲבֹתָ֔יִךְ וְגַם־אֲנִ֤י אֶגְרַע֙ וְלֹא־תָח֣וֹס עֵינִ֔י וְגַם־אֲנִ֖י לֹ֥א אֶחְמֽוֹל׃

¹¹διὰ
τοῦτο Ζῶ ἐγώ, λέγει κύριος, εἰ μὴ ἀνθ᾽ ὧν τὰ ἅγιά μου ἐμίανας ἐν πᾶσιν τοῖς βδελύγμασίν σου, κἀγὼ ἀπώσομαί σε, οὐ φείσεταί μου ὁ ὀφθαλμός, κἀγὼ οὐκ ἐλεήσω.

Jer 22:24

‎²⁴חַי־אָ֣נִי נְאֻם־יְהוָ֔ה כִּ֣י אִם־יִהְיֶ֞ה כָּנְיָ֤הוּ בֶן־יְהֽוֹיָקִים֙ מֶ֣לֶךְ יְהוּדָ֔ה חוֹתָ֖ם עַל־יַ֣ד יְמִינִ֑י כִּ֥י מִשָּׁ֖ם אֶתְּקֶֽנְךָּ׃

²⁴Ζῶ ἐγώ, λέγει κύριος, ἐὰν γενόμενος γένηται Ιεχονιας υἱὸς Ιωακιμ βασιλεὺς Ιουδα ἀποσφράγισμα ἐπὶ τῆς χειρὸς τῆς δεξιᾶς μου, ἐκεῖθεν ἐκσπάσω σε

240: Isa 49:6

‎⁶וַיֹּ֗אמֶר נָקֵ֣ל מִֽהְיוֹתְךָ֣ לִי֮ עֶבֶד֒ לְהָקִים֙ אֶת־שִׁבְטֵ֣י יַֽעֲקֹ֔ב וּנְצִירֵ֥י יִשְׂרָאֵ֖ל לְהָשִׁ֑יב וּנְתַתִּ֙יךָ֙ לְא֣וֹר גּוֹיִ֔ם לִהְי֥וֹת יְשׁוּעָתִ֖י עַד־קְצֵ֥ה הָאָֽרֶץ׃

⁶καὶ εἶπέν μοι Μέγα σοί ἐστιν τοῦ κληθῆναί σε παῖδά μου τοῦ στῆσαι τὰς φυλὰς Ιακωβ καὶ τὴν διασπορὰν τοῦ Ισραηλ ἐπιστρέψαι· ἰδοὺ τέθεικά σε εἰς διαθήκην γένους εἰς φῶς ἐθνῶν τοῦ εἶναί σε εἰς σωτηρίαν ἕως ἐσχάτου τῆς γῆς.

241: Isa 49:8

‎⁸כֹּ֣ה ׀ אָמַ֣ר יְהוָ֗ה בְּעֵ֤ת רָצוֹן֙ עֲנִיתִ֔יךָ וּבְי֥וֹם יְשׁוּעָ֖ה עֲזַרְתִּ֑יךָ וְאֶצָּרְךָ֗ וְאֶתֶּנְךָ֙ לִבְרִ֣ית עָ֔ם לְהָקִ֣ים אֶ֔רֶץ לְהַנְחִ֖יל נְחָל֥וֹת שֹׁמֵמֽוֹת׃

⁸οὕτως λέγει
κύριος Καιρῷ δεκτῷ ἐπήκουσά σου καὶ ἐν ἡμέρᾳ σωτηρίας ἐβοήθησά σοι καὶ ἔδωκά σε εἰς διαθήκην ἐθνῶν τοῦ καταστῆσαι τὴν γῆν καὶ κληρονομῆσαι κληρονομίαν ἐρήμου,

242: Isa 49:18

see Isa 45:23 [239]

243: Isa 52:5

‎⁵וְעַתָּ֣ה מי־לי־פֹה֙ נְאֻם־יְהוָ֔ה כִּֽי־לֻקַּ֥ח עַמִּ֖י חִנָּ֑ם מֹשְׁלָ֤יו יְהֵילִ֙ילוּ֙ נְאֻם־יְהוָ֔ה וְתָמִ֥יד כָּל־ הַיּ֖וֹם שְׁמִ֥י מִנֹּאָֽץ׃

⁵καὶ νῦν τί ὧδέ
ἐστε; τάδε λέγει κύριος. ὅτι ἐλήμφθη ὁ λαός μου δωρεάν, θαυμάζετε καὶ ὀλολύζετε· τάδε λέγει κύριος. δι᾽ ὑμᾶς διὰ παντὸς τὸ ὄνομά μου βλασφημεῖται ἐν τοῖς ἔθνεσιν.

[a]Acts 13:47

47 οὕτως γὰρ ⌜ἐντέταλται ἡμῖν ὁ κύριος·
τέθεικά σε εἰς φῶς ἐθνῶν
   τοῦ εἶναί σε εἰς σωτηρίαν ἕως ἐσχάτου τῆς γῆς.

Isa 49:6; MT = LXX = Acts 13:47 which, however, omits quite a few words in between. (*A*)

[a]2 Cor 6:2

2 λέγει γάρ·
   καιρῷ δεκτῷ ἐπήκουσά σου
   καὶ ἐν ἡμέρᾳ σωτηρίας ἐβοήθησά σοι.
ἰδοὺ νῦν καιρὸς ⌜εὐπρόσδεκτος, ἰδοὺ νῦν ἡμέρα σωτηρίας.

Isa 49:8; MT = LXX = 2 Cor 6:2. (*A*)

[a]Rom 2:24

24 τὸ γὰρ ὄνομα τοῦ θεοῦ δι' ὑμᾶς βλασφημεῖται ἐν τοῖς ἔθνεσιν, καθὼς γέγραπται.

Isa 52:5; MT מִנֹּאָץ כִּי־לֻקַּח עַמִּי חִנָּם מֹשְׁלָו יְהֵילִילוּ נְאֻם־יהוה וְתָמִיד כָּל־הַיּוֹם; LXX τάδε λέγει κύριος· . . . δι' ὑμᾶς διὰ παντὸς τὸ ὄνομά μου βλασφημεῖται ἐν τοῖς ἔθνεσιν; Rom 2:24 τὸ γὰρ ὄνομα τοῦ θεοῦ δι' ὑμᾶς βλασφημεῖται ἐν τοῖς ἔθνεσιν, καθὼς γέγραπται. Here we see that Rom picks up all of the LXX verse except for the διὰ παντός (which = תָּמִיד in the MT). Obviously Paul is simply quoting from the LXX (*B*). The problems arise in comparing the LXX with the MT. We note the following: (1) MT does not indicate who is scorning or reviling God's name; no agent is expressed, which suggests that in general the name of Yahweh is reviled or scorned among the Gentiles; (2) MT also does not indicate the occasion or ground for this revilement. The LXX supplies δι' ὑμᾶς, which is an important element in Paul's discussion here in Rom 2. But perhaps Paul was content to let the insertion stand (even though he knew it was not in the Hebrew text) because of the close parallel in Ezek 36:23: וְקִדַּשְׁתִּי אֶת־שְׁמִי הַגָּדוֹל הַמְחֻלָּל בַּגּוֹיִם אֲשֶׁר חִלַּלְתֶּם בְּתוֹכָם "And I will

243 (continued)

244: Isa 52:7

⁷ מַה־נָּאווּ עַל־הֶהָרִים רַגְלֵי מְבַשֵּׂר
מַשְׁמִיעַ שָׁלוֹם מְבַשֵּׂר טוֹב מַשְׁמִיעַ יְשׁוּעָה
אֹמֵר לְצִיּוֹן מָלַךְ אֱלֹהָיִךְ:

⁷ ὡς ὥρα ἐπὶ τῶν ὀρέων, ὡς πόδες εὐαγγελιζομένου ἀκοὴν
εἰρήνης, ὡς εὐαγγελιζόμενος ἀγαθά, ὅτι ἀκουστὴν ποιήσω τὴν σωτηρίαν σου λέγων Σιων Βασιλεύσει σου ὁ θεός·

Nahum 2:1

¹ הִנֵּה עַל־הֶהָרִים רַגְלֵי מְבַשֵּׂר מַשְׁמִיעַ שָׁלוֹם
חָגִּי יְהוּדָה חַגַּיִךְ שַׁלְּמִי נְדָרָיִךְ
כִּי לֹא יוֹסִיף עוֹד לַעֲבָר־בָּךְ בְּלִיַּעַל
כֻּלֹּה נִכְרָת:

¹ Ἰδοὺ ἐπὶ τὰ ὄρη οἱ πόδες εὐαγγελιζομένου καὶ ἀπαγγέλλοντος
εἰρήνην· ἑόρταζε, Ιουδα, τὰς ἑορτάς σου, ἀπόδος τὰς εὐχάς σου,
διότι οὐ μὴ προσθήσωσιν ἔτι τοῦ διελθεῖν διὰ σοῦ εἰς παλαίωσιν
Συντετέλεσται, ἐξῆρται.

245: Isa 52:11

¹¹ סוּרוּ סוּרוּ צְאוּ מִשָּׁם טָמֵא אַל־תִּגָּעוּ
צְאוּ מִתּוֹכָהּ הִבָּרוּ נֹשְׂאֵי כְּלֵי יְהוָה:

¹¹ ἀπόστητε ἀπόστητε ἐξέλθατε ἐκεῖθεν καὶ ἀκαθάρτου μὴ ἅπτεσθε,
ἐξέλθατε ἐκ μέσου αὐτῆς ἀφορίσθητε, οἱ φέροντες τὰ σκεύη κυρίου·

Ezek 20:34, 41

³⁴ וְהוֹצֵאתִי אֶתְכֶם מִן־הָעַמִּים וְקִבַּצְתִּי
אֶתְכֶם מִן־הָאֲרָצוֹת אֲשֶׁר נְפוֹצֹתֶם בָּם בְּיָד חֲזָקָה וּבִזְרוֹעַ נְטוּיָה
וּבְחֵמָה שְׁפוּכָה:

³⁴ καὶ ἐξάξω ὑμᾶς ἐκ τῶν λαῶν καὶ
εἰσδέξομαι ὑμᾶς ἐκ τῶν χωρῶν, οὗ διεσκορπίσθητε ἐν αὐταῖς, ἐν
χειρὶ κραταιᾷ καὶ ἐν βραχίονι ὑψηλῷ καὶ ἐν θυμῷ κεχυμένῳ·

⁴¹ בְּרֵיחַ
נִיחֹחַ אֶרְצֶה אֶתְכֶם בְּהוֹצִיאִי אֶתְכֶם מִן־הָעַמִּים וְקִבַּצְתִּי אֶתְכֶם מִן־
הָאֲרָצוֹת אֲשֶׁר נְפֹצֹתֶם בָּם וְנִקְדַּשְׁתִּי בָכֶם לְעֵינֵי הַגּוֹיִם:

⁴¹ ἐν ὀσμῇ εὐωδίας προσδέξομαι ὑμᾶς ἐν τῷ ἐξαγαγεῖν με
ὑμᾶς ἐκ τῶν λαῶν καὶ εἰσδέχεσθαι ὑμᾶς ἐκ τῶν χωρῶν, ἐν αἷς
διεσκορπίσθητε ἐν αὐταῖς, καὶ ἁγιασθήσομαι ἐν ὑμῖν κατ᾽ ὀφθαλμοὺς τῶν λαῶν.

sanctify My great name which is profaned among the Gentiles, which you have profaned in their midst" (B). This passage makes it clear enough that God had to reproach His covenant people Israel for the way they had profaned His name by idolatry and moral depravity in the promised land, thus making inevitable the fall of Jerusalem in 587 B.C. and the Babylonian captivity that ensued.

---

[a]Rom 10:15

15 πῶς δὲ κηρύξωσιν ἐὰν μὴ
ἀποσταλῶσιν; ⌜καθὼς γέγραπται· ὡς ὡραῖοι οἱ πόδες ⊤
τῶν εὐαγγελιζομένων ○[τὰ] ἀγαθά.

Isa 52:7; in Rom 10:15 Paul is much closer to the MT than the LXX is: מַה־נָּאווּ עַל־הֶהָרִים רַגְלֵי מְבַשֵּׂר מַשְׁמִיעַ שָׁלוֹם מְבַשֵּׂר טוֹב; LXX ὡς ὥρα ἐπὶ τῶν ὀρέων, ὡς πόδες εὐαγγελιζομένων ἀκοὴν εἰρήνης, ὡς εὐαγγελιζόμενος ἀγαθά; NT reads ὡς ὡραῖοι οἱ πόδες τῶν εὐαγγελιζομένων [τὰ] ἀγαθά. Thus LXX construes it: "Like spring upon the mountains, like the feet of those bringing as good news the report of peace, like one who brings tidings of good things." Paul's quotation of Isa 52:7 may be somewhat abbreviated, but his ὡραῖοι for נָּאווּ is much better than "spring upon the mountains," which may possibly be the result of textual error (i.e., ὥρα for ὡραῖοι) since it is far off base. But like the LXX, Paul takes the singular participle מְבַשֵּׂר as a collective, and therefore renders it as a plural, τῶν εὐαγγελιζομένων. This is perfectly justifiable in the context. (C)

Nahum 2:1. This passage parallels Isa 52:7 in all respects except that an opening הִנֵּה ("Behold!") replaces מַה־נָּאווּ, but it actually contributes nothing distinctive to the quotation in Rom 10:15.

---

[a]2 Cor 6:17

17 διὸ ἐξέλθατε ἐκ μέσου αὐτῶν
καὶ ἀφορίσθητε, λέγει κύριος,
καὶ ἀκαθάρτου μὴ ἅπτεσθε·
κἀγὼ εἰσδέξομαι ὑμᾶς

Isa 52:11; MT = LXX. NT (2 Cor 6:17) contains most of the LXX text, but in a different word order (B). The reason for the altered word order is not apparent, although the NT rearrangement is certainly more poetic. (D[a], a conflate quote).

Ezek 20:34; The final line of 2 Cor 6:17 is taken from this passage, which contains a similar exhortation and promise to that of Isa 52:11, but includes the assurance וְקִבַּצְתִּי אֶתְכֶם, "I will *gather* you (from among the Gentiles)," which is slightly altered in meaning to εἰσδέξομαι ὑμᾶς, "I will *receive* you." But Schl. 692 points out that εἰσδέξεσθαι is similarly used for קבץ in Ezek 20:34; 22:20; Zech 10:8, and so it was apparently a common interpretation on the part of the Alexandrian Jews. (A[d])

246: Isa 52:15

¹⁵ כֵּ֤ן יַזֶּה֙ גּוֹיִ֣ם רַבִּ֔ים עָלָ֛יו יִקְפְּצ֥וּ מְלָכִ֖ים פִּיהֶ֑ם
כִּ֠י אֲשֶׁ֨ר לֹֽא־סֻפַּ֤ר לָהֶם֙ רָא֔וּ וַאֲשֶׁ֥ר לֹֽא־שָׁמְע֖וּ הִתְבּוֹנָֽנוּ׃

¹⁵οὕτως θαυμάσονται ἔθνη πολλὰ ἐπ᾽ αὐτῷ, καὶ συνέξουσιν βασιλεῖς τὸ στόμα αὐτῶν · ὅτι οἷς οὐκ ἀνηγγέλη περὶ αὐτοῦ, ὄψονται, **καὶ οἱ οὐκ ἀκηκόασιν, συνήσουσιν.** —

247: Isa 53:1

¹ מִ֥י הֶאֱמִ֖ין לִשְׁמֻעָתֵ֑נוּ וּזְר֥וֹעַ יְהוָ֖ה עַל־מִ֥י נִגְלָֽתָה׃

¹κύριε, τίς ἐπίστευσεν τῇ
ἀκοῇ ἡμῶν; καὶ ὁ βραχίων κυρίου τίνι ἀπεκαλύφθη;

248: Isa 53:4–5

⁴ אָכֵ֤ן חֳלָיֵ֙נוּ֙ ה֣וּא נָשָׂ֔א וּמַכְאֹבֵ֖ינוּ סְבָלָ֑ם
וַאֲנַ֣חְנוּ חֲשַׁבְנֻ֔הוּ נָג֖וּעַ מֻכֵּ֥ה אֱלֹהִ֖ים וּמְעֻנֶּֽה׃

⁴οὗτος τὰς ἁμαρτίας ἡμῶν φέρει καὶ περὶ ἡμῶν ὀδυνᾶται, καὶ ἡμεῖς ἐλογισάμεθα αὐτὸν εἶναι ἐν πόνῳ καὶ ἐν πληγῇ καὶ ἐν κακώσει.

⁵ וְהוּא֙ מְחֹלָ֣ל מִפְּשָׁעֵ֔נוּ מְדֻכָּ֖א מֵעֲוֺנֹתֵ֑ינוּ
מוּסַ֤ר שְׁלוֹמֵ֙נוּ֙ עָלָ֔יו וּבַחֲבֻרָת֖וֹ נִרְפָּא־לָֽנוּ׃

⁵αὐτὸς δὲ ἐτραυματίσθη διὰ τὰς ἀνομίας ἡμῶν καὶ μεμαλάκισται δια τὰς ἁμαρτίας ἡμῶν · παιδεία εἰρήνης ἡμῶν ἐπ᾽ αὐτόν, τῷ μώλωπι αὐτοῦ ἡμεῖς ἰάθημεν.

249: Isa 53:7–8

⁷ נִגַּ֨שׂ וְה֣וּא נַעֲנֶה֮ וְלֹ֣א יִפְתַּח־פִּיו֒
כַּשֶּׂה֙ לַטֶּ֣בַח יוּבָ֔ל וּכְרָחֵ֕ל לִפְנֵ֥י גֹזְזֶ֖יהָ נֶאֱלָ֑מָה
וְלֹ֥א יִפְתַּ֖ח פִּֽיו׃
⁸ מֵעֹ֤צֶר וּמִמִּשְׁפָּט֙ לֻקָּ֔ח וְאֶת־דּוֹר֖וֹ מִ֣י יְשׂוֹחֵ֑חַ
כִּ֤י נִגְזַר֙ מֵאֶ֣רֶץ חַיִּ֔ים מִפֶּ֥שַׁע עַמִּ֖י נֶ֥גַע לָֽמוֹ׃

⁷καὶ αὐτὸς διὰ τὸ κεκακῶσθαι οὐκ ἀνοίγει
τὸ στόμα · ὡς πρόβατον ἐπὶ σφαγὴν ἤχθη καὶ ὡς ἀμνὸς ἐναντίον τοῦ κείροντος αὐτὸν ἄφωνος οὕτως οὐκ ἀνοίγει τὸ στόμα αὐτοῦ.
⁸ἐν τῇ ταπεινώσει ἡ κρίσις αὐτοῦ ἤρθη · τὴν γενεὰν αὐτοῦ τίς διηγήσεται; ὅτι αἴρεται ἀπὸ τῆς γῆς ἡ ζωὴ αὐτοῦ, ἀπὸ τῶν ἀνομιῶν τοῦ λαοῦ μου ἤχθη εἰς θάνατον.

^aRom 15:21

21 ἀλλὰ καθὼς γέγραπται ·
ˢοἷς οὐκ ἀνηγγέλη περὶ αὐτοῦ ὄψονται⸌,
καὶ οἳ οὐκ ἀκηκόασιν συνήσουσιν.

Isa 52:15; MT = LXX = Rom 15:21 (A). Quite properly LXX and NT have rendered רָאוּ and הִתְבּוֹנָנוּ as futures, regarding them as prophetic perfects.

^aJn 12:38

38 ἵνα ὁ λόγος Ἠσαΐου
τοῦ προφήτου πληρωθῇ ⸋ὃν εἶπεν⸌ ·
   κύριε, τίς ἐπίστευσεν τῇ ἀκοῇ ἡμῶν;
   καὶ ὁ βραχίων κυρίου τίνι ἀπεκαλύφθη;

Isa 53:1; MT = LXX = John 12:38 and Rom 10:16, except that the Greek texts begin with the vocative κύριε, which was probably inserted to clarify to the reader that the prophet begins his query to God. (A)

^bRom 10:16

16 Ἀλλ' οὐ πάντες
ὑπήκουσαν τῷ εὐαγγελίῳ. Ἠσαΐας γὰρ λέγει · κύριε, τίς ἐπίστευσεν τῇ ἀκοῇ ἡμῶν;

^aMt 8:17

17 ὅπως πληρωθῇ
τὸ ῥηθὲν διὰ Ἠσαΐου τοῦ προφήτου λέγοντος ·
   αὐτὸς τὰς ἀσθενείας ἡμῶν ἔλαβεν
   καὶ τὰς νόσους ἐβάστασεν.

Isa 53:4; Here the Mt quotation is much closer to the MT than the LXX is. MT חֳלָיֵנוּ הוּא נָשָׂא וּמַכְאֹבֵינוּ סְבָלָם which becomes in LXX οὗτος τὰς ἁμαρτίας ἡμῶν φέρει καὶ περὶ ἡμῶν ὀδυνᾶται (MT: "He Himself has borne our griefs/illnesses, and as for our sufferings, He has loaded Himself with them"; LXX: "This man bears our sins and suffers anguish for our sake"). Mt 8:17 furnishes a rendering completely distinct from the LXX: αὐτὸς τὰς ἀσθενείας ἡμῶν ἔλαβεν καὶ τὰς νόσους ἐβάστασεν; ἡμῶν after νόσους (which is used for מַכְאֹבֵינוּ) is a completely literal rendering. Matthew probably translated this directly from the Hebrew text. (C)

Isa 53:5; MT וּבַחֲבֻרָתוֹ נִרְפָּא־לָנוּ = LXX except that LXX inserts ἡμεῖς before ἰάθημεν = 1 Pet 2:24 οὗ τῷ μώλωπι ἰάθητε. Thus we see that Peter in applying this to his readers naturally uses the second person plural rather than the first person plural. (A)

^aActs 8:32–33

32 ἡ δὲ περιοχὴ
τῆς γραφῆς ἣν ἀνεγίνωσκεν ἦν αὕτη ·
   ὡς πρόβατον ἐπὶ σφαγὴν ἤχθη
     καὶ ὡς ἀμνὸς ἐναντίον τοῦ ⸉κείραντος αὐτὸν ἄ-
     φωνος,
   οὕτως οὐκ ἀνοίγει τὸ στόμα αὐτοῦ.
   33 Ἐν τῇ ταπεινώσει ᵒ[αὐτοῦ] ἡ κρίσις αὐτοῦ
   ἤρθη ·
   τὴν ᵀ γενεὰν αὐτοῦ τίς διηγήσεται;
   ὅτι αἴρεται ἀπὸ τῆς γῆς ἡ ζωὴ αὐτοῦ.

Isa 53:7–8; in v. 7 the LXX and Acts 8:32–33 are identical: (1) LXX uses aorist ἤχθη for imperfect passive יוּבָל (Hp 20); (2) ἀμνός is not the right gender for רָחֵל "ewe"; (3) τοῦ κείραντος αὐτόν is singular, whereas MT's גֹּזְזֶיהָ is plural; (4) οὐκ ἀνοίγει is not quite the same as נֶאֱלָמָה, which could more accurately be ἀφωνεῖ. (A^d)

v. 8 Here again the LXX = Acts 8:33. MT: "As a result of coercion and a judicial process he was taken away, and as for his generation, who was considering that he

249 (continued)

⁹καὶ δώσω τοὺς πονηροὺς
ἀντὶ τῆς ταφῆς αὐτοῦ καὶ τοὺς πλουσίους ἀντὶ τοῦ θανάτου αὐ-
τοῦ· ὅτι ἀνομίαν οὐκ ἐποίησεν, οὐδὲ εὑρέθη δόλος ἐν τῷ στόματι
αὐτοῦ.

250: Isa 53:9

⁹ וַיִּתֵּ֤ן אֶת־רְשָׁעִים֙ קִבְר֔וֹ וְאֶת־עָשִׁ֖יר בְּמֹתָ֑יו
עַ֚ל לֹא־חָמָ֣ס עָשָׂ֔ה וְלֹ֥א מִרְמָ֖ה בְּפִֽיו׃

⁹καὶ δώσω τοὺς πονηροὺς
ἀντὶ τῆς ταφῆς αὐτοῦ καὶ τοὺς πλουσίους ἀντὶ τοῦ θανάτου αὐ-
τοῦ· ὅτι ἀνομίαν οὐκ ἐποίησεν, οὐδὲ εὑρέθη δόλος ἐν τῷ στόματι
αὐτοῦ.

251: Isa 53:12

¹² לָכֵ֞ן אֲחַלֶּק־ל֣וֹ בָרַבִּ֗ים וְאֶת־עֲצוּמִים֮ יְחַלֵּ֣ק שָׁלָל֒
תַּ֗חַת אֲשֶׁ֨ר הֶעֱרָ֤ה לַמָּ֙וֶת֙ נַפְשׁ֔וֹ וְאֶת־פֹּשְׁעִ֖ים נִמְנָ֑ה
וְהוּא֙ חֵטְא־רַבִּ֣ים נָשָׂ֔א וְלַפֹּשְׁעִ֖ים יַפְגִּֽיעַ׃

¹²διὰ τοῦτο αὐτὸς
κληρονομήσει πολλοὺς καὶ τῶν ἰσχυρῶν μεριεῖ σκῦλα, ἀνθ᾽ ὧν
παρεδόθη εἰς θάνατον ἡ ψυχὴ αὐτοῦ, καὶ ἐν τοῖς ἀνόμοις ἐλογίσθη·
καὶ αὐτὸς ἁμαρτίας πολλῶν ἀνήνεγκεν καὶ διὰ τὰς ἁμαρτίας αὐτῶν
παρεδόθη.

was cut off from the land of the life/the living . . . (?)."
LXX: "In his humiliation his judgment was taken
away. Who will recount his generation/race? Because
his life is taken away from the earth." Note the following: (1) עֹצֶר is interpreted as ταπείνωσις, "humiliation."
Perhaps it could be understood as involving humiliating
maltreatment of the accused prisoner, in which case it is
not too far from עֹצֶר "coercion, constraint" (cf. Schl.
235A); (2) κρίσις (מִשְׁפָּט) is made into "His" (αὐτοῦ)
judgment and treated as the *subject* of לֻקָּח, rather than
as a second *object* of מִן (i.e., מֵ before עֹצֶר); (3) γενεά is
made the object of יְשׂוֹחֵחַ, since דּוֹרוֹ is preceded by אֶת־.
But it makes far better sense to take אֶת־דּוֹרוֹ as the
anticipated, emphasized subject of יְשׂוֹחֵחַ; (4) נִגְזַר "was
cut off" is poorly rendered αἴρεται "is taken away";
(5) חַיִּים in construct with אֶרֶץ is wrongly taken as the
subject of αἴρεται; (6) נֶגַע לָמוֹ is wrongly treated as נֶגַע
לָמֶת (ἤχθη εἰς θάνατον). Here, we have a gravely
deviant translation quoted from the LXX. This, however, poses no problem for biblical inerrancy, since Acts
8 simply records the wording of the LXX which the
Ethiopian eunuch was reading. There is no apostolic
approval or endorsement of the errors in this rendition, and no doctrinal teaching is built upon them. The
facts in this confrontation between Philip and the eunuch are accurately narrated. And enough of the truth
of Isa 53 came through, even in this somewhat defective
translation, to lead the Ethiopian to a saving knowledge
of Christ. This furnishes a classic example, incidentally,
of the missionary strategy used by the early apostles in
making the best use they could of the Septuagint—
which with all of its faults was still the only form of the
OT available to Diaspora Jews and to the Gentile
converts. (*E*)

---

[a]1 Pet 2:22

22 ὃς ἁμαρτίαν οὐκ ἐποίησεν
οὐδὲ εὑρέθη δόλος ἐν τῷ στόματι αὐτοῦ,

Isa 53:9; MT וְלֹא מִרְמָה בְּפִיו "And there was no deceit in
his mouth" = LXX, which supplies εὑρέθη before
δόλος, a verb that is clearly implied, unless one wishes
to use ἦν. LXX = 1 Pet 2:22. (*A*[d])

---

[a]Lk 22:37

37 λέγω γὰρ ὑμῖν ὅτι ᵀ τοῦτο τὸ γεγραμμένον δεῖ
τελεσθῆναι ἐν ἐμοί, τό· *καὶ μετὰ ἀνόμων ἐλογίσθη·* καὶ
ᵒγὰρ ⌐τὸ περὶ ἐμοῦ τέλος ἔχει.

Isa 53:12; MT = Lk 22:37; LXX reads the same except
that it uses ἐν τοῖς ἀνόμοις, which is not as close to
אֶת־פֹּשְׁעִים נִמְנָה as the NT's μετὰ ἀνόμων. (*A*)

252: Isa 54:1

¹ רָנִּי עֲקָרָה לֹא יָלָדָה פִּצְחִי רִנָּה וְצַהֲלִי לֹא־חָלָה
כִּי־רַבִּים בְּנֵי־שׁוֹמֵמָה מִבְּנֵי בְעוּלָה אָמַר יְהוָה:

¹Εὐφράνθητι, στεῖρα ἡ οὐ τίκτουσα, ῥῆξον καὶ βόησον, ἡ οὐκ ὠδίνουσα, ὅτι πολλὰ τὰ τέκνα τῆς ἐρήμου μᾶλλον ἢ τῆς ἐχούσης τὸν ἄνδρα, εἶπεν γὰρ κύριος.

253: Isa 54:13

¹³ וְכָל־בָּנַיִךְ לִמּוּדֵי יְהוָה וְרַב שְׁלוֹם בָּנָיִךְ:

¹³καὶ πάντας
τοὺς υἱούς σου διδακτοὺς θεοῦ καὶ ἐν πολλῇ εἰρήνῃ τὰ τέκνα σου.

254: Isa 55:3

³ הַטּוּ אָזְנְכֶם וּלְכוּ אֵלַי שִׁמְעוּ וּתְחִי נַפְשְׁכֶם
וְאֶכְרְתָה לָכֶם בְּרִית עוֹלָם חַסְדֵי דָוִד הַנֶּאֱמָנִים:

³προσέχετε τοῖς ὠτίοις ὑμῶν καὶ ἐπ-
ακολουθήσατε ταῖς ὁδοῖς μου· ἐπακούσατέ μου, καὶ ζήσεται ἐν ἀγα-
θοῖς ἡ ψυχὴ ὑμῶν· καὶ διαθήσομαι ὑμῖν διαθήκην αἰώνιον, τὰ ὅσια
Δαυιδ τὰ πιστά.

255: Isa 55:10

¹⁰ כִּי כַּאֲשֶׁר יֵרֵד הַגֶּשֶׁם וְהַשֶּׁלֶג מִן־הַשָּׁמַיִם
וְשָׁמָּה לֹא יָשׁוּב כִּי אִם־הִרְוָה אֶת־הָאָרֶץ
וְהוֹלִידָהּ וְהִצְמִיחָהּ וְנָתַן זֶרַע לַזֹּרֵעַ וְלֶחֶם לָאֹכֵל:

¹⁰ὡς γὰρ ἐὰν καταβῇ ὑετὸς
ἢ χιὼν ἐκ τοῦ οὐρανοῦ καὶ οὐ μὴ ἀποστραφῇ, ἕως ἂν μεθύσῃ τὴν
γῆν, καὶ ἐκτέκῃ καὶ ἐκβλαστήσῃ καὶ δῷ σπέρμα τῷ σπείροντι καὶ
ἄρτον εἰς βρῶσιν,

256: Isa 56:7

⁷ וַהֲבִיאוֹתִים אֶל־הַר קָדְשִׁי וְשִׂמַּחְתִּים בְּבֵית תְּפִלָּתִי
עוֹלֹתֵיהֶם וְזִבְחֵיהֶם לְרָצוֹן עַל־מִזְבְּחִי
כִּי בֵיתִי בֵּית־תְּפִלָּה יִקָּרֵא לְכָל־הָעַמִּים:

⁷εἰσάξω
αὐτοὺς εἰς τὸ ὄρος τὸ ἅγιόν μου καὶ εὐφρανῶ αὐτοὺς ἐν τῷ οἴκῳ
τῆς προσευχῆς μου· τὰ ὁλοκαυτώματα αὐτῶν καὶ αἱ θυσίαι αὐτῶν
ἔσονται δεκταὶ ἐπὶ τοῦ θυσιαστηρίου μου· ὁ γὰρ οἶκός μου οἶκος
προσευχῆς κληθήσεται πᾶσιν τοῖς ἔθνεσιν,

Jer 7:11

¹¹ הַמְעָרַת פָּרִצִים הָיָה הַבַּיִת הַזֶּה אֲשֶׁר־נִקְרָא־שְׁמִי עָלָיו
בְּעֵינֵיכֶם גַּם אָנֹכִי הִנֵּה רָאִיתִי נְאֻם־יְהוָה:

¹¹μὴ σπήλαιον λῃστῶν ὁ οἶκός μου, οὗ ἐπικέ-
κληται τὸ ὄνομά μου ἐπ' αὐτῷ ἐκεῖ, ἐνώπιον ὑμῶν; καὶ ἐγὼ ἰδοὺ
ἑώρακα, λέγει κύριος.

257: Isa 58:6

see Isa 61:1–2 [260]

*a*Gal 4:27

27 γέγραπται γάρ·
  εὐφράνθητι, στεῖρα ἡ οὐ τίκτουσα,
  ῥῆξον καὶ βόησον, ἡ οὐκ ὠδίνουσα·
  ὅτι πολλὰ τὰ τέκνα τῆς ἐρήμου
  μᾶλλον ἢ τῆς ἐχούσης τὸν ἄνδρα.

Isa 54:1; MT = LXX = Gal 4:27. (*A*)

*a*Jn 6:45

45 ἔστιν γεγραμμένον ἐν τοῖς προφήταις· καὶ ἔσονται πάντες διδακτοὶ θεοῦ· πᾶς ᵀ ὁ ⌐ἀκούσας παρὰ τοῦ πατρὸς καὶ μαθὼν ἔρχεται πρὸς ⌐ἐμέ.

Isa 54:13; MT ≠ LXX. John 6:45 supplies an ἔσονται, and more correctly than the LXX makes "the sons" (implied by πάντες) of Israel nominative rather than accusative (object of θήσω in v. 13) in closer conformity to the MT. (*A*ᵈ) or (*C*)

*a*Acts 13:34

34 ⌐ὅτι δὲ ἀνέστησεν αὐτὸν ἐκ νεκρῶν μηκέτι μέλλοντα ὑποστρέφειν εἰς διαφθοράν, οὕτως εἴρηκεν ὅτι δώσω ὑμῖν τὰ ὅσια Δαυὶδ τὰ πιστά.

Isa 55:3; if we reckon the Acts 13:34 quote as beginning with ὑμῖν rather than with δώσω (which differs from the אֶכְרְתָה of the MT, which takes בְּרִית as *object*, to which חַסְדֵי דָוִד is an epexegetic appositive), then apart from that the MT = LXX = NT. (*A*)/(*A*ᵈ)

*a*2 Cor 9:10

10 ὁ δὲ ἐπιχορηγῶν ⌐σπόρον τῷ σπείροντι καὶ ἄρτον εἰς βρῶσιν ⌐χορηγήσει καὶ πληθυνεῖ τὸν σπόρον ὑμῶν καὶ αὐξήσει⌐ τὰ γενήματα τῆς δικαιοσύνης ὑμῶν.

Isa 55:10—1 Cor 9:10. (*F*)

*a*Mt 21:13

13 καὶ λέγει αὐ- τοῖς· γέγραπται·
  ὁ οἶκός μου οἶκος προσευχῆς κληθήσεται,
  ὑμεῖς δὲ αὐτὸν ⌐ποιεῖτε σπήλαιον λῃστῶν.

*b*Mk 11:17

17 καὶ ἐδίδασκεν καὶ ἔλεγεν °αὐτοῖς· οὐ γέγραπται ὅτι
  ὁ οἶκός μου οἶκος προσευχῆς κληθήσεται
  πᾶσιν τοῖς ἔθνεσιν;
  ὑμεῖς δὲ ⌐πεποιήκατε αὐτὸν⌐ σπήλαιον λῃστῶν.

*c*Lk 19:46

46 λέγων αὐτοῖς· γέγραπται·
⌐καὶ ἔσται⌐ ὁ οἶκός μου οἶκος προσευχῆς ᵀ,
  ὑμεῖς δὲ αὐτὸν ἐποιήσατε σπήλαιον λῃστῶν.

Isa 56:7: (1) Mt 21:13 follows perfectly with ὁ οἶκός μου οἶκος προσευχῆς κληθήσεται (MT כִּי בֵיתִי בֵּית־ תְּפִלָּה יִקָּרֵא); (2) Mk 11:17 includes also the final phrase πᾶσιν τοῖς ἔθνεσιν = MT לְכָל־הָעַמִּים; (3) Lk 19:46 includes only through προσευχῆς and uses ἔσται instead of the κληθήσεται (= יִקָּרֵא) of Mt and Mk; LXX = MT. (*A*) and (*A*ᵈ) for Lk 10:46

Jer 7:11 contributes the phrase הַמְעָרַת פָּרִצִים = σπήλαιον λῃστῶν as the final clause in all three of the above: Mt 21:13; Mk 11:17; Lk 19:46. (*A*)

258: Isa 59:7-8

⁷ רַגְלֵיהֶם לָרַע יָרֻצוּ   וִימַהֲרוּ לִשְׁפֹּךְ דָּם נָקִי
מַחְשְׁבוֹתֵיהֶם מַחְשְׁבוֹת אָוֶן   שֹׁד וָשֶׁבֶר בִּמְסִלּוֹתָם:
⁸ דֶּרֶךְ שָׁלוֹם לֹא יָדָעוּ   וְאֵין מִשְׁפָּט בְּמַעְגְּלוֹתָם
נְתִיבוֹתֵיהֶם עִקְּשׁוּ לָהֶם   כֹּל דֹּרֵךְ בָּהּ לֹא יָדַע שָׁלוֹם:

⁷οἱ δὲ πόδες αὐτῶν ἐπὶ πονηρίαν τρέχουσιν
ταχινοὶ ἐκχέαι αἷμα· καὶ οἱ διαλογισμοὶ αὐτῶν διαλογισμοὶ ἀφρόνων,
σύντριμμα καὶ ταλαιπωρία ἐν ταῖς ὁδοῖς αὐτῶν. ⁸καὶ ὁδὸν εἰρήνης
οὐκ οἴδασιν, καὶ οὐκ ἔστιν κρίσις ἐν ταῖς ὁδοῖς αὐτῶν· αἱ γὰρ
τρίβοι αὐτῶν διεστραμμέναι, ἃς διοδεύουσιν, καὶ οὐκ οἴδασιν εἰρήνην.

259: Isa 59:20-21

²⁰ וּבָא לְצִיּוֹן גּוֹאֵל   וּלְשָׁבֵי פֶשַׁע בְּיַעֲקֹב   נְאֻם יְהוָה:
²¹ וַאֲנִי זֹאת בְּרִיתִי אוֹתָם אָמַר יְהוָה רוּחִי אֲשֶׁר עָלֶיךָ וּדְבָרַי אֲשֶׁר־
שַׂמְתִּי בְּפִיךָ לֹא־יָמוּשׁוּ מִפִּיךָ וּמִפִּי זַרְעֲךָ וּמִפִּי זֶרַע זַרְעֲךָ אָמַר יְהוָה
מֵעַתָּה וְעַד־עוֹלָם:

²⁰καὶ ἥξει ἕνεκεν Σιων ὁ ῥυό-
μενος καὶ ἀποστρέψει ἀσεβείας ἀπὸ Ιακωβ. ²¹καὶ αὕτη αὐτοῖς ἡ
παρ' ἐμοῦ διαθήκη, εἶπεν κύριος· τὸ πνεῦμα τὸ ἐμόν, ὅ ἐστιν ἐπὶ
σοί, καὶ τὰ ῥήματα, ἃ ἔδωκα εἰς τὸ στόμα σου, οὐ μὴ ἐκλίπῃ ἐκ
τοῦ στόματός σου καὶ ἐκ τοῦ στόματος τοῦ σπέρματός σου, εἶπεν
γὰρ κύριος, ἀπὸ τοῦ νῦν καὶ εἰς τὸν αἰῶνα.

Isa 27:9

⁹ לָכֵן בְּזֹאת יְכֻפַּר עֲוֹן־יַעֲקֹב   וְזֶה כָּל־פְּרִי הָסִר חַטָּאתוֹ
בְּשׂוּמוֹ ׀ כָּל־אַבְנֵי מִזְבֵּחַ   כְּאַבְנֵי־גִר מְנֻפָּצוֹת
לֹא־יָקֻמוּ אֲשֵׁרִים וְחַמָּנִים:

⁹διὰ τοῦτο ἀφαιρεθήσεται ἡ ἀνομία Ιακωβ, καὶ τοῦτό ἐστιν ἡ εὐ-
λογία αὐτοῦ, ὅταν ἀφέλωμαι αὐτοῦ τὴν ἁμαρτίαν, ὅταν θῶσιν
πάντας τοὺς λίθους τῶν βωμῶν κατακεκομμένους ὡς κονίαν λε-
πτήν· καὶ οὐ μὴ μείνῃ τὰ δένδρα αὐτῶν, καὶ τὰ εἴδωλα αὐτῶν
ἐκκεκομμένα ὥσπερ δρυμὸς μακράν.

^aRom 3:15–17

15 ὀξεῖς οἱ πόδες αὐτῶν ἐκχέαι αἷμα,
16 σύντριμμα καὶ ταλαιπωρία ἐν ταῖς ὁδοῖς αὐτῶν,
17 καὶ ὁδὸν εἰρήνης οὐκ ἔγνωσαν.

Isa 59:7–8; MT v. 7 רַגְלֵיהֶם לָרַע יָרֻצוּ וִימַהֲרוּ לִשְׁפֹּךְ דָּם נָקִי
. . . ; LXX οἱ δὲ πόδες αὐτῶν ἐπὶ πονηρίαν τρέχουσιν
(= יָרֻצוּ) ταχινοὶ ἐκχέαι αἷμα (Rom 3:15 uses ὀξεῖς instead of τρέχουσιν). (B^a)

MT שֹׁד וָשֶׁבֶר בִּמְסִלּוֹתָם; LXX σύντριμμα καὶ ταλαιπωρία ἐν ταῖς ὁδοῖς αὐτῶν = NT. (A)/(A-)

v. 8 MT דֶּרֶךְ שָׁלוֹם לֹא יָדָעוּ = LXX καὶ ὁδὸν εἰρήνης οὐκ οἴδασιν = NT, except ἔγνωσαν for יָדָעוּ. (A)/(A-)

---

^aRom 11:26–27

26 καὶ οὕτως πᾶς Ἰσραὴλ σωθήσεται, καθὼς γέγραπται·
ἥξει ἐκ Σιὼν ὁ ῥυόμενος,
ἀποστρέψει ἀσεβείας ἀπὸ Ἰακώβ.
27 καὶ αὕτη αὐτοῖς ^ʃἡ παρ᾿ ἐμοῦ^ʅ διαθήκη,
ὅταν ἀφέλωμαι τὰς ἁμαρτίας αὐτῶν.

Isa 59:20–21; v. 20 compare MT וּבָא לְצִיּוֹן גּוֹאֵל "Will come to/for Zion" with the LXX καὶ ἥξει ἕνεκεν Σιων ὁ ῥυόμενος "For the sake of/to Zion" and Rom 11:26 ἐκ Σιὼν κτλ. *from Zion the Redeemer.* Also compare MT וּלְשָׁבֵי פֶשַׁע בְּיַעֲקֹב ("and to those who return from ungodliness/transgression in Jacob") with the LXX καὶ ἀποστρέψαι ἀσεβείας ἀπὸ Ἰακωβ, and Rom 11:26b, which reads the same as the LXX "and he will turn away ungodliness from Jacob"—as if וְשָׁב or וְהֵשִׁיב or וְיָשִׁיב. (B^a)

Isa 59:21 MT וַאֲנִי זֹאת בְּרִיתִי אוֹתָם "And as for me, this is/will be my covenant with them" = LXX = Rom 11:27a (καὶ αὕτη αὐτοῖς ἡ παρ᾿ ἐμοῦ διαθήκη "And this is/will be the covenant from me"). (A)

Isa 27:9; MT לָכֵן בְּזֹאת יְכֻפַּר עֲוֹן־יַעֲקֹב "Therefore by this the iniquity of Jacob will be covered/atoned for/removed"; LXX ὅταν ἀφέλωμαι (as if אֲכַפֵּר) αὐτοῦ τὴν ἁμαρτίαν "(And this is his blessing,) when I take away his sin." (B^a)

Here then יְכֻפַּר, a passive (Dp 10), is treated as an active, as if אֲכַפֵּר and עֲוֹן (ἁμαρτίαν) is made the object rather than the subject of the verb. Thus we have a conflate quotation, with four minor variants that do not greatly affect the sense, except perhaps in Isa 59:21, where the LXX and NT make God the subject of the turning (as a transitive), rather than the returnees from the exile. However, if לְשָׁבֵי is pointed לְשׁוּבוּ or לְשֻׁבִי (G 65 s0) then the LXX interpretation is quite valid and *may* indeed be the *correct pointing*. The meaning would then be: "At his turning back the transgression of Jacob." There is also a difference between Rom 11:26 "from Zion," the LXX's "on account of/for the sake of Zion," and the MT's "to/for Zion." It would seem more likely that the Redeemer would come to Zion for the purpose of cleansing God's people from sin—if those people are actual Jews already in the Holy Land. But if to all believers (as members of spiritual Israel) the

127

259 (continued)

260: Isa 61:1–2 (see also [219])

¹ רוּחַ אֲדֹנָי יְהוָה עָלָי   יַעַן מָשַׁח יְהוָה אֹתִי
לְבַשֵּׂר עֲנָוִים שְׁלָחַנִי   לַחֲבֹשׁ לְנִשְׁבְּרֵי־לֵב
לִקְרֹא לִשְׁבוּיִם דְּרוֹר   וְלַאֲסוּרִים פְּקַח־קוֹחַ׃
² לִקְרֹא שְׁנַת־רָצוֹן לַיהוָה   וְיוֹם נָקָם לֵאלֹהֵינוּ   [תַּחַת אֵפֶר
לְנַחֵם כָּל־אֲבֵלִים׃

¹Πνεῦμα κυρίου ἐπ' ἐμέ, οὗ εἵνεκεν ἔχρισέν με· εὐαγγελίσασθαι πτωχοῖς ἀπέσταλκέν με, ἰάσασθαι τοὺς συντετριμμένους τῇ καρδίᾳ, κηρύξαι αἰχμαλώτοις ἄφεσιν καὶ τυφλοῖς ἀνάβλεψιν, ²καλέσαι ἐνιαυτὸν κυρίου δεκτὸν καὶ ἡμέραν ἀνταποδόσεως, παρακαλέσαι πάντας τοὺς πενθοῦντας,

Isa 58:6

⁶ הֲלוֹא זֶה צוֹם אֶבְחָרֵהוּ
פַּתֵּחַ חַרְצֻבּוֹת רֶשַׁע   הַתֵּר אֲגֻדּוֹת מוֹטָה
וְשַׁלַּח רְצוּצִים חָפְשִׁים   וְכָל־מוֹטָה תְּנַתֵּקוּ׃

⁶οὐχὶ τοιαύτην νηστείαν ἐγὼ ἐξελεξάμην,
λέγει κύριος, ἀλλὰ λῦε πάντα σύνδεσμον ἀδικίας, διάλυε στραγγαλιὰς βιαίων συναλλαγμάτων, ἀπόστελλε τεθραυσμένους ἐν ἀφέσει καὶ πᾶσαν συγγραφὴν ἄδικον διάσπα·

261: Isa 61:6

see Ex 19:6 [46]

world over, then it would be appropriate to speak of the Redeemer's coming out of Zion, as the center of authoritative revelation. There is insufficient evidence to establish a decided preference for the one preposition over the other.

---

*a*Lk 4:18–19

18 πνεῦμα κυρίου ἐπ' ⌜ἐμὲ
    οὗ εἵνεκεν ἔχρισέν ⌜με
εὐαγγελίσασθαι πτωχοῖς,
    ἀπέσταλκέν με, ᵀ
κηρύξαι αἰχμαλώτοις ἄφεσιν
    καὶ τυφλοῖς ἀνάβλεψιν,
ἀποστεῖλαι τεθραυσμένους ἐν ἀφέσει,
    19 κηρύξαι ἐνιαυτὸν κυρίου δεκτόν.

Isa 61:1–2; v. 1 MT "Spirit of the Lord Yahweh" = LXX and NT "The Spirit of the Lord." (*A*)

Isa 16:1*b*; MT "because Yahweh has anointed" = LXX "because He has anointed me." The omission of אדני or יהוה in 1*a* or 1*b* constitutes no discrepancy in either case; the quotation is merely selective. (*A*)

Isa 61:1*c*; MT = LXX = NT. (*A*)

Isa 61:1*d* is not included at all in Lk 4:18.

Isa 61:1*e*; MT לַאֲסוּרִים פְּקַח־קוֹחַ = "to prisoners the opening up (of eyes)"; LXX = NT καὶ τυφλοῖς ἀνά-βλεψιν "and the recovery of sight to the blind." It may be that the Greek rendering is justified in inferring from the intensive stem form of פָּקַח (פְּקַח־קוֹחַ is a ἅπαξ) that the imprisonment principally in view here is that which results from blindness rather than from incarceration in a dungeon. פָּקַח is never used elsewhere in any other sense than the opening of blind eyes or deaf ears—or of the eyes and ears of those who are merely obtuse or inattentive. This interpretation certainly fits better with Christ's own earthly ministry, for He healed many who were blind, but did not release any prisoners from jail in any miraculous fashion. Since He applied this passage to His own ministry, the LXX interpretation would seem to be valid. (*B*)

Isa 61:2 is the basis for Lk 4:18*g* MT לִקְרֹא שְׁנַת־רָצוֹן לַיהוה = LXX καλέσαι ἐνιαυτὸν κυρίου δεκτὸν "to proclaim a year of Yahweh's favor" = "proclaim an acceptable year of the Lord." There is a standard relationship between רָצָה and δεκτός in both the MT and LXX (*A*).

Isa 58:6*d* contributes the background for Lk 4:18*f*. MT וְשַׁלַּח רְצוּצִים חָפְשִׁים = LXX ἀπόστελλε (for which NT's infinitive ἀποστεῖλαι is equally valid for שָׁלַח) τεθραυσ-μένους ἐν ἀφέσει (= NT). (*A*)

129

262: Isa 62:11

הִנֵּ֣ה יְהוָ֗ה הִשְׁמִ֙יעַ֙ אֶל־קְצֵ֣ה הָאָ֔רֶץ
אִמְר֣וּ לְבַת־צִיּ֔וֹן הִנֵּ֥ה יִשְׁעֵ֖ךְ בָּ֑א
הִנֵּ֤ה שְׂכָרוֹ֙ אִתּ֔וֹ וּפְעֻלָּת֖וֹ לְפָנָֽיו׃

¹¹ἰδοὺ γὰρ
κύριος ἐποίησεν ἀκουστὸν ἕως ἐσχάτου τῆς γῆς Εἴπατε τῇ θυγατρὶ
Σιων Ἰδού σοι ὁ σωτὴρ παραγίνεται ἔχων τὸν ἑαυτοῦ μισθὸν καὶ
τὸ ἔργον πρὸ προσώπου αὐτοῦ.

Zech 9:9

גִּילִ֙י מְאֹד֙ בַּת־צִיּ֗וֹן הָרִ֙יעִי֙ בַּ֣ת יְרוּשָׁלִַ֔ם
הִנֵּ֤ה מַלְכֵּךְ֙ יָ֣בוֹא לָ֔ךְ צַדִּ֥יק וְנוֹשָׁ֖ע ה֑וּא
עָנִי֙ וְרֹכֵ֣ב עַל־חֲמ֔וֹר וְעַל־עַ֖יִר בֶּן־אֲתֹנֽוֹת׃

⁹Χαῖρε σφόδρα, θύγατερ Σιων· κήρυσσε, θύγατερ Ιερουσαλημ·
ἰδοὺ ὁ βασιλεύς σου ἔρχεταί σοι, δίκαιος καὶ σῴζων αὐτός, πραῢς
καὶ ἐπιβεβηκὼς ἐπὶ ὑποζύγιον καὶ πῶλον νέον.

Isa 35:4

אִמְרוּ֙ לְנִמְהֲרֵי־לֵ֔ב חִזְק֖וּ אַל־תִּירָ֑אוּ
הִנֵּ֤ה אֱלֹֽהֵיכֶם֙ נָקָ֣ם יָב֔וֹא
גְּמ֣וּל אֱלֹהִ֔ים ה֥וּא יָב֖וֹא וְיֹשַׁעֲכֶֽם׃

⁴παρακαλέ-
σατε, οἱ ὀλιγόψυχοι τῇ διανοίᾳ· ἰσχύσατε, μὴ φοβεῖσθε· ἰδοὺ ὁ
θεὸς ἡμῶν κρίσιν ἀνταποδίδωσιν καὶ ἀνταποδώσει, αὐτὸς ἥξει καὶ
σώσει ἡμᾶς.

*a*Mt 21:5

5 εἴπατε τῇ θυγατρὶ Σιών·
    ἰδοὺ ὁ βασιλεύς σου ἔρχεταί σοι
πραῢς καὶ ἐπιβεβηκὼς ἐπὶ ὄνον
    καὶ °ἐπὶ πῶλον °1 υἱὸν ὑποζυγίου.

Isa 62:11; this contributes only the phrase אִמְרוּ לְבַת־
צִיּוֹן = LXX = Mt 21:5. (*A*)

Zech 9:9*c*; MT הִנֵּה מַלְכֵּךְ יָבוֹא לָךְ = LXX ἰδοὺ ὁ
βασιλεύς σου ἔρχεταί σοι "Behold thy King will come
to thee" = NT. The NT omits σοι or πρὸς σε. (*A*)

Zech 9:9*d*; MT צַדִּיק וְנוֹשָׁע הוּא = LXX δίκαιος καὶ
σῴζων αὐτός (not included in the NT quote).

Zech 9:9*e*; MT עָנִי וְרֹכֵב עַל־חֲמוֹר = LXX πραῢς καὶ
ἐπιβεβηκὼς ἐπὶ ὑποζύγιον. Thus for MT's "poor and
riding upon a donkey" LXX reads "gentle and mounted
upon a beast of burden." (The LXX and NT apparently
point to עָנָו as a better reading than עָנִי. These two
words were easily susceptible to scribal confusion, since
waw and *yod* became very similar in appearance after
the return, especially during the Qumran period.
Matthew is more accurate than the LXX in rendering
חֲמוֹר by ὄνον rather than ὑποζύγιον (its only deviation
from the LXX in this colon). (*A*)

Zech 9:9*f*; וְעַל־עַיִר בֶּן־אֲתֹנוֹת "even upon a foal, son of
she-asses" = LXX καὶ πῶλον νέον "even a young foal"
= NT καὶ ἐπὶ πῶλον υἱὸν ὑποζυγίου "even upon a foal,
son of a pack animal/beast of burden." ὑποζυγίου is
not very accurate for "she asses," but it means approximately the same thing so far as the donkey-colt himself
was concerned. Jn 12:15 has a briefer summary: 12:15*a*
"Do not be afraid" (μὴ φοβοῦ is drawn from Isa 35:4
אַל־תִּירָאוּ, which may point to a copyist's error in the
Greek, reading a singular jussive instead of a plural
Hiphil, or else it is merely an adaptation to "daughter
in Zion," which was more appropriate in this conflate
quotation). (*A*)

*b*Jn 12:15

15 μὴ φοβοῦ, ⌐θυγάτηρ Σιών·
    ἰδοὺ ὁ βασιλεύς σου ἔρχεται,
καθήμενος ἐπὶ πῶλον ὄνου.

Jn 12:15*b* = MT and the LXX. (*A*)

Jn 12:15*c* καθήμενος (rather than LXX's ἐπιβεβηκὼς) is an acceptable rendering for רֹכֵב "riding" (*A*)

Isa 35:4 contributes the phrase, "Do not be afraid" in
the plural μὴ φοβεῖσθε as contrasted with the singular
in Jn 12:15. But this seems to be the only element that
enters into the NT quotation from this verse.

263: Isa 64:3 (64:4)

³ וּמֵעוֹלָ֥ם לֹֽא־שָׁמְע֖וּ לֹ֣א הֶאֱזִ֑ינוּ
עַ֣יִן לֹֽא־רָאָ֗תָה אֱלֹהִ֤ים זֽוּלָתְךָ֙ יַעֲשֶׂ֣ה לִמְחַכֵּֽה־לֽוֹ׃

³ἀπὸ τοῦ αἰῶνος οὐκ ἠκούσαμεν οὐδὲ οἱ ὀφθαλμοὶ ἡμῶν εἶδον θεὸν πλὴν σοῦ καὶ τὰ ἔργα σου, ἃ ποιήσεις τοῖς ὑπομένουσιν ἔλεον.

264: Isa 65:1–2

¹ נִדְרַ֙שְׁתִּי֙ לְל֣וֹא שָׁאָ֔לוּ נִמְצֵ֖אתִי לְלֹ֣א בִקְשֻׁ֑נִי
אָמַ֙רְתִּי֙ הִנֵּ֣נִי הִנֵּ֔נִי אֶל־גּ֖וֹי לֹֽא־קֹרָ֥א בִשְׁמִֽי׃
² פֵּרַ֧שְׂתִּי יָדַ֛י כָּל־הַיּ֖וֹם אֶל־עַ֣ם סוֹרֵ֑ר
הַהֹלְכִים֙ הַדֶּ֣רֶךְ לֹא־ט֔וֹב אַחַ֖ר מַחְשְׁבֹתֵיהֶֽם׃

¹ Ἐμφανὴς ἐγενόμην τοῖς ἐμὲ μὴ ζητοῦσιν, εὑρέθην τοῖς ἐμὲ μὴ ἐπερωτῶσιν· εἶπα Ἰδού εἰμι, τῷ ἔθνει οἳ οὐκ ἐκάλεσάν μου τὸ ὄνομα. ² ἐξεπέτασα τὰς χεῖράς μου ὅλην τὴν ἡμέραν πρὸς λαὸν ἀπειθοῦντα καὶ ἀντιλέγοντα, οἳ οὐκ ἐπορεύθησαν ὁδῷ ἀληθινῇ, ἀλλ' ὀπίσω τῶν ἁμαρτιῶν αὐτῶν.

*a*1 Cor 2:9

9 ἀλλὰ καθὼς
γέγραπται·

    ἃ ὀφθαλμὸς οὐκ εἶδεν καὶ οὖς οὐκ ἤκουσεν
    καὶ ἐπὶ καρδίαν ἀνθρώπου οὐκ ἀνέβη,
    ⌈ἃ ἡτοίμασεν ὁ θεὸς τοῖς ἀγαπῶσιν αὐτόν.

Isa 64:3(4); v. 3*c* MT וּמֵעוֹלָם לֹא־שָׁמְעוּ לֹא הֶאֱזִינוּ עַיִן לֹא רָאָתָה זוּלָתְךָ ("And never have they heard, nor has the eye beheld anyone besides Thee"). This is the basis for 1 Cor 2:9 ἃ ὀφθαλμὸς οὐκ εἶδεν καὶ οὖς οὐκ ἤκουσεν. Note that this deviates verbally from the LXX: οὐκ ἠκούσαμεν οὐδὲ οἱ ὀφθαλμοὶ ἡμῶν εἶδον "We have not heard nor have our eyes seen (anyone besides God, i.e., anyone to equal God)." Note that לִמְחַכֵּה is interpreted in 1 Cor 2 as expressing an attitude of loving commitment: τοῖς ἀγαπῶσιν αὐτόν, for which LXX has τοῖς ὑπομένουσιν ἔλεον (*E*). Note that Isa 52:15 also furnishes a basis for καὶ οὖς οὐκ ἤκουσεν (MT כִּי אֲשֶׁר לֹא סֻפַּר לָהֶם רָאָה "For that which had not been told them they shall see"), referring to the wonderful person and work of Christ, the Servant of the Lord.

Isa 65:16; MT כִּי נִשְׁכְּחוּ הַצָּרוֹת הָרִאשֹׁנוֹת: 16*e, f* ("for the former afflictions will have been forgotten") וְכִי נִכְתְּרוּ מֵעֵינָי "and surely they are hidden from my sight." In this case the "my" probably refers not to God, as NAS implies by capitalizing the pronoun, but to the thankful Israelite speaking directly in the first person. If so, this passage looks forward to the glorious future of redeemed Zion at the end of the age.

As for the final line of 1 Cor 2:9, there is apparently no OT source that combines both ἑτοιμάζειν and τοῖς ἀγαπῶσιν αὐτόν (referring to God). Probably, therefore, this clause should not be printed in italics in the Nestle Edition (26th). There is, however, a general background for this concept discoverable in the second Commandment (Ex 20:6). The LXX reads that God presents Himself as ποιῶν ἔλεος εἰς χιλιάδας τοῖς ἀγαπῶσίν με in God's purpose to show His covenant love (ἔλεος = חֶסֶד) to those who love Him.

---

*a*Rom 10:20–21

20 Ἠσαῖας δὲ ⌐ἀποτολμᾷ καὶ⌐ λέγει·
    εὑρέθην °[ἐν] τοῖς ἐμὲ μὴ ζητοῦσιν,
    ἐμφανὴς ἐγενόμην ⊤ τοῖς ἐμὲ μὴ ἐπερωτῶσιν.
21 πρὸς δὲ τὸν Ἰσραὴλ λέγει·
    ὅλην τὴν ἡμέραν ἐξεπέτασα τὰς χεῖράς μου
    ⌈πρὸς λαὸν ἀπειθοῦντα ⌐καὶ ἀντιλέγοντα⌐.

Isa 65:1–2; v. 1*a* MT נִדְרַשְׁתִּי לְלֹא שָׁאָלוּ נִמְצֵאתִי לְלֹא בִקְשֻׁנִי "I allowed myself to be sought out by those who did not ask (for me). I was found by those who did not seek me." The LXX and NT are very close in meaning, but there is a switch in word order: 65:1*a* in LXX Ἐμφανὴς ἐγενόμην τοῖς ἐμὲ μὴ ζητοῦσιν, but in NT εὑρέθην τοῖς ἐμὲ κτλ.; 65:1*b* in LXX εὑρέθην τοῖς ἐμὲ μὴ ἐπερωτῶσιν, but in NT ἐμφανὴς ἐγενόμην τοῖς ἐμὲ μὴ ἐπερωτῶσιν. In other words the two verbs have exchanged places between the two versions, though there is no real difference in the idea presented. (*B⁴*)

Isa 65:2; MT = LXX = Rom 10:21. (*A*)

MASORETIC TEXT	SEPTUAGINT

265: Isa 65:17

¹⁷ כִּי־הִנְנִי בוֹרֵא שָׁמַיִם חֲדָשִׁים וָאָרֶץ חֲדָשָׁה
וְלֹא תִזָּכַרְנָה הָרִאשֹׁנוֹת וְלֹא תַעֲלֶינָה עַל־לֵב:

¹⁷ἔσται γὰρ ὁ οὐρανὸς και-
νὸς καὶ ἡ γῆ καινή, καὶ οὐ μὴ μνησθῶσιν τῶν προτέρων, οὐδ' οὐ
μὴ ἐπέλθῃ αὐτῶν ἐπὶ τὴν καρδίαν,

Isa 66:12

²² כִּי כַאֲשֶׁר הַשָּׁמַיִם הַחֲדָשִׁים וְהָאָרֶץ הַחֲדָשָׁה אֲשֶׁר אֲנִי עֹשֶׂה
עֹמְדִים לְפָנַי נְאֻם־יְהוָה כֵּן יַעֲמֹד זַרְעֲכֶם וְשִׁמְכֶם:

²²ὃν τρόπον γὰρ ὁ οὐρανὸς καινὸς καὶ ἡ γῆ καινή, ἃ ἐγὼ ποιῶ,
μένει ἐνώπιόν μου, λέγει κύριος, οὕτως στήσεται τὸ σπέρμα ὑμῶν
καὶ τὸ ὄνομα ὑμῶν.

266: Isa 66:1–2

¹ כֹּה אָמַר יְהוָה
הַשָּׁמַיִם כִּסְאִי וְהָאָרֶץ הֲדֹם רַגְלָי
אֵי־זֶה בַיִת אֲשֶׁר תִּבְנוּ־לִי וְאֵי־זֶה מָקוֹם מְנוּחָתִי:
² וְאֶת־כָּל־אֵלֶּה יָדִי עָשָׂתָה וַיִּהְיוּ כָל־אֵלֶּה נְאֻם־יְהוָה
וְאֶל־זֶה אַבִּיט אֶל־עָנִי וּנְכֵה־רוּחַ וְחָרֵד עַל־דְּבָרִי:

¹Οὕτως λέγει κύριος Ὁ οὐρανός μοι θρόνος, ἡ δὲ γῆ ὑποπόδιον
τῶν ποδῶν μου · ποῖον οἶκον οἰκοδομήσετέ μοι; ἢ ποῖος τόπος
τῆς καταπαύσεώς μου; ²πάντα γὰρ ταῦτα ἐποίησεν ἡ χείρ μου,
καὶ ἔστιν ἐμὰ πάντα ταῦτα, λέγει κύριος · καὶ ἐπὶ τίνα ἐπιβλέψω
ἀλλ' ἢ ἐπὶ τὸν ταπεινὸν καὶ ἡσύχιον καὶ τρέμοντα τοὺς λόγους
μου;

267: Isa 66:22 | see Isa 65:17 [265]

268: Jer 5:21

²¹ שִׁמְעוּ־נָא זֹאת עַם סָכָל וְאֵין לֵב
עֵינַיִם לָהֶם וְלֹא יִרְאוּ אָזְנַיִם לָהֶם וְלֹא יִשְׁמָעוּ:

²¹ἀκούσατε δὴ ταῦτα, λαὸς μωρὸς καὶ ἀκάρδιος, ὀφθαλμοὶ αὐτοῖς
καὶ οὐ βλέπουσιν, ὦτα αὐτοῖς καὶ οὐκ ἀκούουσιν.

269: Jer 7:11 | see Isa 56:7 [256]

270: Jer 9:23 (9:24)

²³ כִּי אִם־בְּזֹאת יִתְהַלֵּל הַמִּתְהַלֵּל
הַשְׂכֵּל וְיָדֹעַ אוֹתִי כִּי אֲנִי יְהוָה עֹשֶׂה חֶסֶד
מִשְׁפָּט וּצְדָקָה בָּאָרֶץ כִּי־בְאֵלֶּה חָפַצְתִּי נְאֻם־יְהוָה:

²³ἀλλ' ἢ ἐν τούτῳ καυχάσθω ὁ
καυχώμενος, συνίειν καὶ γινώσκειν ὅτι ἐγώ εἰμι κύριος ποιῶ κ ἔλεος
καὶ κρίμα καὶ δικαιοσύνην ἐπὶ τῆς γῆς, ὅτι ἐν τούτοις τὸ θέλημά
μου, λέγει κύριος.

271: Jer 10: 6–7 | see Psalm 86:9 [173] and Psalm 111:2 [187]

272: Jer 12:15 | see Amos 9:11–12 [297]

273: Jer 18:2–3 | see Zech 11:12–13 [307]

NEW TESTAMENT	COMMENTARY
^a2 Pet 3:13 13 καινοὺς δὲ οὐρανοὺς καὶ ⌐γῆν καινὴν⌐ ⌐κατὰ τὸ ἐπάγγελμα⌐ αὐτοῦ προσδοκῶμεν, ἐν οἷς δικαιοσύνη κατοικεῖ.	Isa 65:17 and Isa 66:22; the only item quoted in 2 Pet 3:13 is the phrase καινοὺς δὲ οὐρανοὺς καὶ γῆν καινήν, which appears as שָׁמַיִם חֲדָשִׁים וָאָרֶץ חֲדָשָׁה in the two Isaiah passages. (*A*)
^aActs 7:49–50 49 ὁ οὐρανός ⌐μοι θρόνος, ⌐ἡ δὲ⌐ γῆ ὑποπόδιον τῶν ποδῶν μου· ποῖον οἶκον οἰκοδομήσετέ μοι, λέγει κύριος, ἢ ⌐τίς τόπος τῆς καταπαύσεώς μου; 50 οὐχὶ ἡ χείρ μου ἐποίησεν ⌐ταῦτα πάντα⌐;	Isa 66:1–2; v. 1*b*–*c* MT = LXX = Acts 7:49*a*–*b*. (*A*) Isa 66:1*d*–*e*; MT = LXX = Acts 7:49*c*–*d* except that the LXX's ποῖος τόπος is τόπος in Acts. (*A*) Isa 66:2*a*; MT makes a statement: "My hand made all these things"; so also the LXX; Acts 7:50 makes it a question introduced by οὐχὶ: "Did not my hand make all these things?" (*A*). In this case the question is entirely equivalent to the statement in actual meaning.
^aMk 8:18 18 ὀφθαλμοὺς ἔχοντες οὐ βλέπετε καὶ ὦτα ἔχοντες οὐκ ἀκούετε; καὶ οὐ μνημονεύετε,	Jer 5:21; MT עֵינַיִם לָהֶם וְלֹא יִרְאוּ אָזְנַיִם לָהֶם וְלֹא יִשְׁמָעוּ, which is rendered literally in LXX ὀφθαλμοὶ αὐτοῖς . . . ὦτα αὐτοῖς; but Mk 8:18 is quite independent of the LXX, using the more idiomatic ὀφθαλμοὺς ἔχοντες and ὦτα ἔχοντες. (*A*)
^a1 Cor 1:31 31 ἵνα καθὼς γέγραπται· ὁ καυχώμενος ἐν κυρίῳ καυχάσθω. **^b2 Cor 10:17** 17 Ὁ δὲ καυχώμενος ἐν κυρίῳ καυχάσθω·	Jer 9:23(24); MT "Let him who glories glory in this, in understanding and knowing me that I am Yahweh . . ." = LXX = 1 Cor 1:31, which has shortened it to: "Let him who glories glory in the Lord." (*A*) 2 Cor 10:17 has the same wording. (*A*)

274: Jer 22:24

see Isa 45:23 [239]

275: Jer 31:9

see 2 Sam 7:8 [120]

276: Jer 31:15

(Jer 38:15)

15 כֹּה ׀ אָמַר יְהוָה
קוֹל בְּרָמָה נִשְׁמָע נְהִי בְּכִי תַמְרוּרִים
רָחֵל מְבַכָּה עַל־בָּנֶיהָ מֵאֲנָה לְהִנָּחֵם
עַל־בָּנֶיהָ כִּי אֵינֶנּוּ׃

15 Οὕτως εἶπεν κύριος Φωνὴ ἐν Ραμα ἠκούσθη θρήνου καὶ κλαυθμοῦ καὶ ὀδυρμοῦ · Ραχηλ ἀποκλαιομένη οὐκ ἤθελεν παύσασθαι ἐπὶ τοῖς υἱοῖς αὐτῆς, ὅτι οὐκ εἰσίν.

277: Jer 31:31–34

(Jer 38:31–34)

31 הִנֵּה יָמִים בָּאִים נְאֻם־יְהוָה וְכָרַתִּי אֶת־בֵּית יִשְׂרָאֵל וְאֶת־בֵּית יְהוּדָה בְּרִית חֲדָשָׁה׃ 32 לֹא כַבְּרִית אֲשֶׁר כָּרַתִּי אֶת־אֲבוֹתָם בְּיוֹם הֶחֱזִיקִי בְיָדָם לְהוֹצִיאָם מֵאֶרֶץ מִצְרָיִם אֲשֶׁר־הֵמָּה הֵפֵרוּ אֶת־בְּרִיתִי וְאָנֹכִי בָּעַלְתִּי בָם נְאֻם־יְהוָה׃ 33 כִּי זֹאת הַבְּרִית אֲשֶׁר אֶכְרֹת אֶת־בֵּית יִשְׂרָאֵל אַחֲרֵי הַיָּמִים הָהֵם נְאֻם־יְהוָה נָתַתִּי אֶת־תּוֹרָתִי בְּקִרְבָּם וְעַל־לִבָּם אֶכְתֲּבֶנָּה וְהָיִיתִי לָהֶם לֵאלֹהִים וְהֵמָּה יִהְיוּ־לִי לְעָם׃ 34 וְלֹא יְלַמְּדוּ עוֹד אִישׁ אֶת־רֵעֵהוּ וְאִישׁ אֶת־אָחִיו לֵאמֹר דְּעוּ אֶת־יְהוָה כִּי־כוּלָּם יֵדְעוּ אוֹתִי לְמִקְּטַנָּם וְעַד־גְּדוֹלָם נְאֻם־יְהוָה כִּי אֶסְלַח לַעֲוֹנָם וּלְחַטָּאתָם לֹא אֶזְכָּר־עוֹד׃

31 Ἰδοὺ ἡμέραι ἔρχονται, φησὶν κύριος, καὶ διαθήσομαι τῷ οἴκῳ Ισραηλ καὶ τῷ οἴκῳ Ιουδα διαθήκην καινήν, 32 οὐ κατὰ τὴν διαθήκην, ἣν διεθέμην τοῖς πατράσιν αὐτῶν ἐν ἡμέρᾳ ἐπιλαβομένου μου τῆς χειρὸς αὐτῶν ἐξαγαγεῖν αὐτοὺς ἐκ τῆς Αἰγύπτου, ὅτι αὐτοὶ οὐκ ἐνέμειναν ἐν τῇ διαθήκῃ μου, καὶ ἐγὼ ἠμέλησα αὐτῶν, φησὶν κύριος · 33 ὅτι αὕτη ἡ διαθήκη, ἣν διαθήσομαι τῷ οἴκῳ Ισραηλ μετὰ τὰς ἡμέρας ἐκείνας, φησὶν κύριος Διδοὺς δώσω νόμους μου εἰς τὴν διάνοιαν αὐτῶν καὶ ἐπὶ καρδίας αὐτῶν γράψω αὐτούς · καὶ ἔσομαι αὐτοῖς εἰς θεόν, καὶ αὐτοὶ ἔσονταί μοι εἰς λαόν · 34 καὶ οὐ μὴ διδάξωσιν ἕκαστος τὸν πολίτην αὐτοῦ καὶ ἕκαστος τὸν ἀδελφὸν αὐτοῦ λέγων Γνῶθι τὸν κύριον · ὅτι πάντες εἰδήσουσίν με ἀπὸ μικροῦ αὐτῶν καὶ ἕως μεγάλου αὐτῶν, ὅτι ἵλεως ἔσομαι ταῖς ἀδικίαις αὐτῶν καὶ τῶν ἁμαρτιῶν αὐτῶν οὐ μὴ μνησθῶ ἔτι.

ᵃMt 2:18

18 φωνὴ ἐν ᾿Ραμὰ ἠκούσθη,
ᵀκλαυθμὸς καὶ ὀδυρμὸς πολύς·
᾿Ραχὴλ κλαίουσα τὰ τέκνα αὐτῆς,
καὶ οὐκ ἤθελεν παρακληθῆναι,
ὅτι οὐκ εἰσίν.

(a) קוֹל בְּרָמָה נִשְׁמָע נְהִי (b) בְּכִי תַמְרוּרִים MT; Jer 31:15;
(c) רָחֵל מְבַכָּה [(d) עַל בָּנֶיהָ] (e) מֵאֲנָה [לְהִנָּחֵם] (f) עַל־בָּנֶיהָ
(g) כִּי אֵינֶנּוּ, which appears as follows in the LXX:
(a) φωνὴ ἐν ᾿Ραμα ἠκούσθη (b) θρήνου καὶ κλαυθμοῦ καὶ ὀδυρμοῦ· (c) ᾿Ραχηλ ἀποκλαιομένη (d) οὐκ ἤθελεν παύσασθαι ἐπὶ τοῖς υἱοῖς αὐτῆς, ὅτι οὐκ εἰσιν. But Mt 2:18 reads (a) *idem*, (b) omits θρήνου καὶ and reads κλαυθμὸς (instead of οὐ, which is really closer to the Hebrew in the use of nominatives here); so also ὀδυρμὸς πολύς ("much grieving") instead of the construct pair ("weeping of bitter lament") in the MT (but a smoother rendering in the Greek), (c) κλαίουσα instead of ἀποκλαίουσα (which is a better rendering of the *Piel* participle), (d) "For her children" = MT as against the LXX, (e) = LXX, (f) omitted as in the MT, as against the LXX, (g) *idem* LXX and MT. Thus, if we overlook a few omissions, Mt 2:18 is closer (especially in word order) to the MT than the LXX is. (*C*)

ᵃHeb 8:8–12

8 μεμφόμενος γὰρ ⌐αὐτοὺς λέγει·
ἰδοὺ ἡμέραι ἔρχονται, λέγει κύριος,
καὶ συντελέσω ἐπὶ τὸν οἶκον ᾿Ισραὴλ
καὶ ἐπὶ τὸν οἶκον ᾿Ιούδα διαθήκην καινήν,
9 οὐ κατὰ τὴν διαθήκην, ἣν ἐποίησα τοῖς πατράσιν αὐτῶν
ἐν ⌐ἡμέρᾳ ἐπιλαβομένου μου τῆς χειρὸς αὐτῶν
ἐξαγαγεῖν αὐτοὺς ἐκ γῆς Αἰγύπτου,
ὅτι αὐτοὶ οὐκ ἐνέμειναν ἐν τῇ διαθήκῃ μου,
κἀγὼ ἠμέλησα αὐτῶν, λέγει κύριος·
10 ὅτι αὕτη ἡ διαθήκηᵀ, ἣν διαθήσομαι τῷ οἴκῳ ᾿Ισραὴλ
μετὰ τὰς ἡμέρας ἐκείνας, λέγει κύριος·
διδοὺς νόμους μου εἰς τὴν διάνοιαν αὐτῶν
καὶ ἐπὶ ⌐καρδίας αὐτῶν ⌐ἐπιγράψω αὐτούς,
καὶ ἔσομαι αὐτοῖς εἰς θεόν,
καὶ αὐτοὶ ἔσονταί μοι εἰς λαόν·
11 καὶ οὐ μὴ διδάξωσιν ἕκαστος τὸν ⌐πολίτην αὐτοῦ
καὶ ἕκαστος τὸν ἀδελφὸν ᴼαὐτοῦ λέγων· γνῶθι τὸν
ὅτι πάντες εἰδήσουσίν με   [κύριον,
ἀπὸ μικροῦ ᵀ ἕως μεγάλου αὐτῶν,
12 ὅτι ἵλεως ἔσομαι ταῖς ἀδικίαις αὐτῶν
καὶ τῶν ἁμαρτιῶν αὐτῶν ᵀ οὐ μὴ μνησθῶ ἔτι.

Jer 31:31–34; this long passage of five verses shows remarkably little variation (with one important exception) between the MT, LXX, and NT. But note (1) the LXX differentiates נְאֻם יהוה by φησὶν κύριος, but the NT makes it λέγει κύριος throughout (not distinguishing from אָמַר יהוה, which, however, does not occur in the MT of this passage), so (*A*); (2) the NT uses συντελεῖν, διαθήκην for כָּרַת בְּרִית in v. 8, but ποεῖν in v. 9, and διαθήσομαι in v. 10. The LXX uses διαθήσομαι, διαθήκην in all three cases very consistently, so (*A-*); (3) the NT and LXX use ἡμέρᾳ ἐπιλαβομένου μου τῆς χειρὸς for the MT's בְּיוֹם חֶחֱזִיקִי בְיָדָם, possibly because ἐν τῷ ἐπιλαβέσθαι would have sounded unfelicitous in Greek, so (*A*); (4) the NT and LXX use ἠμέλησα αὐτῶν ("I did not care for them any longer" or "I left off caring for them") for בָּעַלְתִּי בָם, which is usually rendered "though I was a husband to them." But since this is hardly appropriate in this context, disturbing the flow of thought, it is better to identify בָּעַלְתִּי as from בָּעַל II = "abhor" (so *Gesenius-Buhl Lex.* 106B). If so, then the LXX gives us a valuable clue as to the proper interpretation of this word, so (*Aᵈ*); (5) the NT uses διδοὺς alone instead of the LXX's διδοὺς δώσω (which suggests נָתֹן אֶתֵּן or something similar, so

277 (continued)

278: Ezek 5:11

see Isa 45:23 [239]

279: Ezek 11:20

²⁰לְמַעַן֩
בְּחֻקֹּתַ֨י יֵלֵ֜כוּ וְאֶת־מִשְׁפָּטַ֤י יִשְׁמְר֙וּ וְעָשׂ֣וּ אֹתָ֔ם וְהָיוּ־לִ֣י לְעָ֔ם וַאֲנִ֕י אֶהְיֶ֥ה
לָהֶ֖ם לֵאלֹהִֽים׃

²⁰ὅπως ἐν τοῖς προστάγμασίν μου πορεύωνται καὶ τὰ δικαιώματά μου φυλάσσωνται καὶ ποιῶσιν αὐτά · καὶ ἔσονταί μοι εἰς λαόν, καὶ ἐγὼ ἔσομαι αὐτοῖς εἰς θεόν.

280: Ezek 20:34, 41

see Isa 52:11 [245]

281: Ezek 37:5, 10

⁵ כֹּ֤ה אָמַר֙ אֲדֹנָ֣י יְהֹוִ֔ה לָעֲצָמ֖וֹת
הָאֵ֑לֶּה הִנֵּ֨ה אֲנִ֜י מֵבִ֥יא בָכֶ֛ם ר֖וּחַ וִחְיִיתֶֽם׃

¹⁰ וְהִנַּבֵּ֖אתִי כַּאֲשֶׁ֣ר צִוָּ֑נִי וַתָּבוֹא֩ בָהֶ֨ם הָר֜וּחַ
וַיִּֽחְי֗וּ וַיַּֽעַמְדוּ֙ עַל־רַגְלֵיהֶ֔ם חַ֖יִל גָּד֥וֹל מְאֹד־מְאֹֽד׃

⁵Τάδε λέγει κύριος τοῖς ὀστέοις τούτοις Ἰδοὺ ἐγὼ φέρω εἰς ὑμᾶς πνεῦμα ζωῆς

¹⁰καὶ ἐπροφήτευσα
καθότι ἐνετείλατό μοι · καὶ εἰσῆλθεν εἰς αὐτοὺς τὸ πνεῦμα, καὶ ἔζησαν καὶ ἔστησαν ἐπὶ τῶν ποδῶν αὐτῶν, συναγωγὴ πολλὴ σφόδρα.

282: Ezek 37:27

see Lev 26:12 [71]

283: Dan 3:6

⁶ וּמַן־דִּי־לָ֣א יִפֵּ֑ל
וְיִסְגֻּ֔ד בַּהּ־שַׁעֲתָ֗א יִתְרְמֵ֛א לְגֽוֹא־אַתּ֥וּן נוּרָ֖א יָקִֽדְתָּֽא׃

𝕲
⁶καὶ πᾶς, ὃς ἂν μὴ πεσὼν προσκυνήσῃ, ἐμβαλοῦσιν αὐτὸν εἰς τὴν κάμινον τοῦ πυρὸς τὴν καιομένην.

θ′
⁶καὶ ὃς ἂν μὴ πεσὼν προσ-
κυνήσῃ, αὐτῇ τῇ ὥρᾳ ἐμβληθήσεται εἰς τὴν κάμινον τοῦ πυρὸς τὴν καιομένην.

*b*Heb 10:16–17   only Jer 31:33–34

16 αὕτη ᵀ ἡ διαθήκη ἣν διαθήσομαι πρὸς αὐτοὺς
   μετὰ τὰς ἡμέρας ἐκείνας, λέγει κύριος·
διδοὺς νόμους μου ἐπὶ καρδίας αὐτῶν
   καὶ ἐπὶ ⌐τὴν διάνοιαν⌐ αὐτῶν ἐπιγράψω αὐτούς,
17 ᵀ καὶ τῶν ἁμαρτιῶν ᵒαὐτῶν καὶ τῶν ἀνομιῶν αὐτῶν
   οὐ μὴ ⌐μνησθήσομαι ἔτι.

(*A*ᵈ); (6) both the LXX and NT omit the נְאֻם יהוה after
עַד־גְּדוֹלָם in Jer 31:34 (Heb 8:11 end). (*A*)

Heb 10:16–17 are simply an excerpt from Heb 8:10–12
without verbal change.

---

*a*Rev 21:7

7 ὁ νικῶν ⌐κληρονομήσει ταῦτα καὶ
ἔσομαι ⌐αὐτῷ θεὸς καὶ ⌐αὐτὸς ἔσται μοι υἱός⌐.

Ezek 11:20 furnishes no direct basis for the quote in
Rev 21:7, which draws entirely from 2 Sam 7:14. But
Ezek does furnish an extended application of the personal, covenantal relationship to the people of God in
general, rather than for Solomon in particular. From
this perspective Ezek 11 furnishes a basis for the wider
scope of the promise in Rev 21. (Cf. #121 for the overall
rating for this passage.)

---

*a*Rev 11:11

11 Καὶ μετὰ ᵒτὰς τρεῖς ἡμέρας καὶ ἥμισυ πνεῦμα ζωῆς
ἐκ τοῦ θεοῦ εἰσῆλθεν ⌐ἐν αὐτοῖς⌐, καὶ ἔστησαν ἐπὶ τοὺς
πόδας αὐτῶν, καὶ φόβος μέγας ⌐ἐπέπεσεν ἐπὶ *τοὺς
θεωροῦντας⌐ αὐτούς.

Ezek 37:5, 10; Rev 11:11 is not actually quoting here,
but only using allusive language (*F*). Note the following: (1) πνεῦμα ζωῆς occurs in the LXX of Ezek
37:5, in a passage which apparently misreads the Hebrew *Vorlage* (reading רוּחַ חַיִּים instead of וְחָיִיתֶם);
(2) εἰσῆλθεν ἐν αὐτοῖς in Rev 11:11 is literalistic (וַתָּבוֹא
בָּהֶם), but not as good syntax as LXX's εἰς αὐτούς.

---

*a*Mt 13:42, 50

42 καὶ ⌐βαλοῦσιν αὐτοὺς εἰς τὴν κάμινον
τοῦ πυρός· ἐκεῖ ἔσται ὁ κλαυθμὸς καὶ ὁ βρυγμὸς τῶν ὀδόντων.

50 καὶ ⌐βαλοῦσιν
αὐτοὺς εἰς τὴν κάμινον τοῦ πυρός· ἐκεῖ ἔσται ὁ κλαυθμὸς
καὶ ὁ βρυγμὸς τῶν ὀδόντων.

Dan 3:6; MT יִתְרְמֵא לְגוֹא־אַתּוּן נוּרָא. This again is not a
quote but a mere allusion in Mt 13:42, 50, setting forth a
prophetic fulfillment of an earlier historical event. But
the language is quite close to Daniel's text: βαλοῦσιν
(active instead of passive) αὐτοὺς εἰς τὴν κάμινον τοῦ
πυρός. It is interesting that the LXX uses the same
active form, βαλοῦσιν, but Theodotion shifts to a
passive, ἐμβληθήσεται, since יִתְרְמֵא is a passive *hitpoel*.
(*F*)

MASORETIC TEXT	SEPTUAGINT

284: Dan 7:13   (see also Psalm 110:1 [185],a–e)

𝕾

¹³ חָזֵה הֲוֵית֙ בְּחֶזְוֵ֣י לֵֽילְיָ֔א
וַאֲר֗וּ עִם־עֲנָנֵ֤י שְׁמַיָּא֙ כְּבַ֣ר אֱנָ֣שׁ אָתֵ֣ה הֲוָ֔ה
וְעַד־עַתִּ֤יק יֽוֹמַיָּא֙ מְטָ֔ה וּקְדָמ֖וֹהִי הַקְרְבֽוּהִי׃

¹³ ἐθεώρουν ἐν ὁράματι τῆς νυκτὸς καὶ ἰδοὺ
ἐπὶ τῶν νεφελῶν τοῦ οὐρανοῦ ὡς υἱὸς ἀνθρώπου ἤρχετο, καὶ ὡς
παλαιὸς ἡμερῶν παρῆν, καὶ οἱ παρεστηκότες παρῆσαν αὐτῷ.

θ

¹³ ἐθε-
ώρουν ἐν ὁράματι τῆς νυκτὸς καὶ ἰδοὺ μετὰ τῶν νεφελῶν τοῦ
οὐρανοῦ ὡς υἱὸς ἀνθρώπου ἐρχόμενος ἦν καὶ ἕως τοῦ παλαιοῦ
τῶν ἡμερῶν ἔφθασεν καὶ ἐνώπιον αὐτοῦ προσηνέχθη.

285: Dan 9:27

𝕾

²⁷ וְהִגְבִּ֥יר בְּרִ֛ית לָרַבִּ֖ים שָׁב֣וּעַ אֶחָ֑ד
וַחֲצִ֨י הַשָּׁב֜וּעַ יַשְׁבִּ֣ית׀ זֶ֣בַח וּמִנְחָ֗ה
וְעַ֨ל כְּנַ֤ף שִׁקּוּצִים֙ מְשֹׁמֵ֔ם וְעַד־כָּלָה֙ וְנֶ֣חֱרָצָ֔ה תִּתַּ֖ךְ עַל־שֹׁמֵֽם׃

²⁷ καὶ δυναστεύσει ἡ διαθήκη εἰς πολλούς, καὶ πάλιν
ἐπιστρέψει καὶ ἀνοικοδομηθήσεται εἰς πλάτος καὶ μῆκος · καὶ κατὰ
συντέλειαν καιρῶν καὶ μετὰ ἑπτὰ καὶ ἑβδομήκοντα καιροὺς καὶ ἑξή-
κοντα δύο ἔτη ἕως καιροῦ συντελείας πολέμου καὶ ἀφαιρεθήσεται
ἡ ἐρήμωσις ἐν τῷ κατισχῦσαι τὴν διαθήκην ἐπὶ πολλὰς ἑβδομά-
δας · καὶ ἐν τῷ τέλει τῆς ἑβδομάδος ἀρθήσεται ἡ θυσία καὶ ἡ
σπονδή, καὶ ἐπὶ τὸ ἱερὸν βδέλυγμα τῶν ἐρημώσεων ἔσται ἕως
συντελείας, καὶ συντέλεια δοθήσεται ἐπὶ τὴν ἐρήμωσιν.

θ′

²⁷ καὶ δυναμώσει διαθήκην πολλοῖς,
ἑβδομὰς μία · καὶ ἐν τῷ ἡμίσει τῆς ἑβδομάδος ἀρθήσεταί μου θυσία καὶ σπονδή, καὶ ἐπὶ τὸ ἱερὸν βδέλυγμα τῶν ἐρημώσεων, καὶ
ἕως συντελείας καιροῦ συντέλεια δοθήσεται ἐπὶ τὴν ἐρήμωσιν.

*f*Mt 24:30

30 καὶ τότε φανήσεται τὸ σημεῖον τοῦ υἱοῦ τοῦ ἀνθρώπου ⸂ ἐν οὐρανῷ ⸃, καὶ ⸄ τότε κόψονται ⸅ πᾶσαι αἱ φυλαὶ τῆς
γῆς καὶ ὄψονται *τὸν υἱὸν τοῦ ἀνθρώπου ἐρχόμενον ἐπὶ τῶν νεφελῶν τοῦ οὐρανοῦ* μετὰ δυνάμεως καὶ δόξης πολλῆς·

*g*Mt 26:64

64 λέγει αὐτῷ
ὁ Ἰησοῦς· σὺ εἶπας·. πλὴν λέγω ὑμῖν· ἀπ' ἄρτι ὄψεσθε
τὸν υἱὸν τοῦ ἀνθρώπου καθήμενον ἐκ δεξιῶν τῆς δυνάμεως
καὶ *ἐρχόμενον ἐπὶ τῶν νεφελῶν τοῦ οὐρανοῦ*.

*h*Mk 13:26

26 καὶ τότε ὄψονται *τὸν υἱὸν τοῦ ἀνθρώπου ἐρχόμενον ἐν νε-
φέλαις* μετὰ δυνάμεως πολλῆς *καὶ δόξης*.

*i*Mk 14:62

62 ὁ δὲ Ἰησοῦς εἶπεν· ᵀ ἐγώ εἰμι, καὶ ὄψεσθε *τὸν υἱὸν τοῦ
ἀνθρώπου* ἐκ δεξιῶν καθήμενον τῆς δυνάμεως □καὶ *ἐρχόμενον* ⸃ *μετὰ τῶν νεφελῶν τοῦ οὐρανοῦ*.

*j*Lk 21:27

27 καὶ τότε
ὄψονται *τὸν υἱὸν τοῦ ἀνθρώπου ἐρχόμενον ἐν νεφέλῃ* ⸂μετὰ
δυνάμεως καὶ δόξης πολλῆς ⸃.

*k*Lk 22:69

69 ἀπὸ τοῦ νῦν δὲ ἔσται ὁ υἱὸς τοῦ ἀνθρώπου καθήμενος ἐκ
δεξιῶν τῆς δυνάμεως τοῦ θεοῦ.

Dan 7:13; MT עִם־עֲנָנֵי שְׁמַיָּא כְּבַר אֱנָשׁ אָתֵה הֲוָה = LXX
ἐπὶ τῶν νεφελῶν τοῦ οὐρανοῦ ὡς υἱὸς ἀνθρώπου ἤρ-
χετο = Mt 26:64 ὄψεσθε τὸν υἱὸν τοῦ ἀνθρώπου . . . καὶ
ἐρχόμενον. (*A*)

---

*a*Mt 24:15

15 Ὅταν οὖν ἴδητε *τὸ βδέλυγμα τῆς ἐρημώσεως* τὸ ῥηθὲν
διὰ Δανιὴλ τοῦ προφήτου □ἑστὸς ἐν τόπῳ ἁγίῳ ⸃, ὁ ἀναγινώσκων νοείτω,

*b*Mk 13:14

14 Ὅταν δὲ ἴδητε *τὸ βδέλυγμα τῆς ἐρημώσεως* ἑστηκότα
ὅπου οὐ δεῖ, ὁ ἀναγινώσκων νοείτω ᵀ, * τότε οἱ ἐν τῇ
Ἰουδαίᾳ φευγέτωσαν εἰς τὰ ὄρη,

Dan 9:27; this is simply the celebrated phrase, βδέλυγμα
ἐρημώσεως, which Jesus referred to in the Olivet Dis-
course as prophetic of the last days. The two evangelists
expressly attribute this expression to Daniel as the
personal author (διὰ Δανιὴλ τοῦ προφήτου). In Daniel
this phrase occurs in 9:27 (both the LXX and Θ) (ἐπὶ τὸ
ἱερὸν) Βδέλυγμα τῆς ἐρημώσεως, in 11:31 (the same
for both versions), and in 12:11 the LXX uses the
definite article before βδέλυμα and ἐρημώσεως, whereas
Theodotion uses it before neither. The Hebrew expres-
sion is in 9:27 שִׁקּוּצִים מְשֹׁמֵם, in 11:31 הַשִּׁקּוּץ מְשֹׁמֵם, and
in 12:11 שִׁקּוּץ שֹׁמֵם. (*A*)

286: Dan 11:31

³¹ וּזְרֹעִים מִמֶּנּוּ יַעֲמֹדוּ וְחִלְּלוּ הַמִּקְדָּשׁ הַמָּעוֹז וְהֵסִירוּ הַתָּמִיד וְנָתְנוּ הַשִּׁקּוּץ מְשׁוֹמֵם׃

³¹ καὶ βραχίονες παρ' αὐτοῦ στήσον-
ται καὶ μιανοῦσι τὸ ἅγιον τοῦ φόβου καὶ ἀποστήσουσι τὴν θυσίαν
καὶ δώσουσι βδέλυγμα ἐρημώσεως.

³¹ καὶ σπέρματα
ἐξ αὐτοῦ ἀναστήσονται καὶ βεβηλώσουσιν τὸ ἁγίασμα τῆς δυνα-
στείας καὶ μεταστήσουσιν τὸν ἐνδελεχισμὸν καὶ δώσουσιν βδέλυγμα ἠφανισμένον.

287: Dan 12:11

¹¹ וּמֵעֵת הוּסַר הַתָּמִיד וְלָתֵת שִׁקּוּץ שֹׁמֵם יָמִים אֶלֶף מָאתַיִם וְתִשְׁעִים׃

¹¹ ἀφ' οὗ ἂν ἀποσταθῇ
ἡ θυσία διὰ παντὸς καὶ ἑτοιμασθῇ δοθῆναι τὸ βδέλυγμα τῆς ἐρημώσεως, ἡμέρας χιλίας διακοσίας ἐνενήκοντα.

¹¹ καὶ ἀπὸ
καιροῦ παραλλάξεως τοῦ ἐνδελεχισμοῦ καὶ τοῦ δοθῆναι βδέλυγμα
ἐρημώσεως ἡμέραι χίλιαι διακόσιαι ἐνενήκοντα.

288: Hos 2:1 (1:10b), 3 (2:1b)

¹ וְהָיָה מִסְפַּר בְּנֵי־יִשְׂרָאֵל כְּחוֹל הַיָּם
אֲשֶׁר לֹא־יִמַּד וְלֹא יִסָּפֵר
וְהָיָה בִּמְקוֹם אֲשֶׁר־יֵאָמֵר לָהֶם לֹא־עַמִּי אַתֶּם
יֵאָמֵר לָהֶם בְּנֵי אֵל־חָי׃
³ אִמְרוּ לַאֲחֵיכֶם עַמִּי וְלַאֲחוֹתֵיכֶם רֻחָמָה׃

¹ Καὶ ἦν ὁ ἀριθμὸς τῶν υἱῶν Ισραηλ ὡς ἡ ἄμμος τῆς θαλάσσης,
οὐκ ἐκμετρηθήσεται οὐδὲ ἐξαριθμηθήσεται· καὶ ἔσται ἐν τῷ τόπῳ,
οὗ ἐρρέθη αὐτοῖς Οὐ λαός μου ὑμεῖς, ἐκεῖ κληθήσονται υἱοὶ θεοῦ
ζῶντος.

³ εἴπατε τῷ ἀδελφῷ ὑμῶν
Λαός-μου καὶ τῇ ἀδελφῇ ὑμῶν Ἠλεημένη.

Isa 10:22–23

²² כִּי אִם־יִהְיֶה עַמְּךָ יִשְׂרָאֵל
כְּחוֹל הַיָּם שְׁאָר יָשׁוּב בּוֹ כִּלָּיוֹן חָרוּץ שׁוֹטֵף צְדָקָה׃ ²³ כִּי כָלָה
וְנֶחֱרָצָה אֲדֹנָי יְהוִה צְבָאוֹת עֹשֶׂה בְּקֶרֶב כָּל־הָאָרֶץ׃

²² καὶ ἐὰν γένηται ὁ λαὸς
Ισραηλ ὡς ἡ ἄμμος τῆς θαλάσσης, τὸ κατάλειμμα αὐτῶν σωθή-
σεται· λόγον γὰρ συντελῶν καὶ συντέμνων ἐν δικαιοσύνῃ, ²³ ὅτι
λόγον συντετμημένον ποιήσει ὁ θεὸς ἐν τῇ οἰκουμένῃ ὅλῃ.

*a*Rom 9:25–28

25 ὡς καὶ
°ἐν τῷ Ὡσηὲ λέγει ·
    καλέσω τὸν οὐ λαόν μου λαόν μου
    καὶ τὴν οὐκ ἠγαπημένην ἠγαπημένην ·
26 καὶ ἔσται ἐν τῷ τόπῳ ⌜οὗ ⌐ἐρρέθη αὐτοῖς⌐ ·
    οὐ λαός μου °ὑμεῖς,
    ἐκεῖ κληθήσονται υἱοὶ θεοῦ ζῶντος.
27 Ἡσαΐας δὲ κράζει ὑπὲρ τοῦ Ἰσραήλ ·
    ἐὰν ᾖ ὁ ἀριθμὸς τῶν υἱῶν Ἰσραὴλ ὡς ἡ ἄμμος τῆς θαλάσσης,
    τὸ ⌜ὑπόλειμμα σωθήσεται ·
28 λόγον γὰρ συντελῶν καὶ συντέμνων ⌐ ποιήσει κύριος ἐπὶ τῆς γῆς.

    9:25—only Hos 2:25
      :26—only Hos 2:3
      :27—only Hos 2:3
              Isa 10:22–23
      :28—only Isa 10:22–23

Hos 2:1; MT וְהָיָה בִמְקוֹם אֲשֶׁר־יֵאָמֵר לָהֶם לֹא־עַמִּי אַתֶּם יֵאָמֵר לָהֶם בְּנֵי אֵל־חָי; LXX καὶ ἔσται ἐν τῷ τόπῳ οὗ ἐρρέθη αὐτοῖς οὐ λαός μου ὑμεῖς, ἐκεῖ κληθήσονται υἱοὶ θεοῦ ζῶντος = NT.

Hos 2:3*a*(1*b*); MT אִמְרוּ לַאֲחֵיכֶם עַמִּי; LXX εἴπατε τῷ ἀδελφῷ ὑμῶν Λαός μου (singular "brother" for MT's "brothers"). NT Rom 9:25 καλέσω τὸν οὐ λαόν μου λαόν μου (the affirmation of God in the first person is legitimately inferred from His command to the prophet to declare it). (*B*ᵃ)

Hos 2:3*b*: MT וְלַאֲחוֹתֵיכֶם רֻחָמָה; LXX καὶ τῇ ἀδελφῇ ὑμῶν Ἠλεημένη (again the LXX uses the singular for the MT's plural); NT (Rom 9:25*b*) καὶ τὴν οὐκ ἠγαπημένην ἠγαπημένην. Here ἠγαπημένην is probably influenced by the Aramaic רְחַם "to love." The reference to οὐκ ἠγαπημένη is actually Hos 1:6 "Name her (לֹא־רֻחָמָה) for I will no longer have compassion (אֲרַחֵם) upon the house of Israel." Hence we have an inferential quote here that accurately reflects the concept of the OT passage cited. (*D*ᵃ)

Isa 10:22–23; MT (כִּי) אִם־יִהְיֶה עַמְּךָ יִשְׂרָאֵל כְּחוֹל הַיָּם שְׁאָר יָשׁוּב בּוֹ; for which the LXX reads ἐὰν γένηται ὁ λαὸς Ἰσραὴλ ὡς ἡ ἄμμος τῆς θαλάσσης, τὸ κατάλειμμα αὐτῶν σωθήσεται (wrong for יָשׁוּב); NT (Rom 9:27) ἐὰν ᾖ ὁ ἀριθμὸς τῶν υἱῶν Ἰσραὴλ ὡς ἡ ἄμμος τῆς θαλάσσης τὸ ὑπόλειμμα σωθήσεται. Note the following divergences: (1) Rom uses ᾖ rather than LXX's γένηται, but this is just as good for יִהְיֶה; (2) σωθήσεται is an implication of יָשׁוּב, since it was largely those who

143

288 (continued)

289: Hos 2:25 (2:23)

25 וּזְרַעְתִּיהָ לִּי בָּאָרֶץ   וְרִחַמְתִּי אֶת־לֹא רֻחָמָה
וְאָמַרְתִּי לְלֹא־עַמִּי עַמִּי־אַתָּה   וְהוּא יֹאמַר אֱלֹהָי:

²⁵ καὶ σπερῶ αὐτὴν ἐμαυ-
τῷ ἐπὶ τῆς γῆς καὶ ἐλεήσω τὴν Οὐκ-ἠλεημένην καὶ ἐρῶ τῷ Οὐ-λαῷ-
μου Λαός μου εἶ σύ, καὶ αὐτὸς ἐρεῖ Κύριος ὁ θεός μου εἶ σύ.

290: Hos 6:6

6 כִּי חֶסֶד חָפַצְתִּי וְלֹא־זָבַח   וְדַעַת אֱלֹהִים מֵעֹלוֹת:

⁶ διότι ἔλεος θέλω καὶ οὐ θυσίαν καὶ ἐπίγνωσιν θεοῦ ἢ ὁλοκαυτώματα.

291: Hos 10:8

8 וְנִשְׁמְדוּ בָּמוֹת אָוֶן   חַטַּאת יִשְׂרָאֵל
קוֹץ וְדַרְדַּר יַעֲלֶה   עַל־מִזְבְּחוֹתָם
וְאָמְרוּ לֶהָרִים כַּסּוּנוּ   וְלַגְּבָעוֹת נִפְלוּ עָלֵינוּ:

⁸ καὶ ἐξαρθήσονται βωμοὶ Ων, ἁμαρτήματα τοῦ Ισ-
ραηλ · ἄκανθαι καὶ τρίβολοι ἀναβήσονται ἐπὶ τὰ θυσιαστήρια αὐτῶν·
καὶ ἐροῦσιν τοῖς ὄρεσιν Καλύψατε ἡμᾶς, καὶ τοῖς βουνοῖς Πέσατε
ἐφ' ἡμᾶς.

returned after the fall of Babylon in the 580s B.C who carried on a covenant relationship with the Lord. Their act of returning to the desolate ruin of Jerusalem evidenced a true commitment to the Lord and His covenant promises; (3) The word ἀριθμός ("number of") is clearly implied by the description of the Israelites as the "sand of the sea"; in other words, in number they were like the sand, rather than in their color or their consistency; (4) The connotation of ὑπόλειμμα in Rom 9 is "that which is left remaining," that of the LXX's κατάλειμμα "that which is left behind"; both are equally good for שְׁאָר. It is interesting to observe the similarity of Paul's quotation of Hos and Isa to the wording of the LXX, and yet the minor differences that do occur here and there. (D)

Hos 2:25(23), which is associated with Hos 2:1 (1:10) in furnishing a source for Rom 9:25, contributes to that conflate passage "her who had not received compassion" as the basis for ἐλεήσω τὴν Οὐκ ἠλεημένην. As for "I will call her *beloved* who has not been beloved" in Rom 9, the "beloved" (ἠγαπημένην) seems to rest upon an interpretation of רְחַם in the Aramaic (but not exclusively *beloved* even in that language; yet it predominantly serves as a favored word for "love"). (D)

---

*a*Mt 9:13

13 πορευθέντες δὲ μά-
θετε τί ἐστιν· ἔλεος θέλω καὶ οὐ θυσίαν· οὐ γὰρ ἦλθον καλέσαι δικαίους ἀλλὰ ἁμαρτωλούς ᵀ.

*b*Mt 12:7

7 εἰ δὲ ἐγνώκειτε τί ἐστιν· ἔλεος θέλω καὶ οὐ
θυσίαν, οὐκ ἂν κατεδικάσατε τοὺς ἀναιτίους.

Hos 6:6; MT כִּי חֶסֶד חָפַצְתִּי וְלֹא־זָבַח; LXX διότι ἔλεος θέλω καὶ οὐ θυσίαν = Mt 9:13 and Mt 12:7 (A). The only comment needed here is that חָפֵץ means "take pleasure in—delight in" (the probable meaning here, according to *BDB* 342b), whereas θέλειν = "wish, desire." But θέλειν is quite often used for חָפֵץ in the LXX, e.g. Deut 21:14; 1 Sam 18:22; cf. 2 Sam 15:26; 1 Kings 10:8; 2 Chron 9:8; Isa 17:22; etc.

---

*a*Lk 23:30

30 τότε ἄρ-
ξονται λέγειν τοῖς ὄρεσιν· πέσετε ἐφ᾽ ἡμᾶς, καὶ τοῖς βου-
νοῖς· καλύψατε ἡμᾶς·

*b*Rev 6:16

16 *καὶ λέγουσιν τοῖς ὄρεσιν καὶ ταῖς πέτραις*
πέσετε ἐφ᾽ ἡμᾶς καὶ ⌜*κρύψατε ἡμᾶς ἀπὸ προσώπου τοῦ*
καθημένου ἐπὶ ⌜*τοῦ θρόνου*⌝ *καὶ ἀπὸ τῆς ὀργῆς τοῦ ἀρ-*
νίου,

Hos 10:8; 8*c* MT וְאָמְרוּ לֶהָרִים כַּסּוּנוּ וְלַגְּבָעוֹת נִפְלוּ עָלֵינוּ = LXX καὶ ἐροῦσιν τοῖς ὄρεσιν, καλύψατε ἡμᾶς, καὶ τοῖς βουνοῖς πέσατε ἐφ᾽ ἡμᾶς (cf. Lk 23:30 ἄρξονται λέγειν τοῖς ὄρεσιν, πέσετε ἐφ᾽ ἡμᾶς, καὶ τοῖς βουνοῖς· καλύψατε ἡμᾶς, so (A). Note the following: (1) ἐροῦσιν in the LXX is fine for וְאָמְרוּ, but ἄρξονται λέγειν is also a justifiable, more sophisticated rendering of the perfect conversive (A^d); (2) καλύψατε in the LXX is a possible inference, but Luke's "fall on us" is exactly what the Hebrew says. Rev 6:16, which is not really a quotation but simply an allusion, uses κρύψατε rather than the LXX's and Luke's καλύψατε before ἡμᾶς. (F)

292: Hos 11:1

¹ כִּי נַעַר יִשְׂרָאֵל וָאֹהֲבֵהוּ וּמִמִּצְרַיִם קָרָאתִי לִבְנִי׳׳:

¹Διότι νήπιος Ισραηλ, καὶ ἐγὼ ἠγάπησα αὐτὸν καὶ ἐξ Αἰγύπτου μετεκάλεσα τὰ τέκνα αὐτοῦ.

293: Hos 13:14

¹⁴ מִיַּד שְׁאוֹל אֶפְדֵּם מִמָּוֶת אֶגְאָלֵם
אֱהִי׳ דְבָרֶיךָ׳ מָוֶת אֱהִי׳ קָטָבְךָ׳ שְׁאוֹל
נֹחַם יִסָּתֵר מֵעֵינָי:

¹⁴ἐκ χειρὸς ᾅδου ῥύσομαι αὐτοὺς καὶ ἐκ θανάτου λυτρώσομαι αὐτούς· ποῦ ἡ δίκη σου, θάνατε; ποῦ τὸ κέντρον σου, ᾅδη; παράκλησις κέκρυπται ἀπὸ ὀφθαλμῶν μου.

294: Joel 3:1–5 (2:28–32)

¹ וְהָיָה אַחֲרֵי־כֵן
אֶשְׁפּוֹךְ אֶת־רוּחִי עַל־כָּל־בָּשָׂר וְנִבְּאוּ בְּנֵיכֶם וּבְנוֹתֵיכֶם
זִקְנֵיכֶם חֲלֹמוֹת יַחֲלֹמוּן בַּחוּרֵיכֶם חֶזְיֹנוֹת יִרְאוּ: [רוּחִי]
² וְגַם עַל־הָעֲבָדִים וְעַל־הַשְּׁפָחוֹת בַּיָּמִים הָהֵמָּה אֶשְׁפּוֹךְ אֶת־
רוּחִי:
³ וְנָתַתִּי מוֹפְתִים בַּשָּׁמַיִם וּבָאָרֶץ דָּם וָאֵשׁ וְתִימֲרוֹת עָשָׁן:
⁴ הַשֶּׁמֶשׁ יֵהָפֵךְ לְחֹשֶׁךְ וְהַיָּרֵחַ לְדָם
לִפְנֵי בּוֹא יוֹם יְהוָה הַגָּדוֹל וְהַנּוֹרָא:
⁵ וְהָיָה כֹּל אֲשֶׁר־יִקְרָא בְּשֵׁם יְהוָה יִמָּלֵט
כִּי בְּהַר־צִיּוֹן וּבִירוּשָׁלַםִ׳ תִּהְיֶה פְלֵיטָה כַּאֲשֶׁר אָמַר יְהוָה
וּבַשְּׂרִידִים׳ אֲשֶׁר יְהוָה קֹרֵא:

¹Καὶ ἔσται μετὰ ταῦτα καὶ ἐκχεῶ ἀπὸ τοῦ πνεύματός μου ἐπὶ πᾶσαν σάρκα, καὶ προφητεύσουσιν οἱ υἱοὶ ὑμῶν καὶ αἱ θυγατέρες ὑμῶν, καὶ οἱ πρεσβύτεροι ὑμῶν ἐνύπνια ἐνυπνιασθήσονται, καὶ οἱ νεανίσκοι ὑμῶν ὁράσεις ὄψονται· ²καὶ ἐπὶ τοὺς δούλους καὶ ἐπὶ τὰς δούλας ἐν ταῖς ἡμέραις ἐκείναις ἐκχεῶ ἀπὸ τοῦ πνεύματός μου. ³καὶ δώσω τέρατα ἐν τῷ οὐρανῷ καὶ ἐπὶ τῆς γῆς, αἷμα καὶ πῦρ καὶ ἀτμίδα καπνοῦ· ⁴ὁ ἥλιος μεταστραφήσεται εἰς σκότος καὶ ἡ σελήνη εἰς αἷμα πρὶν ἐλθεῖν ἡμέραν κυρίου τὴν μεγάλην καὶ ἐπιφανῆ. ⁵καὶ ἔσται πᾶς, ὃς ἂν ἐπικαλέσηται τὸ ὄνομα κυρίου, σωθήσεται· ὅτι ἐν τῷ ὄρει Σιων καὶ ἐν Ιερουσαλημ ἔσται ἀνασῳζόμενος, καθότι εἶπεν κύριος, καὶ εὐαγγελιζόμενοι, οὓς κύριος προσκέκληται.

aMt 2:15

15 καὶ ἦν ἐκεῖ ἕως τῆς τελευτῆς Ἡρῴδου·
ἵνα πληρωθῇ τὸ ῥηθὲν ὑπὸ κυρίου διὰ ᵀ τοῦ προφήτου
λέγοντος·
ἐξ Αἰγύπτου ἐκάλεσα τὸν υἱόν μου.

Hos 11:1; MT מִמִּצְרַיִם קָרָאתִי לִבְנִי; LXX ἐξ Αἰγύπτου μετεκάλεσα τὰ τέκνα αὐτοῦ is less accurate than Mt 2:15: ἐκάλεσα τὸν υἱόν μου. But Hos 11:1 seems to refer to the Israelite nation of Moses' day, whereas Mt 2:15 states that the return of the infant Jesus with Mary and Joseph to Judea and Galilee was a fulfillment of Hos 11:1. (E)

It should be observed that fulfillment (ἵνα πληρωθῇ τὸ ῥῆμα) implies that the Exodus deliverance of national Israel was a prophetic event for which the coming of the Messiah as personal Israel was the antitypical fulfillment, in the same sense as Jesus is spoken of in 1 Cor 5:7 as "Christ our passover." That is, the historical event of the deliverance of Israel through the sprinkled blood of the passover lamb found its antitypical fulfillment in the shedding of Jesus' blood on the cross.

a1 Cor 15:55

55 ποῦ σου, θάνατε, τὸ ⸀νῖκος;
ποῦ σου, θάνατε, τὸ κέντρον⸃;

Hos 13:14; MT אֱהִי דְבָרֶיךָ מָוֶת אֱהִי קָטָבְךָ שְׁאוֹל; LXX ποῦ ἡ δίκη σου, θάνατε; ποῦ τὸ κέντρον σου, ᾅδη; 1 Cor 15:55 ποῦ σου, θάνατε, τὸ νῖκος; ποῦ σου, θάνατε, τὸ κέντρον; (Dᵃ). Observe that: (1) אֱהִי is treated as אַיֵּה "where"; (2) קָטָבְךָ from קֶטֶב = "thy destruction," for which the LXX's δίκη "justice" is quite wrong; but the NT's τὸ νῖκος indicates the positive result of the destruction of mortal men, namely victory over the opposition of God's foes; (2) the second θάνατε is not as accurate as the ᾅδη of the LXX as a rendering of שְׁאוֹל, and it creates a nonvariation in the parallelism that is hardly a stylistic improvement. But insofar as Hades is a metonymic correspondent of "death," it can hardly be classified as conceptually inaccurate. But the choice of the second θάνατε is hard to account for.

aActs 2:17–21

17 καὶ ἔσται ⸀ἐν ταῖς ἐσχάταις ἡμέραις⸃, λέγει ⸂ὁ θεός⸃,
ἐκχεῶ ἀπὸ τοῦ πνεύματός μου ἐπὶ ⸀πᾶσαν σάρκα⸃,
καὶ προφητεύσουσιν οἱ υἱοὶ ⸀ὑμῶν καὶ αἱ θυγατέρες ⸀ὑμῶν
καὶ οἱ νεανίσκοι °ὑμῶν ὁράσεις ὄψονται
καὶ οἱ πρεσβύτεροι °ὑμῶν ἐνυπνίοις ἐνυπνιασθήσονται·
18 καί γε ἐπὶ τοὺς δούλους μου καὶ ἐπὶ τὰς δούλας μου ⸀ἐν ταῖς ἡμέραις ἐκείναις⸃
ἐκχεῶ ἀπὸ τοῦ πνεύματός μου, ⸀ᵀκαὶ προφητεύσουσιν⸃.
19 καὶ δώσω τέρατα ἐν τῷ οὐρανῷ ἄνω
καὶ σημεῖα ἐπὶ τῆς γῆς κάτω,
□αἷμα καὶ πῦρ καὶ ἀτμίδα καπνοῦ⸃.

Joel 3:1–5; MT 1a וְהָיָה אַחֲרֵי־כֵן = LXX Καὶ ἔσται μετὰ ταῦτα; Acts 2:17a καὶ ἔσται ἐν ταῖς ἐσχάταις ἡμέραις, λέγει ὁ θεός. . . .

MT 1b; אֶשְׁפּוֹךְ אֶת־רוּחִי; LXX καὶ ἐκχεῶ ἀπὸ τοῦ πνεύματός μου = NT. (A)

MT 1c; MT = LXX = NT.

MT 1d; זִקְנֵיכֶם וגו׳ = LXX καὶ οἱ πρεσβύτεροι ὑμῶν κτλ.; NT καὶ οἱ πρεσβύτεροι ὑμῶν κτλ. (NT reverses the order of LXX-MT).

294 (continued)

295: Amos 3:13

see Psalm 111:2 [187]

Acts 2:17–21 (continued)

20 ὁ ἥλιος μεταστραφήσεται εἰς σκότος
   καὶ ἡ σελήνη εἰς αἷμα,
   πρὶν ᵀ ἐλθεῖν ᵀ ἡμέραν κυρίου τὴν μεγάλην ☐καὶ ἐπιφανῆ ⌐.
21 καὶ ἔσται πᾶς ὃς ἂν ἐπικαλέσηται τὸ ὄνομα κυρίου σωθήσεται.

ᵇRom 10:13   only Joel 3:5

13 πᾶς γὰρ ὃς ἂν ἐπικαλέσηται τὸ ὄνομα κυρίου σωθήσεται.

MT 1e וגו׳ בַּחוּרֵכֶם = LXX καὶ οἱ νεανίσκοι ὑμῶν κτλ.; NT καὶ οἱ νεανίσκοι ὑμῶν κτλ. (*B*).

MT 2a; . . . וְגַם עַל־הָעֲבָדִים = LXX except for καὶ ἐπὶ τοὺς δούλους = Acts 2:18 καί γε ἐπὶ τ.δ.

MT 2b; בַּיָּמִים הָהֵמָּה . . . אֶת־רוּחִי = LXX except for ἀπὸ τοῦ πνεύματός μου = Acts 2:19.

MT 3a; וְנָתַתִּי מוֹפְתִים וגו׳ = LXX = NT except that after οὐρανῷ it adds ἄνω and after γῆς it adds κάτω, inserting also σημεῖα before ἐπὶ τῆς γῆς. (*A*ᵈ or *D*)

MT 3b; דָּם וָאֵשׁ וגו׳ = LXX = NT (αἷμα . . . καπνοῦ) v. 20. (*A*)

MT 4a; הַשֶּׁמֶשׁ יֵהָפֵךְ וגו׳ = LXX = NT. (*A*)

MT 4b לִפְנֵי בּוֹא = LXX except ἐπιφανῆ for נוֹרָא = NT καὶ ἐπιφανῆ (reading נִרְאָה—although this phrase is omitted in א + D) v. 20. (*B*)

MT 5a וְהָיָה כֹל אֲשֶׁר־וגו׳ = LXX = NT. (*A*)

Note: (1) Acts 2:17 inserts "in the last days" by infer-ence from the setting in Joel 2; (2) the LXX and NT insert ἀπό before "Spirit" perhaps in order to avoid the false impression that all of the third Person of the Trinity would be poured out into believers; (3) there is a switch in the order of "old men . . . young men" in Joel 2:28 to "young men . . . old men" in Acts 2:17, a variant that was apparently without significance unless per-chance Peter was aiming at a better climactic progres-sion than Joel had (*D*ᵃ); (4) note the use of καί γε for גַם at the beginning of v. 18, where the LXX merely has καί. Barthélemy has done research in the matter of what he calls a καί γε recension regarded as proto-Theodotionic (Cf. Cross and Talmon *Qumran and the History of the Biblical Text*, Harvard, 1975, 313); (5) in Acts 2:19 Peter uses a few insertions for greater clarity and impact; therefore he distinguishes heaven as above and earth as beneath, and he also inserts σημεῖα (a natural parallelistic word to τέρατα, corresponding to the frequent pair in the OT: אֹתוֹת and מוֹפְתִים). (*A*)

296: Amos 5:25–27

[יִשְׂרָאֵל:]

25 הַזְּבָחִים וּמִנְחָה֩ הִגַּשְׁתֶּם־לִ֨י בַמִּדְבָּ֜ר אַרְבָּעִ֤ים שָׁנָ֖ה בֵּ֥ית
26 וּנְשָׂאתֶ֗ם אֵ֚ת סִכּ֣וּת מַלְכְּכֶ֔ם וְאֵ֖ת כִּיּ֣וּן צַלְמֵיכֶ֑ם כּוֹכַ֣ב
[אֱלֹֽהֵיכֶ֔ם אֲשֶׁ֥ר עֲשִׂיתֶ֖ם לָכֶֽם:]
27 וְהִגְלֵיתִ֥י אֶתְכֶ֖ם מֵהָ֣לְאָה לְדַמָּ֑שֶׂק אָמַ֤ר יְהוָ֖ה
אֱלֹהֵֽי־צְבָא֥וֹת שְׁמֽוֹ:

25 μὴ σφάγια καὶ θυσίας προσηνέγκατέ μοι ἐν τῇ ἐρήμῳ τεσσαράκοντα ἔτη, οἶκος Ισραηλ; 26 καὶ ἀνελάβετε τὴν σκηνὴν τοῦ Μολοχ
καὶ τὸ ἄστρον τοῦ θεοῦ ὑμῶν Ραιφαν, τοὺς τύπους αὐτῶν, οὓς
ἐποιήσατε ἑαυτοῖς. 27 καὶ μετοικιῶ ὑμᾶς ἐπέκεινα Δαμασκοῦ, λέγει
κύριος, ὁ θεὸς ὁ παντοκράτωρ ὄνομα αὐτῷ.

*a*Acts 7:42–43

42 Ἔστρεψεν δὲ ὁ θεὸς καὶ παρ-
έδωκεν αὐτοὺς λατρεύειν τῇ στρατιᾷ τοῦ οὐρανοῦ καθὼς
γέγραπται ἐν βίβλῳ τῶν προφητῶν·
μὴ σφάγια καὶ θυσίας προσηνέγκατέ μοι
ἔτη τεσσεράκοντα ἐν τῇ ἐρήμῳ, οἶκος Ἰσραήλ;
43 καὶ ἀνελάβετε τὴν σκηνὴν τοῦ Μόλοχ
καὶ τὸ ἄστρον τοῦ θεοῦ ᵒ[ὑμῶν] ⌐ᵉῬαιφάν,
τοὺς τύπους οὓς ἐποιήσατε προσκυνεῖν αὐτοῖς,
καὶ μετοικιῶ ὑμᾶς ᶠἐπέκεινα Βαβυλῶνος.

Amos 5:25–27; for the most part Acts 7:42–43*a* is an exact reproduction of the LXX; two variations occur in v. 43*b*. But in the deity names in Amos 5:26 there are startling discrepancies between the MT and LXX (= NT): (1) Amos 5:25 the only variant is the plural θυσίας for the MT's singular מִנְחָה (E), which the LXX translator may have regarded as a collective; (2) Amos 5:26*a* MT סִכּוּת מַלְכְּכֶם; LXX τὴν σκηνὴν τοῦ Μολοχ. This rendering of the LXX assumes the equivalence of סִכּוּת to סֻכָּה ("booth, lodge, tent"). But since this ἅπαξ (apparently not discussed at all in *BDB*) is thought to be equivalent to the Babylonian god Sakkut (K-B 657a), it is possible that the LXX translator, unfamiliar with this name, assumed that the word should be pointed סֻכַּת or סֻכּוֹת ("booth of" or "booths of")—and he may well have been right. As for מַלְכְּכֶם, it is highly probable that this refers not to any human being (since Israel had no king in Mosaic times) but to a divine king, such as the מֶלֶךְ of the Canaanites. (Since Punic inscriptions suggest the vocalization *molch*, there is no need to assume that a qerê reading of בֹּשֶׁת was necessarily intended by the pointing of מֹלֶךְ, which was really to be pronounced *Malku*.) Hence the LXX's Μόλοχ is quite justified, and the phrase should be translated "the booth/shrine of your Moloch (or possibly King-god)"; (3) Amos 5:26*b* MT וְאֵת כִּיּוּן צַלְמֵיכֶם; LXX καὶ τὸ ἄστρον τοῦ θεοῦ ὑμῶν Ῥαιφάν. Here there seems to be an incorporation of an early gloss, which perhaps read for כִּיּוּן—ἄστρον, т.е., Ῥαιφάν (which would have been understood as the name of the god of some planet). But as transmitted, the LXX text first used the general term ἄστρον (a term that does not always differentiate between a planet and a fixed star), and then an appositional gloss may have contributed the actual name of the planet, Ῥαιφάν. On the other hand, כִּיּוּן might not have been a name at all, but simply a derivative of כּוּן ("be established") and hence meaning a stand or standard for the various idols to be carried on. But since there is no other occurrence of this word, it is more likely to be a spelling of the Mesopotamian deity *Kaimānu* or *Kaiwānu*, and the god associated with Saturn. This would be written כִּיוּן in the Hebrew consonants. But how can we account for the totally different spelling in the LXX as Ῥαιφάν? The easiest explanation is found in a careful examination of the form of the Aramaic alphabet used by the Jews of the Elephantine colony in the 5th century B.C. This shows that *kaph* was very similar to *resh* in appearance, and *pe* was much like *waw*. Thus ךיכ (כיון) could easily be misread by a copyist as ךפר (ריפן). Since this was a non-Hebraic name of a pagan deity, there was no way a

151

297: Amos 9:11–12

¹¹ בַּיּוֹם הַהוּא אָקִים אֶת־סֻכַּת דָּוִיד הַנֹּפֶלֶת [עוֹלָם
וְגָדַרְתִּי אֶת־פִּרְצֵיהֶן וַהֲרִסֹתָיו אָקִים וּבְנִיתִיהָ כִּימֵי
¹² לְמַעַן יִירְשׁוּ אֶת־שְׁאֵרִית אֱדוֹם וְכָל־הַגּוֹיִם אֲשֶׁר־נִקְרָא שְׁמִי
עֲלֵיהֶם נְאֻם־יְהוָה עֹשֶׂה זֹּאת:

¹¹ ἐν τῇ ἡμέρᾳ ἐκείνῃ ἀναστήσω τὴν σκηνὴν Δαυιδ τὴν πεπτωκυῖαν καὶ ἀνοικοδομήσω τὰ πεπτωκότα αὐτῆς καὶ τὰ κατεσκαμμένα αὐτῆς ἀναστήσω καὶ ἀνοικοδομήσω αὐτὴν καθὼς αἱ ἡμέραι τοῦ αἰῶνος, ¹² ὅπως ἐκζητήσωσιν οἱ κατάλοιποι τῶν ἀνθρώπων καὶ πάντα τὰ ἔθνη, ἐφ᾽ οὓς ἐπικέκληται τὸ ὄνομά μου ἐπ᾽ αὐτούς, λέγει κύριος ὁ θεὸς ὁ ποιῶν ταῦτα.

Jer 12:15

¹⁵ וְהָיָה אַחֲרֵי נָתְשִׁי אוֹתָם אָשׁוּב וְרִחַמְתִּים וַהֲשִׁבֹתִים
אִישׁ לְנַחֲלָתוֹ וְאִישׁ לְאַרְצוֹ:

¹⁵ καὶ ἔσται μετὰ τὸ ἐκβαλεῖν με αὐτοὺς ἐπιστρέψω καὶ ἐλεήσω αὐτοὺς καὶ κατοικιῶ αὐτοὺς ἕκαστον εἰς τὴν κληρονομίαν αὐτοῦ καὶ ἕκαστον εἰς τὴν γῆν αὐτοῦ.

later copyist could have corrected a garbled spelling in the *Vorlage* of the LXX. Thus the reading 'Ραιφάν developed from כיון. This perpetuation of the misreading in Stephen's speech in Acts 7 involved no error in doctrine or message; whatever may have been the name of the idol clandestinely worshipped by the heretical fringe of the Hebrews in Moses' congregation, the principle was the same. Secret idol worship showed a sinful and unregenerate heart within a significant segment of the covenant people of God. If Stephen had corrected the spelling of 'Ραιφάν to Καιουν or Καιουαν, he would have needlessly distracted his Greek-speaking audience of Diaspora Jews from his message with an apparent discrepancy in the text of the LXX, which was the form of the OT to which they generally turned in matters of religion. It was in harmony with his evangelistic purpose for Stephen to avoid diverting attention to a misspelled name that would encourage the protest of his audience to his quoting from a Bible that read differently from their own (*E*); (4) Amos 5:26 uses צַלְמֵיכֶם "your images"—a term often translated by the LXX as τύποι; hence there is no discrepancy in the τοὺς τύπους of Acts 7:43; (5) Amos 5:27 MT (וְהִגְלֵיתִי אֶתְכֶם) מֵהָלְאָה לְדַמָּשֶׂק is correctly rendered by the LXX as ἐπέκεινα Δαμασκοῦ whereas Stephen is quoted as extending it to ἐπέκαινα Βαβυλῶνος. This variant seems to be a valid inference from Damascus, because the captive Jews dragged off to Babylonia by the Chaldeans in 586 B.C. had to pass through Damascus on their way, so Babylon was indeed beyond Damascus. The highway to Babylon went north-northeast to Tadmor or Tiphsah to the Euphrates River, and then southeast down to Babylon itself. Stephen's purpose was to bring out the implication of Amos 5:27 that the Assyrian and Babylonian captivities would result from Israel's sin.

---

*a*Acts 15:16–17

16 μετὰ ταῦτα ⌐ἀναστρέψω
 καὶ ἀνοικοδομήσω τὴν σκηνὴν Δαυὶδ τὴν πεπτωκυῖαν
 καὶ τὰ ⌐κατεσκαμμένα αὐτῆς ἀνοικοδομήσω
 καὶ ἀνορθώσω αὐτήν,
17 ὅπως ἂν ἐκζητήσωσιν οἱ κατάλοιποι τῶν ἀνθρώπων τὸν
  κύριον
 καὶ πάντα τὰ ἔθνη ἐφ' οὓς ἐπικέκληται τὸ ὄνομά μου
  ἐπ' αὐτούς,
λέγει κύριος ⌐ποιῶν ⌐ταῦτα

Amos 9:11–12; v. 11a MT בַּיּוֹם הַהוּא אָקִים אֶת־סֻכַּת דָּוִיד; LXX ἀναστήσω; Acts 15:16 μετὰ ταῦτα (for "in that day") LXX (= NT) expand to ἀναστρέψω καὶ ἀνοικοδομήσω ("I will return and I will build again"). This locution fully brings out that בָּנָה means "rebuild" here, not simply "build." James makes clear and explicit what is implied by the Amos text. The first ἀναστήσω similarly brings out that אָקִים = "*re*-establish" (*E*).

v. 11b MT וְגָדַרְתִּי אֶת־פִּרְצֵיהֶן "their breaches" becomes in LXX πεπτωκότα αὐτῆς "*her* fallen portions"; Acts 15:16 τὴν σκηνὴν Δαυὶδ τὴν πεπτωκυῖαν (the tent of David which has fallen down").

298: Jonah 2:1 (1:17)

2 ¹ וַיְמַן יְהוָה דָּג גָּדוֹל לִבְלֹעַ אֶת־יוֹנָה וַיְהִי יוֹנָה בִּמְעֵי הַדָּג שְׁלֹשָׁה יָמִים וּשְׁלֹשָׁה לֵילוֹת:

¹ Καὶ προσέταξεν κύριος κήτει μεγάλῳ καταπιεῖν τὸν Ιωναν· καὶ ἦν Ιωνας ἐν τῇ κοιλίᾳ τοῦ κήτους τρεῖς ἡμέρας καὶ τρεῖς νύκτας.

Here the NT varies somewhat from the LXX, for while it uses the same perfect active participle of πίπτω, it modifies the tent itself, rather than specific portions of it which may have been damaged. The MT implies either broken down stone walls, or gaping rents in the tent (פְּרָצִים). The LXX is less definite about the areas of damage, but James uses more summary language. If gaping breaches have been made through the walls, then the city or house itself has to all intents and purposes fallen down. As for הֲרֹסֹתָיו, the term τὰ κατεσκαμμένα (LXX and NT) is quite satisfactory.

v. 11c MT וּבְנִיתִיהָ כִּימֵי עוֹלָם; LXX καὶ ἀνοικοδομήσω αὐτὴν καθὼς αἱ ἡμέραι τοῦ αἰῶνος. But Acts 15:16d stops with ἀνοικοδομήσω ... αὐτήν, omitting כִּימֵי עוֹלָם.

v. 12a MT לְמַעַן יִירְשׁוּ אֶת־שְׁאֵרִית אֱדוֹם; LXX ὅπως ἐκζητήσωσιν οἱ κατάλοιποι τῶν ἀνθρώπων = NT plus τὸν κύριον. Here it is apparent that the LXX read אָדָם rather than אֱדוֹם and that despite the preceding אֶת־, שְׁאֵרִית is taken as the *subject* of ἐκζητήσωσιν and rendered "the remainder of mankind will eagerly seek"— no object expressed. But Acts 15:17 introduces τὸν κύριον as the object of the "seeking." This strongly suggests the following emendation to the MT: (a) read MT's יִירְשׁוּ as יִדְרְשׁוּ, quite possibly relying on the LXX *Vorlage* that read (in the Qumran period, perhaps) ידרשו rather than יירשו. "In order that the rest of *mankind* might seek him" fits in much better with the context than a promise of taking possession of *Edom*! (b) read אֶת־ before שְׁאֵרִית as אֹתוֹ or אֹתִי. In the course of scribal transmission it would be quite possible for a final *waw* or *yod* to drop out because of a worn spot in the *Vorlage* of the Sopherim text. As amended then, Amos 9:12 should read as follows: לְמַעַן יִדְרְשׁוּ אֹתוֹ שְׁאֵרִית אָדָם וְכָל־הַגּוֹיִם וגו׳. Thus the rendering of the LXX (= NT) would be completely accurate, and we may feel grateful that in this verse we have access to the earlier and more authentic reading: "In order that the remainder of mankind might seek him/me (אֹתִי ?), and all the Gentiles (upon whom my name is called)."

---

*a*Mt 12:40

40 ὥσπερ γὰρ ⌜ἦν Ἰωνᾶς ἐν τῇ κοιλίᾳ τοῦ κήτους τρεῖς ἡμέρας καὶ τρεῖς νύκτας, οὕτως ἔσται ᵀ ὁ υἱὸς τοῦ ἀνθρώπου ἐν τῇ καρδίᾳ τῆς γῆς τρεῖς ἡμέρας καὶ τρεῖς νύκτας.

Jonah 2:1(1:17); This is not a quotation, but Jesus is quoted as referring to Jonah's experience with the fish in terms identical with Jonah 2:1 in the LXX and also with the MT, with which it is identical (Mt 12:40). (*A*) or (*F*)

299: Micah 5:1 (5:2)

¹ וְאַתָּ֞ה בֵּֽית־לֶ֣חֶם אֶפְרָ֗תָה צָעִיר֙ לִֽהְיוֹת֙ בְּאַלְפֵ֣י יְהוּדָ֔ה מִמְּךָ֙ לִ֣י יֵצֵ֔א לִֽהְי֥וֹת מוֹשֵׁ֖ל בְּיִשְׂרָאֵ֑ל וּמוֹצָאֹתָ֥יו מִקֶּ֖דֶם מִימֵ֥י עוֹלָֽם׃

¹ Καὶ σύ, Βηθλεεμ οἶκος τοῦ Εφραθα, ὀλιγοστὸς εἶ τοῦ εἶναι ἐν χιλιάσιν Ιουδα· ἐκ σοῦ μοι ἐξελεύσεται τοῦ εἶναι εἰς ἄρχοντα ἐν τῷ Ισραηλ, καὶ αἱ ἔξοδοι αὐτοῦ ἀπ' ἀρχῆς ἐξ ἡμερῶν αἰῶνος.

2 Sam 5:2

² גַּם־אֶתְמ֣וֹל גַּם־שִׁלְשׁ֗וֹם בִּֽהְי֤וֹת שָׁאוּל֙ מֶ֙לֶךְ֙ עָלֵ֔ינוּ אַתָּ֗ה יָיִיתָה מוֹצִ֥יא וְהַמֵּבִ֖יא אֶת־יִשְׂרָאֵ֑ל וַיֹּ֨אמֶר יְהוָ֜ה לְךָ֗ אַתָּ֤ה תִרְעֶה֙ אֶת־עַמִּ֣י אֶת־יִשְׂרָאֵ֔ל וְאַתָּ֛ה תִּֽהְיֶ֥ה לְנָגִ֖יד עַל־יִשְׂרָאֵֽל׃

² καὶ ἐχθὲς καὶ τρίτην ὄντος Σαουλ βασιλέως ἐφ' ἡμῖν σὺ ἦσθα ὁ ἐξάγων καὶ εἰσάγων τὸν Ισραηλ, καὶ εἶπεν κύριος πρός σέ Σὺ ποιμανεῖς τὸν λαόν μου τὸν Ισραηλ, καὶ σὺ ἔσει εἰς ἡγούμενον ἐπὶ τὸν Ισραηλ.

*a*Mt 2:6

6 καὶ σὺ Βηθλέεμ*,* γῆ Ἰούδα*,*
  οὐδαμῶς ἐλαχίστη εἶ ἐν τοῖς ἡγεμόσιν Ἰούδα·
ἐκ σοῦ γὰρ ἐξελεύσεται ἡγούμενος,
  ὅστις ποιμανεῖ τὸν λαόν μου τὸν Ἰσραήλ.

Micah 5:1(2); MT 5:1*a* וְאַתָּה בֵּית־לֶחֶם אֶפְרָתָה צָעִיר לִהְיוֹת בְּאַלְפֵי יְהוּדָה; LXX καὶ σύ, βηθλέεμ οἶκος τοῦ Εφραθα, ὀλιγοστὸς (very small) εἶ τοῦ εἶναι ἐν χιλιάσιν Ιουδα. MT מִמְּךָ לִי יֵצֵא לִהְיוֹת מוֹשֵׁל בְּיִשְׂרָאֵל; LXX ἐκ σοῦ μοι ἐξελεύσεται τοῦ εἶναι εἰς ἄρχοντα ("from thee shall one come forth for/to me in order to become a ruler").

MT וּמוֹצָאֹתָיו מִקֶּדֶם מִימֵי עוֹלָם; LXX καὶ αἱ ἔξοδοι αὐτοῦ ἀπ᾽ ἀρχῆς ἐξ ἡμερῶν αἰῶνος. The LXX furnishes a very accurate rendering of the MT. But Mt 2:6 has an entirely independent rendering that provides some challenging deviations: (1) NT καὶ σὺ Βηθλέεμ, γῆ Ιουδα (instead of אֶפְרָתָה). Perhaps Ephrathah was taken as an identifier as to which of the two Bethlehems was to be the Messiah's birthplace, whether that of Zebulon to the north (Josh 19:15) up near Nazareth, or the one to the south of Jerusalem. Therefore Matthew, or the advisors of King Herod, saw fit to identify it as Judah, bringing out the implication of Ephrathah, which was the name of the region in which the town was located; (2) NT οὐδαμῶς ἐλαχίστη εἶ ἐν τοῖς ἡγεμόσιν; the LXX states that Bethlehem was very small to be among the 1000-family (or 1000 militiamen) towns of Judah. But Matthew understands from the next clause that if the messianic ruler himself is to come from Bethlehem, then it is—regardless of its size—to be regarded as a town of outstanding importance and glory. So he uses the negative to bring out the implication that it is after all a very important town within the tribe of Judah, despite the modest size of its population.

The next change was in the term ἡγεμόνες, "rulers," instead of אֲלָפִים "thousands," referring to a community that could number 1000 families or even 1000 men at arms. (From this it was but a step to refer to the commander of these troops as a רֹאשׁ אֶלֶף (prince of 1000), or אֶלֶף for short, just as the Roman *centurio* was derived from *centurium*, or a company of 100 soldiers). But to the Greek reader it may have been more helpful to use a less confusing term than χιλιάδες, i.e., ἡγεμών as the commander of 1000 soldiers. While it is true that in the first century ἡγεμών was often used of a procurator like Pontius Pilate, it could also refer to the commander of a cohort, for which a more technical equivalent would be χιλιάρχων. But since the term ἡγεμών several times is used in the LXX for the Hebrew אַלּוּף (Gen 36:15; Ex 15:1; 1 Chron 1:50; Psalm 54:14), some have suggested that Matthew may have read אַלְפֵי as אַלּוּפֵי or אַלֻּפֵי. This is certainly a good possibility, for it would involve no consonantal change of the received consonantal text. (*E*)

300: Micah 7:6

⁶ כִּי־בֵן מְנַבֵּל אָב בַּת קָמָה בְאִמָּה
כַּלָּה בַּחֲמֹתָהּ אֹיְבֵי אִישׁ אַנְשֵׁי בֵיתוֹ:

⁶διότι υἱὸς ἀτιμάζει πατέρα, θυγάτηρ ἐπαναστήσεται
ἐπὶ τὴν μητέρα αὐτῆς, νύμφη ἐπὶ τὴν πενθερὰν αὐτῆς, ἐχθροὶ
ἀνδρὸς πάντες οἱ ἄνδρες οἱ ἐν τῷ οἴκῳ αὐτοῦ.

301: Nahum 2:1

see Isa 52:7 [244]

302: Hab 1:5

⁵ רְאוּ בַגּוֹיִם וְהַבִּיטוּ וְהִתַּמְּהוּ תְּמָהוּ
כִּי־פֹעַל פֹּעֵל בִּימֵיכֶם לֹא תַאֲמִינוּ כִּי יְסֻפָּר:

⁵ἴδετε, οἱ καταφρονηταί, καὶ ἐπιβλέψατε καὶ θαυμάσατε θαυμάσια
καὶ ἀφανίσθητε, διότι ἔργον ἐγὼ ἐργάζομαι ἐν ταῖς ἡμέραις ὑμῶν,
ὃ οὐ μὴ πιστεύσητε ἐάν τις ἐκδιηγῆται.

303: Hab 2:3–4

see Isa 26:20 [220]

NEW TESTAMENT

ᵃMt 10:35–36

35 ἦλ-
θον γὰρ διχάσαι ⌜ἄνθρωπον κατὰ τοῦ πατρὸς αὐτοῦ καὶ θυγατέρα κατὰ τῆς μητρὸς αὐτῆς καὶ νύμφην κατὰ τῆς πενθερᾶς αὐτῆς, **36** καὶ ἐχθροὶ τοῦ ἀνθρώπου οἱ οἰκιακοὶ αὐτοῦ.

ᵃActs 13:41

41 ἴδετε, οἱ καταφρονηταί,
καὶ θαυμάσατε καὶ ἀφανίσθητε,
ὅτι ἔργον ἐργάζομαι ἐγὼ ἐν ταῖς ἡμέραις ὑμῶν,
ᵒἔργον ὃ οὐ μὴ πιστεύσητε ἐάν τις ἐκδιηγῆται
ὑμῖν.ᵀ

COMMENTARY

Micah 7:6—Mt 10:35–36; this is not a quotation, but only allusive language, derived from an OT verse dealing with tensions within the home during the reign of Ahaz, which was an age of sagging morality, presenting a pattern of apostasy which Micah had to denounce. Actually the wording is so close as to deserve a rating of (A) even though technically it is an (F).

Hab 1:5—Acts 13:41 (cited in v. 40 as τὸ εἰρημένον ἐν τοῖς προφήταις:) MT רְאוּ בַגּוֹיִם וְהַבִּיטוּ וְהִתַּמְּהוּ; LXX ἴδετε, οἱ καταφρονηταί, καὶ ἐπιβλέψατε καὶ θαυμάσατε θαυμάσια καὶ ἀφανίσθητε. So also Acts 13:41a, which omits καὶ ἐπιβλέψατε and θαυμάσια, and ends up with καὶ ἀφανίσθητε (D). Note: (1) that the NT omits what the LXX has inserted, and is therefore closer to the MT in leaving out καὶ ἐπιβλέψατε (C); (2) But both the LXX and NT read בּוֹגְדִים ("You treacherous ones!"), rather than the MT's בַגּוֹיִם (which could mean either "Behold the Gentiles/nations!" or "Gloat over the discomfiture of the nations!"); the vocative בּוֹגְדִים would harmonize much better with the context than בַגּוֹיִם does; it is therefore quite possible that this was the reading in the Hebrew *Vorlage* of the LXX. καταφρονητής is "despiser; an imposter who acts cleverly and treacherously" (Sch. 228B). It is used in Zeph 3:5 to mean "perfidy," and its verb, καταφρονέω = "act treacherously" (בָּגַד) in Prov 13:16; Hos 6:7; Hab 1:13. Therefore we must consider the distinct possibility that בּוֹגְדִים or בֹּגְדִים is indeed the original reading. It is more likely that the MT scribe would have inadvertently omitted ד than that the scribe of the LXX *Vorlage* accidentally inserted a ד. (It is therefore best to amend MT to בֹּגְדִים.); (3) ἀφανίσθητε is from ἀφανίζειν, a verb used for over ten different Hebrew verbs in BH. Note that it renders תָּמַהּ in Baruch 3:11 "they perished"; i.e., תָּמְהוּ becomes ἠφανίσθησαν, according to Sch. 412; (4) Acts 13:41 inserts ἔργον before ὃ οὐ μὴ πιστεύσητε, thus picking up an antecedent for ὃ that is clearly implied by the previous ἔργον ἐργάζομαι. We class this as (D) or (Dᵃ), in view of the omission of καὶ ἐπιβλέψατε. As for כִּי־פֹעַל פֹּעֵל, it lacks an explicit subject, which the LXX supplies with ἐγώ and ἐργάζομαι, understanding an implicit אֲנִי as the subject.

159

304: Haggai 2:6, 21

כִּ֣י כֹ֤ה אָמַר֙ יְהוָ֣ה צְבָא֔וֹת ע֥וֹד אַחַ֖ת מְעַ֣ט הִ֑יא ⁶
וַאֲנִ֗י מַרְעִישׁ֙ אֶת־הַשָּׁמַ֣יִם וְאֶת־הָאָ֔רֶץ וְאֶת־הַיָּ֖ם וְאֶת־
הֶחָרָבָֽה׃

⁶διότι τάδε λέγει κύριος
παντοκράτωρ Ἔτι ἅπαξ ἐγὼ σείσω τὸν οὐρανὸν καὶ τὴν γῆν καὶ
τὴν θάλασσαν καὶ τὴν ξηράν·

אֱמֹ֗ר אֶל־זְרֻבָּבֶ֛ל פַּחַֽת־יְהוּדָ֖ה לֵאמֹ֑ר ²¹
אֲנִ֣י מַרְעִ֔ישׁ אֶת־הַשָּׁמַ֖יִם וְאֶת־הָאָֽרֶץ׃

²¹Εἰπὸν πρὸς Ζορο-
βαβελ τὸν τοῦ Σαλαθιηλ ἐκ φυλῆς Ιουδα λέγων Ἐγὼ σείω τὸν
οὐρανὸν καὶ τὴν γῆν καὶ τὴν θάλασσαν καὶ τὴν ξηρὰν

305: Zech 8:16

אֵ֥לֶּה הַדְּבָרִ֖ים אֲשֶׁ֣ר תַּעֲשׂ֑וּ ¹⁶
דַּבְּר֤וּ אֱמֶת֙ אִ֣ישׁ אֶת־רֵעֵ֔הוּ אֱמֶת֙ וּמִשְׁפַּ֣ט שָׁל֔וֹם שִׁפְט֖וּ
בְּשַׁעֲרֵיכֶֽם׃

¹⁶οὗτοι οἱ λόγοι, οὓς ποιήσετε· λαλεῖτε ἀλήθειαν
ἕκαστος πρὸς τὸν πλησίον αὐτοῦ καὶ κρίμα εἰρηνικὸν κρίνατε ἐν
ταῖς πύλαις ὑμῶν

306: Zech 9:9

see Isa 62:11 [262]

307: Zech 11:12-13

וָאֹמַ֣ר אֲלֵיהֶ֗ם ¹²
אִם־ט֧וֹב בְּעֵינֵיכֶ֛ם הָב֥וּ שְׂכָרִ֖י וְאִם־לֹ֑א חֲדָ֑לוּ וַיִּשְׁקְל֥וּ אֶת־שְׂכָרִ֖י
שְׁלֹשִׁ֥ים כָּֽסֶף׃ ¹³ וַיֹּ֨אמֶר יְהוָ֜ה אֵלַ֗י הַשְׁלִיכֵ֙הוּ֙ אֶל־הַיּוֹצֵ֔ר אֶ֣דֶר
הַיְקָ֗ר אֲשֶׁ֣ר יָקַ֖רְתִּי מֵעֲלֵיהֶ֑ם וָֽאֶקְחָה֙ שְׁלֹשִׁ֣ים הַכֶּ֔סֶף וָאַשְׁלִ֥יךְ אֹת֛וֹ
בֵּ֥ית יְהוָ֖ה אֶל־הַיּוֹצֵֽר׃

¹²καὶ ἐρῶ
πρὸς αὐτούς Εἰ καλὸν ἐνώπιον ὑμῶν ἐστιν, δότε στήσαντες τὸν
μισθόν μου ἢ ἀπείπασθε· καὶ ἔστησαν τὸν μισθόν μου τριάκοντα
ἀργυροῦς. ¹³καὶ εἶπεν κύριος πρός με Κάθες αὐτοὺς εἰς τὸ χωνευτήριον, καὶ σκέψαι εἰ δόκιμόν ἐστιν, ὃν τρόπον ἐδοκιμάσθην ὑπὲρ
αὐτῶν. καὶ ἔλαβον τοὺς τριάκοντα ἀργυροῦς καὶ ἐνέβαλον αὐτοὺς
εἰς τὸν οἶκον κυρίου εἰς τὸ χωνευτήριον.

Ex 9:12

וַיְחַזֵּ֤ק יְהוָה֙ ¹²
אֶת־לֵ֣ב פַּרְעֹ֔ה וְלֹ֥א שָׁמַ֖ע אֲלֵהֶ֑ם כַּאֲשֶׁ֛ר דִּבֶּ֥ר יְהוָ֖ה אֶל־מֹשֶֽׁה׃

¹²ἐσκλήρυνεν δὲ κύριος τὴν καρδίαν Φαραω,
καὶ οὐκ εἰσήκουσεν αὐτῶν, καθὰ συνέταξεν κύριος.

Jer 18:2-3

ק֣וּם ²
וְיָרַדְתָּ֖ בֵּ֣ית הַיּוֹצֵ֑ר וְשָׁ֕מָּה אַשְׁמִיעֲךָ֖ אֶת־דְּבָרָֽי׃ ³ וָאֵרֵ֖ד בֵּ֣ית הַיּוֹצֵ֑ר
וְהִנֵּה־ה֛וּא עֹשֶׂ֥ה מְלָאכָ֖ה עַל־הָאָבְנָֽיִם׃

²Ἀνά-
στηθι καὶ κατάβηθι εἰς οἶκον τοῦ κεραμέως, καὶ ἐκεῖ ἀκούσῃ τοὺς
λόγους μου. ³καὶ κατέβην εἰς τὸν οἶκον τοῦ κεραμέως, καὶ ἰδοὺ
αὐτὸς ἐποίει ἔργον ἐπὶ τῶν λίθων·

^aHeb 12:26

26 οὗ ἡ φωνὴ τὴν γῆν ἐσάλευσεν τότε,
νῦν δὲ ἐπήγγελται λέγων·
   ἔτι ἅπαξ ἐγὼ ⌜σείσω⌝ οὐ μόνον τὴν γῆν ἀλλὰ καὶ τὸν
   οὐρανόν.

Haggai 2:6, 21; MT = LXX = Heb 12:26 (which inserts οὐ μόνον . . . ἀλλὰ καὶ "not only . . . but also" in an otherwise literal reading. (A)

---

^aEph 4:25

25 °Διὸ ἀποθέμενοι τὸ ψεῦδος λαλεῖτε ἀλήθειαν ἕ-
καστος μετὰ τοῦ πλησίον αὐτοῦ, ὅτι ἐσμὲν ἀλλήλων μέ-
λη.

Zech 8:16; Eph 4:25 does not announce itself as a quote, but in point of fact it follows the LXX perfectly, and LXX = MT. (F) or (A)

^aMt 27:9–10

9 τότε ἐπληρώθη τὸ ῥηθὲν διὰ ⌜Ἰερεμί-
ου τοῦ προφήτου λέγοντος· καὶ ἔλαβον τὰ τριάκοντα ἀργύρια, τὴν τιμὴν τοῦ τετιμημένου ὃν ἐτιμήσαντο ἀπὸ υἱῶν
Ἰσραήλ, 10 καὶ ⌜ἔδωκαν⌝ αὐτὰ εἰς τὸν ἀγρὸν τοῦ κεραμέως, καθὰ συνέταξέν μοι κύριος.

Zech 11:12-13; MT v. 13c וָאֶקְחָה שְׁלֹשִׁים הַכֶּסֶף וָאַשְׁלִיךְ אֹתוֹ בֵּית יהוה אֶל־הַיּוֹצֵר; LXX καὶ ἔλαβον τοὺς τριάκοντα ἀργυροῦς καὶ ἐνέλαβον (poor for וָאַשְׁלִיךְ "and I threw") αὐτοὺς εἰς τὸν οἶκον κυρίου εἰς τὸ χωνευτήριον (forced air furnace/kiln); Mt 27:9–10 καὶ ἔλαβον τὰ τριάκοντα ἀργύρια, τὴν τιμὴν τοῦ τετιμημένου ὃν ἐτιμήσαντο ἀπὸ υἱῶν Ἰσραήλ (E). However, this second clause is not really a quote at all, but a summary of the preceding action narrated earlier in this verse: καὶ ἔστησαν τὸν μισθόν μου τριάκοντα ἀργυροῦς ("And they weighed out my reward/price—30 pieces of silver"). This is vividly expressed by the ironical phrase "the fine price at which they rated me from the children of Israel" (a clause omitted in the LXX but well preserved in Mt 27:9). Then Mt 27:10 continues with a clause not part of the quotation: "and I gave them to the field of the potter," and closes with καθὰ συνέταξέν μοι κύριος ("just as the Lord had commanded me"). But since even the last clause is not found in Zech 11:13, we should understand the evangelist as allusively picking up this phraseology from Ex 9:12 (LXX καθὰ συνέταξεν κύριος; MT כַּאֲשֶׁר דִּבֶּר יהוה) in an entirely different context from that of Zech 11:13.

Lastly, we note that Mt 27:10 relates "And they (and high priests) gave them (the 30 silver pieces) for the purchase of the field of the potter, as the Lord commanded me." There is in Zech 11 no mention of a potter's field, which is a cardinal item in the fulfillment of this prophecy that took place in connection with Judas' betrayal of Jesus. This key element, totally missing in Zech, is supplied by Jeremiah (hence the citing of

307 (continued)

308: Zech 12:10

10 וְשָׁפַכְתִּי עַל־בֵּית דָּוִיד וְעַל ׀ יוֹשֵׁב יְרוּשָׁלַם רוּחַ חֵן
וְתַחֲנוּנִים וְהִבִּיטוּ אֵלַי אֵת אֲשֶׁר־דָּקָרוּ וְסָפְדוּ עָלָיו כְּמִסְפֵּד עַל־
הַיָּחִיד וְהָמֵר עָלָיו כְּהָמֵר עַל־הַבְּכוֹר:

¹⁰ καὶ ἐκχεῶ ἐπὶ τὸν οἶκον Δαυιδ καὶ ἐπὶ τοὺς κατοικοῦντας Ιερουσαλημ πνεῦμα χάριτος καὶ οἰκτιρμοῦ, καὶ ἐπιβλέψονται πρός με ἀνθ' ὧν κατωρχήσαντο καὶ κόψονται ἐπ' αὐτὸν κοπετὸν ὡς ἐπ' ἀγαπητὸν καὶ ὀδυνηθήσονται ὀδύνην ὡς ἐπὶ πρωτοτόκῳ.

309: Zech 13:7

7 חֶרֶב עוּרִי עַל־רֹעִי וְעַל־גֶּבֶר עֲמִיתִי נְאֻם יְהוָה צְבָאוֹת
הַךְ אֶת־הָרֹעֶה וּתְפוּצֶיןָ הַצֹּאן וַהֲשִׁבֹתִי יָדִי עַל־הַצֹּעֲרִים:

⁷ Ῥομφαία, ἐξεγέρθητι ἐπὶ τοὺς ποιμένας μου καὶ ἐπ' ἄνδρα πολίτην μου, λέγει κύριος παντοκράτωρ· πατάξατε τοὺς ποιμένας καὶ ἐκσπάσατε τὰ πρόβατα, καὶ ἐπάξω τὴν χεῖρά μου ἐπὶ τοὺς ποιμένας.

Jeremiah by name at the beginning of Mt 27:9), for Jer 18:2–3 records how the prophet himself went down to the workshop of the potter to observe how he would deal with a vessel that became marred on the potter's wheel. Jer 19:2 speaks of the potter employed by the temple as possessing a workshop in the valley of Hinnom. We may therefore understand Zechariah's casting of the money in the temple for the purchase the potter's real property as the renewal of a pre-exilic symbolic action dating back to the reign of Jehoiakim or Zedekiah. Since Mt 27 is therefore combining elements from both Jer and Zech, we see him simply conforming to contemporary literary custom when he cites the name of the more famous of the two. Even so, Mk 1:2 cites only Isa (40:3) in his combination quote that mostly consists of Mal 3:1.

---

^aJn 19:37

37 καὶ πάλιν ἑτέρα γραφὴ λέγει·
ὄψονται εἰς ὃν ἐξεκέντησαν.

Zech 12:10; the quoted portion is very brief, only four words in John 19:37: ὄψονται εἰς ὃν ἐξεκέντησαν. This corresponds quite closely to the MT וְהִבִּיטוּ אֵלַי אֵת אֲשֶׁר־דָּקָרוּ, except that the MT uses first person singular: "and they will look upon *me* whom they have pierced through." But in John's context, since it is not God who is speaking, the third person "They shall look unto *Him* whom they have pierced through" is used. It is therefore quite uncalled for to amend אֵלַי to אֵלָיו on the basis of the wording in this passage (as certain scholars have suggested). The LXX misread דָּקָרוּ as רָקָדוּ (exchanging ר with ד, which looked very similar in the Hebrew alphabet of intertestamental times), with near nonsense resulting in their rendition (ἀνθ' ὧν κατωρχήσαντο "on account of their having danced in derision of [*me*]"). Despite their error in reading דקרו as רקדו, they at least confirmed the reading of אֵלַי after וְהִבִּיטוּ by translating καὶ ἐπιβλέψονται πρός με. (*C*)

---

^aMt 26:31

31 Τότε λέγει αὐτοῖς ὁ Ἰησοῦς· πάντες ὑμεῖς σκανδαλισθήσεσθε ἐν ἐμοὶ ἐν τῇ νυκτὶ ταύτῃ, γέγραπται γάρ·
πατάξω τὸν ποιμένα,
καὶ ⌐διασκορπισθήσονται τὰ πρόβατα τῆς ποίμνης⌐.

^bMk 14:27

27 καὶ λέγει αὐτοῖς ὁ Ἰησοῦς * ὅτι πάντες σκανδαλισθήσεσθε^T, ὅτι γέγραπται·
πατάξω τὸν ποιμένα,
καὶ ⌐τὰ πρόβατα διασκορπισθήσονται⌐.

Zech 13:7; Mt 26:31 and Mk 14:27: MT הַךְ אֶת־הָרֹעֶה וּתְפוּצֶיןָ הַצֹּאן, for which LXX uses πατάξατε (plural imperative instead of the singular) τοὺς ποιμένας (plural instead of singular) καὶ ἐκσπάσατε (imperative "scatter ye" the sheep). Mk 14:27 recasts πατάξατε as πατάξω ("I will smite"), deriving this from the final clause in Zech 13:7 וַהֲשִׁבֹתִי יָדִי עַל־הַצֹּעֲרִים, where Yahweh speaks of Himself as bringing about the smiting of the messianic shepherd. Thus this is a mere summation of the verse, for brevity's sake, and first person singular (returning to God) is validly brought in from the final clause, וַהֲשִׁבוֹתִי אָדִי וגו', which shows that those who

309 (continued)

310: Mal 1:2-3

אָהַבְתִּי אֶתְכֶם אָמַר יְהוָה וַאֲמַרְתֶּם בַּמָּה אֲהַבְתָּנוּ [עֵשָׂו שָׂנֵאתִי
הֲלוֹא־אָח עֵשָׂו לְיַעֲקֹב ²נְאֻם־יְהוָה ³וָאֹהַב אֶת־יַעֲקֹב: ³וְאֶת־
וָאָשִׂים אֶת־הָרָיו שְׁמָמָה וְאֶת־נַחֲלָתוֹ לְתַנּוֹת מִדְבָּר:

²Ἠγάπησα ὑμᾶς, λέγει κύριος. καὶ εἴπατε Ἐν τίνι ἠγάπησας
ἡμᾶς; οὐκ ἀδελφὸς ἦν Ησαυ τοῦ Ιακωβ; λέγει κύριος · καὶ ἠγάπησα τὸν Ιακωβ, ³τὸν δὲ Ησαυ ἐμίσησα καὶ ἔταξα τὰ ὅρια αὐτοῦ
εἰς ἀφανισμὸν καὶ τὴν κληρονομίαν αὐτοῦ εἰς δόματα ἐρήμου.

311: Mal 3:1

¹הִנְנִי שֹׁלֵחַ מַלְאָכִי וּפִנָּה־דֶרֶךְ לְפָנָי
וּפִתְאֹם יָבוֹא אֶל־הֵיכָלוֹ הָאָדוֹן אֲשֶׁר־אַתֶּם מְבַקְשִׁים
וּמַלְאַךְ הַבְּרִית אֲשֶׁר־אַתֶּם חֲפֵצִים הִנֵּה־בָא אָמַר יְהוָה
[צְבָאוֹת:

¹ἰδοὺ ἐγὼ ἐξαποστέλλω τὸν ἄγγε-
λόν μου, καὶ ἐπιβλέψεται ὁδὸν πρὸ προσώπου μου, καὶ ἐξαίφνης
ἥξει εἰς τὸν ναὸν ἑαυτοῦ κύριος, ὃν ὑμεῖς ζητεῖτε, καὶ ὁ ἄγγελος
τῆς διαθήκης, ὃν ὑμεῖς θέλετε · ἰδοὺ ἔρχεται, λέγει κύριος παντοκράτωρ.

Ex 23:20

²⁰הִנֵּה אָנֹכִי שֹׁלֵחַ מַלְאָךְ לְפָנֶיךָ לִשְׁמָרְךָ בַּדָּרֶךְ וְלַהֲבִיאֲךָ אֶל־
הַמָּקוֹם אֲשֶׁר הֲכִנֹתִי:

²⁰Καὶ ἰδοὺ ἐγὼ ἀποστέλλω τὸν ἄγγελόν μου πρὸ προσώπου σου,
ἵνα φυλάξῃ σε ἐν τῇ ὁδῷ, ὅπως εἰσαγάγῃ σε εἰς τὴν γῆν, ἣν ἡτοί-
μασά σοι.

|

earlier in the verse are bidden to smite are to do so only as God's agents in carrying out His plan. Mt 26:31 adheres to the singular of the MT, τὸν ποιμένα, rather than the LXX's plural τοὺς ποιμένας. Note also that NT διασκοπισθήσονται is more accurate that the LXX's ἐκσπάσατε in handling the MT's וּתְפוּצֶיךָ ("and they shall be scattered"); the LXX takes it as a jussive *hiphil*, apparently reading it as תְּפִיצוּנָה rather than the 2nd plur. fem. sufformative. But the NT follows the MT in making the "sheep" the subject of this verb. Here then we have a completely non-Septuagintal reading in Mk 14:27. (*C*)

*a*Rom 9:13

13 ⌜καθὼς γέγραπται· τὸν Ἰακὼβ ἠγάπησα, τὸν δὲ Ἠσαῦ ἐμίσησα.

Mal 1:2–3; MT = LXX = Rom 9:13. (*A*)

*a*Mt 11:10

10 οὗτός ᵀ
ἐστιν περὶ οὗ γέγραπται·
 ἰδοὺ ἐγὼ ἀποστέλλω τὸν ἄγγελόν μου πρὸ προσώπου σου,
 ὃς κατασκευάσει τὴν ὁδόν σου ἔμπροσθέν σου.

*b*Mk 1:2

□**2** Καθὼς γέγραπται ἐν ⸆τῷ Ἠσαΐᾳ τῷ προφήτῃ ⸄·
 ἰδοὺ ᵀ ἀποστέλλω τὸν ἄγγελόν μου πρὸ προσώπου σου,
 ὃς κατασκευάσει τὴν ὁδόν σου ᵀ·

*c*Lk 7:27

27 οὗτός ᵀ ἐστιν
περὶ οὗ γέγραπται·
 ἰδοὺ ἀποστέλλω τὸν ἄγγελόν μου πρὸ προσώπου σου,
 ὃς κατασκευάσει τὴν ὁδόν σου □ἔμπροσθέν σου\.

Mal 3:1; we should observe first of all that the three Synoptic quotations of this passage are in literal agreement with one another, except that Mk 1:2 omits the final ἔμπροσθέν σου. Therefore we may discuss the NT quotation as if it were one and the same vis-a-vis the MT source. Second, the variations from the LXX rendering are quite minor, and consist of the following: (1) the LXX uses an ἐγώ before ἐξαποστέλλω; (2) the LXX uses the compound ἐξαποστέλλω for the MT's הִנְנִי שֹׁלֵחַ, without any special superiority over the Synoptist's ἀποστέλλω (*C*); (3) the LXX uses ἐπιβλέψεται for the converted perfect וּפִנָּה (i.e. "and he will look to") as a rendition of "and he shall prepare," rather than the NT's more accurate κατασκευάσει (*C*); (4) the LXX follows the word order of the MT a little more closely than the NT does, in that it places πρὸ προσώπου μου in the same position as Malachi's לְפָנָי, i.e., right after דֶּרֶךְ (= ὁδόν); whereas the NT defers it to after τὸν ἄγγελόν μου. Note that this language in Mal 3:1 seems to follow very closely the wording of Ex 23:20, at least so far as the first five Hebrew words are concerned. But since it does not continue with the rest of the Malachi promise (which clearly predicts the coming of John the Baptist), and since it relates to that angel of the Lord (possibly the preincarnate Christ Himself), it furnishes a purely verbal resemblance rather than a direct hermeneutical relationship. But it does not give support to πρὸ προσώπου σου (which Malachi's לְפָנָי does not). (*Dª*)

312: Mal 3:23-24

²³ יְהוָה אָנֹכִי שֹׁלֵחַ לָכֶם אֵת אֵלִיָּה הַנָּבִיא
לִפְנֵי בּוֹא יוֹם יְהוָה הַגָּדוֹל וְהַנּוֹרָא:
²⁴ יְהָשִׁיב לֵב־אָבוֹת עַל־בָּנִים וְלֵב בָּנִים עַל־אֲבוֹתָם
פֶּן־אָבוֹא וְהִכֵּיתִי אֶת־הָאָרֶץ חֵרֶם:

²³ὃς ἀποκαταστήσει καρ-
δίαν πατρὸς πρὸς υἱὸν καὶ καρδίαν ἀνθρώπου πρὸς τὸν πλησίον
αὐτοῦ, μὴ ἔλθω καὶ πατάξω τὴν γῆν ἄρδην. ²⁴μνήσθητε νόμου
Μωυσῆ τοῦ δούλου μου, καθότι ἐνετειλάμην αὐτῷ ἐν Χωρηβ πρὸς
πάντα τὸν Ισραηλ προστάγματα καὶ δικαιώματα.

*a*Mt 17:10–11

10 Καὶ ἐπηρώτησαν αὐτὸν οἱ μαθηταὶ ᵀ λέγοντες · τί οὖν οἱ γραμματεῖς λέγουσιν ὅτι 'Ηλίαν δεῖ ἐλθεῖν πρῶτον; **11** ὁ δὲ ᵀ ἀποκριθεὶς εἶπεν · 'Ηλίας μὲν ἔρχεται ⸆ ⸀καὶ ἀποκαταστήσει⸃ πάντα:

Mal 3:23–24; this is not really a straight quotation at all, so far as Mt 17 is concerned, but simply a report of the teaching of the scribes of Jesus' day. To be sure, their teaching concerning the return of Elijah to earth to prepare for the coming of the Messiah was really derived from this passage in Malachi, and accurately represented its intent: "Elijah must come first!" This is clearly implied also by Mal 3:23: "Behold I am going to send to you Elijah the prophet before the great and terrible day of the Lord will come." Jesus commented that this scribal inference was absolutely correct: "Elijah, on the one hand (μέν), will come, and he shall restore (ἀποκατάστησει) all things." The verb itself, ἀποκαταστήσει, is found at the commencement of the LXX's Mal 3:23 (MT's 3:24) as a rendering of וְהֵשִׁיב, but the object πάντα ("all things") is found neither in the MT nor the LXX. But this is no problem at all, since it is not a direct quotation that is involved in this passage—only a reference to the teaching of Mal 3:23–24. (C) and (D)

DATE DUE

APR 01 1995			
APR 11 1996			
			Printed in USA